Economic Efficiency and Productivity Growth in the Asia-Pacific Region

ACADEMIA STUDIES IN ASIAN ECONOMIES

General Editor: Sheng-Cheng Hu, *Director, Institute of Economics, Academia Sinica, Taiwan*

Titles in the series include:

Economic Efficiency and Productivity Growth in the Asia-Pacific Region
Edited by Tsu-Tan Fu, Cliff J. Huang and C.A. Knox Lovell

Economic Efficiency and Productivity Growth in the Asia-Pacific Region

Edited by

Tsu-Tan Fu
Research Fellow, Institute of Economics, Academia Sinica, Taipei, Taiwan, ROC

Cliff J. Huang
Professor of Economics, Vanderbilt University, Nashville, Tennessee, USA

C.A. Knox Lovell
Terry Professor, Department of Economics, University of Georgia, Athens, Georgia, USA and Professor, School of Economics, University of New South Wales, Sydney, Australia

ACADEMIA STUDIES IN ASIAN ECONOMIES

Edward Elgar
Cheltenham, UK • Northampton, MA, USA

Published by
Edward Elgar Publishing Limited
Glensanda House
Montpellier Parade
Cheltenham
Glos GL50 1UA
UK

Edward Elgar Publishing, Inc.
6 Market Street
Northampton
Massachusetts 01060
USA

A catalogue record for this book
is available from the British Library

Library of Congress Cataloguing in Publication Data

Economic efficiency and productivity growth in the Asia-Pacific region / edited by Tsu-Tan Fu, Cliff J. Huang, C.A. Knox Lovell.
(Academia studies in Asian economies)
1. Asia—Economic conditions. 2. Pacific Area—Economic conditions. 3. Gross domestic product—Asia. 4. Gross domestic product—Pacific Area. 5. Economic development. 6. Industrial productivity—Asia. 7. Industrial productivity—Pacific Area. I. Fu, Tsu-Tan. II. Huang, Cliff J., 1938– . III. Lovell, C.A. Knox. IV. Series.
HC412.E217 1999
330.95'0429—dc21 98–27884
CIP

ISBN 1 85898 857 8

Printed and bound in Great Britain by MPG Books Ltd, Bodmin, Cornwall

Contents

Figures

Tables

Contributors

Seung C. Ahn, *Associate Professor of Economics, Arizona State University, Tempe, Arizona, US*

Been-Lon Chen, *Associate Research Fellow, Institute of Economics, Academia Sinica, Taipei, Taiwan, ROC*

Jing-Yi Chen, *Senior Clerk, Credit Card Center, Shanghai Commercial and Savings Bank, Taipei, Taiwan, ROC*

Clifford D. Clark, *University Professor and President Emeritus, Binghamton University, Binghamton, New York, USA*

Sébastien Dessus, *Economist, OECD Development Centre, Paris, France*

W.E. Diewert, *Professor of Economics, The University of British Columbia, Vancouver, BC, Canada*

Chrys Dougherty, *Assistant Professor of Public Affairs, University of Texas, Austin, Texas, USA*

Kevin J. Fox, *Senior Lecturer, School of Economics, The University of New South Wales, Sydney, Australia*

Tsu-Tan Fu, *Research Fellow, Institute of Economics, Academia Sinica, Taipei, Taiwan, ROC*

James H. Gapinski, *Professor of Economics, Florida State University, Tallahassee, Florida, USA, and Curtin University of Technology, Perth, Western Australia*

David H. Good, *Associate Professor, School of Public and Environmental Affairs, Indiana University, Bloomington, Indiana, USA*

Mei Hsu, *Associate Professor of Economics, National Chung-Hsing University, Taipei, Taiwan, ROC*

Cliff J. Huang, *Professor of Economics, Vanderbilt University, Nashville, Tennessee, USA*

Mei-Ying Huang, *Professor of Economics, Chung-Hsing University, Taipei, Taiwan, ROC*

Dale W. Jorgenson, *Frederic Eaton Abbe Professor of Economics, Harvard University, Massachusetts, USA*

Masahiro Kuroda, *Professor, Faculty of Business and Commerce, Keio University, Tokyo, Japan*

Jonathan E. Leightner, *Associate Professor, College of Business Administration, Augusta State University, Augusta, Georgia, USA*

Chi-yuan Liang, *Research Fellow, Institute of Economics, Academia Sinica, Taipei, Taiwan, ROC*

Jung-Chao Liu, *Professor of Economics, Binghamton University, Binghamton, New York, USA*

C.A. Knox Lovell, *Professor of Economics, University of Georgia, Athens, Georgia, USA, and University of New South Wales, Sydney, Australia*

M. Ishaq Nadiri, *Professor of Economics, New York University, New York, USA*

Koji Nomura, *Assistant, Keio Economic Observatory, Keio University, Tokyo, Japan*

Robin C. Sickles, *Professor of Economics and Statistics, Department of Economics, Rice University, Houston, Texas, USA*

Wanpyo Son, *Professor of Economics, Hanshin University, Osan Kyounggi, Korea*

Yih Pin Tang, *Graduate Student, University of Georgia, Athens, Georgia, USA*

David L. Western, *Lecturer, School of Economics and Finance, Curtin University of Technology, Perth, Western Australia, Australia*

Yanrui Wu, *Research Fellow in Economics, University of Western Australia, Nedlands, West Australia, Australia*

Acknowledgment

Academia Studies in Asian Economies serves to assimilate the findings of research conducted by the faculty of the Institute of Economics, Academia Sinica and studies presented at conferences sponsored by the Institute.

The Institute of Economics is one of the 24 research units of Academia Sinica, the leading academic institution in Taiwan. Its goals are to conduct and promote academic research in economics. Its faculty conducts research in all areas of economics, with emphasis on issues related to Asian economies. To promote economic research, each year the Institute organizes a number of international conferences on Asian economies. The papers included in this volume were selected from those presented at the Taipei International Conference on Efficiency and Productivity Growth, held at the Institute in June 1997. Over one hundred and sixty conference participants from 14 countries contributed papers and discussed issues concerning efficiency and productivity growth in the Asia-Pacific region.

Many individuals and institutions contributed to the success of the conference and this volume. We own a special debt of gratitude to Dr Yuan-Tseh Lee, President of Academia Sinica and Dr Sheng-Cheng Hu, Director of the Institute of Economics, for their encouragement and support. We are grateful to the Department of Economics of the National Taiwan University, the National Science Council and the Ministry of Education for generous financial support. Our thanks also go to the staff of the Institute of Economics for their efficient logistic support.

1. Editors' Introduction

Tsu-Tan Fu, Cliff J. Huang, C.A. Knox Lovell

1 INTRODUCTION

The primary objective of this book is to provide new insights into the performance of various economies in the Asia-Pacific region. By performance we generally mean economic growth, defined as the rate of growth of some aggregate indicator of economic activity, such as gross domestic product (GDP) or gross national product (GNP) or GDP per capita or GNP per capita. By any indicator, most economies in the region have experienced unprecedented economic growth for the last three decades or more. Whether this remarkable performance can be sustained into the twenty-first century is a matter of conjecture. Currently, the dramatic financial upheavals of 1997 are still reverberating throughout the region. The economies of Thailand, Indonesia, Malaysia and South Korea are badly shaken, and others are threatened. Japan remains mired in an economic stagnation that has lasted eight years. These events notwithstanding, however, it is still worthwhile to examine the performance of the region's economies prior to 1997. Regardless of what some of them may have done wrong, clearly each of them managed to get a lot of things right, and their sustained successes deserve examination.

Economic growth has two basic sources. One source is factor accumulation; mobilizing economic resources enables an economy to increase its output of goods and services. Factor accumulation occurs through increases in the quantity of labor (through increases in labor force participation rates and increases in employment rates), and through increases in the quality of labor (through investments in education and training). It also occurs through increases in capital stocks as a result of both private and public domestic investment and foreign direct investment. There is no doubt that factor accumulation has been a major contributor to economic growth in the region.

The other source of economic growth is productivity growth, which enables an economy to increase its output of goods and services at a faster rate than its resource base grows. Productivity growth itself is multi-faceted, being an amalgamation of improvements in technology, the exploitation of scale economies, and improvements in the efficiency with which resources are allocated. In contrast to the role of factor accumulation, the role of productivity growth in fostering economic growth in the region has been a matter of considerable debate. The debate is of substantial consequence, because economies cannot continue to grow indefinitely without the fruits of productivity growth; resource-driven growth is inherently constrained by the availability of resources.

A simple model may serve to fix ideas. Suppose the time path of a nation's aggregate economic activity can be summarized by the relationship

$$Y_t = A_t \cdot f(K_t, L_t, t), \; t = 1, \ldots, T,$$

where Y_t is some measure of real aggregate economic output (for example, GDP or GNP) in year t, K_t is a measure of the capital stock in use in year t, L_t is a measure of labor employment in year t, t is a time index intended to capture the level of technology in place in year t, A_t is an index of the efficiency with which K and L are utilized in year t, and $f(\cdot)$ is a production function describing how capital, labor and technology are used to produce output. The relationship can also be expressed in per capita terms by normalizing Y_t, K_t and L_t. The rate of growth of aggregate output can be expressed as

$$G_Y = \varepsilon_K G_K + \varepsilon_L G_L + G_A + G_f,$$

where G_Y, G_K and G_L denote rates of growth of Y_t, K_t and L_t, $\varepsilon_K = \partial lnf(\cdot)/\partial lnK_t$ denotes the elasticity of Y_t with respect to K_t, $\varepsilon_L = \partial lnf(\cdot)/\partial lnL_t$ denotes the elasticity of Y_t with respect to L_t, G_A denotes the rate at which the efficiency of resource use is changing, and G_f denotes the rate at which technology is changing (that is, the rate of technical progress or regress).

Accounting for the sources of economic growth is facilitated by a further decomposition of the above expression into

$$G_Y = s_K G_K + s_L G_L + S + G_A + G_f,$$

where $s_K = \varepsilon_K/(\varepsilon_K + \varepsilon_L)$, $s_L = 1 - s_K$, and $S = [1-(\varepsilon_K + \varepsilon_L)^{-1}][s_K G_K + \varepsilon_L G_L]$ provides a measure of the contribution of scale economies to output growth. If constant returns to scale in production prevail, then $\varepsilon_K + \varepsilon_L = 1 \Rightarrow S = 0$, and the above equation decomposes output growth into two sources: factor accumulation ($\varepsilon_K G_K + \varepsilon_L G_L$) and productivity change ($G_A + G_f$). In this formulation productivity change consists of efficiency change and technical change, either of which enables output growth to exceed input growth (if 'change' is 'improvement' or 'progress'). However if production is subject to nonconstant returns to scale, $\varepsilon_K + \varepsilon_L \neq 1 \Rightarrow S \neq 0$. Output growth is decomposed into the same two sources, factor accumulation and productivity change, but in this formulation productivity change consists of efficiency change, technical change and a scale effect. If aggregate resource use is growing $[(s_K G_K + s_L G_L) > 0]$, the scale effect enhances ($S > 0$) or retards ($S < 0$) output growth according to whether returns to scale are increasing $[(\varepsilon_K + \varepsilon_L) > 1]$ or decreasing $[(\varepsilon_K + \varepsilon_L) < 1]$.

To summarize, a nation's aggregate output increases for either or both of two reasons. Factor accumulation, through capital investment and employment growth, is the main engine of economic growth in most economies. However economic growth can be further enhanced through productivity growth. We have identified three potential sources of productivity growth: an improvement in the efficiency with which resources are allocated, perhaps as a result of deregulation of labor and product markets, privatization, reduced trade barriers and the like; an improvement in the general level of production technology, perhaps through increased domestic innovative activity or technology transfer; and economies of scale in production, which might be exploited as a result of amalgamations or the lowering of trade barriers, for example.

A secondary objective of this book is to expose the reader to the wide variety of empirical techniques economists use to measure economic growth and to decompose measured growth into its various sources. Traditional growth accounting remains the most popular empirical technique, but it is demanding of data, and it provides limited insight into the sources of economic growth. The use of econometric and mathematical programming techniques offers an alternative approach. These techniques are generally less demanding of data, and they typically provide greater insight into the sources of economic growth, although they do require estimation or computation of the underlying technology by which resources are transformed into goods and services. We do not conduct a tutorial on these techniques, but we do alert the reader to the wide variety of empirical techniques which are used in the chapters to follow.

This introductory chapter is organized as follows. In section 2 we provide a brief overview of the evidence on economic growth in the region. In section 3 we review the conventional laudatory interpretation of this evidence, primarily as exposited by the World Bank. In section 4 we review the revisionist interpretation of this evidence. In section 5 we review the post-revisionist (but pre-1997) optimistic view of the future prospects for the region. In section 6 we provide a brief overview of the events of 1997, events which somewhat ironically were not foreseen by the optimists, the revisionists or the post-revisionists. Finally in section 7 we provide a brief overview of the chapters included in this book.

2 THE ECONOMIC GROWTH RECORD IN THE ASIA-PACIFIC REGION SINCE 1965

The recent record of economic growth established by countries in the Asia-Pacific region is remarkable. Many empirical investigations have been conducted, and their findings are in general agreement: the economies of the region have sustained rapid rates of economic growth for a long period of time, much more rapid than those sustained by the wealthy industrialized countries of Europe and North America.

Based on its own data, the World Bank (1993) reports that during the period from 1965 through 1990, the economies of Japan, the four tigers (Hong Kong, Singapore, South Korea and Taiwan), and the newly industrializing economies (Indonesia, Malaysia and Thailand) managed to increase their GNP per capita by an average annual rate of 5.5 percent. In contrast, the economies of the Organization for Economic Cooperation and Development (OECD) managed an average annual growth rate of GNP per capita of just 2.4 percent during the same period.

The regional average annual growth rate of 5.5 percent conceals surprisingly little variation across countries. Using Penn World Table data, the World Bank also reports that Taiwan, Indonesia, Hong Kong, Singapore, South Korea and Japan each managed to increase their GDP per capita by average annual rates in excess of 3 percent during the 1960-1985 period, while Malaysia and Thailand managed increases in excess of 1.5 percent. Comparable figures for Canada, (West) Germany, the USA and the UK were well beneath 1 percent.

The Economist (1997a) reports similar figures, both for economies of the region and for an undefined group of rich industrial countries. These figures, presented in Table 1.1 below, show very high rates of growth of GDP in the region during the slightly more recent period from 1970 through 1996. Although growth has slowed in some countries (for example, Hong Kong and Taiwan), it has held steady or increased in others (for example, Malaysia, Thailand and China) and even the slowest of the growth rates in the region dwarf growth rates achieved by the rich industrial countries.

Table 1.1 GDP growth in the Asia-Pacific region, 1970-1996

	Average Annual Rates(%)		
	1970-1979	1980-1989	1990-1996
China	7.5	9.3	10.1
Hong Kong	9.2	7.5	5.0
Indonesia	7.8	5.7	7.2
Korea	9.3	8.0	7.7
Malaysia	8.0	5.7	8.8
Philippines	6.1	1.8	2.8
Singapore	9.4	7.2	8.3
Taiwan	10.2	8.1	6.3
Thailand	7.3	7.2	8.6
Rich Industrial Countries	3.4	2.6	2.0

It is of course possible to quibble about the accuracy of these and other related figures, perhaps to as much as a few tenths of a percentage point here and there, but the substantive message of the figures would remain. Many economies in the region have grown at extremely rapid rates for a very long time, and these rates of economic growth have been far greater than those achieved by most, if not all, advanced economies.

The question is *how* the economies in the region have managed to achieve such rapid rates of economic growth over such a long period of time, and the question has perhaps unsurprisingly led to a debate. The debate is not about the impressive rates of economic growth achieved by the economies in the region; on this point there is widespread agreement. Rather, the debate concerns the attribution of observed rates of economic growth to the two sources mentioned in the previous section, factor accumulation and productivity change. Consequently the challenging empirical problem is to decompose observed rates of economic growth into their two components. In the next two sections we summarize the positions of the two sides of the debate.

3 THE CONVENTIONAL INTERPRETATION

In a very influential book, the World Bank (1993) sought explanations for the rapid rates of growth achieved by countries in the region, principally Japan, the four tigers and the three newly industrializing economies. Unfortunately the title of the book, *The East Asian Miracle*, has received considerably more attention than the subtitle, *Economic Growth and Public Policy*. Whether the postwar performance of these eight economies has been miraculous or merely impressive is a matter of semantics. What is important is how it came to pass, and the World Bank emphasized the role of public policies which established a framework within which rapid economic growth was achieved.

The basic claim is that these eight economies managed to sustain high rates of economic growth 'by getting the basics right'. Not all economies got all the basics equally right, of course, and some economies paid dearly in 1997 for their failures. Among the basics which these economies did manage to get right are policies which encouraged rapid rates of factor accumulation, and policies which enhanced productivity growth. We briefly consider each set of policies.

Gross domestic savings rates increased from less than 20 percent of GDP to nearly 40 percent of GDP during the 1965-1990 period. These high savings rates were achieved through a combination of fundamental and interventionist policies. Fundamental policies included the maintenance of relative price stability and, in some (but evidently not all) countries, the maintenance of strong prudential regulation and supervision of financial institutions. Interventionist policies included the maintenance of artificially high interest rates on savings and the imposition of mandatory savings requirements.

High savings rates enabled gross domestic investment rates to climb from less than 20 percent of GDP to over 35 percent of GDP during the same period. Private domestic investment was encouraged by a variety of means, including the creation of public infrastructures complementary to private investment, the establishment of tax policies which favored investment, and the maintainance of low tariffs on imported capital goods.

The eight economies also invested heavily in education, with the share of GNP allocated to public expenditure on education increasing from 2.5 percent in 1960 to 3.7 percent in 1989. Generally speaking, investment in human capital took the form of providing universal primary education, and then by increasing the availability of secondary education. Spending on tertiary education focused on the development of technical skills.

These three factors, high savings rates, high rates of private domestic investment, and high rates of investment in human capital, contributed greatly to the rapid rates of economic growth achieved by the region's economies. Indeed the World Bank (1993: 5) observed that '... there is little that is "miraculous" about the ... superior record of growth; it is largely due to superior accumulation of physical and human capital'. But factor accumulation does not explain all observed growth in any of the economies; productivity growth has made a contribution as well, although its contribution has varied, both across economies and through time. Based on a cross-economy growth accounting regression exercise, the World Bank concluded that, on average across the eight economies during the 1960-1985 period, roughly two-thirds of observed growth in GDP per capita can be explained by factor accumulation. The remaining one-third must be attributed to productivity growth. Since the rate of growth of GDP per capita in these economies averaged 5.5 percent per year, this implies a regional average productivity growth rate of about 1.8 percent per year. Implied productivity growth rates vary widely across economies, however, from a low of 0.5 percent in Malaysia to a high of 3.4 percent in Hong Kong. The results for each economy are summarized in Table 1.2.

Table 1.2 Sources of economic growth in the Asia-Pacific region, 1960-1985

		% of Real Per Capita GDP Growth, Accounted for by	
Country	Growth (%)	Factor Accumulation	Productivity Growth
Hong Kong	6.09	44	56
Indonesia	3.72	60	40
Japan	5.69	82	18
Korea	5.89	63	37
Malaysia	4.00	87	13
Singapore	6.03	65	35
Taiwan	6.38	58	42
Thailand	3.82	66	34

The World Bank provided a long list of institutional and policy features which established a framework within which productivity growth flourished. Briefly, these include an openness to foreign trade, particularly to foreign technology and foreign direct investment, the maintenance of flexible labor markets, the enforcement of secure property rights embodied in legal frameworks, generally effective systems of public administration and largely competent and honest bureaucracies. The fact that these features vary from country to country, as well as through time for each country, may help explain some of the variation in the role of productivity growth across countries.

4 THE REVISIONIST INTERPRETATION

The rosy view propounded by the World Bank has supporters and critics. Foremost among the critics is Alwyn Young. In a pair of papers, Young (1992, 1995) has called into question the World Bank claim that as much as one-third of economic growth in the region can be attributed to productivity growth. Based on detailed data from published and unpublished sources which enabled him to make a variety of adjustments to conventional capital and labor input series, Young (1995) used conventional growth accounting techniques to derive estimates of productivity growth rates for each of the Four Tigers during the 1966-1990 period and for various subperiods. His findings are summarized in Table 1.3.

Table 1.3 Productivity growth rates for the Four Tigers

	Annual Growth Rates (percent)			
Country	GDP	Weighted Capital	Weighted Labor	Productivity
Hong Kong (1966-1991)	7.3	8.0	3.2	2.3
Korea (1966-1990)	10.3	13.7	6.4	1.7
Singapore (1966-1990)	8.7	11.5	5.7	0.2
Taiwan (1966-1990)	8.9	12.3	4.9	2.1

Young's calculations for Hong Kong, Korea and Taiwan are more or less in line with those of the World Bank, and imply that productivity growth has accounted for 31 percent of GDP growth in Hong Kong, 16 percent of GDP growth in Korea and 24 percent of GDP growth in Taiwan. However his calculations for Singapore are much lower, essentially zero, and have been quite controversial. Nonetheless, they have an air of plausibility. Simply put, factor accumulation was sufficiently rapid to account for virtually all of Singapore's growth during the period. For example, the employed share of the population rose from 27 percent to over 50 percent, massive investments in human capital led to two-thirds of the labor force having completed secondary education by 1990, as compared with 16 percent in 1966, and capital investment increased from 11 percent of GDP in 1966 to over 40 percent of GDP by 1990. Very little, if any, output growth is left unexplained by such rapid factor accumulation.

The controversy grew when Krugman (1994) popularized Young's findings, and added his own interpretation of them. It is worth quoting

Krugman at length (p. 71):

> Even without going through the formal exercise of growth accounting, these numbers should make it obvious that Singapore's growth has been based largely on one-time changes in behavior that cannot be repeated. Over the past generation the percentage of people employed has almost doubled; it cannot happen again. A half-educated work force has been replaced by one in which the bulk of workers has high school diplomas; it is unlikely that a generation from now most Singaporeans will have Ph.D.s. And an investment share of 40 percent is amazingly high by any standard; a share of 70 percent would be ridiculous. So one can immediately conclude that Singapore is unlikely to achieve future growth rates comparable to those of the past.

The implication of Krugman's interpretation is not backward-looking, although Young's findings themselves were certainly backward-looking. Rather, the implication is forward-looking, and ominous: since Singapore's sustained factor accumulation cannot continue, its future growth prospects are bleak. However this prognosis misses an important point: even if Singapore has experienced little or no productivity growth in the past, it is possible that future productivity growth will enable it to continue growing, albeit at slower but still respectable rates.

Collins and Bosworth (1996) have obtained results which are broadly consistent with those of Young (with the notable exception of Singapore), and which extend Young's backward-looking findings to economies other than those of the Four Tigers. For the region as a whole, they found productivity to have grown by 1.1 percent per year during the 1960-1994 period, and to have accounted for nearly 25 percent of growth in output per worker. They also found considerable variation in rates of productivity growth across economies, ranging from 2.1 percent in Taiwan, 1.9 percent in Thailand and 1.6 percent in Singapore down to 1.0 percent in Malaysia, 0.8 percent in Indonesia and −0.4 percent in the Philippines. In contrast to Krugman's pessimism, however, they also find evidence that these economies are gradually beginning to pursue policies which place greater emphasis on productivity gains, so that their future growth can be sustained in the face of declining rates of factor accumulation. Their findings for the most recent 1984-1994 subperiod suggest that productivity growth has increased to 1.6 percent per annum, and has accounted for over one-third of growth in output per worker.

Nonetheless, the popular press has voiced concerns for the region's near-term growth prospects. These concerns post-date and reinforce Krugman's prognosis, although they pertain less to Singapore than to some of the other economies in the region. It is noteworthy that they were voiced prior to the financial disturbances of 1997. Among the concerns expressed by *Business Week* (1996) and *The Economist* (1996, 1997a) are the following:

- excess capacity in sectors such as autos, petrochemicals, consumer electronics and semiconductors
- inadequate human capital, particularly in engineering and management, attributable to rigidities and other inadequacies of public education and to inadequate training programs
- rising costs attributable to tightening labor markets and skill shortages
- poor infrastructure, such as transportation networks and power systems
- inefficient financial markets, which frequently allocate capital to state-owned enterprises, overextended conglomerates, tall buildings and big dams rather than to small businesses
- excessive red tape and widespread corruption, which among other things deter foreign investment
- large current account deficits, as in Indonesia, Malaysia, the Philippines and Thailand, and particularly if it is financed by short-term portfolio capital rather than by foreign direct investment, as in Thailand.

5 THE OPTIMISTIC VIEW

In sharp contrast to the concerns expressed by the revisionists, there remains considerable optimism concerning the region's economic prospects. This optimism springs from such diverse sources as the World Economic Forum, the International Institute for Management Development, a group of institutes led by the Fraser Institute, and the Third International Maths and Science Study. These sources provide rankings of various economies on the basis of their international competitiveness, their economic freedom, and the mathematics and science education they provide their youth. In each of the rankings, the countries of the region fare rather well, and their lofty rankings bode well for their future economic performance.

The World Economic Forum (WEF) has ranked 49 countries on the basis of an index of 155 indicators of their economic competitiveness ('the ability of a country to achieve sustained high rates of growth in GDP per capita'). The International Institute for Management Development (IIMD) has ranked 46 countries on the basis of an index of 224 indicators of their economic competitiveness ('the ability of a country to create value added and thus increase national wealth by managing assets and processes, attractiveness and aggressiveness, globality and proximity, and by integrating these relationships into an economic and social model'). (Both as reported in *The Economist*, 1996b.) A group of 11 institutes, led by the Fraser Institute (FI) has published a ranking of 102 countries on the basis of 17 indicators of their economic freedom (the indicators include measures of money and inflation, government operations and regulations, takings and discriminatory taxation, and international exchange). (As reported in *The Economist*, 1996a.) Finally, the Third International Maths and Science Study (TIMSS) ranked 41 countries on the basis of the performance of their 13-year old students on examinations in mathematics and science. (As reported in *The Economist*, 1997b.)

On the reasonable assumption that economic competitiveness, economic freedom and educational achievement are good indicators of future economic prospects, then most of the countries in the region appear to be well-positioned to continue their recent rapid growth rates. The results of these studies are summarized in Table 1.4. They suggest that the long-term prospects are bright for Hong Kong, Japan and Singapore, and not exactly bleak for the remaining economies in the region.

Additional evidence in support of the optimistic view is provided by demographic trends in the region. Dependency ratios, the proportion of the population not of prime working age, are declining throughout the region and are expected to continue declining for a generation. This factor augurs well for continued high rates of employment, and also for continued high savings rates, which in turn provide the funds for rapid rates of investment.

Table 1.4 Future prospects for the Asia-Pacific economies

	Rank According to				
Country	WEF	IIMD	FI	TIMSS Maths	TIMSS Science
Hong Kong	2	3	1	4	24
Indonesia			31		
Japan	13	4	10	3	3
Korea	20	27	12	2	4
Malaysia	10	23	6		
Philippines			27		
Singapore	1	2	2	1	1
Taiwan	9	18	16		
Thailand	14	30	8	20	21

6 THE YEAR OF THE ASIAN FU: 1997

The financial turmoil began in Thailand in July, and spread rapidly to Indonesia, Malaysia and South Korea and, to a lesser extent, to several other economies in the region. Krugman (1998: 2, 9) describes the events as being brought on by 'financial excess and then financial collapse', and by 'bad banking and its consequences'. A popular argument has it that sustained rapid economic growth had concealed, and probably encouraged, serious shortcomings in financial infrastructures throughout the region. The general nature of the problem was a classic example of moral hazard: risky lending on the part of poorly regulated financial intermediaries operating with implicit government guarantees. In Thailand the problem was excessive lending, on the part of most finance companies and some banks, to property developers. In Indonesia and Korea the problem was excessive lending to those with connections to the government, and to the overextended *chaebol*, respectively. Eventually asset price bubbles burst, creating mountains of bad debt. Currency depreciations followed, making timely repayment of private foreign debts increasingly improbable. Political instability in several countries only made economic uncertainties worse. Finally the International Monetary Fund entered, providing financial assistance to the hardest-hit countries.

The Far Eastern Economic Review (1997, 1998), in its year-end review of the region's economic affairs, commented that '... the biggest surprise of the region's crisis was that it came as a surprise'. Regardless of whether or why it came as a surprise, the crisis raises two fundamental questions: first, what does it imply for the academic research praising and questioning the East Asian Miracle, and second, what does it imply for the near-term growth prospects in the region?

Much of the academic research has been based on growth accounting or on the estimation of production relationships. Both types of exercise employ data on the inputs and outputs of economies, but not on the quality of the financial infrastructures in these economies. Consequently they were able to quantify growth performances to a reasonable degree of accuracy, although they were unable to reach a consensus on the apportionment of growth to its constituent sources. They had no chance of predicting the events of 1997 with the data they were using.

What, then, are the near-term growth prospects in light of the events of 1997? The *Wall Street Journal* (1998), citing 'two surveys of economists', predicts GDP growth rates for 1998 dramatically lower than in previous years. Estimates range from −3.3 percent for Indonesia, −2.7 percent for Thailand and −0.2 percent for South Korea up to 2.7 percent for Malaysia, 2.9 percent for the Philippines, 3.3 percent for Hong Kong and

3.9 percent for Singapore. Only China and Taiwan are expected to enjoy relatively robust growth, at 8.2 percent and 6.0 percent respectively. *The Economist* (1998), in an informative survey of the events of 1997 and a guardedly optimistic look into the future, provided very similar dire predictions for 1998, although their predictions for 1999 are considerably more optimistic. These predictions appear in Table 1.5.

Table 1.5 Predicted future rates of GDP growth in the region

	Actual and Predicted Rates of GDP Growth (%)			
Country	1970-1996	1997	1998	1999
China	9.1	8.9	6.3	7.5
Hong Kong	7.5	5.1	1.8	3.8
Indonesia	6.8	5.4	−5.2	2.9
Korea	8.4	5.6	−2.5	1.7
Malaysia	7.4	7.4	1.6	1.8
Philippines	3.6	4.8	1.9	4.0
Singapore	8.2	7.6	2.7	5.0
Taiwan	8.3	6.3	5.0	5.7
Thailand	7.5	−0.7	−4.0	3.7
Rich Industrial Countries	2.7	2.8	2.6	2.6

The future outlook depends largely on the quality of governance, and more specifically on the quality of macroeconomic management so highly praised by the World Bank. According to *The Economist* (1998), the quality of macroeconomic management in much of the region has not been as high as previously thought. Much of the enormous investment has been misallocated and squandered; several governments, though relatively small, still have managed to interfere in economic affairs; not all labor and capital markets have been sufficiently flexible; not all legal systems have been reliable; a widespread lack of corporate transparency and accountability has bred corruption; and financial institutions have been inadequately regulated. A return to rapid rates of economic growth requires that governments in the region make serious efforts to rectify these and other structural problems that the miracle years concealed. Or, as *The Economist* (1997a) warned prior to the onset of the Asian flu epidemic, 'The biggest challenge to the Asian economic miracle is not economic, but political: the risk that governments take bad policy decisions in response to the current slowdown'.

The task of measuring and explaining growth rates in the region prior to 1997 was difficult, but with so much riding on political will, the task of explaining growth through the millennium promises to be even more challenging.

7 AN INTRODUCTION TO THE CHAPTERS IN THIS VOLUME

The 14 studies included in this volume are organized into two groups, one consisting of five international studies and the other consisting of nine national studies. The international studies are divided into three which focus on the economies of the Asia-Pacific region, and two with a different geographic perspective. The national studies each focus on individual economies in the region, and we have somewhat arbitrarily organized them into six macroeconomic productivity studies and three microeconomic efficiency studies. A distinguishing characteristic of these studies is their diversity. Collectively they touch on every economy in the region (although some economies receive considerably more attention than others), occasionally by way of comparison with other economies outside the region. Levels of aggregation at which empirical analysis is conducted range from national economies to specific regions, sectors or industries all the way down to individual enterprises. Empirical techniques employed range from growth accounting to econometric estimation (frequently based on duality theory) to linear programming calculations to input-output analysis to nonquantitative investigation. A characteristic which unites many of the studies is an emphasis on the influential role of international trade, a welcome feature of studies which focus on the performance of trade-dependent economies in the region.

Of the three international studies which focus on the Asia-Pacific region, one examines the performance of the two city-states of Hong Kong and Singapore, one examines the performance of six economies in the region, and one sets the performance of several of the region's international airlines in international perspective. In Chapter 2 Lovell and Tang tell an alternative tale (to that told by Young and Krugman) of the two city-states. Their tale is alternative not in the sense that it attempts to challenge previous estimates of productivity growth, but in the sense that it offers a fresh perspective on the past performance and future prospects of these two economies. Using data covering a dozen economies over a lengthy period of time, they construct backward-looking and forward-looking indexes of the quality of macroeconomic management, as revealed by its observable consequences. They find the quality of macroeconomic management to have been relatively good in Hong Kong, somewhat better in Singapore, and best of all in Taiwan. In Chapter 3 Nadiri and Son examine the post-1960 growth experience of seven regional economies (Japan, three of the Four Tigers, and Malaysia and Thailand). They provide estimates of the sources of output growth and productivity growth in each economy, and they also examine various factors which contributed to a convergence in per capita incomes in these economies. An important feature of their analysis is their concentration on the multiple roles of international trade; labor, human capital, physical capital, imports and foreign capital are treated as inputs in the production of domestic output and exports. They find considerable variability, both across economies and through time, in the importance of various sources of growth. In Chapter 4 Ahn, Good and Sickles study the performance of a group of 11 Pacific Rim and 12 North American airlines over the period 1976-1994. Their analysis is based on a dynamic specification of a stochastic production frontier in which performance, as measured by productive efficiency, is allowed to vary across airlines and through time. Only four Pacific Rim carriers (Qantas, Singapore Airlines, Air New Zealand and Cathay Pacific) rank in the upper half of the performance distribution, although the Pacific Rim carriers as a group are converging toward best practice twice as fast as the group of North American carriers.

Although the two remaining international studies have little to do with the Asia-Pacific region, they both have much to offer in the way of analytical techniques which might usefully be applied by others to the region's economies. In Chapter 5 Dougherty and Jorgenson develop a model for allocating the sources of economic growth between endogenous investment and productivity growth. They then apply this model to the G-7 economies (Canada, France, Germany, Italy, Japan, the UK and the US) over the 1960-1973 and 1973-1989 periods, aggregating 21 capital categories and 20 labor categories. Their analytical approach is quite different from conventional growth accounting or production function estimation exercises and, given suitable data, could shed interesting new light on the ongoing debate about the sources of productivity growth among the economies in the Asia-Pacific region. In Chapter 6 Fox and Diewert also take a somewhat unconventional approach, by estimating both rates and biases of technical change in a sample of 18 OECD economies over the 1960-1992 period. Their framework is similar to that of Nadiri and Son, in that they specify an open model including three outputs (exports, investment and combined private and government consumption), two variable inputs (labor and imports) and one fixed input (capital). Unlike Nadiri and Son, who use a cost function to represent the structure of technology, Fox and Diewert base their analysis on a variable profit function. Once again, however, international trade plays a pivotal role in the analysis. In light of the significance of international trade in the Asia-Pacific region, the application of the Fox and Diewert model to a sample of economies in the region would be a particularly useful exercise, one which would also be less demanding of data sources than would the Dougherty and Jorgenson model.

Among the national studies are six macroeconomic productivity studies. In Chapter 7 Gapinski and Western explore Hong Kong's growth prospects subsequent to reversion to Chinese rule. They begin by estimating a labor productivity equation based on data from 120 countries during the 1951-1990 period. Output growth in Hong Kong is attributed primarily to international trade, and to a lesser extent to capital investment and labor growth. Since in their model trade is a component of productivity growth, their results suggest that productivity growth has accounted for roughly half of output growth in Hong Kong, and this share is rising. Gapinski and Western conclude with some conjectures concerning the effects of reversion under alternative scenarios ranging from worst case to best case values of five factors influencing growth. Wu examines the Panda itself, focusing on the performance of 27 of China's 30 provinces over the 1981-1995 period. In Chapter 8 Wu uses a stochastic production frontier framework and aggregate provincial data on GDP, capital and employment to estimate productivity change, and to decompose it into contributions attributable to efficiency change and technical change. Unsurprisingly he finds considerable regional variation in performance, with the three city economies (Beijing, Shanghai and Tianjin) having registered the best performances. He also finds productivity to have declined through 1986, and to have increased thereafter, with technical progress becoming an increasingly important factor influencing China's future growth prospects. Returning to the role of foreign trade, in Chapter 9 Dessus examines the relationship between productivity growth and outward orientation in Taiwan. Using Penn World Tables data covering the 1951-1990 period, Dessus estimates a productivity growth rate of just over 3 percent per year for Taiwan. Among the determinants of productivity growth, Dessus finds imports of technology and the reduction of domestic labor market distortions to have been the most important. In Chapter 10 Chen, Hsu and Chen also examine the impact of outward orientation on productivity in Taiwan, but their measure of productivity is labor productivity, and they use both industry- and firm-level data from 1986 and 1991 censuses. They find that export performance enhances labor productivity, whereas in contrast to conventional wisdom (as well as the findings of Dessus), foreign direct investment tends to reduce labor productivity, and this finding is robust across industries and levels of aggregation. In Chapter 11 Kuroda and Nomura provide estimates of productivity growth in 43 sectors of the Japanese economy over the 1955-1992 period. Unlike the majority of studies in this volume, which are regression-based, Kuroda and Nomura adopt an analytical framework based on the dynamic inverse approach to input-output analysis. In this framework new technologies are embodied in private and social overhead capital, and the objective is to evaluate the impacts of new technologies on capital coefficients, and on productivity change in each sector. They find that the use of a 'dynamic unit TFP' measure of productivity change, which incorporates direct and indirect spillover effects, largely eliminates the productivity paradox (an apparent inverse relationship between investment and productivity change) in these sectors. Finally in Chapter 12 Liang and Jorgenson estimates and decomposes productivity change in Taiwan's 20 manufacturing sectors over the 1961-1993 period. Within each sector Liang aggregates six types of capital input, four types of labor input, five types of intermediate input and four types of energy input, and specifies both total output and value added productivity measures. He finds productivity growth to have varied widely across sectors, and he finds its contribution to economic growth to have varied widely across sectors and through time periods.

The concluding section of the book contains three microeconomic efficiency studies. In Chapter 13 Leightner, in a presciently titled chapter, uses linear programming techniques to evaluate the performance of the vast majority of Thailand's finance and securities companies over the 1990-1995 period. He finds considerable variation in performance, and a common shortcoming: an inefficiently small size which made it difficult for them to compete with the much larger banks. Leightner argues that this shortcoming led them to take unwise risks in order to grow, which led directly to their aforementioned 1997 problems, which Leightner discusses in some detail. In Chapter 14 Huang, Fu and Huang examine another undersized segment of the financial sector, Taiwan's farmers' credit unions. The authors estimate a stochastic shadow cost frontier, using a two-year panel of 283 credit unions, in order to estimate economies of scale and scope and to estimate cost efficiency. They find evidence of scale economies, and scope economies for large credit unions only, and they find considerable cost inefficiency due to loan quality and input allocative distortions, and they discuss the policy implications of their findings. The concluding chapter by Clark and Liu in Chapter 15 is unique in a number of respects. It seeks to measure the 'social productivity', of township and village enterprises in China, social productivity referring to largely unmeasurable externalities (such as providing rural employment opportunities which moderate migration to already overcrowded urban areas) generated by their measurable productive activities. These enterprises have grown tenfold since 1978, and now account for nearly one third of China's industrial output. The authors also discuss some external costs associated with the rapid growth of township and village enterprises, and propose some steps which might alleviate these problems.

REFERENCES

Business Week (1996), 'Time for a reality check in Asia', 2 December.

Collins, S.M. and B.P. Bosworth (1996), 'Economic growth in East Asia: accumulation versus assimilation', *Brookings Papers on Economic Activity*, **2**, 135-91.

Far Eastern Economic Review (1997)(1998), 'Blown away', 25 December and 1 January.

Krugman, P. (1994), 'The myth of Asia's miracle', *Foreign Affairs*, **73** (6), 62-78.

Krugman, P. (1998), 'What happened to Asia?', http://web.mit.edu/krugman/www/DISINTER.html.

The Economist (1996), 'Economic freedom: of liberty and prosperity', 13 January.

The Economist (1996b), 'The C-word strikes back', 1 June.

The Economist (1996c), 'Emerging Asia's sombre era', 24 August.

The Economist (1997a), 'The Asian miracle: is it over?', 1 March.

The Economist (1997b), 'World education league: who's top?', 29 March.

The Economist (1998), 'Frozen miracle', 7 March.

The Wall Street Journal (1998), 'Asian-growth forecasts are pared even as signs emerge of recovery', 26 February.

World Bank (1993), *The East Asian Miracle: Economic Growth and Public Policy*, New York: Oxford University Press.

Young, A. (1992), 'A tale of two cities: factor accumulation and technical change in Hong Kong and Singapore', *NBER Macroeconomics Annual 1992*, 13-54.

Young, A. (1995), 'The tyranny of numbers: confronting the statistical realities of the East Asian growth experience', *Quarterly Journal of Economics*, **110**, 641-80.

PART I

International Studies

A. The Asia-Pacific Region

2. An Alternative Tale of Two Cities*

C.A. Knox Lovell and Yih Pin Tang

1 INTRODUCTION

Hong Kong and Singapore are similar in a number of ways, and different in others. Both were at one time British colonies serving as international trading centers. Eventually both developed export-dependent domestic manufacturing sectors. Both passed through a similar set of industries, graduating from textiles to electronics to financial services. Both are city-states, with little in the way of agricultural activity. Both have grown rapidly in recent decades, and have participated fully in the East Asian economic miracle. However they have followed very different paths to their economic success. The Hong Kong economy has developed within a freewheeling *laissez-faire* framework, with growth having been driven largely by relatively unfettered domestic entrepreneurs, while the Singapore economy has to a much greater degree been guided by an interventionist government policy which has relied on high rates of domestic saving and direct foreign investment to funnel resources into the sectors it has favored.

The value of output per capita in both economies has grown at roughly the same rapid rate during the past several decades. Estimates vary but all agree that GDP in both economies has grown at rates in excess of 6 percent per annum since 1960. This raises the obvious question of what factors might explain such high and sustained rates of economic growth in two economies which have taken such different approaches to development. The World Bank has attributed high rates of growth in Hong Kong and Singapore (and several other Asian economies as well) to

* This chapter is based on a paper presented to the Taipei International Conference on Efficiency and Productivity Growth held at the Institute of Economics, Academia Sinica, Taipei, Taiwan, ROC, 20-21 June, 1997, and to the Council for Economic Planning and Development, Taipei, Taiwan, ROC, 16 December, 1997. We received many helpful comments at both presentations, and we are also grateful for advice and guidance received from Tsu-Tan Fu and Cliff Huang.

generally sound macroeconomic management. Growth accountants, on the other hand, have tended to attribute high rates of economic growth in the region to rapid, and ultimately unsustainable, factor accumulation in the face of unimpressive rates of productivity growth (essentially zero in the case of Singapore). Although much is made of these two divergent interpretations, they are not necessarily inconsistent. Sound macroeconomic management can of course establish an institutional framework within which productivity growth flourishes. However in the absence of significant productivity growth, sound macroeconomic management in other respects would seem to be a prerequisite for rapid economic growth. Since productivity growth is neither necessary nor sufficient for economic growth, much less growth in economic well-being, and since the Asian productivity growth literature is already vast, we prefer to focus on the quality of macroeconomic management in Asia in general, and in the two city-states in particular.

The quality of a country macroeconomic management is difficult to define, and even more difficult to observe directly. However it is possible to evaluate the quality of a country's macroeconomic management indirectly, by evaluating the observable outcomes of policy decisions undertaken by its economic decision-makers. This is the approach we take in this study. We make no contribution to the contentious issue concerning the contribution of productivity growth to economic growth in Hong Kong and Singapore. Our contribution is to conduct a pair of empirical exercises in which we examine the quality of macroeconomic management in Hong Kong and Singapore, relative to that in a number of other relevant countries. One exercise is backward-looking, and the other is forward-looking.

This chapter is organized as follows. In section 2 we briefly review the various competing interpretations of the recent economic performances of Hong Kong and Singapore. In section 3 we conduct our backward-looking evaluation of the quality of macroeconomic management these two city-states have enjoyed. We find evidence that the Singapore interventionist approach has been just as effective as the Hong Kong hands-off approach, although we also find that neither approach has been as effective as that of Taiwan. In section 4 we conduct our forward-looking evaluation of the quality of macroeconomic management in the two city-states as they position themselves for the twenty-first century. Results of this evaluation suggest that despite certain shortcomings, Hong Kong appears much better prepared than Singapore for continued rapid economic growth in the near future.[1] Section 5 contains a summary of our findings, and some speculative ruminations in light of the tumultuous events of 1997.

2 COMPETING INTERPRETATIONS OF THE RECENT ECONOMIC PERFORMANCE OF HONG KONG AND SINGAPORE

Impressions of the recent economic performance of Hong Kong and Singapore, and of the role of productivity change in this performance, come from four sources. The World Bank (1993) has adopted a laudatory stance. Young (1992, 1995) and Krugman (1994) have questioned the World Bank's favorable view. The rest of the academic community has, perhaps not surprisingly, expressed divergent opinions. Finally, regardless of past performance, the nonacademic community is optimistic about future prospects. In this section we briefly review each of these positions.

The World Bank has referred admiringly to the 'economic miracle' achieved by the high performing Asian economies, which it categorizes as the Four Tigers (Hong Kong, the Republic of Korea, Singapore and Taiwan) and the newly industrializing economies (Indonesia, Malaysia and Thailand). It attributes the economic miracle to the fact that they got the basics right. Among the basics these seven economies have got right are, to varying degrees in various countries, (i) declining rates of population growth and declining income inequality, (ii) secure property rights embodied in the legal framework, (iii) high domestic savings rates which sustained high rates of private domestic investment, (iv) an openness to foreign technology and foreign direct investment, (v) investment in human capital and flexible labor markets, (vii) competent and honest bureaucracies and effective systems of public administration, and (viii) sound macroeconomic management. We will return to the claim of sound economic management in sections 3 and 4.

However recently a revisionist view has emerged. Originally propounded by Young (1992, 1995), and popularized by Krugman (1994), this view claims that (i) the East Asian economic miracle is overrated, particularly in Singapore, and (ii) output growth in Singapore, and to a lesser extent in Hong Kong, has been due to unsustainable input growth, and the days in which Singapore can continue to sustain accumulation-driven growth are clearly numbered. Or, as *The Economist* (1995) so eloquently put it, 'If you invest in more sausage machines and employ more sausage-makers, of course you will make more sausages. Where's the miracle? Growth will slow down when you run out of extra sausage-makers.'

The following calculations, taken from Young (1995), illustrate the revisionist contention that economic growth in these two city-states has been accumulation-driven, particularly in Singapore. Over the period 1966-1990 Young calculates that Singapore's real GDP grew at an average annual rate of 8.7 percent, while its average annual growth rates of quality-adjusted capital and labor were 11.5 percent and 5.7 percent respectively. For productivity to have grown at a 2 percent average annual rate would have required an average labor expenditure share of 83 percent. However Young calculates that labor expenditure share averaged 51 percent over the period, which implies an average productivity growth rate of just 0.2 percent. It follows that Singapore's rapid economic growth during the period was due almost exclusively to rapid factor accumulation rather than to productivity growth.

Young paints a somewhat brighter picture for Hong Kong, for which he calculates that real GDP growth averaged 7.3 percent per annum over the same period, while growth rates of quality-adusted capital and labor averaged 8.0 percent and 3.2 percent respectively. With an estimated average labor expenditure share of 63 percent, a 2.3 percent average annual productivity growth rate is implied. While Hong Kong's productivity growth has been far more impressive than that of Singapore, it still appears that less than a third of Hong Kong's economic growth can be attributed to productivity growth.

The search for an explanation for rapid rates of economic growth in the region has attracted a substantial academic effort. Perhaps not surprisingly, findings have been mixed, although there has been some support for the revisionists' claim of negligible productivity growth in Singapore. Kim and Lau (1994) used a meta-production function approach and concluded that (i) capital accumulation accounted for the vast majority of economic growth achieved by the Four Tigers; and (ii) the hypothesis of no technological progress could not be rejected for these economies collectively. This conclusion was questioned by Harberger (1996), who noted that differences in GDP growth rates between high-growth subperiods and low-growth subperiods were highly correlated with, and perhaps caused by, differences in productivity growth rates between these subperiods. Thus the Young finding of negligible productivity growth in Singapore over a three-decade period is not inconsistent with the assertion that variation in growth rates from one decade to the next are attributable to variation in productivity growth rates from one decade to the next. The Harberger point is echoed by Hsiao and Hsiao (1997).

Easterly (1995) ran a variety of conventional growth regressions based on a large number of countries over several decades. He found persistent large positive growth regression residuals for Hong Kong and Singapore. However he attributed these residuals not to productivity growth, but to (i) the fact that both economies are city-states which are likely to have benefited from externalities associated with migration, urbanization and density; and (ii) quantitatively and statistically significant effects of various government policies on growth. We will take up Easterly's emphasis on government policies in sections 3 and 4.

Nadiri and Son (1998) specified a model with two outputs (domestic output and exports), five inputs (labor, physical capital, human capital, foreign capital and imports), and a time trend to account for technical change. They used data from six countries (Singapore, Korea, Taiwan, Thailand, Malaysia and Japan; requisite data were unavailable for Hong Kong) over the 1969-1990 period. They found that most of Singapore's output growth was associated with international trade, only 5 percent being attributable to technical progress. International trade was also emphasized by Gapinski (1997), who defined productivity growth to include all sources of economic growth other than growth in input quantities, primarily growth in input quality and international trade. On the basis of this definition he found that productivity growth accounted for well over half of output growth in both Hong Kong and Singapore during the 1961-1990 period. Gapinski and Western (1998) applied a similar approach to modeling economic growth in Hong Kong, and again found growth in international trade and growth in input quality to account together for over half of Hong Kong's economic growth.

More recently still, a more optimistic view has emerged from a variety of sources. The World Economic Forum ranks Singapore and Hong Kong first and second in terms of economic competitiveness based on 155 indicators for 49 countries. The International Institute for Management Development ranks Singapore and Hong Kong second and third in terms of an alternative notion of economic competitiveness based on 224 indicators for 46 countries.[2] A group of 11 institutes, led by the Fraser Institute, the Cato Institute and the Institute of Economic Affairs, ranks Singapore and Hong Kong second and first in terms of economic freedom based on 17 indicators for 102 countries.[3] Finally the Third International Maths and Science Study ranks Singapore and Hong Kong first and fourth in maths education and first and twenty-fourth in science education among 41 nations.[4]

It is hard to know what to make of all these conflicting claims. Singapore and Hong Kong apparently 'got the basics right' in the past, and they currently rank at or near the top of international rankings in terms of economic competitiveness and economic freedom. Yet productivity growth, which is the engine of economic growth and prosperity, has apparently lagged in Hong Kong and gone AWOL in Singapore. Perhaps the World Bank is off the mark, and Singapore and, to a lesser degree, Hong Kong, failed to get the basics right after all. In section 3 we conduct our own backward-looking investigation into the quality of macroeconomic management in these two countries during the recent past. Perhaps the optimists are also off the mark, and Singapore and Hong Kong are not well positioned to achieve rapid productivity gains in the near future. In section 4 we conduct a forward-looking investigation into the future potential of these two economies.

3 AN ALTERNATIVE TALE OF TWO CITIES

Easterly (1995) concluded that the success of the Four Tigers was due largely to 'the old prosaic fundamentals' of sound macroeconomic management. Our objective in this section is to follow up on the Easterly conclusion by taking yet another look backward at the past performance of Hong Kong and Singapore, by conducting an evaluation of three conventional backward-looking indicators of the quality of macroeconomic management in these two countries. The common logic underlying the three indicators is that if the unobservable quality of a country macroeconomic management has been high, then the observable consequences of its macroeconomic policies should be favorable. The three indicators differ only in their specification of the observable consequences. The three indicators are

- Okun's 'Misery Index' $M = I + U,$
- Calmfors' Index $C = U - (X-M)/GDP,$
- the OECD's 'Magic Diamond' $D = G_{GDP} + (X-M)/GDP - U - I,$

where I is the rate of inflation, U is the unemployment rate, $(X-M)$ is the real trade balance, GDP is real gross domestic product and G_{GDP} is the rate of growth of real GDP. Okun's Misery Index and Calmfors' Index are perverse indicators of the quality of macroeconomic management, since each adds undesirable consequences. The OECD's Magic Diamond is a positive indicator, since it subtracts undesirable consequences from desirable consequences. The components of each indicator are expressed in percentage terms, and so each indicator can be compared across countries and through time without concern for exchange rate fluctuations. Each indicator can be constructed from readily available data sources, and each is frequently reported in the popular press.

However each of these indicators suffers from the same problem: by simply adding components to create an indicator, each implicitly assigns constant and equal weights to each component. This arbitrary weighting scheme does not allow for intertemporal and intercountry variation in macroeconomic policy which, under varying economic circumstances, would tend to favor one component over another. It is therefore desirable to generalize each indicator so as to allow weights attached to each component to vary, both across countries and through time, as economic circumstances warrant.[5]

Our solution to the problem is to employ a linear programming technique known as data envelopment analysis (DEA) to aggregate the components of each index in a non-arbitrary fashion. A great virtue of DEA is that it permits weights attached to each component to be variable and unequal, across countries and through time. Country-year observations are allowed to select component weights which put them in the most favorable light relative to other country-year observations in the sample, subject to some restrictions to be discussed below. A second virtue of DEA is that it simultaneously constructs a best practice macroeconomic performance frontier which envelops all country-year performances from above. At the same time it measures the distance of each country-year observation to the best practice frontier, and these distances provide the basis for a ranking of country-year observations in terms of their ability to optimize each indicator.[6]

Suppose we observe a sample of $i = 1, ..., I$ countries over a span of $t = 1, ..., T$ years. Denote by the vector $y = (y_1, ..., y_M)$ a set of M desirable outcomes of macroeconomic policy, and by the vector $x = (x_1, ..., x_N)$ a set of N undesirable outcomes of macroeconomic policy. Then a DEA formulation of a problem intended to minimize undesirable outcomes with given desirable outcomes can be expressed as

$$\min_{\theta, \lambda^j} \quad \theta$$

subject to

$$\begin{aligned} \theta x_n^o &\geq \textstyle\sum_j \lambda^j x_n^j & \quad n &= 1, ..., N \\ \textstyle\sum_j \lambda^j y_m^j &\geq y_m^o & m &= 1, ..., M \\ \lambda^j &\geq 0 & j &= 1, ..., I \cdot T \\ \textstyle\sum_j \lambda^j &= 1 \end{aligned}$$

This linear program is solved $I \cdot T$ times, once for every country-year observation in the sample. The program constructs a best practice macroeconomic performance frontier, and measures the distance of each observation from the frontier. For a country-year with data (y_m^o, x_n^o) the program seeks the maximum feasible equiproportionate contraction in its undesirable outcomes, subject to the constraint that it does not violate best practice observed in the sample. If at optimum $\theta = 1$, this country-year is best practice relative to all country-years in the sample. If at optimum $\theta < 1$, this country-year is not best practice, and to have achieved best-practice status it would have had to decrease its undesirable outcomes to $(100 \times \theta)$ percent of their observed values. Thus $\theta \in (0,1]$ provides a convenient ranking of country-year observations on the basis of their ability to minimize undesirable outcomes. Also at optimum, the nonzero elements of λ identify the best practice country-year observation(s) with which the country-year being evaluated is compared. Thus high-performing country-years have two characteristics: they have optimal values of θ at or near unity, and they appear frequently as role models for other country-years.

Since the DEA problem is a linear program, it has a dual linear program. This program can be expressed as

$$\max_{\nu_m, \nu_*, \mu_n} \quad \sum_m \nu_m y_m^o + \nu_*$$

subject to

$$\begin{aligned} \sum_n \mu_n x_n^o &= 1 \\ \sum_m \nu_m y_m^j - \sum_n \mu_n x_n^j + \nu_* &\leq 0, \qquad j = 1, \ldots, o, \ldots, I \cdot T \\ \nu_m \geq 0, \ \mu_n \geq 0, \ \nu_* \ &\text{free.} \end{aligned}$$

For the country-year under evaluation the dual program seeks a set of nonnegative weights which, when attached to each of its outcomes, maximizes the 'value' of its desirable outcomes, subject to a normalization on the value of its undesirable outcomes and subject to a set of $I \cdot T$ feasibility constraints. It is these feasibility constraints, together with the nonnegativity constraints, which restrict the ability of country-year observations to select large weights for their desirable outcomes and small, even negative, weights for their undesirable outcomes. Nonetheless the weights for each outcome are allowed to vary across countries and through time. Thus country-year observations are allowed to attach different values to a particular outcome as economic circumstances warrant.[7]

Okun's Misery Index M is a special case of the DEA problem indicated above, in which the orientation of the primal problem is toward minimizing two undesirable outcomes [I and U] and there are no desirable outcomes. The Calmfors' Index C is a different special case of the DEA problem, in which the orientation of the primal problem is toward minimizing the sole undesirable outcome U, with $(X-M)/GDP$ as the sole desirable outcome. Finally the OECD Magic Diamond D is a third special case of the DEA problem, in which the orientation is toward minimizing the two undesirable outcomes [I and U], with two desirable outcomes [G_{GDP} and $(X-M)/GDP$].

Our strategy is to proceed in two stages. In the first stage we construct Okun's Misery Index M, Calmfors' Index C, and the OECD Magic Diamond D, directly from the data for various countries over a period of time. These three indicators have weights which are constant across countries and through time, and so they provide rankings of country-year observations under the constraint that all country-year observations are forced to agree that each component of the indicator is equally important. In the second stage we delete this equality constraint, by using DEA to calculate variable-weight variants of each indicator. These DEA-based indicators provide alternative rankings which allow country-year observations to attach varying degrees of importance to components as economic circumstances warrant.

We are interested in the degree of concordance of rankings based on the fixed-weight and the variable-weight performance indicators. We are also interested in the extent to which the variable-weight performance indicators vary across countries and through time, and in the extent to which the component weights themselves vary across countries and through time. Finally we are interested in how frequently a country appears as a role model for other countries. Throughout our investigation we are particularly interested in the performance of Hong Kong and Singapore.

We use a conventional data set derived from annual issues of the Statistical Yearbook for Asia and the Pacific, and various country Statistical Yearbooks. The sample countries and years are listed in Table 2.1. All of the World Bank high-performing Asian economies are represented, as are the Philippines, Australia and New Zealand, and Japan and the USA. Since not all countries report all components of the three indicators for all years, some DEA calculations of the three indicators are based on fewer than 270 observations. Since some countries report data as far back as 1964 and others report data only as far back as 1978, we report results for the common time span 1981-1993. Only Indonesia is missing the terminal year.[8]

A summary of the DEA-based calculations of the three variable-weight macroeconomic performance indicators appears in Table 2.2. There we report temporal means of GGDP, which can be compared with temporal

Table 2.1 Countries included in the backward-looking analysis

Australia	(1965-1993)	29
Hong Kong	(1977-1993)	17
Indonesia	(1978-1992)	15
Japan	(1964-1993)	30
Korea	(1965-1993)	29
Malaysia	(1978-1993)	16
New Zealand	(1974-1993)	20
Philippines	(1978-1994)	17
Singapore	(1966-1994)	29
Taiwan	(1965-1994)	30
Thailand	(1977-1993)	17
USA	(1975-1995)	21

means of each of the three indicators. The impressive growth rates achieved by the high performing Asian economies are apparent, ranging from over 8 percent per annum in Korea to just under 6 percent per annum in Indonesia. Singapore and Hong Kong rank fourth and sixth, both among the seven high performing Asian economies and overall.

Temporal mean values of the DEA-based Okun's Misery Index M appear in the second column of Table 2.2. Taiwan turned in the best overall performance at keeping inflation and unemployment under control, while the Philippines performed the worst. Singapore and Hong Kong ranked third and fifth, slightly better than their G_{GDP} rankings. To illustrate the interpretation of these results, on average during the period Singapore would have had to reduce its inflation and unemployment rates to approximately two-thirds of their observed values in order to have achieved best practice status. Of the seven best practice observations in the sample, those to which both Singapore and Hong Kong are most frequently compared are Japan (1966) and Taiwan (1988).[9] Neither Singapore nor Hong Kong appears as a best practice role model for any other country-year observation during the 1981-1993 period.

Temporal mean values of the DEA-based Calmfors' Index C appear in the third column of Table 2.2. Again Taiwan turned in the best overall performance, in this case in terms of its ability to minimize its inflation rate given its normalized trade balance, while Australia, the Philippines and the USA performed the worst. Hong Kong and Singapore ranked second and sixth. The interpretation for Hong Kong is that, on average during the period, and given its normalized trade balances, it could have

Table 2.2 Summary of backward-looking findings, 1981-1993

Country	[GDP Growth]	[M]	[C]	[D]
Australia	2.78	0.28	0.14	0.28
Hong Kong	6.07 (6)	0.56 (5)	0.55 (2)	0.69 (5)
Indonesia	5.88	0.50	0.46	0.58
Japan	3.61	0.76	0.45	0.77
Korea	8.24 (1)	0.51	0.36	0.53
Malaysia	6.54	0.41	0.28	0.49
New Zealand	1.52	0.32	0.20	0.34
Philippines	1.54	0.26	0.16	0.30
Singapore	7.26 (4)	0.68 (3)	0.40 (6)	0.69 (4)
Taiwan	7.71	0.84 (1)	0.70 (1)	0.93 (1)
Thailand	7.94	0.67	0.48	0.72
USA	2.56	0.34	0.16	0.34

decreased its inflation rates to 55 percent of their observed values without violating best practice observed in the sample. Of the four best practice observations in the sample, by far the most frequent role model for Hong Kong and Singapore during the period was Hong Kong (1988) itself.[10]

Temporal mean values of the DEA-based Magic Diamond *D* appear in the final column of Table 2.2. No country comes close to Taiwan. Singapore and Hong Kong rank fourth and fifth. The interpretation is that both Singapore and Hong Kong could have reduced their inflation and unemployment rates to 69 percent of their observed values on average, given their normalized trade balances and their GDP growth rates, without violating best practice observed in the sample. Of the 16 best practice observations in the sample, the role models to which Singapore and Hong Kong are most frequently compared include Taiwan (various years) and Hong Kong (1988).

The three DEA-based macroeconomic performance indicators have dual weights attached to each component. Ratios of weights indicate tradeoffs between pairs of components. We do not report detailed results for each indicator. Rather, to illustrate the variability of weights across countries and through time, we report selected results for Hong Kong and Singapore. Table 2.3 contains temporal means and ranges of the ratio of the optimal weights attached to unemployment and inflation in the two indicators (*M* and *D*) containing both outcomes. These calculations suffice to demonstrate that optimal weights vary through time for each country, and that they also vary across countries. They indicate that both

Hong Kong and Singapore have attached greater weight to low unemployment rates than to low inflation rates as a macroeconomic policy objective. They also indicate that Hong Kong has placed greater emphasis on full employment relative to price stability than has Singapore.[11]

Table 2.3 Selected weight ratio means

Misery Index Weight Ratio Means and Ranges
(μ UNEMPLOYMENT/μ INFLATION)

Hong Kong	6.31 (2.68-18.09)
Singapore	2.87 (0.91-4.84)

Magic Diamond Weight Ratio Means and Ranges
(μ UNEMPLOYMENT/μ INFLATION)

Hong Kong	18.41 (2.68-44.36)
Singapore	7.94 (0.00-17.89)

Since optimal weights attached to indicator components vary through time and across countries, we expect the DEA-based variable-weight macroeconomic performance indicators to diverge from their fixed-weight counterparts. They do, but not by as much as we had expected. We do not report detailed results for the fixed-weight versions of the three macroeconomic performance indicators. Instead, in Table 2.4 we report rank correlation coefficients between fixed-weight and variable-weight versions of each indicator. Rank correlations are positive as expected, and unexpectedly high in light of the variability of the component weights in each indicator.

Table 2.4 Rank correlations between fixed-weight and variable-weight macroeconomic performance indicators

Misery Index	0.83
Calmfors' Index	0.62
Magic Diamond	0.74

Although we have shed no light on the question of the magnitude of productivity growth in Singapore and Hong Kong, this has not been our objective in this section. Our objective has been to evaluate the quality of macroeconomic management in the two city-states, as reflected by variable-weight versions of three popular macroeconomic performance indicators. Our analysis leads us to four backward-looking conclusions. First the quality of macroeconomic policy-making, as judged by various combinations of its observable consequences, has been substantially higher in Taiwan than in any other country in our sample. Second the macroeconomic performances of Singapore and Hong Kong rank them no better than in the middle of the group of seven high performing Asian economies. Third if Young's productivity growth calculation for Hong Kong is reasonably accurate, then Hong Kong's policy-makers have done a fairly mediocre job of converting its respectable rate of productivity growth into successful macroeconomic performance. Finally if Young's productivity growth calculation for Singapore is reasonably accurate, then Singapore's policy-makers have done a respectable job of converting its negligible rate of productivity growth into successful macroeconomic performance.

4 AN ALTERNATIVE TALE OF TWO CITIES, PART II

Lee Kuan Yew, Singapore senior minister, is reported to have stated (to Krugman) that 'you're right so far, but our total factor productivity growth will be much higher in the future because of the investments we're making in education' (and other growth-enhancing areas?).[12]

To the extent that Singapore and Hong Kong have been investing heavily in education and other growth-enhancing areas, their future productivity growth prospects may be enhanced. Our objective in this section is to take a look into the future, by conducting an evaluation of less conventional forward-looking indicators of the quality of macroeconomic management in these two countries. These indicators have as their components various measures of investment in human and physical capital which, it can be argued, ought to enhance productivity growth in the future.

Our forward-looking sample is essentially the same as our backward-looking sample: nine countries for various time periods extending back from 1993. Variables, which are taken from the same sources we used in section 3, include the share of gross domestic investment in GDP, the share of gross domestic savings in GDP, the share of health expenditure in GDP, the share of housing expenditure in GDP, the share of transport and communication expenditure in GDP, the share of education expenditure in

GDP, high school enrollment as a percent of the population, and university enrollment as a percent of the population. We have run a number of experiments with various combinations of these measures. Some of the more interesting experiments are indicated in Table 2.5. The first two models include the share of gross domestic investment in GDP, while the second two models replace investment with savings. One of the first two models includes the share of education expenditure in GDP, and the other uses enrollment ratios. This pattern is reversed in the second two models. The shares of GDP accounted for by health, housing and transport expenditure are included in all four models. Unfortunately Japan, Taiwan and the USA are excluded from the analysis because they do not report comparable data.

Table 2.5 Variables included in selected forward-looking models

	Models			
Outputs	1	2	3	4
Investment as % of GDP	x	x		
Savings as % of GDP			x	x
Health Expenditure as % of GDP	x	x	x	x
Housing Expenditure as % of GDP	x	x	x	x
Transport Expenditure as % of GDP	x	x	x	x
Education Expenditure as % of GDP	x			x
HS Enrollment as % of Population		x	x	
Univ Enrollment as % of Population		x	x	

Our strategy is to use a variant of the generic DEA model introduced in section 3 to evaluate the propensity of sample country-year observations to undertake the productivity-enhancing investments in human and physical capital indicated in each of the models. Thus we report the results of four DEA models. The orientation of each model is toward maximizing the investment variables, which are treated as desirable outputs. There are no inputs in these models. We use data covering different time periods for different countries in the DEA exercises, but to enhance comparability we report results for the 1977-1992 time period common to all countries. Results are summarized in Table 2.6, where we report rankings based on temporal mean performances.

Table 2.6 Selected forward-looking model results

Country	Rank by Model (1977-1992)			
	1	2	3	4
Australia	8	4	3	8
Hong Kong	3	3	2	3
Indonesia	9	8	8	6
Korea	5	2	1	9
Malaysia	2	7	6	2
New Zealand	1	1	4	1
Philippines	6	6	5	5
Singapore	4	5	7	4
Thailand	7	9	9	7

Rankings vary across models, but when all four models are considered the overall top investor in human and physical capital has been New Zealand, followed by Hong Kong and Korea. Singapore ranks fifth. Indonesia and Thailand are at the bottom of the overall ranking.

In Table 2.7 we report somewhat more detailed results for Hong Kong and Singapore. There it is clear that Hong Kong is at or very near best practice in all four models. Singapore, on the other hand, falls well short of best practice in models 3 and 4, which include the saving rate rather than the investment rate.

From Tables 2.6 and 2.7 it is apparent that the outlook is brighter for Hong Kong with models which contain savings rather than investment (models 3 and 4), and which contain enrollments rather than educational expenditures (models 2 and 3). Although Hong Kong has had relatively high investment and savings rates (29 percent and 11 percent respectively), its saving rate has been higher relative to the rest of the sample than has its investment rate. And although Hong Kong has had relatively high enrollment ratios, its education expenditure share of GDP has been among the lowest in the sample.[13] Conversely, the outlook is brighter for Singapore with models which contain investment rather than savings (models 1 and 2), and which contain educational expenditure rather than enrollments (models 1 and 4). Like Hong Kong, Singapore has had high rates of investment and saving (39 percent and 12 percent respectively), but its investment rate has consistently been among the highest in the region. Unlike Hong Kong, Singapore has had relatively high rates of education expenditure, despite relatively low enrollment ratios. Singapore's low enrollment ratios have been due to the fact that it has only one university and a few colleges, and consequently many of its students are trained overseas.

Table 2.7 Detailed forward-looking results for Hong Kong and Singapore

Model	Country		
	Hong Kong	Singapore	Winner
1	0.89	0.89	0.96
2	0.96	0.90	0.99
3	0.96	0.78	0.96
4	0.91	0.80	0.94

It is possible that the results reported in Tables 2.6 and 2.7 overstate Singapore's future growth potential. This is because Singapore allocates a relatively large share of GDP to investment in housing (1.8 percent on average during the period), and this share exceeds the shares it allocates to health and transport. While it is plausible that investment in health, transport and education will enhance future growth prospects, it is less likely that investment in housing will do likewise. While it will certainly enhance living standards, the opportunity cost of housing investment in Singapore may be high.

5 SUMMARY AND CONCLUSIONS

This study originated in deep skepticism of the revisionist claim of unimpressive rates of productivity growth in East Asia in general, and in Singapore in particular. Our skepticism remains, despite the fact that we have no alternative estimates of productivity growth to offer. We have, however, formed some impressions of the past performance and the future prospects for Singapore and Hong Kong. Our impressions are based on a series of backward-looking and forward-looking evaluations of the quality of macroeconomic management in these two economies. Since management quality is not directly observable, we base our two sets of evaluations on observable consequences of economic policies.

Our backward-looking evaluations were based on variable-weight versions of three conventional indicators of macroeconomic performance: Okun's Misery Index, Calmfors' Index and the OECD Magic Diamond. We found Hong Kong and Singapore to rank no better than in the middle of the seven high performing Asian economies, well behind Taiwan. That

Singapore managed to achieve its success despite the apparent absence of productivity growth is impressive. It is also noteworthy that the seven high performing Asian economies outperformed the USA, Australia and New Zealand, typically by wide margins.

Our forward-looking evaluations were based on various combinations of investments in human and physical capital, since such investments should pave the way for future economic success. On these criteria Hong Kong ranked second behind New Zealand, and Singapore ranked fifth. To the extent that past investments do augur well for future economic success, and subject to the current uncertainties surrounding Hong Kong's reversion to Chinese sovereignty, the future looks bright for Hong Kong.

The data on which this study is based extend only through 1994, but the tumultuous events of 1997 are still reverberating throughout the region. Can the results of this study shed any light on 1997? It is clear that 1997 was not about productivity growth, but about the quality of macroeconomic management. Thus even though our notions of the quality of macroeconomic management do not include indicators of the quality of the financial infrastructure, or of the opaque linkages between the financial sector and business and government, it is perhaps worth revisiting our findings in light of 1997. We gave the highest backward-looking marks to Taiwan, which has weathered the storm in relatively good economic shape. We gave above average marks to Hong Kong and Singapore, both of which have done likewise. We gave below average marks to Indonesia, Korea, Malaysia and the Philippines, all of which have suffered greatly. Only Thailand, which started the financial difficulties, received relatively high backward-looking marks, and it received poor forward-looking marks. There thus appears to be a degree of concordance between the quality of macroeconomic management as we have defined it and performance during and immediately after 1997.

NOTES

1. Hong Kong reverted to the sovereignty of China on 1 July 1997, and the impact this reversion has on Hong Kong's economic future is uncertain. Although we do not speculate in this chapter, Gapinski and Western (1998) do.
2. The World Economic Forum and the International Institute for Management Development studies are discussed in *The Economist* (1996b).
3. As reported in *The Economist* (1996a).
4. As reported in *The Economist* (1997a).
5. This observation was apparently first made by Melyn and Moesen (1991).
6. DEA was introduced by Charnes *et al.* (1978). A good recent reference is

Charnes *et al.* (1994).

7. The analogy to the revealed preference approach to demand analysis should be apparent; in this formulation country-years reveal their preferences for components of indicators. We owe this point to Kevin Fox.
8. Several country-year observations have negative values of one or more of the components of each indicator. This presents no difficulty in calculating fixed-weight versions of the three indicators, but it does present a problem in calculating the DEA-based variable-weight versions of the three indicators. We have therefore translated each component by adding to every country-year value the smallest value observed in the sample to assure that all values of each component are nonnegative. Lovell and Pastor (1995) have shown that under certain conditions, satisfied here, DEA is invariant to such a translation of variables.
9. Japan (1966) had $U = 0.9$ and $I = 5.1$, while Taiwan (1988) had $U = 1.7$ and $I = 1.28$; these two observations served as joint role models for the majority of the remaining observations.
10. Hong Kong (1988) had $(X - M)/GDP = 0.07$ and $U = 1.1$, and served as the sole role model for the majority of the remaining observations.
11. As evidence of this greater emphasis, during the period Hong Kong's mean unemployment rate was 2.45 percent, while Singapore was 3.17 percent. The tradeoff Hong Kong experienced was a higher mean rate of inflation, 10.03 percent compared with 4.35 percent in Singapore.
12. The quote is taken from *The Wall Street Journal* (1995). The parenthetical phrase is ours.
13. *Business Week* (1997) notes that 85 percent of Hong Kong's primary school students attend school part time because of insufficient investment in schools. Thus the popular view that throwing money at existing schools may be unproductive may not apply to Hong Kong, where investments in new schools may be very productive.

REFERENCES

Business Week (1997), 'Hong Kong', 9 June, 44-62.

Charnes, A., W.W. Cooper, A.Y. Lewin and L.M. Seiford (eds) (1994), *Data Envelopment Analysis: Theory, Methodology and Applications*, Boston, Dordrecht and London: Kluwer Academic Publishers.

Charnes, A., W.W. Cooper and E. Rhodes (1978), 'Measuring the efficiency of decision making units', *European Journal of Operational Research*, **2** (6), 429-44.

The Economist (1995), 'The miracle of the sausage-makers', 9 December, 33-34.

The Economist (1996a), 'Of liberty, and prosperity', 13 January, 21-3.

The Economist (1996), 'The C-word strikes back', **76**, 1 June,

The Economist (1997), 'Who's top?', 29 March, 21-3.

Easterly, W. (1995), 'Explaining miracles: growth regressions meet the gang of four', in T. Ito and A.O. Krueger (eds), *Growth Theories in Light of the East Asian Experience*, Chicago and London: The University of Chicago Press for the National Bureau of Economic Research.

Gapinski, J.H. (1997), 'Economic growth in the Asian-Pacific region', *Asia Pacific Journal of Economics and Business 1*, forthcoming.

Gapinski, J.H. and D.L. Western (1998), 'A tiger in the land of the panda: growth prospects for Hong Kong under reversion to China', this volume.

Harberger, A.C. (1996), 'Reflections on economic growth in Asia and the Pacific', *Journal of Asian Economics*, **7** (3), 365-92.

Hsiao, F.S.T. and Hsiao, M.-C.W. (1997), 'Miracle or myth of Asican NICs' growth - the irony of numbers', Working paper, Department of Economics, University of Colorado, Boulder, CO 80309, USA.

Kim, J.-I. and L.J. Lau (1994), 'The sources of economic growth of the East Asian newly industrialized countries', *Journal of the Japanese and International Economies*, **8**, 235-71.

Krugman, P. (1994), 'The myth of Asia miracle', *Foreign Affairs*, **73** (6), 62-78.

Lovell, C.A.K. and J.T. Pastor (1995), 'Units invariant and translation invariant DEA models', *Operations Research Letters*, **18** (3), 147-51.

Melyn, W. and W. Moesen (1991), 'Towards a synthetic indicator of macroeconomic performance: unequal weighting when limited information is available', public economics research paper No. 17, Centrum voor Economische Studien, Katholieke Universiteit Leuven, Leuven, BELGIUM.

Nadiri, M.I. and W. Son (1998), 'Sources of growth in East Asian economies', this volume.

The Wall Street Journal (1995), 'Is the vaunted "Asian miracle" really just an illusion?', 20 October.

World Bank (1993), *The East Asian Miracle: Economic Growth and Public Policy,* New York: Oxford University Press.

Young, A. (1992), 'A tale of two cities: factor accumulation and technical change in Hong Kong and Singapore', NBER Macroeconomics Annual 1992, 13-54.

Young, A. (1995), 'The tyranny of numbers: confronting the statistical realities of the East Asian growth experience', *Quarterly Journal of Economics*, **110**, 641-80.

3. Sources of Growth in East Asian Economies*

M. Ishaq Nadiri and Wanpyo Son

1 INTRODUCTION

There has been considerable interest in the growth and productivity literature in explaining whether there is a tendency for per capita income or aggregate productivity levels to converge, and whether this tendency and the slower growth of productivity experienced in recent years are related. The theoretical analysis and empirical evidence on the subject have been controversial. Three different theoretical explanations have been proposed. 'New Growth Theory' proposed by Romer (1987) and Lucas (1988) stresses how factor accumulation makes growth rates endogenous so that differences in growth rates between countries may persist. There are possibilities of multi-equilibria, that is, some countries may catch up to the leader but others may get stuck on low-level equilibrium paths and may not have the opportunity to do so (Hulten, 1992). The second approach, proposed by Abramovitz (1986), emphasizes the role of catch-up in the growth process and has been examined empirically by Barro and Sala-i-Martin (1991), Dowrick and Nguyen (1989) and others. The third approach is the political economy of institutional sclerosis (Olson, 1982) which stresses the rent seeking and anti-growth practices of special interest groups that over time lead to slower growth and differential rates of growth among different economies. The empirical application of the endogenous growth models have often been analyzed using a large cross-section of data covering ninety to a hundred highly heterogeneous countries (see, for example, Lichtenberg, 1993 and Mankiw, Romer and Weil, 1992 for recent contributions).

The various aspects of the growth experience of East Asian economies

* We would like to thank Hui Guo and Frances Hui for their helpful assistance. Support from the C.V. Starr Center for Applied Economics of New York University is also gratefully acknowledged.

have been discussed with great fascination and controversy in the literature. Some have argued that substantial investment boom in plant and equipment have been the source of the Asian 'growth miracles'. High levels of human capital and relatively equal distribution of income created the conditions under which government intervention stimulated investment that led to growth.[1] Another standard explanation of the success of these countries is one of export led growth. As the story goes, in the 1950s these countries engaged in import substitution policies with high levels of trade protection, multiple exchange rates and tight regulation of the financial markets. In the early 1960s the 'easy stage' of import substitution had been exhausted and the policy makers were forced into adopting an export-oriented policies. Policies such as liberalization of the exchange rate controls and of import regimes and various incentives for exports were accompanied with macroeconomic policies to stabilize the economy and promote public investment and investment in human capital. In this environment the economies of East Asia specialized according to comparative advantage which resulted in turn to rising incomes investment, saving and productivity.[2]

Another potential source of growth in recent years is the possible role of foreign direct investment in these economies. The size of this type of investment is still not very large but it is increasing rapidly. However, looked at as a vehicle for technology transfer and management skills and integrating these economies into the global markets, foreign direct investment can become a critical element of the growth process and a major source of dynamism of these economies. Finally, a number of studies have focused on the contribution of technical progress as a source of growth in the countries. The growth rate of technical change, according to these studies, has played a negligible or very small role in the growth of these economies. Kim and Lau (1995) report that 'the hypothesis of zero technical progress cannot be rejected for the East Asian newly industrialized countries (NICS)'. It is the rapid rate of capital accumulation that is the major source of growth of these economies. Young (1995) also reports that the productivity growth of East Asian fast-growing economies are not extraordinarily high compared with those of other postwar economies.

Finally, the issue of international competitiveness and its contribution to growth and prosperity of the whole economy has been a subject of considerable controversy. Krugman (1994) has contended that concerns about competitiveness in international markets is misguided, and may lead to skewing domestic policies and international economic system. However, he provides no empirical evidence on the contribution domestic and export markets toward the 'competitiveness' of an economy. One way to address this issue is to examine the contributions of exports to the output and productivity growth and compare them with those of the domestic economic activity in a country.

Our objective is to look at the growth experience of a group of countries-South Korea, Japan, Taiwan, Singapore, Thailand and Malaysia - which have achieved extraordinary growth rates since early 1960s.

1. We are interested in developing a framework to examine the implications of the various hypotheses, noted earlier, on growth of these countries. In particular, we are interested to know how different rates of capital accumulation in physical capital, foreign capital, and human capital, labor and the rate of technical change have contributed to output and productivity growth in these economies over the period 1969-1990.[3]
2. In contrast to much of the catch-up literature we consider in some detail the question of what factors may have contributed to the narrowing of the gaps in the levels of productivity and income per capita among these countries. Basically, the issue of catch-up or convergence depends on how different economies have deployed their resources and invested in technology and physical capital.

The convergence possibilities among these countries are of interest because of special features of this region. First, Japan is the leading economy with a high standard of living and economic power that other countries in the region aspire to. Japan is also the main provider of capital to these economies as increasing number of Japanese firms locate and invest in East Asian economies. Also, the convergence process in this region may be different from the standard analysis. In the analysis of convergence the US economy or industries serve as the leaders that others would want to catch up. However, the growth of the US economy is not high and therefore it makes an easier target to catch-up with than would be the case if the US economy had experienced a sustained high growth rate. Japan in the period under consideration was expanding rapidly and therefore is a more difficult leader to catch up.

The rest of this chapter is organized as follows. In section 2 we provide a brief description of the behavior of output (both domestic output and exports) and productivity growth as well as input growth in the six countries over the period 1967-1990. Section 3 describes the theoretical model and discusses the basic estimation results. In this section we also report estimates of cost elasticities with respect to labor, physical capital, human capital, and foreign capital and the rate of technical change for each of the countries. Section 4 is devoted to examining the sources of output and productivity growth in each of the countries. We present estimates of the contributions of domestic economy and exports' growth to total factor productivity growth. Also we proved estimates of the contributions of domestic capital, labor, human capital, foreign capital and technological change to the growth of output and labor productivity in these countries. In section 5 we explore the factors that may have led to a possible convergence in labor productivity or per capita income among these economies. Summary and conclusions are presented in section 6. The data used in estimating the model are described in the Appendix.

2 SOME DESCRIPTIVE CHARACTERISTICS

In this section, we provide a brief description of labor and total factor productivity (TFP) growth and the growth of domestic output, exports and imports. We also discuss factor accumulation such as the growth of labor, domestic capital and foreign direct investment and human capital. Table 3.1 shows the size of the population, GDP and level of GDP per capita as

Table 3.1 Population size, levels of output and inputs, trade in East Asian countries (average 1967-1990)

	Korea	Japan	Taiwan	Singapore	Thailand	Malaysia
Population	37.048	114.04	17.19	2.36	45.16	13.40
GDP	101.25	970.57	54.56	18.37	87.13	47.08
GDP Per Capita	2612	8384	3003	7504	1846	3376
Import	39.89	134.03	28.65	32.86	32.20	27.10
Total Output (Y)	141.139	1104.59	83.11	51.23	119.33	74.20
Domestic Output (Y_D)	104.303	983.72	50.68	18.69	94.72	42.76
Export (Y_E)	36.83	120.88	32.43	32.53	24.61	31.42
Employment	13.13	54.89	6.24	0.96	21.39	4.89
Physical Capital (K)	152.40	2508.69	74.51	33.94	161.70	60.65
Foreign Capital (F)	1.77	2.34	1.52	7.13	4.81	9.60
Human Capital (H)	6.47	10.48	7.20	6.62	6.17	6.40

well as the average levels of output, export, imports' employment and capital stock for the six countries over the period 1967-1990. Also, the level of foreign capital and an index of human capital are presented.

These economies clearly differ in size measured by the size of population or GDP. The largest economy is obviously Japan and the smallest is Singapore. But in terms of per capita income it is Japan that leads the group but in recent years surpassed by Singapore. Malaysia and Taiwan rank a distant second in terms of per capita income to Japan and Singapore. The income per capita in Korea and Thailand, is smaller by one-third from those in the second group. The size of employment, capital stock and foreign capital also vary considerably across countries. Japan leads in terms of size of capital stock and employment followed by Thailand and Korea. But in terms of capital-labor ratio, Japan and Singapore are the leaders followed by Korea, Taiwan and Malaysia. Thailand has the lowest capital-labor ratio among the countries. Similar diversity is observed in terms of foreign capital. In terms of size of foreign capital Malaysia and Singapore lead the group followed by Thailand and Japan and surprisingly the size of foreign capital in Korea and Taiwan is relatively small. The indicator for human capital measured by the number of years of education of working population, are quite similar among the economies with the exception of Japan.

These economies are major participants in international trade. Exports and imports as percentages of GDP are very high for every country in the group except for Japan. The export to GDP ratio is 1.77 for Singapore, 0.66 for Malaysia, 0.59 for Taiwan, 0.36 for Korea, and 0.29 for Thailand. The import-GDP ratio for these countries are often higher than their export-GDP ratio. Japan is of course a major player in world trade in terms of size of its trade transactions.

The growth rates are shown in Table 3.2. The growth rates of GDP in these economies are impressive. The average rate of increase in GDP ranged between 5 percent for Malaysia to over 9 percent for Korea over the sample period. Japan had the slowest growth compared to others partly because the other East Asian countries had started from a low base. The growth rate of exports was extremely high in all of the six countries ranging from 8.6 percent (Malaysia) to 17 percent (Korea). Imports grow also very rapidly in each country but often less than exports. Employment increased at an annual rate of 4 percent in Thailand and Singapore, followed by a 3 percent growth rate in Korea and Taiwan. Malaysia experienced a 2 percent increase in employment while the least expansion of employment took place in Japan - about 1 percent per annum. Human capital grew at about 3 percent per annum in Korea, Singapore, and Malaysia. In Taiwan it grew at about 2 percent and Thailand had the

Table 3.2 Annual average growth rates of variables in the period 1965-1990

	Korea	Japan	Taiwan	Singapore	Thailand	Malaysia
Population	0.016	0.009	0.020	0.014	0.020	0.030
GDP	0.090	0.056	0.087	0.087	0.070	0.060
GDP Per Capita	0.074	0.047	0.067	0.073	0.050	0.030
Import	0.14	0.07	0.13	0.11	0.09	0.09
Foreign Capital	0.10	0.06	0.13	0.16	0.09	0.09
Domestic Output	0.09	0.05	0.08	0.077	0.07	0.07
Export	0.17	0.086	0.14	0.11	0.10	0.08
Labor	0.03	0.01	0.03	0.039	0.04	0.02
Physical Capital	0.13	0.087	0.11	0.11	0.08	0.09
Human Capital	0.036	0.009	0.02	0.03	0.01	0.03
TFP	0.025	0.024	0.03	0.017	0.019	0.016
LP	0.081	0.049	0.08	0.06	0.048	0.066

Notes:

1. The base year is 1985. Constant US dollar is obtained by multiplying PPP of 1985 to the series in 1985 domestic constant price.
2. The unit of population and employment is million; the unit of human capital is years; the unit of GDP/capita is US dollar in 1985 price; the unit of price is real number; the unit of other variables is billion US dollars in 1985 price.
3. TFP is total factor productivity and LP is labor productivity.

lowest growth rate in human capital of almost 1 percent. The growth of physical capital was very high in all countries ranging between a low of 8.6 percent in Japan to a high of 13.4 percent in Korea. Foreign capital also grew rapidly in all countries at a rate of about 10 to 11 percent per annum. Japan was an exception, where foreign capital grew at 6.6 percent, which is still impressive.

Labor productivity and total factor productivity growth rates in these countries were also remarkable. The growth of labor productivity was very high in Korea and Taiwan at about 8 percent per annum followed by Singapore and Malaysia - about 6 percent per annum. In Japan and Thailand labor productivity increased by almost 5 percent per year. The

TFP growth rates for Taiwan, Korea and Japan were between 3 percent to 2.4 percent while those for the rest of the countries were about 1.6 percent to 1.9 percent.

The growth rates of the variables shown in Table 3.2 varied considerably over time and across countries. Such variations are particularly visible in the case of aggregate output, exports and imports. Looking at these variations a pattern emerges. With one or two exceptions, the output growth rates surged to over double digit numbers for a few years, then the economies slowed down to rates of 1 to 2 percent (in some cases to negative rates). Then the pattern of boom and slowdown followed once again. All six countries experienced very high growth rates in almost all of the variables shown in Table 3.2 during 1969-1973 period. The growth rates remained fairly high in the second sub-period 1974-1980. But in the period 1981-1985, the growth rates of output and labor productivity slowed down considerably in all the countries before rebounding in the last sub-period 1985-1990.

3 MODEL SPECIFICATION AND ESTIMATION

Since international economic activities and markets have played an important role in the growth process of these countries, we carry out our analysis in an open economy framework. To do so, we utilize the methodologies developed in Burgess (1974), Kohli (1978), Diewert and Morrison (1988), and Lawrence (1990), which are based on the GNP function approach.[4] As in Lawrence (1990) and Diewert and Morrison (1988), the current and constant dollar GDP is decomposed by type of purchaser into domestic market (Y_D) and foreign market (Y_E). The rationale for treating imported goods as intermediate input to domestic technology has been stated in the previous studies: (i) many imports are intermediate goods and (ii) even if imports are for the final consumption, they have to go through distribution and retail channels before getting to the household. The value of domestic output in current price is obtained from the accounting identity of $p_D \cdot Y_D = p_G \cdot GDP - p_E \cdot Y_E + w_M \cdot IM$.[5]

To model the technology, we use a multi-product translog cost function with labor, physical capital, imports, human capital and foreign capital considered as inputs to produce two outputs, domestic output and exports. Human capital is measured by the average years of schooling by working age population, and is treated as a quasi-fixed input. A time trend is also included to capture the effect of disembodied technical change. A full blown multi-product translog cost function could not be supported by the data and therefore some restrictions were imposed. The specific cost function estimated is given by (3.1):

$$
\begin{aligned}
lnVC = {} & \gamma_0 + \gamma_L \ln W_L^* + \gamma_K \ln W_K + \gamma_D \ln Y_D + \gamma_E \ln Y_E + \gamma_T \ln T \\
& + 0.5\{ \gamma_{LL}(\ln W_L^*)^2 + \gamma_{KK}(\ln W_K)^2 + \gamma_{DD}(\ln Y_D)^2 + \gamma_{EE}(\ln Y_E)^2 + \gamma_{TT}(\ln T)^2 \} \\
& + \gamma_{LK} \ln W_L^* \ln W_K + \gamma_{LD} \ln W_L^* \, ln Y_D + \gamma_{LE} \ln W_L^* \ln Y_E + \gamma_{LT} \ln W_L^* \ln T \qquad (3.1) \\
& + \gamma_{KD} \ln W_K \ln Y_D + \gamma_{KE} \ln W_K \ln Y_E + \gamma_{KT} \ln W_K \ln T \\
& + \gamma_{DE} \ln Y_D \ln Y_E + \gamma_{DT} \ln Y_D \ln T \\
& + \gamma_{ET} \ln Y_E \ln T.
\end{aligned}
$$

where W_L and W_K respectively are the price of labor and capital normalized by the price of imports, W_M. Costs and input prices are normalized with the price of imports to ensure the condition of linear homogeneity in prices is met. $\ln W_L^*$ is defined as $(\ln W_L + \delta \ln H)$ and $\ln T$ as $(t + \varphi \ln F)$ where H is an index of human capital; t is the rate of disembodied technical change proxied by a time variable; and F is the stock of foreign capital. These expressions suggest that human capital is embodied in labor and that foreign capital serves as a carrier of technological and managerial and organizational knowledge.

Assuming competitive output markets and setting marginal costs equal output price we can obtain a set of revenue share equations:

$$S_{Y_D} = \gamma_D + \gamma_{LD} \ln W_L^* + \gamma_{KD} \ln W_K + \gamma_{DD} \ln Y_D + \gamma_{DE} \ln Y_E + \gamma_{DT} \ln T \qquad (3.2)$$

$$S_{Y_E} = \gamma_E + \gamma_{LE} \ln W_L^* + \gamma_{KE} \ln W_K + \gamma_{DE} \ln Y_D + \gamma_{EE} \ln Y_E + \gamma_{ET} \ln T. \qquad (3.3)$$

where S_{YD} and S_{YE} are cost shares of domestic output and exports respectively.

Using Shephard's Lemma a set of cost share equations are derived as,

$$S_L = \gamma_L + \gamma_{LL} \ln W_L^* + \gamma_{LK} \ln W_K + \gamma_{LD} \ln Y_D + \gamma_{LE} \ln Y_E + \gamma_{LT} \ln T \qquad (3.4)$$

$$S_K = \gamma_K + \gamma_{LK} \ln W_L^* + \gamma_{KK} \ln W_K + \gamma_{KD} \ln Y_D + \gamma_{KE} \ln Y_E + \gamma_{KT} \ln T \qquad (3.5)$$

where S_L and S_K denote the cost shares of labor and capital respectively.

Stochastic disturbance terms were added to the equations (3.2)-(3.5). Using dummy variables to capture intercountry differences, the parameters γ_0, γ_L, γ_K, γ_D, γ_E, γ_T, and δ are estimated individually for each country. The three stage least squares method is used to avoid the potential simultaneity problem at this level of aggregation. The instrumental variables used are: country dummies, all exogenous variables and their squared values lagged one and two periods, time and its square, population, stock of foreign direct investment lagged one period and world population. The sample period for estimation was 1968-1990.

Estimated parameter values and their standard errors are presented in Table 3.3. The model fits the data well and the curvature conditions are

*Table 3.3 Parameters of estimation**

Parameter	Estimate	Standard Error
γ_O	2.453395	0.5238111
γ_L	0.7154751	9.64E-01
γ_K	0.3293902	6.29E-01
γ_D	0.2044647	0.1481608
γ_E	0.4624252	8.19E-01
γ_T	8.79E-02	1.41E-01
γ_{LL}	0.1323001	1.09E-01
γ_{KK}	7.93E-01	1.39E-01
γ_{DD}	0.285707	3.75E-01
γ_{EE}	0.2050175	1.84E-01
γ_{TT}	1.05E-02	4.89E-03
γ_{LK}	−5.81E-01	1.02E-01
γ_{LD}	−1.95E-01	1.40E-01
γ_{KD}	−1.02E-01	1.22E-01
γ_{LE}	−1.12E-02	9.06E-02
γ_{LZ}	−2.91E-01	8.07E-02
γ_{LT}	−7.99E-02	1.49E-02
γ_{KT}	7.99E-02	1.18E-02
γ_{DE}	−0.1880731	1.93E-01
γ_{DT}	−6.71E-02	2.83E-02
γ_{ET}	−4.08E-02	2.04E-02
δ	−0.6094408	0.3615142
ϕ	0.4059381	0.292036

Equation	R^2
Cost Function	0.99
Labor Share	0.99
Capital Share	0.99
Domestic Output	0.99
Export	0.99

Note: * Coefficients of the dummy variables are not reported.

Table 3.4 Average cost elasticities, returns to scale and technical change

	Korea	Japan	Taiwan	Singapore	Thailand	Malaysia
EIVCL	0.39	0.57	0.38	0.19	0.49	0.42
EIVCK	0.27	0.34	0.24	0.10	0.22	0.18
EIVCM	0.34	0.09	0.37	0.71	0.29	0.40
EIVCH	−0.24	−0.35	-0.23	−0.11	−0.30	−0.25
EIVCF	−0.008	−0.003	−0.009	−0.002	−0.01	−0.003
EIVCAA	−0.020	−0.027	−0.023	−0.005	−0.025	−0.007
EIVCYD	0.84	0.97	0.71	0.41	0.92	0.64
EIVCYE	0.26	0.11	0.39	0.69	0.22	0.45
Scale	1.13	1.25	1.12	1.02	1.13	1.15

met at all data points. The elasticities of outputs, inputs, returns to scale and technical change are shown in Table 3.4. The cost elasticities with respect to human capital vary across countries; it is about −0.30 for Japan and Thailand followed by an estimate of approximately −0.24 for Korea, Taiwan and Malaysia. Surprisingly the value of the cost elasticity of human capital for Singapore is only −0.11. The effect of human capital on the demand for labor, physical capital and imports are all negative suggesting that the increase in education or quality of labor is cost saving by reducing demand for these inputs. However, the magnitudes of the elasticities differ across countries among the inputs. The estimates of the physical capital elasticity with respect to human capital are generally very small in all countries except Singapore; the largest impact of increase in human capital is on labor; labor elasticity with respect to human capital is about −0.35 to −0.40 while those of imports range between −0.23 to −0.30.

The cost elasticities with respect to foreign capital is generally small at about −0.01 for Korea, Taiwan and Thailand and about −0.003 for the other countries. The estimated rate of technical change, that is, shift of the cost function, varies across countries. Japan, Korea, Taiwan and Thailand have similar rates of technical change about −0.02 to −0.025 while the rate of technical progress is very small in the other countries. Singapore has the lowest rate of technical change of −0.005 while that for Malaysia is about −0.007.

The response of costs to changes in domestic output and exports vary considerably among countries and over time. The cost elasticities with respect to output used in domestic economy greatly dominate those with respect to exports in all countries except in Singapore. The ratio of cost elasticities of domestic output to those of exports is three times in Korea, nine times in Japan and four times in Thailand. In Taiwan and Malaysia the ratio is 2 and 1.4 respectively. In the case of Singapore the relation is reversed because of the dominance of exports over domestic output in Singapore's economy. Another point to note is that the cost elasticities with respect to these two outputs show a clear trend over time in all countries. The elasticity with respect to output used in domestic economy has a downward trend while that for exports exhibits a strong upward trend, which suggests that these economies are facing rising costs in their attempt to penetrate the world markets.

4 DECOMPOSITION OF OUTPUT AND LABOR PRODUCTIVITY GROWTH

Using the estimates shown in Table 3.5, two sets of closely related issues can be quantitatively explored: we decompose the sources of output, labor productivity growth and TFP growth. Second, we analyze the contributions of labor, physical and human capital, foreign direct investment and technical change to the catch-up process.

The contributions of the factor accumulations *vis-à-vis* the exogenous technical change to output growth are shown in Table 3.6 for each of the six countries for the period 1969-1990. The decomposition is based on the approximation given in (3.6).

$$\Delta \ln Y_t = \frac{1}{2}\sum_{i=1}^{4}[\varepsilon_{YZ_i}(t) + \varepsilon_{YZ_i}(t-1)]\Delta \ln Z_{it} + \frac{1}{2}[\varepsilon_{YF}(t) + \varepsilon_{YF}(t-1)]\Delta \ln F_t + \frac{1}{2}[\lambda(t) + \lambda(t-1)] \quad (3.6)$$

where $Z_1 = L$, $Z_2 = K$, $Z_3 = IM$, $Z_4 = H$ and ε_{YZ_i}'s denote respective output elasticities with respect to labor, physical capital, imports, human capital, and foreign capital, and $\lambda(t) = \partial \ln Yt/\partial T_t$ denotes cost-based disembodied technical change. As noted earlier, the average growth of output in all six countries was very rapid ranging between 5 percent to 11 percent per annum for the period 1969-1990. The average rates of growth of output were particularly high for Korea, Singapore and Taiwan. The average growth of output varied considerable over the respective subperiods.

Table 3.5 Output growth decomposition average yearly growth rates for period 1969-1990

	Korea	Japan	Taiwan	Singapore	Thailand	Malaysia
Output Growth	9.70	5.07	9.71	9.60	7.158	7.62
			Percentage Contribution to Output Growth			
Labor	7.09	7.19	6.86	7.19	17.01	5.76
Capital	33.57	50.65	24.30	9.47	27.42	20.77
Import	38.12	8.66	41.50	69.69	40.60	48.02
Human Capital	7.66	5.45	4.95	3.40	7.13	7.97
Foreign Capital	0.69	0.24	0.94	0.34	0.94	0.26
Tech Progress	18.44	30.93	21.52	5.00	10.81	7.90

The contributions of the various inputs to the growth of output differed considerably among countries and over time. The contribution of labor was the largest in Thailand (17 percent) and smallest in Malaysia (6 percent). Labor's contribution to output growth in other countries was approximately 7 percent. Over the period the contribution of labor input has decreased in each country. Physical capital, on the other hand, contributed significantly to growth of output in all countries except in Singapore.[6] Fifty percent of output growth in Japan was due to capital accumulation. In Korea capital growth contributed about 34 percent of output growth and in other countries except for Singapore the contribution of capital accumulation was about 20 percent. The contribution of growth in physical capital to growth of output was about 10 percent in Singapore again because of the preponderant importance of the foreign sector in Singapore's economy.

The contribution of imports to the growth of output was very high in all countries except in Japan. It ranged between 30 percent of output growth in Thailand to approximately 70 percent in Singapore. In Japan it was about 9 percent. These estimates reflect the degree of dependence of these economies on trade. The contribution of human capital was much lower than that of physical capital. It ranged from 3.4 to 8 percent of output growth; its contribution to output growth was largest in Malaysia and

Korea and smallest in Singapore. In other countries the contribution was in the 3.5 to 5.5 percent range. The contribution of foreign capital to output growth was approximately 1 percent in Taiwan and Thailand, 0.7 percent in Korea, and about 0.2 to 0.3 percent in other countries. Considering a relatively very small share of foreign direct investment in GDP for these economies, this is not an insignificant contribution.

Next to physical capital and imports the most significant contributor to the growth of output in all countries except Singapore over the period 1969-1990, was the disembodied technical change. Its contribution to output growth ranged from 5 percent to over 30 percent. The contribution of technical change to output growth was very large in Japan, Taiwan and Korea. Its contribution to output growth in Thailand and Malaysia was approximately 11 percent and 8 percent respectively. Surprisingly, its contribution was smallest in Singapore. Also it should be noted that the contribution of technical change has been rising over time in most of these countries.

The contributions of the factor accumulation and exogenous technical change to labor productivity growth are obtained from the decomposition based on the following approximation:

$$\begin{aligned}\Delta \ln(Y_t / L_t) = {} & \tfrac{1}{2}\textstyle\sum_{i=2}^{4}[\varepsilon_{YZ_i}(t) + \varepsilon_{YZ_i}(t-1)]\,\Delta \ln(Z_{it} / L_t) \\ & + \tfrac{1}{2}[\varepsilon_{YF}(\mathrm{t}) + \varepsilon_{YF}(\mathrm{t}-1)]\,\Delta \ln F_{\mathrm{t}} \\ & + \tfrac{1}{2}[\lambda(t) + \lambda(t-1)] \\ & + \tfrac{1}{2}[\rho(\mathrm{t}) + \rho(\mathrm{t}-1) - 2]\,\Delta \ln L_t\end{aligned} \tag{3.7}$$

where ρ is the scale measure which is equal to the sum of output elasticities.

The growth rates of labor productivity over the period 1969-1990 were high for Korea and Taiwan at about 8 percent. In the other countries, labor productivity growth ranged between 5 percent to 6 percent over the period 1969-1990. Labor productivity growth was very rapid for all countries over the period 1969-1973 with Japan leading the group. Over the subsequent years some decline in the growth rates of labor productivity is observed in all countries. We note that the decomposition of labor productivity growth is the same as those noted for output growth. The pattern that emerges is that the three major contributors to labor productivity growth are physical capital imports and disembodied technical change. The contribution from the scale economies depicted by the second term in equation (3.7) was between 1 percent (Singapore) and

8 percent (Thailand) to labor productivity growth. The contribution of human capital growth followed the same pattern as shown in Table 3.4. The contribution of foreign capital growth to labor productivity ranged from a low of 0.27 percent in Japan to about 1.5 percent in Thailand.

Thus the main contributors to the growth of output and labor productivity at the total economy level in the six counties have been physical capital accumulation, imports and disembodied technical change. The contributions of human capital and foreign capital at the total economy level are modest, reflecting their small shares in total output.

The decomposition of the conventional measure of total factor productivity growth is shown in Table 3.6. The magnitudes of TFP growth vary across countries with Taiwan having the highest (0.032) and Singapore the lowest (0.011) TFP growth rates. TFP growth rates in other countries are about 0.023 to 0.027. The TFP growth represents a shift in the production function, that is, technological progress, only under specified circumstance such as constant returns to scale technology. In the presence of scale economies we can decompose the traditional measure of TFP growth. We have estimated the degree of return to scale for each country.

Table 3.6 TFP growth decomposition average yearly growth rates (1969-1990)

	Korea	Japan	Taiwan	Singapore	Thailand	Malaysia
TFP Growth	2.45	2.23	3.15	1.17	1.90	1.60
	Percentage Contribution to TFP Growth					
Domestic Output	27.00	31.84	16.46	13.4	25.37	21.01
Exports	13.52	5.16	14.88	29.95	12.06	18.92
Technical Change	64.83	56.57	59.03	40.48	62.50	24.86
Foreign Capital	2.70	0.58	2.89	2.83	2.39	0.95

The contributions of exports and output used in domestic economy to TFP growth show that both contributed to TFP growth. However, the contribution of domestic economy clearly dominates that of exports by a margin of 2 to 1 in Korea, 6 to 1 in Japan, 2 to 1 in Thailand, slightly greater than 1 in Malaysia. In Singapore it is the contribution of exports which dominates. The contribution of technical change is a major component of TFP growth. Its contribution is about 60 percent in Korea, Japan, Taiwan and Thailand. In Singapore autonomous technical change contributes about 40 percent, and about 25 percent in Malaysia. Finally, about 2 to 3 percent of the conventional TFP growth can be attributed to the contribution of foreign capital in these countries. Japan and Malaysia are the exceptions where the contribution of foreign capital is approximately 0.6 percent and 1 percent respectively.

5 ANALYSIS OF THE CATCHING-UP PROCESS

We have used two measures of labor productivity to analyze the catching up process among East Asian countries. One is to use the ratio of our GDP to our measure of labor input and the other is to use per capita income. In Figure 3.1 we show the cumulative effect of the differences in labor productivity growth by plotting the levels of per capita income, measured as GDP per capita, for the respective countries relative to Japan over time. The reason for choosing per capita income rather than our measure of labor productivity is to relate the discussion more closely to the existing literature on catch-up. We note that the two measures are highly correlated. The graph shows that some countries have narrowed the gap in GDP per capita relative to Japan over the period 1969-1990. This is particularly visible in the case of Singapore where the relative per capita income has moved from a ratio of about 60 percent in 1969 to more than parity with Japan in 1990. Taiwan and Korea have also been able to make significant strides and were able to move from relative productivity levels of 28 and 23 percent respectively in 1969 to almost 47 percent in 1990. Unlike other East Asian countries that have made much less progress in narrowing the gap in labor productivity or per capita income, Thailand and Malaysia have only been able to sustain their initial positions.

A decomposition of the annual rate of change of the gap in the levels of labor productivity of the respective countries relative to Japan involves weighted differences between the respective contributions by labor, physical and human capital and disembodied technical change to labor productivity growth. At this point we have not computed the proper weights and therefore cannot provide an exact decomposition. However, abstracting from the problem of using the proper weights, a comparison of the relative contributions of the respective factors to the productivity growth in Japan and the other countries will give a first indication of the sources that led to the catch-up in the levels of labor productivity and in

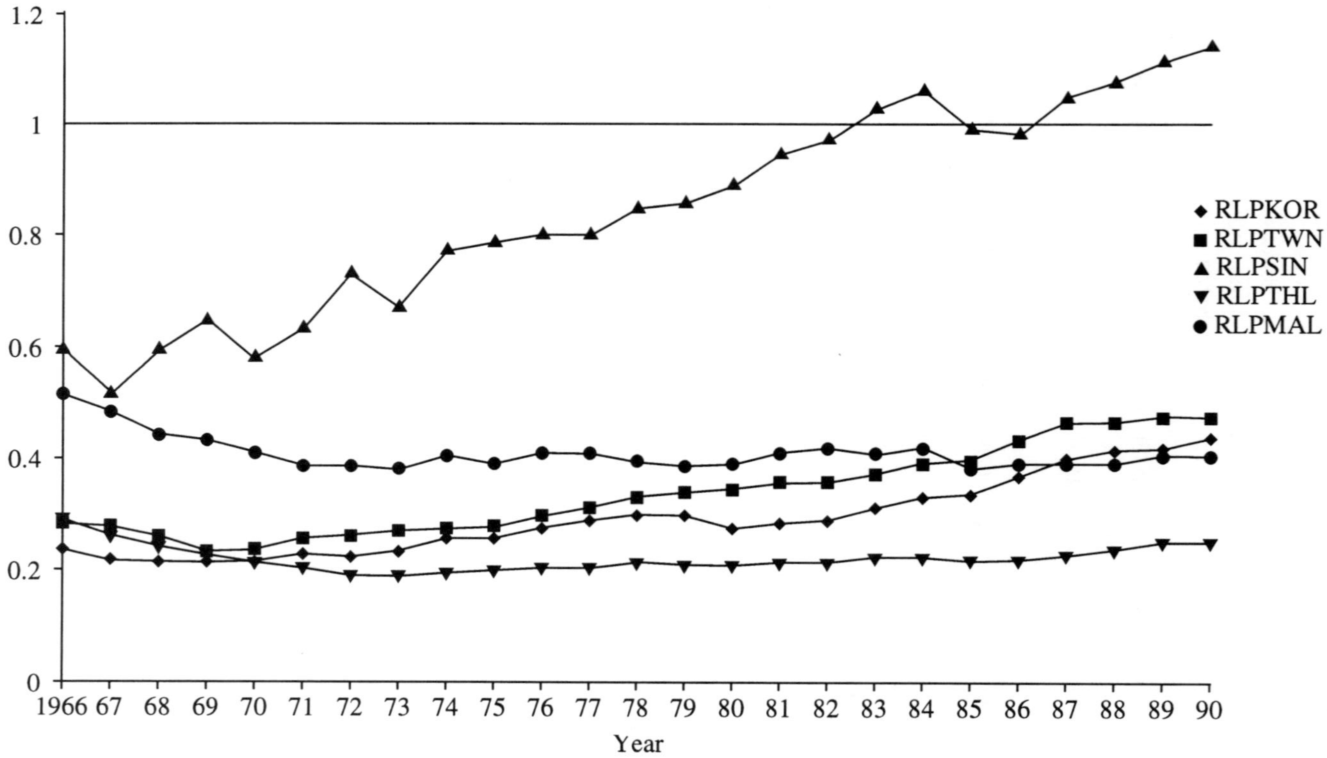

Figure 3.1 Labor productivity relative to Japan (GDP/POP)

GDP per capita. It seems that disembodied technical change and capital accumulation were the major contributors towards narrowing the productivity gap relative to Japan. Also the weakening of those forces seem to be responsible for the deceleration of the catch-up process after 1980.

To give some quantitative meaning to the degree of the convergence over time we have calculated the sample variance of the GDP per capita level of the six countries in each period. More explicitly, we calculated the following statistic:

$$V_t = \frac{1}{6}\sum_{i=1}^{6}[(P_{ti} - \overline{P}_t]^2 ,$$

where P_{ti} denotes the GDP per capita of the ith country in year t and

$$\overline{P}_t = \frac{1}{6}\sum_{i=1}^{6} P_{ti}$$

denotes the corresponding sample average of six countries in year t. Figure 3.2 shows the movement of V_t over time. The variance measure V_t declined from 1969-1990, reflecting the sizable catch-up by Taiwan, Korea and particularly Singapore over this period due to the forces discussed above. However, because Thailand and Malaysia did not take part in the catching up process, the decline in value of the variance, V_t, over time was not dramatic at all.

6 CONCLUSION

In this chapter we have modeled the production structure of six East Asian countries in order to analyze the sources of their output and labor productivity growth. We also attempted to identify the major contributing factors to the catch-up process in the level of labor productivity or GDP per capita. Some countries experienced very high rates of output and productivity growth over the period 1969-1990, and had devoted a considerable portion of their national income to capital accumulation and have received (except for Japan) a growing amount of foreign direct investment. A large portion of their foreign investment has come from Japan, a member of the group. Also these countries had experienced extraordinary growth rates of output for the domestic and export markets. The growth rates of imports and exports in most of these countries were truly spectacular.

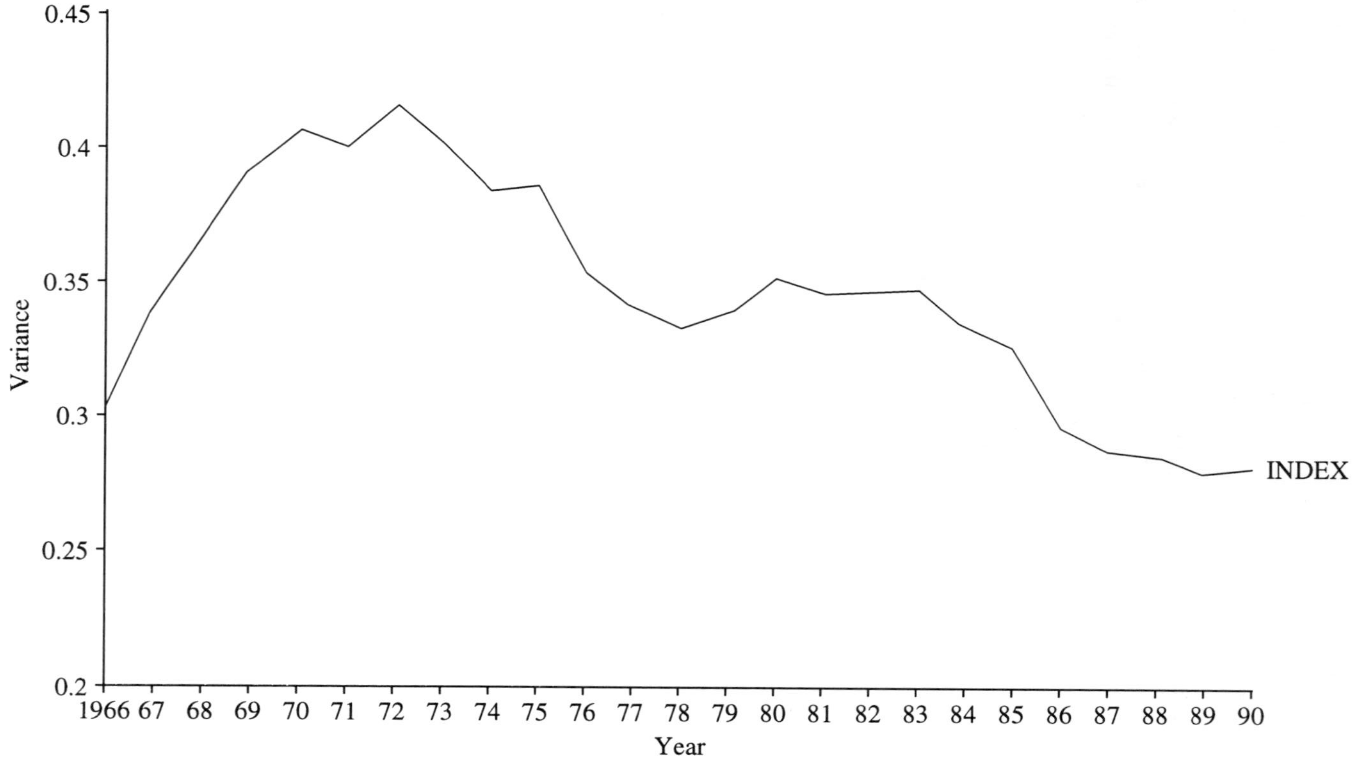

Figure 3.2 Variance of relative productivity (GDP/POP)

Based on the structural estimates of this model we find capital formation, disembodied technical change, labor and human capital (education) to be the most important sources of output growth. Foreign capital plays an increasingly important role in the growth of output and productivity growth in all countries. The contributions of labor and physical capital were particularly large during the period 1969-1973 for some countries. It seems that the rate of capital accumulation slowed down in the 1980s but the rate of technical change has increased in some countries.

However, even with the substantial growth in physical capital and the high rate of technical change, the economies of Korea, Taiwan, Thailand and Malaysia have not achieved a substantial narrowing in the gap between their levels of GDP per capita relative to Japan. In fact between 1966-1972 the gap between the Asian countries and Japan increased mainly due to vigorous expansion of the Japanese economy. Since 1972, however, there has been a general narrowing of the gap. The variance of GDP per capita since the early 1970s did not decline dramatically. There was a decline, but at a very modest pace. There were two basic reasons for the modest pace of convergence among East Asian countries. One, the Japanese economy continued its vigorous expansion during the sample period. The slowdown in the growth of the Japanese economy came after 1990. The second reason is that while some countries like Korea and Taiwan increased their labor productivity compared to that of Japan but others like Thailand and Malaysia could not sustain their relative position over time.

APPENDIX: DESCRIPTION OF THE DATA

The data for GDP, exports, imports, and gross investment and its components were taken from the *Yearbook of National Accounts statistics* (UN) for each country except for Taiwan. For Taiwan the data for these variables were obtained from the Yearbook of Republic of China. The deflators for the variables mentioned are calculated by dividing the current values by constant values; all deflators are of base year 1985 = 1. The data from the Yearbook of National Accounts were checked against the corresponding series provided in *World Tables* (World Bank) and *International Financial Statistics* (IMF). These sources were also used to update various series.

The labor input is defined as the total annual man-hours. To construct this variable we obtained data on total employment from the *Yearbook of Labor Statistics* of ILO (1991). Data on average hours worked per week are also obtained from this source. Total man hours worked are then calculated as the product of total employment and average hours worked per week multiplied by 50 (as a proxy for the number of weeks worked annually). Data on the compensation of employees was obtained from the *National Accounts.* The series on the hourly wage rate was constructed as the ratio of compensation of employees and total man hours worked.

The data on the gross investment expenditures in billions of 1985 national currency for each individual country were derived from the *Yearbook of National Account Statistics* and various issues of the UN *Statistical YearBook* (UN). To derive capital stock series, disaggregated investment data on non-residential buildings, other construction, transportation equipment, and machinery and equipment, were obtained from these sources. The depreciation rates provided by Jorgenson and Yun (1991) (0.0287 for nonresidential buildings, 0.0333 for other construction, 0.2113 for transportation equipment and 0.1329 for machinery and equipment) were used to calculate the capital stock of each category by the perpetual inventory method. The estimates of the base year capital stock of each category were calculated by using the formula $K_0 = INV_0/(\delta_i + g)$ where INV_0 is base year fixed capital formation of each category, δ_i is depreciation rate of category, and g is the average growth rate of GDP over the sample period. Non-residential capital stock was obtained by adding up these categorized capital stocks. The price of the non-residential capital stock has been calculated by using the formula $W_K = P_K*(\delta + r)$, where P_K is the price deflator for non-residential fixed investment, δ is depreciation rate of nonresidential capital stock (calculated as a weighted average of individual δs) and r is the real interest rate which is nominal interest rate minus the average inflation rate calculated from the price deflator for gross fixed investment.

Human capital is measured as the average of total years of education per person of the working age population series for Korea, Japan, Taiwan and Singapore have been obtained from Kim and Lau (1995). The human capital series for Malaysia has been generated following Kim and Lau's procedure. The data are obtained from *International Historical Statistics* (Mitchell, 1995).

Foreign capital stock has been generated using the perpetual inventory method. The foreign direct investment data were obtained from *World Directory of Investment,* and the depreciation rate and price deflator for constructing the stock of foreign capital are assumed to be the same as those used in constructing the domestic capital stock series. The benchmark value for foreign capital is estimated in the same way as for domestic capital. To avoid double counting the aggregate domestic capital stock is redefined by subtracting foreign capital stock.

The purchasing power parity (PPP) values for 1985 are obtained from Summers and Heston (1991). Those values are used to convert all data to US dollars for reasons of comparability.

NOTES

1. For a comprehensive discussion see World Bank (1993).
2. See World Bank (1993) and Sephton (1989).
3. See Nadiri and Prucha (1997) for similar analysis for the OECD countries.
4. A translog cost function is used in Burgess (1974), a translog profit function in Kohli (1978), and Diewert and Morrison (1988) and Lawrence (1990) used a biquadratic profit function. A dynamic aspect of production technology is modeled in Lawrence (1990) by having an adjustment cost associated with changes in the capital stock.
5. From the domestic absorption identity, $C + I + G = GDP - (EX - IM) - Y_D$, the price of domestic output is computed as a chain price index of C, I, and G.
6. The magnitudes of the contributions varied over the subsamples and often explained more than 50 percent of output growth, although in absolute terms the growth rates of physical capital fell substantially since the mid-1970s in most countries.

REFERENCES

Abramovitz, M.A. (1986), 'Catching up. Forging ahead and falling behind', *Journal of Economic History*, **46**, 385-406.

Barro, R.J. and X. Sala-i-Martin (1991), 'Convergence across states and regions', *Brookings Papers on Economic Activity*, **1**, 407-44.

Burgess, D.F. (1974), 'A cost minimization approach to import demand equations,' *The Review of Economics and Statistics*, **56** (2), 225-34.

Diewert, W.E. and C.J. Morrison (1988), 'Export supply and import demand functions: a production theory approach', in Robert C. Feenstra ed. *Empirical Methods for International Trade*, Cambtidge, MA: MIT Press, 207-22.

Dowrick, S. and D. Nguyen (1989), 'OECD comparative economic growth 1950-85: catch up and convergence,' *American Economic Review*, **76** (1), 141-54.

Hulten, C.R. (1992), 'From productiocity slowdown to new investment opportunities?', in H. Siebert (ed.), *Capital Flows in the World Economy: Symposium 1990*, Tubingen: Mohr, 67-83.

International Labor Organization (1991), *Yearbook of Labor Statistics*, (annual issues 1970, 1981 and 1991).

International Monetary Fund (1997), *International Financial Statistics*, (Various issues).

Jorgensen, D.W. and K.Y. Yun (1991), *Tax Policy and the Cost of Capital*, New York: Oxford University Press.

Kim, J.I. and L.J. Lau (1995), 'The role of human capital in the economic growth of the East Asian newly industrialized countries', *Asia Pacific Economic Review*, **1** (3), 3-22.

Kohli, U.R. (1978), 'A gross national product function and the derived demand for imports and supply of exports', *The Canadian Journal of Economics*, **11**, 167-82.

Krugman, P.R. (1994), 'Competitiveness: a dangerous observation', *Foreign Affairs*, **73** (2), 28-44.

Lawrence, D. (1990), 'An adjustment-costs model of export supply and import demand', *Journal of Econometrics*, **46**, 381-98.

Lichtenberg, F.R. (1993), 'R&D investment and international productivity differences', in Horst Siebert (ed.), *Economic Growth in the World Economy: Symposium 1992*, Kiel Institut fur Weltwirtschaft Symposien-und Konferenzbande series, Tubingen: Mohr (Siebeck), 89-110.

Lucas, R.E. (1988), 'On the mechanics of economic development,' *Journal of Monetary Economics*, **22** (1), 3-42.

Mankiw, N.G., D. Romer and D.N. Weil (1992), 'A contribution to the emprics of economic growth,' *Quarterly Journal of Economics*, **107** (2), 407-37.

Mitchell, B.R. (1995), *International Historical Strtistics: Africa, Asia & Oceania, 1750-1988*, New York: Stockton Press.

Nadiri, M.I. and I.R. Prucha, (1997), 'Sources of growth of output and convergence of productivity in major OECD countries,' *International Journal of Production Economics*, **52** (1-2), 133-46.

Olson, M. (1982), *The Rise and Decline of Nations*, New Haven: Yale University Press.

Romer, P. (1987), 'Crazy explanations for the productivity slowdown,' in S. Fischer (ed.), *NBER macroeconomics annual: 1987*, Cambridge: MIT Press, 163-202.

Sephton, P.S. (1989), 'Causality between export growth and industrial development: empirical evidence from NICs - a comment,' *Journal of Development Economics*, **31** (2), 413-15.

Summers, R. and A. Heston (1991), 'The penn world table (mark 5), an expanded set of international comparisons, 1950-1988,' *Quarterly Journal of Economics*, **106** (2), 327-68.

United Nations (1995), *Statistical Yearbook*, (various issues).

United Nations (1995), *World Investment Directory*, (various issues).

United Nations (1995), *Yearbook of National Accounts Statistics*, (various issues).

World Bank (1993), *The East Asian Miracle: Economic Growth and Public Policy*, New York: Oxford University Press.

World Bank (1995), *World Tables*, (various issues).

Young, A. (1995), 'The tyranny of numbers: confronting the statistical realities of the East Asian growth experience,' *Quarterly Journal of Economics*, **110** (3), 641-80.

4. The Relative Efficiency and Rate of Technology Adoption of Asian and North American Airline Firms*

Seung C. Ahn, David H. Good and Robin C. Sickles[1]

1 INTRODUCTION

The nature of international trade has changed dramatically over the last decade. Where once the world was a place of nations seeking their own interests individually, this has been replaced by large trading blocs. The European Community has embarked on an ambitious effort to remove economic barriers among the 12 Member States and to establish an integrated market system. The 1992 EC integration presages the momentum of global changes in international trading arrangements which place special demands on the global economic community. It is hard to argue that these developments in Europe have not been pivotal factors in the North American Free Trade Agreement, GATT, and trading blocs in the Americas and the Pacific Rim.

The changing international economic environment would suggest that governments and industries, which have enjoyed success in some international and/or domestic markets, will find that terms of trade are altered. Continuation of current subsidies and business as usual may prove infeasible. On the other hand, economic entities that may have been unable to successfully compete in some markets may find new business opportunities and avenues for their profitable exploitation. As countries around the world have developed under this new environment, so have the patterns of air traffic. For example, the share of international traffic

---

* This chapter was based on a paper presented at the Taipei International Conference on Efficiency and Productivity Growth, 20-21 June, 1997. The chapter relies heavily on the paper entitled 'Estimation of long-run inefficiency levels: a dynamic frontier', by Ahn *et al.* (1997). Those interested in a more detailed discussion of the econometric model presented therein can contact R.C. Sickles via e-mail, fax or regular mail.

generated over and near the Pacific Ocean has been increasing at a rate of more that 10 percent per year, far above the 6.6 percent annual growth rate for the rest of the world. Projections indicate that by the end of the century over one third of all international flights will emanate from the Pacific. No doubt another important factor behind this growth in air travel has been the emergence of strong industrial economies in the region, including Hong Kong, Indonesia, Singapore, Japan, South Korea and Taiwan. In China, the region contains the world's largest unexploited market. As these newly industrialized economies grow, so too do their demands for air travel and their ability to produce it. In fact, it can be argued that these countries already possess a comparative advantage because of low labor costs, an ability to increasingly exploit the advantages of large equipment size, and recent improvements in their productive efficiency. Moreover, the 8 billion ($) losses in the US industry during 1991-1994 and the strong open sky policy of the USA in its bilateral negotiations point to strong forces for change in government policies toward shared equity stakes, interlining and integration of networks among international airlines.

The domestic industrial policy of the USA has also undergone changes which have spread worldwide. A major turning point in policy was the Airline Deregulation Act of 1978. The Act influenced moves toward deregulation in trucking and rail, as well as deregulation in nontransport sectors such as banking and telecommunications. It is doubtful that these latter movements toward deregulation would have proceeded so quickly had the early experience with airline deregulation been less positive. Domestic deregulation of the US airlines also has been influential in the policies of other countries. Since 1978, there has been deregulation of the domestic air transportation sectors in Canada and Australia and the discussion currently continues about how, not if, deregulation will be fully implemented within Europe and how it will be extended to EFTA countries.

The impact of differing carrier-specific institutional constraints due to varying regulatory climates and efficiency incentives have been studied in a series of papers by Good *et al.* (1993a, b, 1995), Captain and Sickles (1997), Roeller and Sickles (1996), Park *et al.* (1997) for Europe and the USA during the 1970s and 1980s, and by Coelli *et al.* (1997), Oum and Yu (1997) and Good *et al.* (1997a) for a set of international carriers through more recent periods. These dynamic analyses are based largely on structural econometric. A complimentary literature on convergence at the country level (Färe *et al.*, 1994) and at the firm level (Alam and Sickles, 1997) provides a rich menu of dynamic possibilities for productivity and efficiency patterns and interpretations but is based on index numbers and not on econometric estimates of productivity and efficiency.

There have been some efforts to introduce dynamics of inefficiencies to production frontier models. Examples are Cornwell *et al.* (1990), Kumbhakar (1990), Battese and Coelli (1992) and Lee and Schmidt (1993). Although these studies provide reasonable approximations for the dynamics of short-run technical inefficiency, they have two major limitations. First, the models utilized do not in general allow for the analysis of long-run dynamics in technical inefficiency. Second, the studies do not provide a theoretical or structural explanation of the sources of the variations in firms technical inefficiency.

The motivation of this chapter is to study a dynamic panel data model which allows flexible and economically meaningful dynamics, and by which researchers can estimate firms' long-run technical inefficiency levels. Specifically, we consider a model in which technical inefficiency levels are serially correlated (possibly) with different patterns among regions of the world. One possible source of such variations in technical inefficiency is technical innovations in the industry. Technical innovations may affect both short and long-run efficiency levels. Specifically, in an industry which faces technical innovation over time, firms may adopt such innovations in a sluggish manner. By modeling these differences, we allow for a form of rigidity that keeps firms from optimally choosing input levels in each period, because they are unable to adjust instantly. Our assumption that firms may adopt continuous technical innovations in a sluggish manner naturally leads to a dynamic panel data model. We estimate this model to identify and test for long-run differences in inefficiency.

Section 2 describes the institutional setting for competition among airlines in the pacific rim region of the world. In section 3, we discuss the Ahn *et al.* (1997) model and show how it can be used to estimate long-run technical inefficiency of firms in an industry facing continuous technical innovations. Section 4 describes the estimation procedure applied to the model and gives insight into the inefficiency measures. Section 5 provides a discussion of sources of data and variable construction while section 6 describes estimation results and offers concluding remarks.

2 INSTITUTIONAL BACKGROUND

A major turning point in the industrial policy of the USA was the Airline Deregulation Act of 1978. Not only did this act have a direct influence on the way airline services are delivered domestically, in the USA, the Act, and the early experience with deregulation, influenced deregulation in trucking and rail, as well as deregulation in nontransport sectors, such as banking and telecommunications. The domestic deregulation of airlines also had international repercussions. Since 1978, there has been deregulation of the domestic air transportation sectors in Canada, Australia and major advancements toward deregulation within the EC with at least nominal deregulation in place. Practical deregulation will, of course, follow a much slower path.

Not only has the US been a leader in allowing market forces to shape the domestic air transport industry, it has also historically been an advocate of allowing competition to shape international travel as well. Over the last 50 years it has been stalwart in its preference for a competitive international aviation industry (an 'open skies' policy), although its aggressiveness in pursuing that end has wavered from time to time.

US international aviation policy has evolved over the years. Prior to World War II, the policy took the form of the 'chosen instrument' doctrine. This policy, in effect, prohibited domestic airlines from offering international service, and prohibited Pan American, which was typically the chosen international carrier on a route, from offering domestic service. By allowing a carrier to negotiate for landing rights, it also blurred the distinctions between a government and its airlines. Many argued that a private company should not have the ability to negotiate for such important instruments of international policy especially when it involved the right to provide exclusive service. During this era, advantages of US technology, particularly the flying boat, made Pan American an unquestioned dominant firm in international air travel over the Pacific.

Near the end of World War II, a conference was organized in Chicago with the express purpose of obtaining a multinational agreement on the exchange of international aviation rights. The US position at the Chicago conference was that open competition, rather than the chosen instrument policy, was the appropriate model for the international aviation markets. This position, it can be argued, was the result of an overwhelming competitive advantage. During the war the US had concentrated much more heavily on producing transports rather than fighters and bombers like the British. Furthermore, the US economy and manufacturing sectors, contrary to the rest of the world, were expected to emerge from the war largely intact. Smaller countries were in favor of stricter fare and capacity regulation designed to ensure their airlines a fair share of the traffic on particular routes, even though they could not hope to offer as extensive a set of services globally as larger countries could. The US position for open competition was the result of a belief that the US carriers would be one of the clear winners in such a regime. The position of other nations stemmed from a belief that their airlines would be losers under open competition.

While there were some successes at the Chicago conference, notably the establishment of the International Civil Aviation Organization (ICAO) and the development of a standard format for bilateral agreements, it failed to reach a multilateral agreement for international aviation. This failure left each nation to negotiate bilateral agreements with all of the nations where service was desired. In the US, the first and most pivotal of these negotiations was with the UK, called the Bermuda Agreement. The negotiations ended with a compromise from the positions the two nations held in Chicago. The two major issues were the regulation of fares and the regulation of capacity. The British had wanted explicit restrictions on capacity, while the Americans wanted no restrictions at all. The settlement allowed individual airlines to set their own fare and capacity decisions subject to *ex post* review by the two governments.

The Chicago conference also led to the establishment of the International Air Transport Association (IATA). This organization had two functions. First, they were a trade association, and lobbied for the airlines as a group before various governments. As a trade association they also helped to set standards and provided coordination for the industry with things such as interlining of passengers and baggage. The second role for IATA was fundamentally economic. They provided assistance to the member airlines for the coordination of schedules, capacity and fares. In effect, they were the information clearing house for international airline cartels. IATA could react to changes in conditions, such as increasing fuel prices, much more quickly than the long drawn out bilateral negotiation process. Consequently, this organization was initially granted antitrust immunity by the USA.

During the 1950s, 1960s and 1970s the USA has been able to negotiate bilateral agreements with the majority of nations in the Pacific Rim. While the Bermuda Agreement formed a model for these negotiations, such as those with New Zealand and Australia, there were often significant variations in the agreements actually reached. Some of these were much less competitive than the US-UK accord. Notably, several countries - Japan, Peru, Pakistan, India and Argentina - contained specific a priori capacity limitation clauses and generally required strict equality. Pakistan even went so far as to permit their citizens only one international flight on a foreign carrier. Other countries did not allow the scheduling of any flights which interfered with the operations of their national carrier. With the mitigation of tension between China and the USA, a bilateral was negotiated in the late 1970s. Unfortunately, service for either US or Chinese carriers was delayed for years because China did not have a sufficient number of aircraft which met safety standards (such as seat-belts) to offer the service.

Still other nations, such as Singapore, South Korea and Taiwan, arrived at settlements that permitted more competition than the Bermuda Agreement. Singapore had also taken a very pro-competitive position with the rest of the world. They have even permitted Quantas to establish a hub in Singapore.

In 1977 the Bermuda Agreement was renegotiated after the British claimed that US carriers were earning a disproportionate share of the revenues on these routes. The new accord had much stricter capacity and fare restrictions. The USA was insistent that this was an aberration, not a change in policy. It appeared to be starkly at odds with the strides toward domestic deregulation and over the next two years repeatedly reaffirmed its commitment to an open skies policy in international aviation markets.

In 1978 the US Civil Aeronautics Board issued a show cause order as to why IATA should not have its antitrust immunity revoked. Later that year they organized another conference, much like that in Chicago 34 years earlier to convince that an open and competitive and multilateral international aviation policy was better. In the end, only one country, Chile, sided with the USA. IATA countered that the USA was trying to usurp its authority by attempting to dictate policy for other countries. Several US airlines chose to end their participation in IATA's rate-making functions, although they remained participants in the trade organization.

Ultimately, in 1980, the USA passed the International Air Transportation Competition Act. The stated purpose of the Act was to promote several goals which include: (1) to increase the competitive positions and profitability of US airlines; (2) to ensure freedom to offer fares which correspond to consumer demand; (3) to reduce restrictions on capacity by encouraging charter operations, multiple carrier designations, and eliminating flight frequency restrictions; and (4) to eliminate discrimination and unfair competitive practices against US carriers (such as differential fuel charges and differential landing fees and government subsidy). The act formed a clear statement of US objectives. However, the success of this policy toward meeting these objectives appears to have been quite limited. Not the least of these was that the USA was still left in a position of negotiating bilateral agreements, and the act did nothing to change the abilities of foreign flag carriers to openly compete.

One often cited characteristic for the productivity differences of firms is the extent of government ownership. Ownership patterns of airlines has traditionally been different among Asian than North American carriers. Governments often maintain national airlines for political rather than economic reasons. When these airlines are not competitive and cannot sustain themselves, governments act to maintain them politically through regulation, or implicit or explicit subsidy. The political motivations for maintaining an unprofitable airline are numerous. Governments, especially those responsible for developing economies, often wish to enhance national prestige, generate hard currency to improve the balance of payments, or to promote tourism to the country. Military reasons range from extending the careers of pilots to the improvement of aviation infrastructure, such as airports and navigational aids. In many cases, these objective are so strong as to require government ownership of the airline.

In our sample, all of the North American carriers have no government ownership and have their stocks listed on an exchange. For our Asian carriers, Air India and Garuda are completely government owned as of December 1995. Air New Zealand, Quantas, JAL, Japan Asia Airways, and Quantas have no government ownership. Others have a significant stake of government ownership (Philippines Airlines, 33 percent, Singapore Airlines 54 percent, and Thai International 93 percent). Cathay Pacific and KAL were both privately owned, but with ownership very concentrated.

Good and Rhodes (1991) have also noted that countries tend to negotiate significantly different kinds of bilateral agreements depending on the perceived ability to compete. They note that some Asian countries, notably Singapore, Hong Kong, Australia and New Zealand, have negotiated very pro-competitive bilateral agreements while others, notably Pakistan, India, the Philippines and Indonesia, have had much more restrictive bilaterals.

3 SPECIFICATION

3.1 Basic Model

We consider an industry, each firm of which produces a homogeneous product, with the following Cobb-Douglas production technology in logarithm form:

$$y_{it}^{F} \equiv X_{it}\beta + \alpha_{t}^{F} + v_{it} \equiv X_{it}\beta + \beta_0 + \gamma t + v_{it} \qquad (4.1)$$

Here i (= 1, ..., N) indexes firms and t (= 1, ... , T_i) denotes time. The y_{it}^{F} denote logarithms of the frontier output levels, the X_{it} are vectors of logarithms of input levels, the β_j are parameters describing the technology, and the v_{it} are random noises independently distributed over different i and t with zero mean. Consistent with other stochastic production frontier studies, we assume that the input vectors X_{it} are strictly exogenous to the v_{it}. The term $\alpha_t^F \equiv \beta_0 + \gamma t$ denotes the time-varying component of technology which is common to every firm: β_0 is the overall intercept term and γ is the common growth rate of productivity by technical innovations in the industry.

A firm's technical inefficiency may hinder full usage of its production capacity. In such cases, the actual productivity level, which we denote by α_{it} could be below α_t^F; that is, $\alpha_{it} = \alpha_t - u_{it}$, where u_{it} (≥ 0) is firm i's technical inefficiency level at time t. With this notation, we can define the actual production by

$$y_{it} = X_{it}\beta + \alpha_{it} = X_{it}\beta + \beta_0 + \gamma t - u_{it} - v_{it}. \tag{4.2}$$

Specifications of the dynamic evolution of u_{it} (or α_{it}) are central to the choice of an appropriate estimation procedure for the frontier production function and firms' long-run average inefficiency levels. We here demonstrate how continuous technical innovations undergoing in an industry may result in autoregressive technical inefficiency. To begin with, we consider the cases in which firms can adopt all undergoing technical innovations timely. Let a random variable η_{it} (≥ 0) denote firm i's inefficiency score induced by the technology innovated at time t. The η_{it} are both firm- and time-specific. We assume that the η_{it} are independently distributed over different i and t. Further, we assume $E(\eta_{it} \mid \Omega_{i,t-1}) = \kappa_i \geq 0$, where $\Omega_{i,t-1}$ is the information set available to firm i at the very beginning of time t. With the η_{it}, we define

$$\alpha_{it}^* \equiv \alpha_t^F - \eta_{it} = \beta_0 + \gamma t - \eta_{it}, \tag{4.3}$$

where α_{it}^* is firm i's productivity level which could be achieved if the firm would adopt technology innovations timely. The term κ_i can be conceived of as firm i's technical inefficiency due to its failure to utilize full capacity. This expected measure of inefficiency κ_i is compatible to the time-invariant inefficiency assumed frequently in previous studies (for example, Schmidt and Sickles, 1984). There would be several factors which determine the size of κ_i for an airline firm, among which are the quality of a carrier's major hub airport facilities, quality of air traffic control, access to government subsidies and rationalization of business practices via market discipline.

Another possible source of technical inefficiency is firms' sluggish adoption of technical innovations. An implicit assumption in the bulk of frontier literature is that adjustment rates are instantaneous and therefore that the data is generated from a firm in long-run static equilibrium. Were there costs that inhibit instantaneous adjustment, inefficiency measures developed by previous studies may in fact be proxies for differing adjustment costs and misspecification of the long- and short-run dynamics. Based on this intuition, we consider cases in which firms adjust their production technology only slowly over time. Specifically, we assume that technical innovations introduced at the beginning of time t are only partially adopted, while the adoption speed, ρ_i, may differ across firms:

$$\alpha_{it} = (1-\rho_i)\,\alpha_{i,t-1} + \rho_i\,\alpha^*_{it} \tag{4.4}$$

where $0 \le \rho_i \le 1$.

When a firm adjusts its production technology following (4.4), the inefficiency level u_{it} must be correlated with its lagged levels. If we substitute $u_{it} = \alpha^F_t - \alpha_{it}$ into (4.4), we can easily show

$$u_{it} = (1-\rho_i)u_{i,t-1} + \xi_{it}\,;\; E(\xi_{it} \mid \Omega_{i,t-1}) = \lambda_i > 0\,, \tag{4.5}$$

where $\xi_{it} \equiv (1-\rho_i)\gamma + \rho_i\,\eta_{it}$ and $\lambda_i \equiv (1-\rho_i)\gamma + \rho_i\kappa_i$. Accordingly, the long-run average technical inefficiency level of firm i equals

$$u_i^{LR} \equiv \frac{\lambda_i}{\rho_i} = \kappa_i + \frac{(1-\rho_i)\gamma}{\rho_i} \tag{4.6}$$

which is finite unless $\rho_i = 0$. The first component of u_i^{LR}, κ_i captures the long-run inefficiency due to firm i's inability to comprehend and fully utilize available production technologies. The second component $(1-\rho_i)\gamma/\rho_i$ captures the long-run efficiency loss due to the firm's sluggish adoption of technical innovations, which is negatively related with the adjustment speed ρ_i.

3.2 Empirical Dynamic Model and Specification Test

Our autoregressive assumption on the dynamics of u_{it} (4.5) is consistent with the production function of usual fixed effects form but with autocorrelated errors. To see this, define the short-run deviation of technical inefficiency from the long-run level $u_i^{LR} \equiv \lambda_i/\rho_i$ by $u^d_{it} = u_{it} - u_i^{LR}$. With this notation, we can rewrite the production function defined in (4.2) as

$$y_{it}=X_{it}\beta+\gamma t+(\beta_0-u_i^{LR})-\in_{it}, \quad (4.7)$$

where $\in_{it}=u_{it}^{d}-v_{it}$. However, assumption (4.5) implies

$$u_{it}^{d}=(1-\rho_i)u_{i,t-1}^{d}+\xi_{it}^{d}, \quad (4.8)$$

where $\xi_{it}^{d}=\xi_{it}-\lambda_i$. Thus, the error term $\in_{it}$ in (4.7) should be autocorrelated unless $\rho_i=1$.

The conventional within estimation procedure, which is equivalent to the least squares with dummy variables for each individual firms, might be used to consistently estimate the production function (4.7) if the input variables in X_{it} were exogenous (predetermined) to $\in_{it}$. However, this condition could be violated even if firms are assumed to maximize expected profits as in Zellner *et al.* (1966). To illustrate this point, suppose that each firm is rational and determines its input levels at the beginning of each production time period to maximize its conditional expectation of profits (π_{it}) given the information set Ω_{it}; that is, firm i maximizes $E(\pi_{it}\mid\Omega_{it})$ with respect to the input vector X_{it} given output and input prices.[2] If a firm can observe its previous-period inefficiency level ($u_{i,t-1}$) at the beginning of time t as we assume for specification (4.7), the firm's input usages at time t must depend on $u_{i,t-1}^{d}$. Thus, X_{it} must be correlated with $\in_{it}$ since the latter is a function of u_{it}^{d} which is serially correlated.

As a treatment of the problem, we may transform (4.7) into a nonlinear dynamic function. Specifically, solving (4.7) and (4.8), we can obtain

$$y_{it}=X_{it}\beta+(1-\rho_i)y_{i,t-1}+X_{i,t-1}[-(1-\rho_i)\beta]+\rho_i\lambda t+\rho_i\delta_i-e_{it}, \quad (4.9)$$

where,

$$\delta_i=\beta_0-u_i^{LR}+(1-\rho_i)\gamma/\rho_i;\ e_{it}=\xi_{it}^{d}-[v_{it}-(1-\rho_i)v_{i,t-1}]. \quad (4.10)$$

Note that if $\rho_i=1$ for all i, that is, all firms can promptly adjust their inefficiencies, model (4.9) reduces to that of Schmidt and Sickles (1984), a panel model with time and firm effects. Note that e_{it} is $MA(1)$,[3] and thus, $y_{i,t-1}$ is not a predetermined variable in (4.9). Accordingly, use of nonlinear least squares will lead to biased estimates. Because of this problem, we use generalized methods of moments (GMM) to estimate the model (4.9). More detailed estimation procedures are discussed in section 3.

A possible criticism to our $AR(1)$ assumption (4.5) on firms' inefficiencies is that it is observably equivalent to an alternative $AR(1)$ assumption imposed on the stochastic components of the frontier v_{it} ; that is, an alternative assumption that $u_{it}=u_i^{LR}$ for any t and $v_{it} = (1-\rho_i)v_{i,t-1} + h_{it}$ also leads to the production function specified in (4.7) and (4.8). Our response to this possible criticism is two-fold. Firstly, whichever assumption is correct, firms' long-run average inefficiencies can be recovered from any consistent estimates of the parameters of (4.9). Secondly, it is possible to test for the alternative AR assumption against ours. In the stochastic frontier literature, the v_{it} are nothing but statistical noises (Schmidt, 1984, p. 304); that is, the v_{it} are unexplainable error components which should not be systematically related with firms' input decisions. Accordingly, a firm's input decisions X_{it} should be strictly exogenous to the v_{it}; all leads and lags of X_{it} are uncorrelated with v_{it}. Thus, when the v_{it}, not u_{it}, are $AR(1)$, $X_{i,t-1}$ and X_{it} should be uncorrelated with $\in_{it}$ in (4.7), since $\in_{it}$ simply equals v_{it}. In contrast, our assumption (4.5) implies that all the lagged values of X_{it} are correlated with $\in_{it}$ by the same reason as X_{it} is not predetermined in (4.7). In short, a test for exogeneity of X_{it} and $X_{i,t-1}$ in (4.7) enables us to determine which of the u_{it} and v_{it} are autocorrelated. Following Ahn (1997), we can derive a convenient statistic for testing exogeneity of both X_{it} and $X_{i,t-1}$: we first estimate the model (4.7) by *OLS* including $X_{i,t-1}$ as additional regressors, and then conduct a Wald test for the significance of $X_{i,t-1}$. Intuitively, this test makes sense, because $X_{i,t-1}$ should not explain y_{it} if the v_{it}, not the u_{it}, are autocorrelated. In addition, Theorem 1 of Ahn (1997) implies that the Wald test is numerically identical to a Hansen test (1982) for the exogeneity of X_{it} and $X_{i,t-1}$. For the Wald test we need a heteroskedasticity and/or autocorrelation-robust covariance matrix for the *OLS* estimates. This covariance matrix can be estimated by a method introduced in section 4.

4. ESTIMATION OF THE DYNAMIC STOCHASTIC PANEL FRONTIER MODEL

We estimate and test for our dynamic stochastic panel frontier model using generalized methods of moments (GMM). The results are based on a newly developed panel of international airline firms discussed in Good *et al.* (1997) and utilize carriers from Asia and North America. The GMM estimates are compared to the Schmidt and Sickles (1984) within estimator which is consistent under the special case in which firms adjust their inefficiencies timely ($\rho_i = 1$).

GMM estimation of the dynamic production function (4.9) requires a set of instrumental variables that are uncorrelated with the error e_{it}. Possible instruments are, for example, two-period (or more) lagged output levels, current and lagged input levels, time (t), $1 \times N$ dummy variables (d_i) for each firms. Let W_{it} denote a set of such instruments; and let $W_i = [W_{i1}', \dots, W_{i,Ti}']'$. Define $\theta = (\beta', \delta_1, \rho_1, \dots, \delta_N', \rho_N')'$, $e_{it}(\theta) = y_{it} - X_{it}\beta - (1-\rho_i)y_{i,t-1} + X_{i,t-1}[(1-\rho_i)\beta] - \rho_i\gamma t - \rho_i\delta_i$, and $e_i(\theta) = (e_{i1}(\theta)', \dots, e_{iTi}(\theta)')'$. We also define $f_i(\theta) = W_i' e_i(\theta)$ for each i; and $m(\theta) = \Sigma_i f_i(\theta)$. If the instruments W_i are legitimate, it must be the case that $E[m(\theta)] = 0$. Under this condition and other standard GMM assumptions, we can have

$$\frac{1}{\Sigma_i T_i} m(\theta) \overset{d}{\to} N(0, \Lambda), \tag{14.11}$$

as $\Sigma_i T_i \to \infty$. This result implies that the optimal GMM estimator of θ, $\hat{\theta}_{GMM}$, is obtained by minimizing

$$J(\theta) = \frac{1}{\Sigma_i T_i} m(\theta)' \Lambda^{-1} m(\theta). \tag{14.12}$$

In practice, Λ must be estimated to construct the criterion function $J(\theta)$. However, when each T_i is large, it is straightforward to show that $\Lambda = \Sigma_i r_i \Omega_i$, where Ω_i is the asymptotic covariance of $\sqrt{T_i} f_i(\theta)$ and $r_i = \lim \Sigma_{iTi \to \infty} T_i / \Sigma_i T_i$. This result implies that a simple consistent estimate of Λ can be obtained by $\hat{\Lambda} = \Sigma_i (T_i / \Sigma_i T_i) \hat{\Omega}_i$, where $\hat{\Omega}_i$ is a consistent estimate of Ω_i. We can estimate Ω_i by applying the Newey and West (1987) method to each $f_i(\theta)$ evaluated at an initial consistent estimator of θ.[4] In our empirical study, we obtain the initial consistent estimator by nonlinear two-stage least squares using instruments W_i.

Once $\hat{\Omega}_i$ is computed, the legitimacy of instruments and our stochastic frontier specification can be jointly tested using the Hansen statistic (1982), $J(\hat{\theta}_{GMM})$. We also use an exogeneity test method which tests for predeterminedness (exogeneity) of two-period lagged dependent variable ($y_{i,t-2}$), which is constructed following Newey (1985: 243). In our model, technical inefficiency is assumed to be $AR(1)$. If inefficiency follows an autoregressive process of higher order, two-period lagged output levels are no longer predetermined. While the Hansen test has power to detect such possible misspecification, the exogeneity test may have better power properties (see Newey, 1985).

5 DATA

The primary sources for our data are the Digest of Statistics for Commercial Air Carriers from the International Civil Aviation Organization and the Penn World Table (Mark 5.6). There are frequent instances where this source was not complete. Consequently, data was supplemented with other sources such as the International Air Transport Association's World Air Transport Statistics and the Federal Express Aviation Service's Commercial Jet Fleets. Using these sources, we construct a set of four airline inputs: labor, energy, materials and aircraft fleet. In addition we construct several aggregate airline outputs along with characteristics of these outputs.

The materials index is based on the financial data from ICAO. It uses total operating expenses minus the amounts spent on aircraft rental, depreciation, fuel and labor (from ICAO fleet and personnel). Because the data is in different currencies, with different bundles of goods and services that those currencies will purchase, we need to put amounts in common terms. Simply using exchange rates does not adequately make expenditures comparable across countries since exchange rates are heavily influenced by the narrower sets of goods that are imported and exported. Instead, we use purchasing power parities. Unlike data for the USA based on Form 41, the ICAO data does not have much detail about detailed subcomponents. While expenses are broken up along functional lines (ticketing, passenger services and so on), there generally is not adequate information to remove other physical inputs (primarily labor) from these categories, nor are there always separate price indices for them. This leaves the materials index with a single subcomponent.

Inconsistencies in the definition of labor categories, differences in aggregation and missing data (primarily expenditure data) demand that the labor index is also constructed from a single subcomponent. The labor index uses the number of employees at mid-year as the measure of quantity. Prices are calculated by dividing expenditures by this quantity. Unlike the US Form 41 data, we do not have independent, carrier specific measures of either quantities and prices or quantities and expenditures for aircraft fuel. This is particularly problematic since fuel prices vary widely around the world, primarily the result of tax differences. ICAO does compile annual information about jet fuel prices within each of its 12 regions. We use this information as a price measure in cents/liter. Quantities are calculated by dividing the fuel expenses by this price. For consistency, we use ICAO's prices even when we have carrier specific information available from other sources (such as US DOT Form 41). The US and ICAO prices compare fairly closely.

Because of the importance of flying capital in our model, we have described this input in considerably more detail, providing several characteristics of the fleet in addition to its quantity and user price. We use an inventory of aircraft fleets provided by ICAO to determine the number of aircraft in over 80 separate aircraft types. For each aircraft type, we construct a user price, roughly comparable to an annual rental price. Total expenses are then the sum of these user prices, weighted by the number of aircraft in a carrier's fleet in each category. We considered several alternatives in constructing these user prices. We rejected the traditional approach of basing cost on book value since this is not responsive to changing demands for different types of aircraft at different points in time. For example, following deregulation in the USA the demand for small aircraft increased dramatically (along with their selling price) while wide bodied aircraft had a dramatic decrease in price. Valuation of individual aircraft types is based on the average of Avmark's January and July subjective valuations of each type of aircraft for every year. These valuations are based on recent sales and perceptions of changing market conditions for aircraft in half-time condition. The primary liability of this approach is that it does not capture benefits (for example, reduced maintenance) for newer rather than older aircraft within a particular type. This approach also poses some problems for aircraft which are not widely traded or for aircraft that are not jets. For aircraft that are not widely traded, we used the most comparable aircraft that was traded in order to get a market value. For the BAC/SUD Concorde, we used the Boeing747-200. While the 747 is a much larger aircraft, because of its speed, the revenue-generating capability of these two aircraft is roughly comparable. Soviet equipment also posed some problems. Most airlines do not consider this equipment very desirable and its market values are considered to be fairly low. We value it as comparable to the oldest Western equipment of a comparable size. For example we value the Tupelov Tu-154 at the same rate as the Boeing B727-100 and the Tu-134 as the same as a BAC-111. We value the Ilyushin Il-62 the same as a Douglas DC-8-10. Avmark also provides some limited information about turboprop aircraft. We divided turboprop aircraft into six categories (YS-11, Lockheed Electra, Lockheed Hercules, Fairchild F-227, Fokker 27, and Saab 340) and allocated different types to these categories based on age and size. (For example we allocated the Fokker 50 into the Saab 340 category since they are both relatively new design commuter aircraft. We allocated the HS-748 to the YS-11 category since they are both a 1960's design 50-passenger aircraft.) We had a final residual type of aircraft which could not conveniently be categorized this way. Some carriers operate a small fleet of single engine aircraft. Others operate one or two helicopters. We valued single engine piston aircraft at 100 000 and helicopters at 400 000. These residual aircraft are so small (in terms of the number of seats of capacity) that our cost per seat user price is insensitive to whatever decisions we make about their valuation.

Because we value aircraft in half-time condition, we assume that their remaining useful life is 14 years and use a 1.5 declining balance method to calculate economic depreciation. We considered several alternatives in constructing the interest portion of the rental price: using local and US real interest rates and using fixed depreciation rates versus rates based on changes in the valuation of the asset. We rejected an approach which used country-specific interest rates. It was not possible to find comparable interest and inflation rates across different countries. In some cases real interest rates were always negative and nominal rates did not change over the entire sample period. Under the assumption that marginal decisions about fleet size were based on the international leasing market, and that the leasing market was dominated by US carriers and US prices, we used rates based on Moody's Baa rate for a six-month commercial paper. An alternative to using our depreciation method described above, is to construct the depreciation portion by viewing an aircraft as both a financial and economic asset. Under this approach the cost of holding and using the aircraft would be the difference in market value at the end of the year compared to the beginning of the year plus the nominal interest rate. We ultimately rejected this approach because it led to several instances where the capital price fluctuated dramatically near periods when the price for a particular aircraft was depressed due to random events (such as the DC-10 grounding in 1979, or the bankruptcy of a carrier leading to lots of a particular aircraft flooding the market). In addition to constructing price and quantity measures, we also generate several characteristics of the capital stock: its size (maximum seats per plane), its speed (cruising miles per hour), its technological age (in years) and a classification of the aircraft as turboprop, jet or wide bodied jet.

Data on these technological characteristics were collected for individual aircraft types from *Jane's* (1945-1996 editions). We use the average number of months since first flight of aircraft designs as our measure of the technological age of the fleet. Our assumption is that the technological innovation in an aircraft does not change significantly after the design is first flown. While it would have been desirable to use certification date of equipment (as in our US data set) not all equipment types are FAA certified. The measure of technological age we adopt does not fully capture the deterioration in capital and increased maintenance costs caused by use. It does capture retrofitting older designs with major innovations, if these innovations were significant enough to lead to a new aircraft designation. (For example, a Convair 580 is a retrofitted Convair 240 with new turboprop engines and wing modifications. A DC-8-72 is a retrofit of a previous version with new engines.) Average equipment size was measured with the highest density seating configuration listed in *Jane's* for each aircraft type. This assumption was necessary for consistency. Over time, the number of seats in a particular aircraft type has increased by decreasing seat pitch. Even within a particular carrier's fleet, the number of seats varied, sometimes significantly, yet we were not able to identify the total number of seats. Further, for aircraft used in combination service, the actual number of seats would seriously understate the aircraft's true capacity and revenue generating capability. Since our purpose was to consistently describe the bulk transport capability of the fleet, we used this single maximum value regardless of the actual seating configuration. This average across the fleet was weighted by the average number of aircraft of each type assigned into service. In some cases, particularly with wide-bodied jets, the actual number of seats was substantially less than described by this configuration.

The measure of speed we utilize captures a third aspect about the productivity of the aircraft. As speed increases, flight crew time can be spread over more aircraft miles. Our measure of speed for individual aircraft types is based on *Jane's* measure of the economic cruising speed (in nautical miles per hour) for the type. This measure has some potential for inconsistency. As fuel prices change, the economic cruising speed slows. Consequently, there is a tendency for newer aircraft types to have slower design cruising speeds than older types.

We also construct the percentage of aircraft in several categories: turboprop, jet and a subgroup of jets: wide-bodied jet (determined by having two aisles in the main cabin). To the extent that turboprop and jet aircraft percentages do not sum to one, it indicates the presence of either piston or rotary wing aircraft. These categories roughly provide measures of the potential productivity of capital as well as its heterogeneity. As more wide-bodied aircraft are used, resources for flight crews, passenger and aircraft handlers, landing slots and so on do not increase proportionately. The percent turboprops also provide a measure of aircraft speed. This type of aircraft flies at approximately one-third of the speed of jet equipment. Consequently providing service in these types of equipment requires proportionately more flight crew resources than with jets. Our data provide for three separate categories of airline output:

scheduled passenger output, nonscheduled and cargo output and incidental output. This third category describes revenues which are attributable to airline related activities but which are not the physical transport of passengers and cargo. An example would be maintenance performed for other airlines. For some carriers this can be a significant component of revenue (and user of resources); for others this category is virtually zero.

Scheduled passenger output is measured in revenue tonne kilometers. This is calculated under the assumption that a passenger, along with checked baggage, constitutes 200 pounds in weight. Nonscheduled output combines charter, mail and cargo operations. Charter passenger traffic again assumes 200 pounds per passenger. For scheduled and nonscheduled outputs, both quantity and expense information is available. For incidental output we use the country's purchasing power parity as a deflator to construct a quantity measure. We combine these in a single output measure for this study.

Finally we construct two traditional measures of the carrier's output: stage length and load factor. Load factor provides a measure of service quality and is often used as a proxy for service competition. Stage length provides a measure of the length of individual route segments in the carrier's network.

The carriers for Asia are: Air India, Air New Zealand, Garuda Airlines, Cathay Pacific, Japan Airlines, Japan Asia Airways, Korean Airlines and Philippines Airlines, Quantas, Singapore Airlines and Thai International. The North American carriers are American Airlines, Air Canada, CP Air, Continental, Delta, Eastern Airlines, Northwest, Pan Am, Trans World Airlines, United Airlines, USAir and Western Airlines.

6 RESULTS AND CONCLUDING REMARKS

Summary statistics for the variables used in the dynamic frontier analysis are provided in Table 4.1 while individual carriers and the years for which we have data are listed in Table 4.2. To be parsimonious, we consider only two different adjustment speeds in our results, one for each of the two regions, instead of estimating separate adjustment speeds for each of the 23 carriers in our sample. Within estimates (Schmidt and Sickles, 1984) of the frontier ignoring potential dynamic adjustments are in Table 4.3. Results are plausible, with long-run returns to scale constant, a recurring empirical finding by researchers in this industry and an assumption utilized in the modeling of long-run industry decision. These results are similar to static results obtained from other studies (Good and Rhodes,

1991; Oum and Yu, 1997). Exogeneity of the lagged inputs, necessary for the consistency of the within estimates when the structure of the dynamic adjustment model is ignored, is rejected at nominal significance levels.[5] Further we find that a test of the equality of long run efficiency levels can resoundingly be rejected. Our within estimates suggest relative efficiencies which are much more homogeneous among North American carriers than Asian (the lowest quartile is made up exclusively of Asian carriers), with no particular pattern suggested in the rest of the distribution of efficiency scores.

GMM estimates are provided in Table 4.4, again based on region-specific adjustment speed parameters. Returns to scale remain insignificantly different from unity. The efficiency levels of carriers is similar to those described by the within estimates with some notable exceptions. North American airlines are in general more efficient in the long-run due in part to the Asian airlines' inability to utilize full capacity (k_i). If public infrastructures' investments, in airport facilities and air traffic control systems, and market-based incentives were encouraged by reducing governmental ownership and subsidies such inefficiencies could be ameliorated. On the other hand, however, Asian airlines adopt new technologies faster and thus the output loss due to tardy adoption is

Table 4.1 Summary statistics

Variable	Mean	Standard deviation	Skewness	Kurtosis	Minimum	Maximum
ln(*Q*)	14.98	1.08	−0.6	3.3	11.41	17.07
ln(*L*)	9.63	1.03	−1.4	6.3	5.99	11.49
ln(*E*)	7.43	1.06	−0.5	2.9	4.26	9.26
ln(*M*)	9.00	0.97	−0.6	3.5	5.59	11.01
ln(*K*)	4.37	1.13	−0.2	2.3	1.39	6.51
ln(*SL*)	0.36	0.46	0.3	2.7	−0.77	1.47
PT	0.04	0.10	2.9	10.3	0.0	0.48
PWB	0.34	0.26	1.3	3.9	0.0	1.0
ln(*AA*)	5.14	0.23	−0.3	2.9	4.45	5.69
ln(*ASZE*)	5.51	0.36	0.1	2.4	4.55	6.19
ln(*ASPD*)	6.28	0.07	−2.5	9.3	5.87	6.34

Table 4.2 Airlines

Airlines	Time Periods
Asia	
Air India	1977-1992
Air New Zealand	1977-1993
Garuda Airlines	1976-1991
Cathay Pacific	1987-1994
Japan Airlines	1976-1994
Japan Asia Airways	1976-1994
Korean Airlines	1976-1994
Philippines Airlines	1976-1994
Quantas	1978-1991
Singapore Airlines	1976-1994
Thai International	1976-1991
North America	
American Airlines	1976-1994
Air Canada	1976-1994
CP Air	1976-1994
Continental	1976-1994
Delta	1976-1994
Eastern Airlines	1976-1990
Northwest	1976-1994
Pan Am	1976-1990
Trans World Airlines	1976-1994
United Airlines	1976-1994
US Air	1979-1995
Western Airlines	1976-1986

Table 4.3 Within estimation results

A. Results for the frontier production function

Variable	Coefficient	Std. Err.	T-Stat.	Variable	Coefficient	Std. Err.	T-Stat
ln(*L*)	0.123	0.023	5..35	*PWB*	−0.120	0.056	−2.15
ln(*E*)	0.355	0.031	11.52	ln(*AA*)	−0.165	0.039	−4.27
ln(*M*)	0.250	0.025	10.13	ln(*ASZE*)	0.365	0.068	5.40
ln(*K*)	0.293	0.032	9.04	ln(*ASPD*)	−0.780	0.340	−2.30
ln(*SL*)	−0.024	0.031	−0.76	Time Trend	0.0028	0.0025	1.10
PT	−0.462	0.202	−2.29	*RTS**	1.021	0.018	55.69
R^2		0.996		Obs.		383	
Significance test for lagged values on inputs** (df = 8)					24.59 (p = 0.017)		

Airline	Estimate	Std. Err.	T-Stat.	Airline	Estimate	Std. Err.	T-Stat.
Quantas	1.000	---	---	Northwest	0.812	0.050	16.23
Cathay Pacific	0.928	0.352	26.36	Japan Airlines	0.780	0.033	24.00
Western Airlines	0.913	0.056	16.34	Eastern Airlines	0.758	0.052	14.57
CP Air	0.882	0.042	20.88	US Air	0.699	0.053	13.11
Pan Am	0.879	0.045	19.63	Air Canada	0.692	0.038	18.41
Air New Zealand	0.867	0.048	18.13	Japan Asia Airways	0.619	0.039	15.73
Continental	0.866	0.052	16.54	Korean Airlines	0.610	0.027	22.73
TWA	0.855	0.050	16.98	Thai Inter.	0.601	0.028	21.48
United Airlines	0.855	0.056	15.39	Garuda	0.564	0.040	14.16
Delta	0.855	0.059	14.46	Philippines Airlines	0.515	0.031	16.80
Singapore Airlines	0.853	0.030	28.86	Air India	0.477	0.021	22.88
American Airlines	0.8421	0.054	15.67				
Wald test for equality of *LR* effects (df = 22)					834.9 (p = 0.000)		

Notes:

**RTS* means 'returns to scale', which is obtained by adding the coefficients of ln(*L*), ln(*E*), ln(*M*) and ln(*K*).

**The test for the exogeneity of regional dummy variables times lagged ln(*L*), ln(*E*), ln(*M*) and ln(*K*) (with bandwidth = 4).

Table 4.4 GMM results for dynamic stochastic panel frontier

A. Results for the frontier production function							
Variable	Coefficient	Std. Err.	T-Stat.	Variable	Coefficient	Std. Err.	T-Stat
ln(L)	0.094	0.030	3.11	PWB	−0.163	0.075	−2.18
ln(E)	0.359	0.048	7.46	ln(AA)	−0.155	0.068	−2.26
ln(M)	0.206	0.046	4.52	Ln($ASZE$)	0.450	0.124	3.61
ln(K)	0.304	0.048	6.37	ln($ASPD$)	−1.17	0.724	−1.61
ln(SL)	−0.027	0.036	−0.77	Time Trend	0.0064	0.0056	1.14
PT	−0.598	0.358	−1.67	RTS	0.964	0.046	20.94
R^2		0.996		Obs.		337	
B. Estimation Results for Adjustment Speed							
Coefficient	Estimate	Std. Err.	T-Stat.	Coefficient	Estimate	Std. Err.	T-Stat.
North America	0.278	0.112	2.47	Asia	0.542	0.114	4.47
C. Specification Tests							
Hansen test (df = 21)	16.90 (p = 0.717)			Exo. Test* (df = 23)	32.70 (p = 0.0865)		
D. Relative long-run (LR) inefficiency							
Airline	Estimate	Std. Err.	T-Stat.	Airline	Estimate	Std. Err.	T-Stat.
Quantas	1.000	---	---	CP Air	0.815	0.090	9.07
United Airlines	0.967	0.114	8.46	Eastern Airlines	0.815	0.101	8.05
Delta	0.933	0.108	8.63	Japan Airlines	0.811	0.048	17.05
American Airlines	0.931	0.115	8.11	US Air	0.744	0.090	8.31
Western Airlines	0.904	0.086	10.50	Air Canada	0.689	0.065	10.68
Continental	0.894	0.098	9.09	Korean Airlines	0.610	0.035	17.45
TWA	0.892	0.084	10.61	Thai International	0.577	0.039	14.63
Pan Am	0.880	0.076	11.53	Garuda	0.558	0.055	10.23
Singapore Airlines	0.878	0.038	22.92	Japan Asia Airlines	0.534	0.064	8.38
Air New Zealand	0.867	0.079	10.94	Philippines Airlines	0.520	0.043	12.19
Cathay Pacific	0.854	0.034	25.44	Air India	0.492	0.033	14.97
Northwest	0.828	0.085	9.72				

Notes: Wald test for equality of LR effects (df = 22); 585.50 (p = 0.000).
*Test for exogeneity of two-period lagged output levels of all 23 firms.

smaller for the Asian airlines. Our estimates of adjustment speeds for Asian carriers which is given by $(1-\rho)\gamma/\rho$ are twice those of North America (0.542 versus 0.278). Therefore if long-run inefficiencies can be reduced the relatively higher speed of technology adoption would allow Asian airlines to catch-up and possibly leap-frog North American carriers. We reject the hypothesis of equal long-run inefficiencies using the Wald test reported in Table 4.3. The composition of the top quartile of the efficiency distribution is 84 percent North American and 16 percent Asian; the composition of the remaining quartiles is 50 percent/50 percent, 30 percent/70 percent, and 0 percent/100 percent. The efficiency levels of United, Delta and American, the only financially successful carriers in the USA, are dramatically improved using the GMM estimates. As with the within estimates, the bottom quartile contains Asian carriers with significant government ownership. Singapore Airlines, with 54 percent government ownership, is an exception. Singapore Airline stands out in two important respects from other carriers in the sample. Like Cathay Pacific, it has a history of maintaining a relatively new fleet which may be reflected in part by its relatively high efficiency level. However, Singapore Airline is noted as a carrier which has one of the highest levels of service in the world. To the extent that providing high quality service uses resources, this would tend to make our estimate of their efficiency lower than if we had been able to quality adjust output for the level of customer service. We find that the efficiency levels for Asian carriers is also reflected by the level of competitiveness of the bilateral agreements. This suggests that airlines' willingness to compete (as measured by the bilateral agreements) tracks closely with their ability to compete (as measured by productive efficiency).

Our results clearly illustrate the advantages of the dynamic frontier model put forth in Ahn *et al.* (1997) by permitting the dynamic convergence of firms within the international aviation industry. GMM estimates of efficiency levels appear to be more consistent with the financial success of carriers than the static within estimates. Our model nests the conventional deterministic and stochastic panel frontier and thus conventional hypothesis tests can be carried out to discriminate among competing specifications, and our results point to the importance of modeling dynamics in frontier analyses.

NOTES

1. The authors wish to thank Anthony Postert for his valuable research assistance. Ahn gratefully acknowledges the financial support of the College of Business and Dean's

Council of 100 at Arizona State University, the Economic Club of Phoenix, and the alumni of the College of Business. Good and Sickles acknowledge the valuable research support from the Logistics Management Institute and the National Aeronautics and Space Administration.

2. For expository convenience, we here assume that all future output and input prices are known. This assumption can be easily relaxed. See Zellner, Kmenta and Drèze (1966).
3. Note that sum of a *MA*(1) process and white noise is also *MA*(1). See Hamilton (1994, pp. 102-5).
4. We fix bandwidth at one to compute the Newey and West estimator of Ω_i, since the errors e_{it} are *MA*(1) under our stochastic frontier assumption.
5. For this test, we fix the bandwidth parameter for Newey-West estimators at four. Many other values are also used, but the Wald test results remains unaffected.

REFERENCES

Ahn, S.C. (1997), 'Orthogonality tests in linear models', *Oxford Bulletin of Economics and Statistics*, **59**, 183-86.

Ahn, S.C., D.H. Good and R.C. Sickles (1997), 'Estimation of long-run inefficiency levels: a dynamic frontier', mimeo.

Alam, I. and R.C. Sickles (1997), 'Long-run properties of technical efficiency in the US airline industry', mimeo.

Battese, G.E. and T.J. Coelli (1992), 'Frontier production functions, technical efficiency and panel data: with application to paddy farmers in India', *Journal of Productivity Analysis*, **3**, 153-69.

Captain, P. and R.C. Sickles (1997), 'Competition and market power in the European airline industry: 1976-1990', *Managerial and Decision Economics*, **18**, 1-17.

Coelli, T., S. Perelman, and E. Romano (1997), 'Airlines environment and technical efficiency: an international comparative study', mimeo.

Cornwell, C., P. Schmidt and R.C. Sickles (1990), 'Production frontiers with cross-sectional and time-series variation in efficiency levels', *Journal of Econometrics*, **46**, 185-200.

Färe, R., S. Grosskopf, M. Norris and Z. Zhang (1994), 'Productivity growth, technical progress, and efficiency change in industrialized countries', *American Economic Review*, **84**, 66-83.

Good, D.H. and E.L. Rhodes (1991), 'Productive efficiency, technological change and the competitiveness of US airlines in the Pacific rim', *Journal of the Transportation Research Forum*, **31** (2), 347-58.

Good, D.H., M.I. Nadiri, L.-H. Roeller and R.C. Sickles (1993a), 'Efficiency and productivity growth comparisons of European and US. air carriers: a first look at the data', *Journal of Productivity Analysis*, **4**, special issue edited by J. Mairesse and Z. Griliches, 115-25.

Good, D.H., L.-H. Roeller and R.C. Sickles (1993b), 'US airline deregulation: implications for European transport', *Economic Journal*, **103**, 1028-41.

Good, D.H., L.-H. Roeller and R.C. Sickles (1995), 'Airline efficiency differences between Europe and the US: implications for the pace of EC integration and domestic regulation', *European Journal of Operational Research*, **80**, special issue edited by A. Lewin and C.A.K. Lovell, 508-18.

Good, D.H., M.I. Nadiri and R.C. Sickles (1997a), 'Index number and factor demand approaches to the estimation of productivity', in M.H. Pesaran and P. Schmidt (eds), *Handbook of Applied Econometrics, Volume II-Microeconometrics*, Cambridge, UK, Basil Blackwell forthcoming.

Good, D.H., A. Postert and R.C. Sickles (1997b), 'A model of world aircraft demand', mimeo.

Hamilton, J. (1994), *Time Series Analysis,* Princeton, NJ: Princeton University Press.

Hansen, L.P. (1982), 'Large sample properties of generalized method of moments estimators', *Econometrica*, **50**, 1029-54.

Kumbhakar, S.C. (1990), 'Production frontiers, panel data, and time-varying technical inefficiency', *Journal of Econometrics*, **46**, 201-2.

Lee, Y.H. and P. Schmidt (1993), A production frontier model with flexible temporal variation in technical efficiency, in H. Fried C.A.K. Lovell and S. Schmidt (eds), *The Measurement of Productive Efficiency Techniques and Applications*, Oxford: Oxford Academic Press, 237-55.

Newey, W.K. (1985), Generalized method of moments specification testing, *Journal of Econometrics*, **29**, 229-56.

Newey, W.K. and K.D. West (1987), 'Hypothesis testing with efficient method of moments estimation', *International Economic Review*, **28**, 777-87.

Oum, T.H. and Chunyan Yu (1997), 'Cost competitiveness of major airlines: an international comparison', mimeo.

Park, B.U., R.C. Sickles and L. Simar (1997), 'Stochastic panel frontiers: a semiparametric approach', *Journal of Econometrics*, forthcoming.

Roeller, L.-H. and R.C. Sickles (1996), 'Competition, market niches, and efficiency: a structural model of the European airline industry', mimeo.

Schmidt, P. (1984), 'Frontier production function', *Econometric Reviews*, **4**, 289-328.

Schmidt, P. and R.C. Sickles (1984), 'Production frontiers and panel data', *Journal of Business and Economic Statistics*, **2**, 367-74.

Zellner, A., J. Kmenta and J. Drèze (1966), 'Specification and estimation of Cobb-Douglas production function models', *Econometrica*, **34**, 784-95.

B. International

5. There is No Silver Bullet: Investment and Growth in the G7

Chrys Dougherty and Dale W. Jorgenson[1]

1. INTRODUCTION

In this chapter we present international comparisons of patterns of economic growth among the G7 countries over the period 1960-1989. We rationalize the important changes that have taken place on the basis of Solow's (1970) neoclassical theory of economic growth, extended to incorporate persistent differences among countries. We greatly reduce the role of exogenous productivity growth, where productivity is defined as output per unit of input, including both capital and labor inputs. We give a much more prominent role to investment, which is endogenous to the theory.

The USA retained its lead in output per capita throughout the period 1960-1989, despite lagging behind other G7 countries - Canada, France, Germany, Italy, Japan and the UK - in economic growth. Perhaps surprisingly, the USA relinquished its position as the country with the highest productivity level and capital-labor ratio. However the USA retained its leadership in capital per capita and the quality of its work force, reflecting high levels of investment in tangible assets and human capital.

Patterns of economic growth among the G7 countries became considerably more uniform during the period 1960-1989. Canada converged toward US levels of output per capita, achieving higher productivity and a substantially greater capital-labor ratio. The sole remaining US advantage was greater labor input per capita. Outside Canada and the USA, the UK was the leader and Japan the laggard in output per capita in 1960, but these two countries interchanged roles by 1989. The UK reached approximate parity with Canada and the USA in productivity, but UK capital per capita was less than half Canadian and US levels as a consequence of underinvestment in tangible assets.

Japan exhibited considerably higher growth rates in output per capita and productivity than the other G7 countries and led the G7 in per capita labor input after 1962; however Japan had the lowest capital-labor ratio and productivity level throughout the period. France had the highest capital-labor ratio after 1976 and led in productivity after 1981, but ranked at the bottom in the quality of its work force, reflecting underinvestment in human capital. Italian labor input per capita languished throughout the period, while German productivity lagged behind productivity in the other G7 countries, except Japan.

Investment greatly predominated as a source of economic growth for Canada and the USA throughout the period 1960-1989. With the conspicuous exception of France investment was the most important source of growth for the G7 countries after 1973. However differences among these countries persist in patterns of investment in tangible assets and human capital. These account for many of the remaining disparities in economic performance and suggest policy initiatives to remedy the deficiencies that have become apparent.

In section 2, we describe our methodology for allocating the sources of economic growth for the G7 countries between investment and productivity. We introduce constant quality indices of capital and labor inputs that incorporate the effects of investments in tangible assets and human capital. The constant quality index of labor input combines different types of hours worked by means of wage rates. The constant quality index of capital input weights different types of capital stock by rental rates, rather than the asset prices appropriate for capital stock.

Differences in wage rates for different types of labor input reflect investments in human capital through education and training, so that a constant quality index of labor input is the channel for the impact of these investments on growth. The constant quality index of capital input includes a perpetual inventory of investments in tangible assets. The index also includes rental prices that capture the impact of these investments on growth.

In section 3, we analyze the role of investment and productivity as sources of economic growth in the G7 countries over the period 1960-1989. We also consider the two subperiods before and after 1973 in order to identify changes in growth patterns after the first oil crisis. We decompose growth of output per capita for each country between growth of productivity and growth of input per capita. Finally, we decompose the growth of input per capita into components associated with investments in tangible assets and human capital.

International comparisons reveal important similarities among the G7 countries. Investments in tangible assets and human capital now account for the major portion of economic growth in the G7 countries and also explain the predominant share of international differences in output per capita. Heterogeneity in capital and labor inputs and changes in the composition of these inputs over time are essential for identifying persistent international differences and accounting for the sources of growth.

In section 4, we test the implication of the neoclassical theory of growth that relative levels of output and input per capita converge over time. For this purpose we employ the coefficient of variation to measure convergence of levels of output per capita, input per capita, and productivity among the G7 countries over the period 1960-1989. As before, we divide the period at 1973. We also analyze the convergence of capital and labor inputs per capita, another implication of the neoclassical theory.

While patterns of growth have become much more similar, differences among the G7 countries persist. Before 1973 output and productivity for the G7 countries gradually converged; however convergence ended after 1973, leaving important differences in levels of output per capita and productivity. Capital input per capita converged until 1977 but differences in the composition of capital remain. Labor input per capita was slower to converge and differences persist in hours worked per capita and the composition of labor input.

In section 5, we summarize the conclusions of our study and suggest alternative approaches to endogenizing economic growth at the aggregate level by broadening the concept of investment. The mechanism for capital accumulation captured in Solow's theory provides the most appropriate point of departure. Investments in human capital, especially investment in education, can be included in theory. When measures of the output of research and development activities become available, investment in intellectual capital can also be made endogenous.

2 INVESTMENT AND PRODUCTIVITY

The ongoing debate over the relative importance of investment and productivity in economic growth coincides with disputes about the appropriate role for the public sector. Productivity can be identified with 'spillovers' of benefits that do not provide incentives for actors within the private sector. Advocates of a larger role for the public sector advance the view that these spillovers can be guided into proper channels only by an all-wise and beneficent government. By contrast proponents of a smaller government search for means to privatize investment decisions by decentralizing these decisions among participants in the private sector.

Profound differences in policy implications militate against any simple resolution of the debate on the relative importance of investment and productivity. Proponents of income redistribution will not lightly abandon the search for a 'silver bullet' that will generate economic growth without the necessity of providing incentives for investment. Advocates of growth strategies based on capital formation will not readily give credence to claims of spillovers to beneficiaries who are difficult or impossible to identify.

To avoid the semantic confusion that pervades popular discussions of economic growth, it is essential to be precise in defining investment. Investment is the commitment of current resources in the expectation of future returns and can take a multiplicity of forms. The distinctive feature of investment as a source of economic growth is that the returns can be internalized by the investor. The most straightforward application of this definition is to invest in tangible assets that creates property rights, including rights to benefit from the incomes that accrue to the owners and transfer the resulting assets.

The mechanism by which tangible investments are translated into economic growth is well understood. For example, an investor in a new industrial facility adds to the supply of these assets and generates a stream of rental income. Investment and income are linked through markets for capital assets and services. The income stream can be divided between the increase in capital input and the marginal product of capital or rental price. The increase in capital contributes to output growth in proportion to the marginal product. This is the basis for construction of a constant quality index of capital input.

Similarly, an individual who completes a course of education or training adds to the supply of people with higher qualifications or skills. The resulting income stream can be decomposed into a rise in labor input and the marginal product of labor or wage rate. The increase in labor contributes to output growth in proportion to the marginal product. This provides the basis for constructing a constant quality index of labor input. While there are no asset markets for human capital, investments in human and nonhuman capital have the common feature, pointed out by Fisher (1906), that returns are internalized by the investor.

The defining characteristic of productivity as a source of economic growth is that the incomes generated by higher productivity are external to the economic activities generating growth. Publicly supported research and development programs are a leading illustration of policies to stimulate productivity growth. These programs can be conducted by government laboratories or financed by public subsidies to private laboratories. The benefits of the resulting innovations are external to the economic units conducting the research and development and must be carefully distinguished from the private benefits of research and development that can be internalized through the creation of intellectual property rights.

The allocation of sources of economic growth between investment and productivity is critical for assessing the explanatory power of growth theory. Only substitution between capital and labor inputs resulting from investment in tangible assets is endogenous in Solow's (1970) neoclassical theory of growth. However substitution among different types of labor input is the consequence of investment in human capital, while investment in tangible assets induces substitution among different types of capital input. Neither form of substitution is included in Solow's (1957) model of production.

The distinction between substitution and technical change emphasized by Solow (1957) parallels the distinction between investment and productivity as sources of economic growth. However Solow's definition of investment, like that of Kuznets (1971), was limited to tangible assets. Both specifically excluded investments in human capital by relying on increases in undifferentiated hours of work as a measure of the contribution of labor input to growth.

Kuznets (1971) and Solow (1970) identified the contribution of tangible assets to growth with increases in the stock, which does not adequately capture substitution among different types of capital input. Constant quality indices of both capital and labor inputs and investment goods output are essential for the allocation of sources of growth between investment and productivity. Failing to employ these measurement techniques, Kuznets and Solow attributed almost all of US economic growth to productivity or the Solow residual.[2]

Investment can be made endogenous within a neoclassical growth model. If productivity growth greatly predominates among sources of economic growth, as indicated by Kuznets (1971) and Solow (1970), most of growth is determined exogenously. Reliance on the Solow residual as an explanatory factor is a powerful indictment of the limitations of the neoclassical framework. This viewpoint was expressed by Abramovitz (1956), who famously characterized productivity growth as 'a measure of our ignorances'.

Jorgenson and Griliches (1967) introduced constant quality indices of capital and labor inputs and a constant quality measure of investment goods output in allocating the sources of growth between investment and productivity. This considerably broadened the concept of substitution employed by Solow (1957) and altered, irrevocably, the allocation of economic growth between investment and productivity. They showed that

85 percent of US economic growth could be attributed to investment, while productivity accounted for the remaining 15 percent.[3]

The constant quality index of labor input employed by Jorgenson and Griliches combined different types of hours worked into a constant quality index of labor input, using methodology Griliches (1960) had developed for US agriculture.[4] The constant quality index of capital input combined different types of capital inputs by means of rental rates, rather than the asset prices appropriate for measuring capital stock. This model of capital as a factor of production was introduced by Jorgenson (1963) and made it possible to incorporate differences in capital consumption and the tax treatment of different types of capital income.

Jorgenson and Griliches identified technology with a production possibility frontier. This extended the aggregate production function to include two outputs, investment and consumption goods. Jorgenson (1966) showed that economic growth could be interpreted, equivalently as 'embodied' in investment in the sense of Solow (1960) or 'disembodied' in productivity growth. Jorgenson and Griliches removed this indeterminacy by introducing constant quality indices for investment goods.

Two studies by Christensen and Jorgenson (1969, 1970) provided a much more detailed implementation of the concept of capital as a factor of production. This utilized a model of the tax structure for corporate capital income developed by Hall and Jorgenson (1967). Christensen and Jorgenson extended this model to noncorporate and household capital incomes in order to capture more adequately the impact of differences in returns to capital due to taxation on substitutions among capital inputs.

Christensen and Jorgenson distinguished between two approaches to the analysis of economic growth. They identified with production account with a production possibility frontier describing technology and the income and expenditure account with a social welfare function describing consumer preferences. They divided the *uses* of economic growth between current consumption and future consumption through saving. Saving was linked to the asset side of the wealth account through capital accumulation equations for each type of asset. Prices for different vintages of assets were linked to rental prices of capital inputs through a parallel set of capital asset pricing equations.

In 1973 Christensen and Jorgenson presented estimates of the *sources* of economic growth within a complete system of US national accounts. They constructed internally consistent income, product and wealth accounts. Separate product and income accounts were integral parts of both the US Income and Product Accounts and the United Nations (1968) *A System of National Accounts*.[5] However neither system included wealth accounts consistent with the income and product accounts.

Christensen and Jorgenson constructed income, product and wealth accounts, paralleling the US National Income and Product Accounts for the period 1929-1969, and implemented a vintage accounting system for the US on an annual basis. The complete system of vintage accounts gave stocks of assets of each vintage and their prices. The stocks were cumulated to obtain asset quantities, providing a perpetual inventory of assets accumulated at different points of time.

The key innovation in the vintage system of accounts was the use of asset pricing equations to link the prices used in evaluating capital stocks and the rental prices employed in the constant quality index of capital input.[6] In a prescient paper on the measurement of welfare Samuelson (1961) had suggested that the link between asset and rental prices was essential for the integration of income and wealth accounting proposed by Fisher (1906). The vintage system of accounts employed the specific form of this relationship developed by Jorgenson (1973).

Christensen *et al.* (1981) presented annual estimates of sources of economic growth for the USA and its major trading partners for the period 1960-1973. These estimates included constant quality indexes of capital and labor input for each country. Our first objective in this chapter is to extend these estimates to 1989 for the G7 countries. We have chosen GDP as a measure of output. We include imputations for the services of consumers' durables as well as land, buildings and equipment owned by nonprofit institutions in order to preserve comparability in the treatment of income from different types of capital.

Our constant quality index of capital input is based on a disaggregation of the capital stock among the 21 categories given in Table 5.1. These are

Table 5.1 Disaggregation of capital by asset characteristics

Asset type	Ownership sector
1. Equipment	1. Corporations and Government
2. Nonresidential Structures	2. Unincorporated Businesses
3. Residential Structures	3. Households and Nonprofit Institutions
4. Nonfarm Inventories	4. General Government
5. Farm Inventories	
6. Consumer Durables	
7. Residential Land	
8. Nonresidential Land	

classified by asset type and ownership to reflect differences in capital consumption and tax treatment among assets. We derive estimates of capital stock and property income for each type of capital input from national accounting data. Similarly our constant quality index of labor input is based on a disaggregation of the work force among the 20 categories presented in Table 5.2. These are classified by sex, educational attainment and employment status. For each country we derive estimates of hours worked and labor compensation for type of labor input from labor force surveys.[7]

Table 5.2 Disaggregation of labor by demographic characteristics

Sex
Educational attainment:
1. 1-8 years' grade school
2. 1-3 years' secondary school
3. Completed secondary school
4. 1-3 years' college
5. 4 or more years of college
Employment status:
1. Business sector employee
2. Self-employed or unpaid family worker
3. General government employee

3 SOURCES OF GROWTH

We summarize growth in output and input per capita and productivity for the G7 countries in Table 5.3. We present annual average growth rates for the period 1960-1989 and the subperiods before and after 1973. Japan was the leader in the growth of output per capita for the period as a whole and both subperiods. The USA grew more slowly than the remaining six countries during the period as a whole and before 1973, but grew slightly faster than the UK after 1973, when growth slowed in all the G7 countries. Differences in growth rates among the G7 countries also declined substantially after 1973.

Canada led the G7 in growth of input per capita for the period 1960-1989 and after 1973, while Japan was the leader in input growth before 1973. There is little evidence of a slowdown in input growth after 1973;

Table 5.3 Growth in output and input per capita and productivity, G7 countries, 1960-1989 (average percentage growth rates)

	USA	Canada	UK	France	Germany	Italy	Japan
Output Per Capita							
1960-1973	2.51	3.32	2.80	4.30	3.77	4.79	8.18
1973-1989	1.72	2.61	1.62	2.01	2.20	2.89	3.12
1960-1989	2.07	2.93	2.15	3.04	2.91	3.74	5.39
Input Per Capita							
1960-1973	1.70	2.23	0.88	1.98	1.20	0.81	2.43
1973-1989	1.39	2.34	0.95	0.62	1.26	2.34	2.06
1960-1989	1.53	2.29	0.92	1.23	1.23	1.65	2.23
Productivity							
1960-1973	0.81	1.09	1.92	2.32	2.57	3.97	5.75
1973-1989	0.32	0.28	0.67	1.40	0.94	0.55	1.07
1960-1989	0.54	0.64	1.23	1.81	1.67	2.09	3.16

Table 5.4 Levels of output and input per capita and productivity, G7 countries, 1960, 1973 and 1989 (USA =100 percent in 1985)

	USA	Canada	UK	France	Germany	Italy	Japan
Output Per Capita							
1960	59.9	44.0	38.9	30.4	34.2	25.6	17.2
1973	83.0	67.7	56.0	53.2	55.9	47.7	49.9
1989	109.2	102.9	72.6	73.4	79.5	75.7	82.2
Input Per Capita							
1960	68.7	50.9	55.6	43.9	62.0	45.1	50.6
1973	85.7	68.0	62.3	56.8	72.5	50.1	69.4
1989	107.1	98.9	72.5	62.7	88.6	72.8	96.5
Productivity							
1960	87.2	86.4	70.1	69.2	55.2	56.8	34.0
1973	96.9	99.5	89.9	93.6	77.1	95.2	71.8
1989	102.0	104.0	100.1	117.0	89.7	104.0	85.2

differences among input growth rates are much less than among output growth rates. Japan led the G7 in productivity growth for the period as a whole and before 1973, while France was the leader after 1973. The slowdown in productivity growth after 1973 parallels the slowdown in output growth. In Table 5.4 we present levels of output and input per capita and productivity relative to the US level in 1985.

Our constant quality index of capital input weights capital stocks for each of the 21 categories of the capital given in Table 5.1 by rental prices, defined as property compensation per unit of capital. By contrast an index of capital stock weights different types of capital by asset prices rather than the rental prices appropriate for capital input. The ratio of capital input to capital stock measures the average quality of a unit of capital, as reflected in its marginal product. This enables us to assess the magnitude of differences between the constant quality index of capital input and the unweighted index of capital stock employed by Kuznets (1971) and Solow (1970).

The picture for capital stock per capita has some similarities to capital input, but there are important differences. Canada overtook the USA in capital stock per capita in 1986, while France, rather than Germany, was the leader among the remaining five countries. Japan ranked last until 1976, but surpassed the UK in that year. Capital stock does not accurately reflect the substitutions among capital inputs that accompany investments in tangible assets.

We summarize growth in capital input and capital stock per capita and capita quality for the G7 countries in Table 5.5. Italy was the international leader in capital input growth and the USA the laggard for the period 1960-1989 and before and after 1973. There was a very modest slowdown in capital input growth after 1973 and a narrowing of differences in growth rates. Although Italy topped the rankings for capital stock growth for the period as a whole, Germany led before 1973 and Japan afterwards, while the USA lagged for the period as a whole and both subperiods. By contrast the slowing of capital stock growth was not substantial although differences in growth rates declined. Italy was the leader in capital quality growth and Japan the laggard. In Table 5.6 we present levels of capital input and capital stock per capita and capital quality relative to the USA in 1985.

Our constant quality index of labor input weights hours worked for each of the twenty categories of hours worked given in Table 5.2 by the wage rate, defined as labor compensation per hour. An index of hours worked adds together different types of hours without taking quality differences into account. The ratio of labor input to hours worked measures the average quality of an hour of labor, as reflected in its

Table 5.5 Growth in capital input and capital stock per capita and capital quality, G7 countries, 1960-1989 (average percentage growth rates)

	USA	Canada	UK	France	Germany	Italy	Japan
Capital Input Per Capita							
1960-1973	2.56	3.37	3.46	4.84	6.12	6.19	2.93
1973-1989	2.45	3.64	2.77	2.69	3.19	4.64	3.64
1960-1989	2.50	3.52	3.08	3.66	4.50	5.33	3.32
Capital Stock Per Capita							
1960-1973	2.08	3.09	3.14	4.40	5.59	5.01	2.97
1973-1989	1.94	3.18	2.63	2.72	2.74	3.44	3.94
1960-1989	2.00	3.14	2.86	3.47	4.01	4.14	3.51
Capital Quality							
1960-1973	0.48	0.27	0.32	0.45	0.53	1.19	−0.04
1973-1989	0.51	0.46	0.14	−0.03	0.45	1.19	−0.30
1960-1989	0.50	0.38	0.22	0.18	0.49	1.19	−0.18

Table 5.6 Levels of capital input and capital stock per capita and capital quality, G7 countries, 1960, 1973 and 1989 (USA = 100 percent in 1985)

	USA	Canada	UK	France	Germany	Italy	Japan
Capital Input Per Capita							
1960	89.3	86.0	98.2	88.6	105.1	71.9	102.3
1973	95.0	89.1	102.4	93.9	112.6	83.9	101.8
1989	103.1	96.0	104.8	93.4	121.1	101.5	97.0
Capital Stock Per Capita							
1960	60.3	45.1	21.6	29.4	23.9	23.9	21.1
1973	79.0	67.4	32.5	52.1	49.3	45.8	31.0
1989	107.7	112.1	49.5	80.5	76.4	79.4	58.3
Capital Quality							
1960	89.3	86.0	98.2	88.6	105.1	71.9	102.3
1973	95.0	89.1	102.4	93.9	112.6	83.9	101.8
1989	103.1	96.0	104.8	93.4	121.1	101.5	97.0

marginal product. This enables us to assess the magnitude of differences between the constant quality index of labor input and the unweighted index of hours worked employed by Kuznets (1971) and Solow (1970).

The picture for hours worked per capita has some similarities to labor input, but there are important differences. Japan was the international leader in hours worked per capita throughout the period, while Germany led the four European countries for most of the period. The US led Italy at the beginning of the period and overtook France in 1975 and Germany and the UK in 1977. Canada overtook Italy in 1965, France in 1978, the UK in 1981, and Germany in 1986. Hours worked do not accurately reflect the substitutions that accompany investments in human capital.

We summarize growth in labor input and hours worked per capita and labor quality in Table 5.7. Japan led the G7 countries in labor input growth before 1973, while Canada was the international leader after 1973 and led for the period 1960-1989 as a whole. Japan led growth in hours worked before 1973, Italy after 1973, and Canada for the period as a whole. Growth was positive throughout the period for Canada and the USA, mostly negative for the four European countries, and alternately positive and negative for Japan. There was no slowdown in the growth of hours worked and growth in labor quality was positive for all seven countries with only a modest decline after 1973. In Table 5.8 we present labor input and hours worked per capita and labor quality relative to the USA in 1985.

Relative differences in output per capita between any two countries are the sum of relative differences in productivity and input per capita. Differences in input per capita can be expressed in turn as the sum of differences in capital-labor ratios, weighted by the average of shares of capital in the value of output in the two countries, and differences in labor input per capita.[8] Initially, the USA had the highest capital-labor ratio, but was overtaken by France in 1976, Canada in 1977 and Italy and Germany in 1984.

The USA retained its lead in output per capita over France, despite lower productivity and a lower capital-labor ratio, through a large and growing lead in labor input per capita. Canada and Italy achieved approximate parity in productivity with the USA and substantially higher capital-labor ratios, but the USA retained a modest advantage in labor input per capita over Canada and a large advantage over Italy. Germany also achieved parity in capital-labor ratios with the USA with lower productivity and much lower and declining labor input per capita. Japan's substantial lead in labor input per capita did not outweigh its lower productivity and considerably lower capital-labor ratio.

Table 5.7 Growth in labor input and hours worked per capita and labor quality, G7 countries, 1960-1989 (average percentage growth rates)

	USA	Canada	UK	France	Germany	Italy	Japan
Labor Input Per Capita							
1960-1973	1.24	1.43	−0.48	0.28	−1.21	−1.24	1.93
1973-1989	0.87	1.38	0.00	−0.75	0.13	1.080	0.82
1960-1989	1.04	1.40	−0.21	−0.29	−0.47	0.04	1.32
Hours Worked Per Capita							
1960-1973	0.37	0.49	−1.01	−0.57	−1.53	−1.38	0.50
1973-1989	0.52	0.81	−0.25	−1.38	−0.35	0.86	−0.13
1960-1989	0.45	0.67	−0.59	−1.02	−0.88	−0.14	0.15
Labor Quality							
1960-1973	0.88	0.94	0.53	0.85	0.32	0.14	1.43
1973-1989	0.35	0.57	0.25	0.62	0.48	0.22	0.95
1960-1989	0.59	0.74	0.38	0.73	0.41	0.19	1.16

Table 5.8 Levels of labor input and hours worked per capita and labor quality, G7 countries, 1960, 1973 and 1989 (USA – 100 percent in 1985)

	USA	Canada	UK	France	Germany	Italy	Japan
Labor Input Per Capita							
1960	77.6	61.8	94.5	60.6	98.6	67.5	94.3
1973	91.2	74.5	88.8	62.8	84.3	57.4	121.2
1989	104.9	92.9	88.9	55.7	86.0	68.3	138.1
Hours Worked Per Capita							
1960	91.4	80.7	110.6	105.3	120.9	89.5	140.3
1973	95.9	85.9	97.0	97.8	99.1	74.8	149.8
1989	104.2	97.9	93.2	78.5	93.7	85.9	146.7
Labor Quality							
1960	84.9	76.7	85.5	57.5	81.6	75.3	67.2
1973	95.2	86.7	91.6	64.3	85.1	76.7	80.9
1989	100.7	95.0	95.4	71.0	91.8	79.5	94.2

In Figure 5.1 we assess the relative importance of investment and productivity in per capita growth for the G7 countries. For Canada and the USA investments in tangible assets and human capital greatly predominated as sources of growth over the period 1960-1989. We attribute less than half of Japanese growth to productivity, while proportions for the four European countries - France, Germany, Italy and the UK - range between 55 percent and 60 percent. Since 1973 growth in output and productivity has declined for all seven countries; however growth in input has not declined, so that the relative importance of productivity has diminished.

In Figure 5.2 we combine estimates of growth in capital input, capital stock and capital quality to assess the importance of changes in quality. Capital input growth is positive for all countries for the period 1960-1989 and before and after 1973. Capital quality growth is positive for the period as a whole for all countries except Japan. Although capital stock greatly predominates in capital input growth, capital quality is quantitatively significant, so that the heterogeneity of capital must be taken into account in assessing the role of investment in tangible assets.

Finally in Figure 5.3 we combine estimates of growth in labor input, hours worked and labor quality to assess the importance of hours and quality. Labor input growth is negative for the period 1960-1989 in France, Germany and the UK and near zero for Italy. Except for positive growth in Italy after 1973, growth in hours worked is negative for all four countries for the period as a whole and before and after 1973. Labor quality growth helps to offset the decline in hours worked in Europe. For Japan and the USA labor quality predominates in the growth of labor input, while hours worked slightly exceeds labor quality in Canada, so that the heterogeneity of labor input is essential in assessing the role of investment in human capital.

4 CONVERGENCE

The objective of modeling economic growth is to explain the *sources* and *uses* of growth endogenously. National income is the starting point for assessments of the uses of growth through consumption and saving. The concept of 'a measure of economic welfare', introduced by Nordhaus and Tobin (1972), is the key to augmenting national income to broaden the concepts of consumption and saving. Similarly GDP is the starting point for attributing the *sources* of economic growth to growth in productivity and investments in tangible assets and human capital.

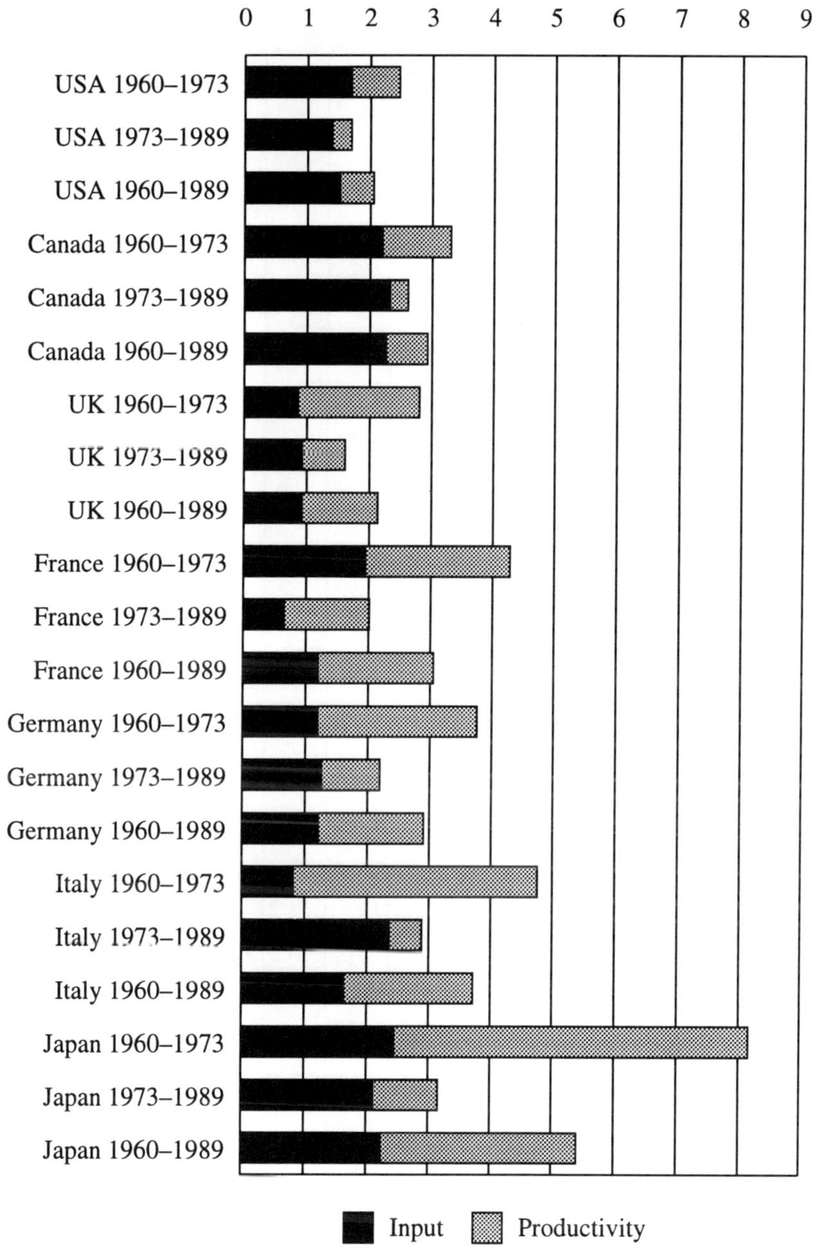

Figure 5.1 Sources of output growth, G7 countries (percent)

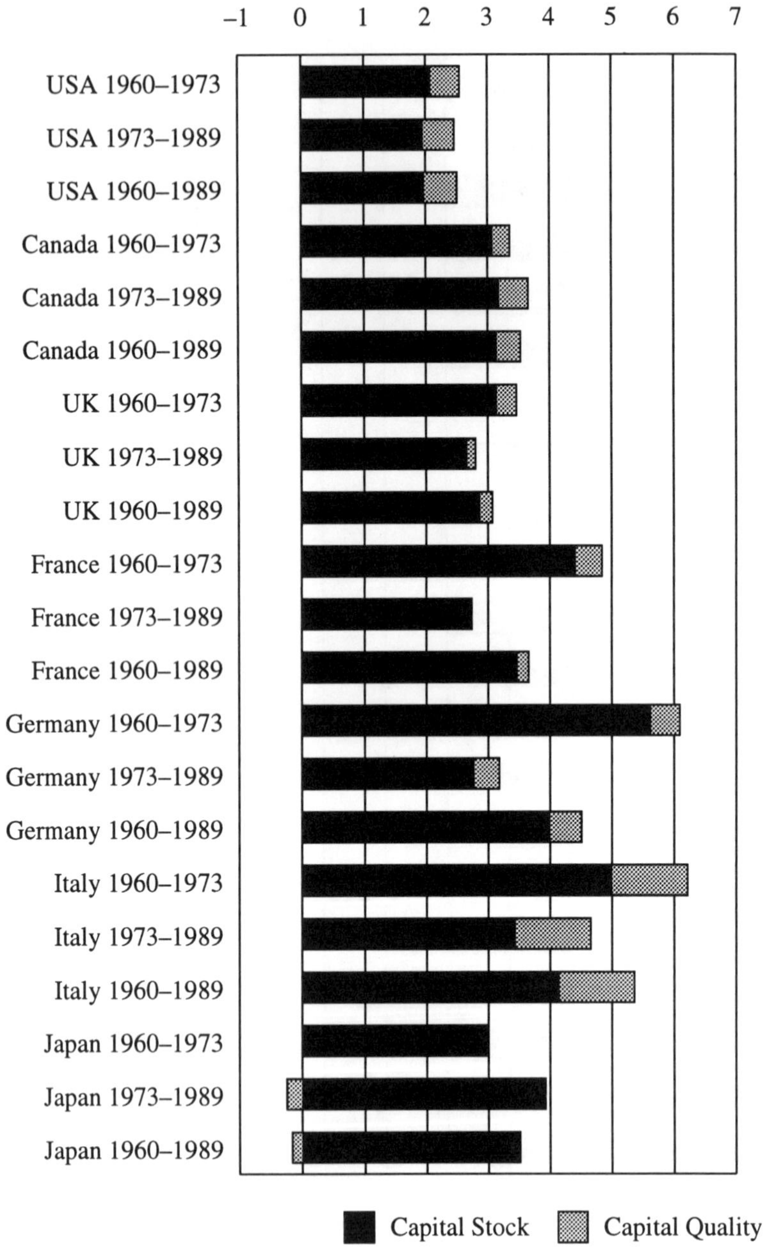

Figure 5.2 Sources of capital input growth, G7 countries (percent)

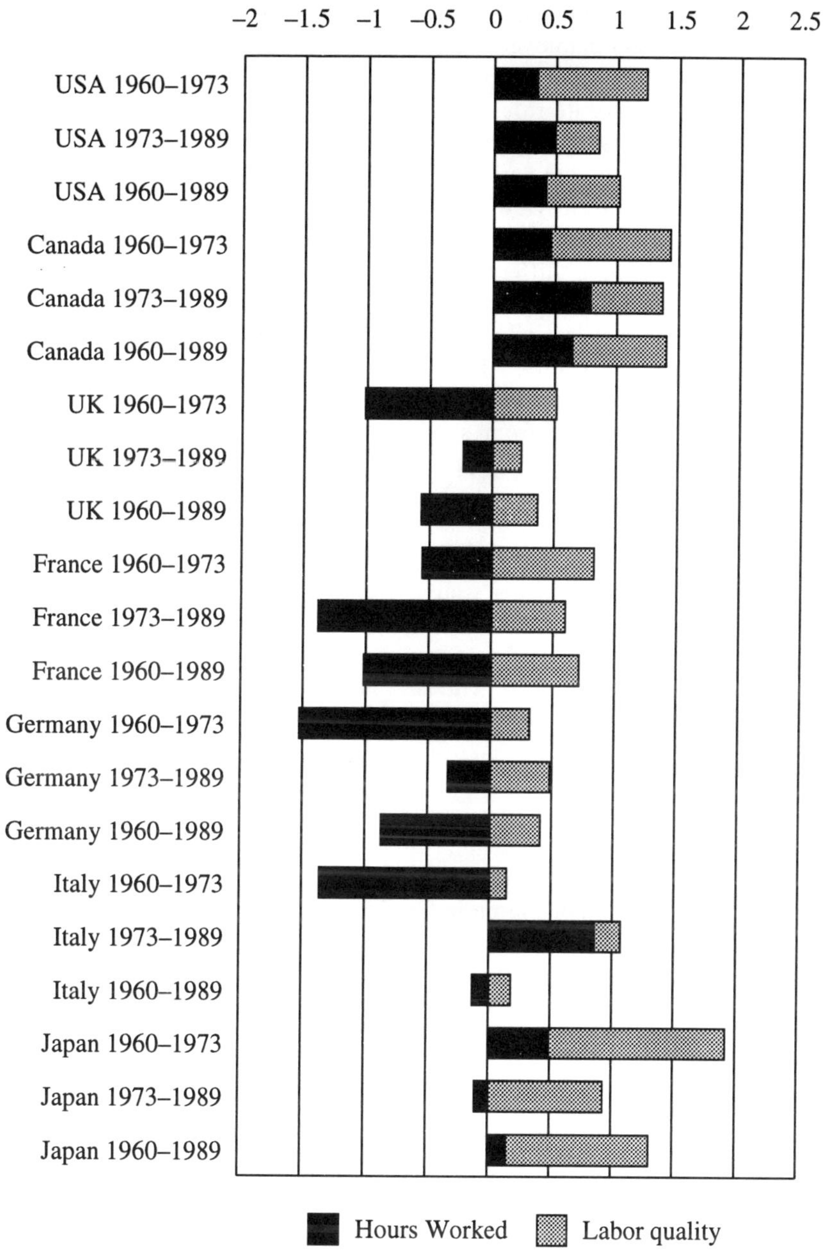

Figure 5.3 Sources of labor input growth, G7 countries (percent)

Denison (1967) compared differences in growth rates for national income per person employed for the period 1950-62 with differences of levels in 1960 for eight European countries and the USA. However he overlooked the separate roles for a production account with the national product and inputs of capital and labor services and an income and expenditure account with national income, consumption and saving. From an economic point of view this ignored the distinction between the sources and uses of economic growth.

Denison compared differences in both growth rates and levels of national income per person employed. The eight European countries as a whole were characterized by more rapid growth and a lower level of national income per capita. Although this association was not monotonic for comparisons between individual countries and the USA, Denison concluded that:[9] 'Aside from short-term aberrations Europe should be able to report higher growth rates, at least in national income per person employed, for a long time. Americans should expect this and not be disturbed by it.'

Kuznets (1971) provided elaborate comparisons of growth rates for the 14 countries included in his study. Unlike Denison (1967), he did not provide level comparisons. Maddison (1982) filled this gap by comparing levels of national product for 16 countries[10] on the basis of estimates of purchasing power parities by Kravis *et al.* (1978).[11] These estimates have been updated by successive versions of the Penn World Table and made it possible to reconsider the issue of convergence of output per capita raised by Denison (1967).[12]

Abramovitz (1986) was the first to take up the challenge of analyzing convergence of output per capita among Maddison's 16 countries. He found that convergence appeared to characterize output levels in the postwar period, but not the period before 1914 and the interwar period. Baumol (1986) formalized these results by running a regression of growth rate of GDP per hour worked over the period 1870-1979 on the 1870 level of GDP per hour worked.[13] A negative regression coefficient is evidence for 'beta-convergence' of GDP levels.

In a notable paper on 'Crazy explanations for the productivity slowdown' Paul Romer (1987) derived a version of the growth regression from Solow's (1970) growth model with a Cobb-Douglas production function. Romer also extended the data set for growth regressions from Maddison's (1982) group of 16 advanced countries to the 115 countries included in Penn World Table (Mark 3), presented by Summers and Heston (1984). Romer's key finding was that an indirect estimate of the Cobb-Douglas elasticity of output with respect to capital was close to three-quarters. The share of capital in output implied by Solow's model was less than half as great on average.

Mankiw *et al.* (1992) undertook a defense of the neoclassical framework of Kuznets (1971) and Solow (1970). The empirical portion of their study is based on data for 98 countries from the Penn World Table (Mark 4), presented by Summers and Heston (1991). Like Romer (1987), Mankiw, David Romer, and Weil derived a growth equation from the Solow (1970) model; however they also augmented this model by allowing for investment in human capital.

The results of Mankiw *et al.* (1992) provided empirical support for the augmented Solow model. There was clear evidence of the convergence predicted by the model, where convergence was conditional on the ratio of investment to GDP and the rate of population growth; both are determinants of steady state output. In addition the estimated Cobb-Douglas elasticity of output with respect to capital coincided with the share of capital in the value of output. However the rate of convergence of output per capita was too slow to be consistent with the 1970 version of the Solow model.

Islam (1995) exploited an important feature of the Summers and Heston (1991) data overlooked in previous empirical studies, namely, benchmark comparisons of levels of the national product at five year intervals, beginning in 1960 and ending in 1985. Using econometric methods for panel data, Islam tested an assumption maintained in growth regressions, such as those of Mankiw, Romer and Weil. Their study, like that of Paul Romer (1987), assumed identical technologies for all countries included in the Summer-Heston data sets.

Substantial differences in levels of productivity among countries have been documented by Denison (1967), Christensen *et al.* (1981) and in section 2 above. By introducing panel data techniques Islam (1995) was able to allow for these differences. He corroborated the finding of Mankiw *et al.* (1992) that the elasticity of output with respect to capital input coincided with the share of capital in the value of output.

In addition, Islam (1995) found that the rate of convergence of output per capita among countries in the Summers and Heston (1991) data set was precisely that required to substantiate the *unaugmented* version of Solow (1970). In short, 'crazy explanations' for the productivity slowdown, like those propounded by Romer (1987, 1994), are not required. Moreover the model did not require augmentation, as suggested by Mankiw *et al.* (1992). However differences in productivity among these countries must be taken into account in modeling differences in growth rates.

The conclusion from Islam's (1995) research is that the Solow model is the appropriate point of departure for modeling the accumulation of tangible assets. For this purpose it is unnecessary to endogenize investment in human capital as well. The rationale for this key empirical finding is that the transition path to balanced growth equilibrium requires decades after a change in policies that affect investment in tangible assets, such as tax policies. By contrast the transition after a change in policies affecting investment in human capital requires as much as a century.

In Figure 5.4 we present coefficients of variation for levels of output and input per capita and productivity for the G7 countries annually for the period 1960-1989. The coefficients for output per capita decline by a factor of two between 1960 and 1974, but then remain stable throughout the rest of the period. Coefficients for productivity decline by more than a factor of two between 1960 and 1970 and then stabilize. Coefficients for input per capita are almost unchanged throughout the period. This is evidence for the 'sigma-convergence' of output and input per capita and productivity implied by Solow's neoclassical theory of growth, allowing for differences in productivity of the type identified by Islam.

Figure 5.5 presents coefficients of variation for levels of capital input and capital stock per capita and capital quality for the G7 countries. The coefficients for capital input decline through 1977 and then stabilize through 1989. Coefficients for capital stock are slightly larger than those for capital input, but behave in a similar manner, also stabilizing around 1977. Coefficients for capital quality are stable until 1970 and then remain almost unchanged at a modestly lower level after 1971. This is also evidence of the sigma-convergence implied by Solow's growth model with persistent differences in levels of capital quality among countries.

Finally coefficients of variation for levels of labor input and hours worked per capita and labor quality for the G7 are given in Figure 5.6. The coefficients for labor input are stable through 1966, rise gradually and then stabilize from 1970 to 1982. These coefficients rise again and stabilize after 1983. The coefficients for hours worked are also stable until 1966 and then rise gradually and stabilize from 1968 to 1973. These coefficients decline and stabilize again after 1974. The coefficients for labor quality are stable throughout the period. Again this is evidence for sigma-convergence with persistent international differences in labor quality.

Productivity levels relative to the USA have stabilized with France as the international leader, Canada, Italy, the UK and the USA at similar levels, and Germany and Japan below. Differences in capital quality have also stabilized with Germany in the lead, Italy and the UK at US levels, and Canada, France and Japan at lower levels. The USA is the international leader in labor quality with Canada, Germany, Japan and the

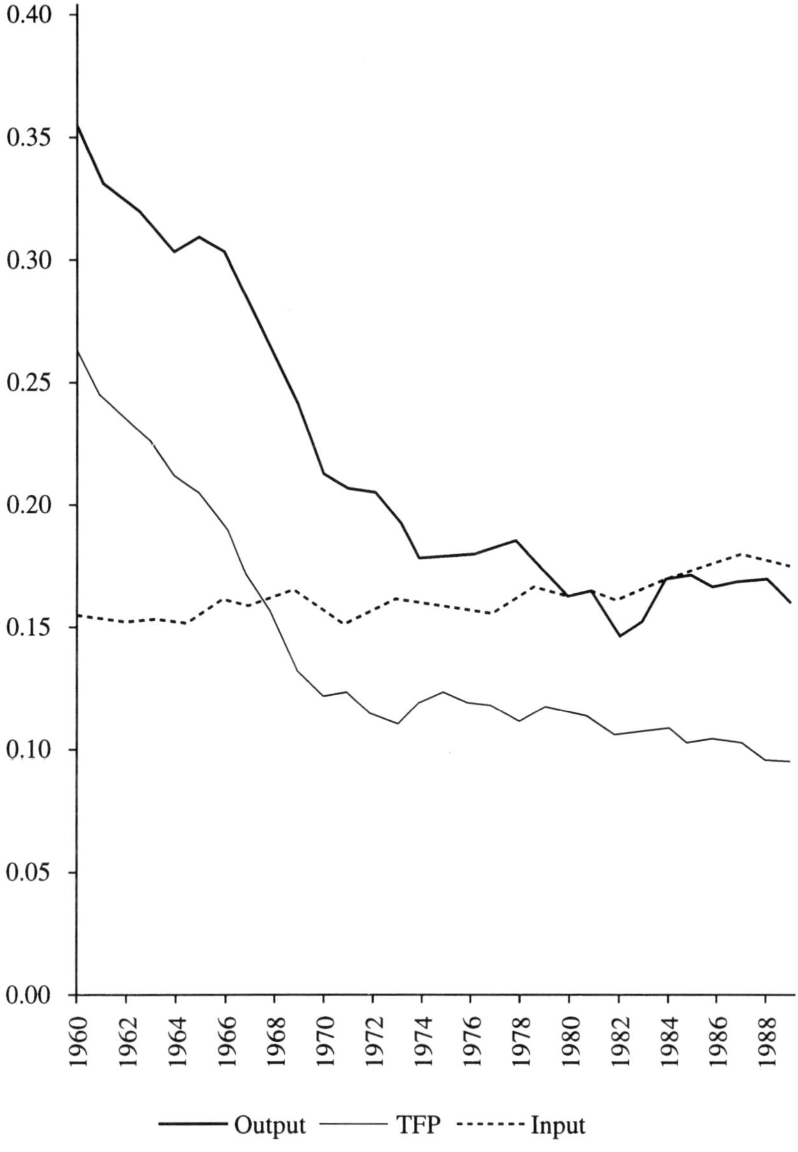

Figure 5.4 Convergence of output and input per capita and productivity (coefficient of variation)

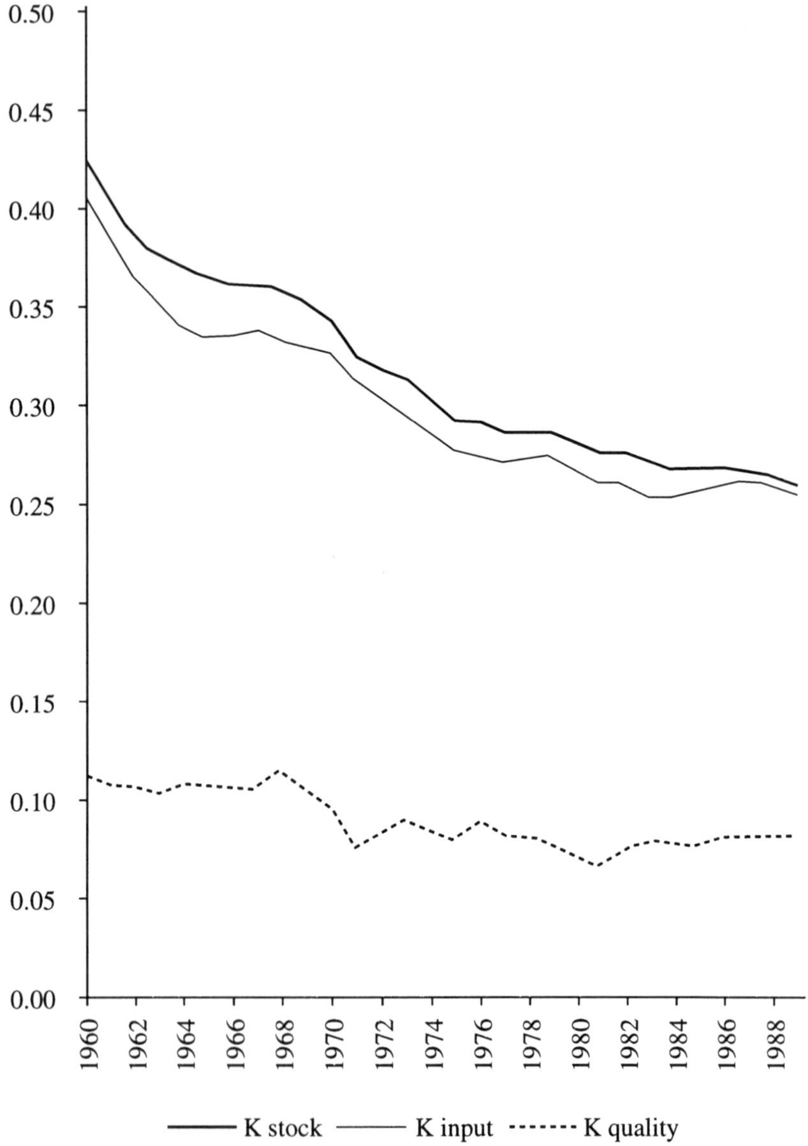

Figure 5.5 Convergence of capital input and capital stock per capita and capital quality (coefficient of variation)

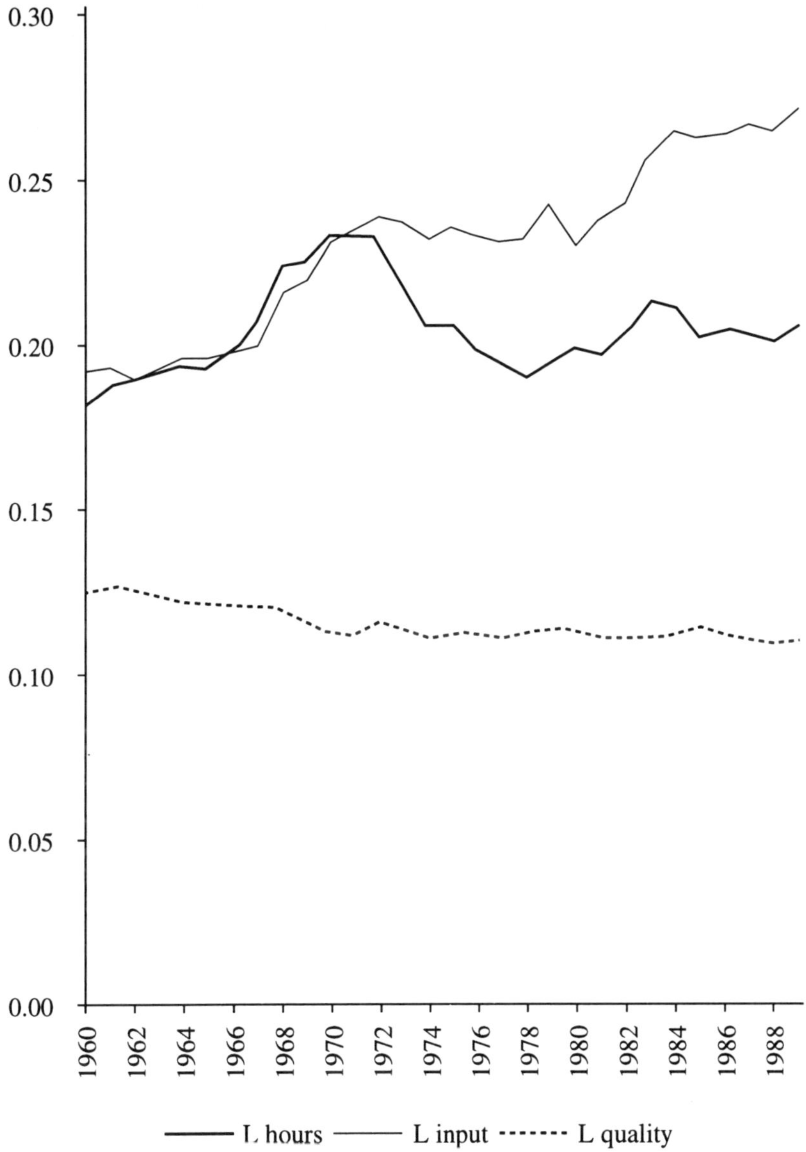

Figure 5.6 Convergence labor input and hours worked per capita and labor quality (coefficient of variation)

UK below, and Italy and France as laggards. Finally Japan leads in hours worked per capita with the USA a distant second, Canada, Germany and the UK grouped below, and Italy and France lagging the others. Differences in labor quality and hours worked per capita have been stable throughout the period.

The evidence of sigma-convergence among the G7 countries presented in Figures 5.4, 5.5 and 5.6 is consistent with a new version of Solow's neoclassical growth model, characterized by persistent but stable international differences in productivity, capital quality, labor quality and hours worked per capita. A simpler version of Solow's model with constant differences in productivity among countries was identified in Islam's research on beta-convergence. This version successfully rationalizes differences in growth of per capita output among a much broader group of countries over the period 1960-1985.

5 ENDOGENOUS GROWTH

Constant quality indices of labor input are an essential first step in incorporating investments in human capital into empirical studies of economic growth. Jorgenson and Fraumeni (1989) extended the vintage accounting system developed by Christensen and Jorgenson (1973) to incorporate these investments. The essential idea is to treat individual members of the US population as human assets with 'asset prices' given by their lifetime labor incomes. Jorgenson and Fraumeni implemented the vintage accounting system for both human and nonhuman capital for the USA on an annual basis for the period 1948-1984.

Asset prices for tangible assets can be observed directly from market transactions in investment goods; intertemporal capital asset pricing equations are used to derive rental prices for capital services. For human capital wage rates correspond to rental prices and can be observed directly from transactions in the labor market. Lifetime labor incomes are derived by applying asset pricing equations to these wage rates. Lifetime incomes are analogous to the asset prices used in accounting for investment in tangible assets.

Jorgenson and Fraumeni (1992b) have developed a measure of the output of the US education sector. The point of departure is that while education is a service industry, its output is investment in human capital. Investment in education can be measured from the impact of increases in educational attainment on lifetime incomes of all individuals enrolled in school. Investment in education, measured in this way, is similar in magnitude to the value of working time for all individuals in the labor force.

Second, Jorgenson and Fraumeni (1992a) measured the inputs of the education sector, beginning with the purchased inputs recorded in the outlays of educational institutions. A major part of the value of the output of educational institutions accrues to students in the form of increases in their lifetime incomes. Treating these increases as compensation for student time, this time is evaluated as an input into the educational process. Given the outlays of educational institutions and the value of student time, the growth of the education sector can be allocated to its sources.

An alternative approach, employed by Nordhaus and Tobin (1972), and many others, is to apply Goldsmith's (1955-6) perpetual inventory method to private and public expenditures on educational services. Unfortunately the approach has foundered on the absence of a satisfactory measure of the output of the educational sector and the lack of an obvious rationale for capital consumption. This fails to satisfy the conditions for integration of income and wealth accounts established by Fisher (1906) and Samuelson (1961).[14]

Given vintage accounts for human and nonhuman capital, Jorgenson and Fraumeni (1989) constructed a system of income, product and wealth accounts, paralleling the system Jorgenson had developed with Christensen. In these accounts the value of human wealth was more than ten times the value of nonhuman wealth, while investment in human capital was five times investment in tangible assets. 'Full' investment in the US economy is defined as the sum of these two types of investment. Similarly the value of nonmarket labor activities is added to personal consumption expenditures to obtain 'full' consumption. The product measure included these new measures of investment and consumption.

Since the complete accounting system included a production account with 'full' measures of capital and labor inputs, Jorgenson and Fraumeni were able to generate a new set of accounts for the *sources* of US economic growth. The system also included an income and expenditure account with income from labor services in both market and nonmarket activities and an allocation of 'full' income between consumption and saving. This provided the basis for the *uses* of US economic growth and a new measure of economic welfare. The system was completed by a wealth account containing both human wealth and tangible assets.

Jorgenson and Fraumeni aggregated the growth of education and noneducation sectors of the US economy to obtain a new measure of US economic growth. Combining this with measures of input growth, they obtained a new set of accounts for the sources of growth. Productivity contributes almost nothing to the growth of the education sector and only a modest proportion to output growth for the economy as a whole, so that productivity accounts for only 17 percent of growth.

The introduction of endogenous investment in education increases the explanatory power of the theory of economic growth to 83 percent. However it is important to emphasize that growth is measured differently. The traditional framework for economic measurement of Kuznets (1971) and Solow (1970) excludes nonmarket activities, such as those that characterize the major portion of investment in education. The intuition is familiar to any teacher, including teachers of economics: what the students do is far more important than what the teachers do, even if the subject matter is the theory of economic growth.

A third approximation to the theory of economic growth results from incorporating all forms of investment in human capital, including education, child-rearing and addition of new members to the population. Child-rearing could be made endogenous by modeling the household as a producing sector along the lines of the model of the educational sector outlined above. The results presented by Jorgenson and Fraumeni (1989) show that this would endogenize 86 percent of US economic growth. This is a significant, but not overwhelming, gain in explanatory power.

In principle investment in new technology could be made endogenous by extending the accounting framework to incorporate investment in new technology.

The standard model for investment in new technology, formulated by Griliches (1973) is based on a production function incorporating inputs of services from intellectual capital accumulated through investment in research and development. Intellectual capital is treated as a factor of production in precisely the same way as tangible assets in section 2, above. Hall (1993) has developed the implications of this model for the pricing of the services of intellectual capital input and the evaluation of intellectual capital assets.

The model of capital as a factor of production first proposed by Jorgenson (1963) has been successfully applied to tangible assets and human capital. However implementation for intellectual capital would require a system of vintage accounts including not only accumulation equations for stocks of accumulated research and development, but also asset pricing equations. These equations are essential for separating the revaluation of intellectual property due to price changes over time from depreciation of this property due to aging. This is required for measuring the quantity of intellectual capital input and its marginal product.

Endogenizing a greater proportion of US economic growth at the aggregate level requires a broader concept of investment. The distinctive feature of investment is that returns can be internalized and decisions can be decentralized to individual investors. Productivity growth is generated by spillovers that cannot be captured by private investors and activities generating spillovers require collective decision-making. We conclude that future extensions of the theory of economic growth will increase the proportion of growth than can be attributed to investment rather than productivity.

NOTES

1. Financial support was provided by the Program on Technology and Economic Policy of Harvard University. Responsibility for any remaining deficiencies rests solely with the authors.
2. The measurement conventions of Kuznets and Solow remain in common use. See the references given by Jorgenson (1990).
3. Jorgenson and Griliches (1967), table IX, p. 272, attributed 13 percent of growth to the relative utilization of capital, measured by energy consumption as a proportion of capacity; however this is inappropriate at the aggregate level. For additional details, see Jorgenson, *et al.* (1987), especially pp. 179-81.
4. Constant quality indices of labor input are discussed in detail by Jorgenson *et al.* (1987), chapters 3 and 8, pp. 69-108 and 261-300.
5. The United Nations System of National Accounts (SNA) is summarized by Stone (1992) in his Nobel Prize address. The SNA has been revised by the Inter-Secretariat Working Group on National Accounts (1993).
6. BEA (1995) has adopted constant quality price indices for investment goods of different ages or vintages in the latest benchmark revision of the US National Income and Product Accounts, following methodology described by Fraumeni (1997).
7. A more detailed description of our constant quality indices of capital and labor input is given by Dougherty (1992).
8. See Christensen, *et al.* (1981) for more detail.
9. See Denison (1967), especially chapter 21: 296-348, 'The Sources of Growth and the Contrast between Europe and the United States'.
10. Maddison added Austria and Finland to Kuznets' list and presented growth rates covering periods beginning as early as 1820 and extending through 1979. Maddison (1991, 1995) has extended these estimates through 1992.
11. For details see Maddison (1982: 159-68).
12. A complete list through Mark 5 is given by Summers and Heston (1991), while the results of Mark 6 are summarized by the World Bank (1994) in the *World Development Report 1993*.
13. This 'growth regression' has spawned a vast literature, summarized by Baumol (1994) and Robert Barro and Xavier Sala-i-Martin (1994). Much of this literature has been based on successive versions of the Penn World Table.
14. For more detailed discussion, see Jorgenson and Fraumeni (1989).

REFERENCES

Abramovitz, M. (1956), 'Resources and output trends in the United States since 1870', *American Economic Review*, **46** (2), 5-23.

Abramovitz, M. (1986), 'Catching up, forging ahead, and falling behind', *Journal of Economic History*, **46** (2), 385-406.

Baumol, W.J. (1986), 'Productivity growth, convergence, and welfare', *American Economic Review*, **76** (5), 1072-85.

Bureau of Economic Analysis (1995), 'Preview of the comprehensive revision of the national income and product accounts: recognition of government investment and incorporation of a new methodology for calculating depreciation', *Survey of Current Business*, **75** (9), 33-41.

Bureau of Labor Statistics (1994), 'Multifactor productivity measures, 1991 and 1992', *News Release USDL 94-327*, 11 July.

Christensen, L.R. and D.W. Jorgenson (1969), 'The measurement of U.S. real capital input, 1929-1967', *Review of Income and Wealth*, **15** (4), 293-320.

Christensen, L.R. and D.W. Jorgenson (1970), 'U.S. real product and real factor input, 1929-1967', *Review of Income and Wealth*, **16** (1), 19-50.

Christensen, L.R. and D.W. Jorgenson (1973), 'Measuring economic performance in the private sector', in M. Moss (ed.), *The Measurement of Economic and Social Performance*, 233-38.

Christensen, L.R., D. Cummings and D.W. Jorgenson (1981), 'Relative productivity levels, 1947-1973', *European Economic Review*, **16** (1), 61-94.

Denison, E.F. (1967), *Why Growth Rates Differ*, Washington: The Brookings Institution.

Dougherty, C. (1992), 'A comparison of productivity and economic growth in the G-7 countries', doctoral dissertation, Harvard University.

Fisher, I. (1906), *The Nature of Capital and Income*, New York: Macmillan.

Fraumeni, B.M. (1997), 'The measurement of depreciation in the U.S. National Income and Wealth Accounts', *Survey of Current Business*, **77** (7), 7-23.

Griliches, Z. (1960), 'Measuring inputs in agriculture: a critical survey', *Journal of Farm Economics*, **40** (5), 1398-1427.

Griliches, Z. (1973), 'Research expenditures and growth accounting', in B.R. Williams (ed.), *Science and Technology in Economic Growth*, London: Macmillan, 59-95.

Hall, B.H. (1993), 'Industrial research in the 1980s: did the rate of return fall?', *Brookings Papers on Economic Activity: Microeconomics*, **2**, 289-331.

Hall, Robert E. and D.W. Jorgenson (1967), 'Tax policy and investment behavior', *American Economic Review*, **57** (3), 391-414.

Inter-Secretariat Working Group on National Accounts (1993), *System of National Accounts 1993*, New York: United Nations, 379-406.

Islam, N. (1995), 'Growth empirics', *Quarterly Journal of Economics*, **110** (4), 1127-70.

Jorgenson, D.W. (1963), 'Capital theory and investment behavior', *American Economic Review*, **53** (2), 247-59.

Jorgenson, D.W. (1966), 'The embodiment hypothesis', *Journal of Political Economy*, **74** (1), 1-17.

Jorgenson, D.W. (1973), 'The economic theory of replacement and depreciation', in W. Sellekaerts (ed.), *Econometrics and Economic Theory*, New York: Macmillan, 189-221.

Jorgenson, D.W. (1990), 'Productivity and economic growth', in E.R. Berndt and J. Triplett (eds), *Fifty Years of Economic Measurement*, Chicago University of Chicago Press, 19-118.

Jorgenson, D.W. and B.M. Fraumeni (1989), 'The accumulation of human and nonhuman capital, 1948-1984', in R.E. Lipsey and H.S. Tice (eds), *The Measurement of Saving, Investment, and Wealth*, Chicago: University of Chicago Press, 227-82.

Jorgenson, D.W. and B.M. Fraumeni (1992a), 'Investment in education and U.S. economic growth', *Scandinavian Journal of Economics*, **94** (supplement), 51-70.

Jorgenson, D.W. and B.M. Fraumeni (1992b), 'The output of the education sector', in Z. Griliches (ed.), *Output Measurement in the Services Sector*, Chicago: University of Chicago Press, 303-8.

Jorgenson, D.W. and Z. Griliches (1967), 'The explanation of productivity change', *Review of Economic Studies*, **34** (99), 249-80.

Jorgenson, D.W., F.M. Gollop and B.M. Fraumeni (1987), *Productivity and U.S. Economic Growth*, Cambridge: Harvard University Press.

Kravis, I.B., A. Heston and R. Summers (1978), *International Comparisons of Real Product and Purchasing Power*, Baltimore: Johns Hopkins University Press.

Kuznets, S. (1971), *Economic Growth of Nations*, Cambridge: Harvard University Press.

Maddison, A. (1982), *Phases of Capitalist Development*, Oxford: Oxford University Press.

Maddison, A. (1991), *Dynamic Forces in Capitalist Development*, Oxford: Oxford University Press.

Maddison, Angus (1995), *Monitoring the World Economy*, Paris: Organization for Economic Cooperation and Development.

Mankiw, N.G., D. Romer and D. Weil (1992), 'A contribution to the empirics of economic growth', *Quarterly Journal of Economics*, **107** (2), 407-37.

Nordhaus, W.D. and J. Tobin (1972), *Is Growth Obsolete?* New York: National Bureau of Economic Research; reprinted in M. Moss: (ed.), *The Measurement of Economic and Social Performance*, New York: Columbia University Press, 1973, 509-32.

Romer, P. (1987), 'Crazy explanations for the productivity slowdown', in Stanley Fischer (ed.), *NBER Macroeconomics Annual*, Cambridge: The MIT Press, 163-201.

Samuelson, P.A. (1961), 'The evaluation of "social income": capital formation and wealth', in F.A. Lutz and D.C. Hague (eds), *The Theory of Capital*, London: Macmillan, 32-57.

Solow, R.M. (1957), 'Technical change and the aggregate production function', *Review of Economics and Statistics*, **39** (3), 312-20.

Solow, R.M. (1960), 'Investment and technical progress', in K.J. Arrow, S. Karlin and P. Suppe (eds), *Mathematical Methods in the Social Sciences, 1959*, Stanford: Stanford University Press, 89-104.

Solow, R.M. (1992), *Growth Theory*, 2nd edn, New York: Oxford University Press (1st edn, 1970).

Summers, R. and A. Heston (1984), 'Improved international comparisons of real product and its composition: 1950-1980', *Review of Income and Wealth*, **30** (2), 207-62.

Summers, R. and A. Heston (1991), 'The Penn World Table (Mark 5): an expanded set of international comparisons, 1950-1988', *Quarterly Journal of Economics*, **106** (2), 327-68.

United Nations (1968), *A System of National Accounts*, New York: United Nations.

World Bank (1994), *World Development Report 1993*, Washington: World Bank.

6. Is the Asia-Pacific Region Different? Technical Progress Bias and Price Elasticity Estimates for 18 OECD Countries, 1960-1992*

Kevin J. Fox and W.E. Diewert

1 INTRODUCTION

Productivity growth and technical progress biases for specific variables are estimated for 18 OECD countries, 1960-1992.[1] Estimates of price elasticities are also reported. Comparisons across countries and time are made, with special attention to the possibility of systematic differences between countries in the Asia-Pacific region and other OECD member countries. The examination of regional economic differences and similarities is of timely interest, in particular due to the current trend of countries identifying economically with other countries in their region through international agreements on economic cooperation (for example, European Union (EU), APEC, NAFTA).

The modeling approach employed follows Diewert and Wales (1992) and Kohli (1994), rather than the usual Solow (1957) style of single-output analysis. The method used allows examination of a multiple-output multiple-input context where the economies are engaging in foreign trade. Hence, it is taken into consideration that the countries in the sample are not closed economies, that multiple outputs exist as well as multiple inputs, and technical progress does not have to occur in a neutral fashion, for example, technical progress may cause not only outward movements in the production possibility frontier, but also twists favoring one output over another. Similarly, technical progress may have asymmetric effects on the use of inputs. Estimates of these technical progress biases and price elasticities for three outputs (consumption, investment and exports) and

* Financial support from the Australian Research Council and the Canadian Donner Foundation is gratefully acknowledged.

two variable inputs (imports and labour) are generated for each observation in the sample, for each of the 18 countries considered. It is envisaged that these estimates will aid researchers in examining the economic experiences of these countries and regions over the very interesting 33 years of the sample. The price elasticities will also be of great interest for general equilibrium modeling.

The approach specifies a Normalized Quadratic[2] profit function for each country in the sample. This functional form is used as it is 'flexible'[3] and globally correct curvature can be imposed without losing the flexibility property. All productivity and elasticity estimates are generated from these estimated functions, which provide estimates that are as comparable as possible across countries.

Section 2 describes the Normalized Quadratic variable profit function, and Section 3 describes the methods for calculating productivity growth, technical progress biases and price elasticities. Readers not interested in the technical details may omit reading these sections. Section 4 discusses some of the results shown in Figures 6.1 to 6.11, and Tables 6.2 to 6.5. Section 5 concludes.

2 NORMALIZED QUADRATIC VARIABLE PROFIT FUNCTION

See the Appendix for the properties which define a variable profit function. The Normalized Quadratic functional form (Diewert and Wales, 1987) is a flexible functional form (Diewert, 1974: 113). The Normalized Quadratic variable profit function can be written in matrix notation as follows:

$$[V(p, k, t) = a \cdot p + b \cdot pk + c \cdot pkt + 1/2 \cdot d \cdot pkt^2 + 1/2 \cdot \frac{p \cdot Bpk}{\alpha \cdot p}] \quad (6.1)$$

where a,b,c and d are parameter vectors, $B = [b_{ij}] = B'$, t is a time trend, $t = 1,\ldots,T$, k denotes capital (taken to be exogenously given), there are N variable goods with prices $p = (p_1,\ldots,p_N)$, including both inputs and outputs, and $a \cdot p \equiv \Sigma_{i=1}^{N} a_i p_i$ is the inner product of the vectors a and p. Input quantities are taken to be negative, that is, inputs are treated as negative outputs. The α vector ($\alpha \geq 0_N$) is a predetermined vector of parameters. Kohli (1991) and Diewert and Wales (1992) experimented with different values for α, but for simplicity it can be set to a vector of ones, that is, $\alpha = 1_N$. Setting the elements of the a vector to zero results in the profit function exhibiting constant returns to scale, which for estimation purposes is the approach taken in the empirical work described in section 4 below. Differentiating (6.1) with respect to p gives the system of net supply equations, through Hotelling's Lemma, which is used in estimation:

$$y(p, k, t) = \nabla_p V(p, k, t)$$

$$= a + bk + ckt + 1/2 \cdot dkt^2 + \frac{Bpk}{\alpha \cdot p} - 1/2 \cdot \frac{p \cdot Bpk}{(\alpha \cdot p)^2} \cdot \alpha$$

$$= a + bk + ckt + 1/2 \cdot dkt^2 + Bwk - 1/2 \cdot w \cdot Bwk\alpha \tag{6.2}$$

where $w \equiv p/\alpha \cdot p$ and ∇p denotes first order differentiation with respect to the vector of prices p. The following restrictions are placed on the elements of B to avoid potential problems with multicollinearity between the elements of b and B:

$$B1_N = 0_N, \tag{6.3}$$

that is, the rows of B are restricted to add to zero. Therefore we have one parameter in each row which is not independently determined. Using these restrictions, we can, for example, solve for the diagonal elements of the B matrix once the other parameters have been obtained by estimation.

Once we have estimated our supply and demand equations, we can multiply the fitted quantities by their respective prices and add them together to derive the fitted variable profit function for each t.

A requirement on the profit function is that it satisfies convexity in prices (see the Appendix). This is satisfied by the Normalized Quadratic if the estimated B matrix of parameters is found to be positive semidefinite. In the model described so far, there is no guarantee that this condition will hold, and in practice it will usually be violated by flexible functional forms such as this and the Translog (Fox, 1996). But one of the main advantages of the Normalized Quadratic form over other flexible functional forms is the ability to impose curvature *globally* without sacrificing flexibility, or any of the other theoretical requirements. Curvature is imposed using the following theorem:

Theorem 1 *Let B be a symmetric $N \times N$ matrix. Then B is positive* *semidefinite if and only if $B = AA'$ for some lower triangular matrix A (that is, $A = [a_{ij}]$, $a_{ij} = 0$ for $i < j$; $i,j = 1,...,N-1$), (Wiley et al., 1973; Diewert and Wales, 1987; Magnus and Woodland, 1988).*

The restriction on the elements of the B matrix that we imposed above, $B1_N = 0_N$, can now be written as $A'1_N = 0_N$, that is, we now have the columns of A adding to zero. Using this restriction, we can express the elements of the B matrix in terms of the elements of the A matrix. Substituting these expressions for the b_{ij} into the estimating equations gives us a system of net supply equations (6.2) whose parent function, the Normalized Quadratic profit function, has assured globally correct curvature.

3 TECHNICAL PROGRESS AND ELASTICITY MEASURES

Differentiating the log of the profit function, V, with respect to t, we get an index of technical progress (productivity growth) for each t:

$$TFP \equiv (\partial V / \partial t)(1 / V) = (c \cdot pk + d \cdot pkt) / V. \tag{6.4}$$

This measures aggregate productivity growth, or total factor productivity change (*TFP*), for an economy. Similarly a measure of the effect of technical change on each variable good can be calculated by taking the derivative of each estimated demand equation with respect to time and dividing by the estimated demands (Diewert and Wales, 1992; Kohli, 1994). Therefore, for the *i*th good we have:

$$\tau_i \equiv (\partial y_i / \partial t)(1/y_i), \tag{6.5}$$

for each period $t = 1,...,T$ and good $i = 1,...,N$. If the good in question is an output, then a positive value indicates that more of the output is being produced due to the passing of time, that is, if $\tau_i > 0$ (< 0) then technical progress is output i augmenting (reducing). If the good in question is an input, then a negative value suggests that less of the input is required due to the passing of time, that is, if $\tau_i < 0$ (> 0) then technical progress is input i reducing (augmenting). We define these τ_is to be technical progress biases for each good. This approach is in the spirit of Hicks (1932) who seems to have been the first to introduce the ideas of input-reducing and output-augmenting technical progress. See Kohli (1994) for an excellent discussion of Hick's contribution and other similar frameworks.

We can get more insight into the interpretation of these biases by noting the following. Due to the linear homogeneity of $V(p, k, t)$, *TFP* and the τ_i are homogenous of degree zero in prices and capital (under the assumption of constant returns to scale). Using the linear homogeneity in prices property of the variable profit function, V, we can write

$$\partial V/\partial t = \sum_{i=1}^{N} (\partial^2 V/\partial t \partial p_i) p_i \tag{6.6}$$

Dividing both sides of (6.6) by V, and using Hotelling's Lemma as in (6.2), yields

$$TFP = \sum_{i=1}^{N} s_i \tau_i \tag{6.7}$$

for each t, where $s_i = (p_i y_i)/V$, and s_i is negative for inputs. If technical progress is completely unbiased (neutral), so that all goods are affected to the same degree by technical progress, then (6.7) becomes

$$TFP = \tau_i = -\tau_j. \tag{6.8}$$

for outputs i and inputs j. This, however, is unlikely to be the case, and the estimates that follow in section 4 certainly show that technical progress is biased in favour of some goods and against others. Equations (6.7) and (6.8) suggest that comparisons between *TFP* and the τ_i are as of much interest as the values themselves.

It should be noted that the above approach only identifies the effects of technical progress on the demands and supplies of goods, not the sources of technical progress. This latter task is far beyond the scope of this paper. It is well known that under the assumptions of constant returns to scale and disembodied technical progress, it is impossible to identify the separate rates of technical progress for each of the inputs and outputs, but it is possible to identify the effects of technical progress on each good.[4]

As demonstrated by Jorgenson and Fraumeni (1981), there is a close relationship between the effects of the march of time on output and input quantities, and the impact of price (and factor endowment) changes on certain definitions of the rate of technological change. We define η_i to be a measure which captures the effects of a change in the price of good i on the rate of technological change, for each t:

$$\eta_i \equiv (\partial^2 \ln \pi)/(\partial t \partial \ln p_i) = \partial TFP/\partial \ln p_i \tag{6.9}$$

$$=s_i(\tau_i - TFP) \tag{6.10}$$

where s_i is negative for inputs, *TFP* is defined by (6.4) and τ_i is defined by (6.5). Therefore, the share weighted difference between τ_i and aggregate technological change captures the effect of changes in the price of good i on the rate of technical progress. From (6.7) it follows that

$$\sum_{i=1}^{N} \eta_i = 0 \tag{6.11}$$

that is, if all prices change by the same proportion, then relative prices have not changed and the aggregate effect of the price changes on technical progress sums to zero.

Table 6.1 presents the possible relationships between τ_i and *TFP* which determine η_i as described by equation (6.10). This table will aid in the interpretation of the results presented in section 4. For example, when *TFP* is positive (as has typically been the case), then $\tau_i < 0$ for an output means that technical progress has been output reducing, and the impact of an increase in the price of output i, *ceteris paribus*, is that technical progress becomes more output reducing ($\eta_i < 0$).

Table 6.1 The relationship between TFP, τ_i and η_i

Condition	Outputs Sign of η_i	Inputs Sign of η_i
TFP > 0		
$\tau_i < 0$	<0	>0
TFP $> \tau_i > 0$	>0	>0
$\tau_i >$ TFP > 0	>0	<0
TFP < 0		
$\tau_i > 0$	>0	<0
$\tau_i <$ TFP < 0	>0	<0
TFP $< \tau_i < 0$	<0	>0

Note: $\eta_i = (\partial^2 \ln V)/(\partial t \partial p_i) = s_i(\tau_i - TFP)$, where *TFP* is defind by (6.4), τ_i is defined by (6.5), V is the profit function defined by (6.1), $s_i = p_i y_i / V$, and s_i is negative for inputs.

Finally, price elasticities are calculated as follows:

$$E_{ij} = \partial y_i / \partial p_j \cdot p_j / y_i \tag{6.12}$$

for goods i and where $i,j = 1,\ldots, N$.

4 RESULTS

The data set consists of prices and quantities for three outputs (exports, investment, and combined private and government consumption), two variable inputs (labour and imports) and one exogenously given input (capital) for 18 OECD countries, 1960-1992. The treatment of imports as an input to the production sector is quite standard (Kohli, 1991). This recognizes that imports are often raw materials or intermediate goods, and even products which are imported as 'finished' products have value added to them locally through transportation, retailing and so forth. The construction of the data set is described in detail in Fox (1997), however it is worth noting that the raw data came from primarily OECD sources. Constant returns to scale and correct curvature were imposed *a priori*. Error terms were appended to the equations (6.2) for estimation. All regularity conditions (see the Appendix) were satisfied by the estimated functions. The parameter estimates for each country are available on request.[5]

Measures of goodness-of-fit (R^2 between observed and predicted) for each equation in each system of equations (that is, each country) estimated, are reported in Table 6.2. Aggregate productivity growth and technical progress biases are reported in Figures 6.1 to 6.6, and summary statistics for each country are reported in Table 6.3.[6] Own price elasticities (that is, $i=j$ in (6.12)) for each year are reported in Figures 6.7 to 6.11, and summary statistics for each country are reported in Table 6.4, while average cross price elasticities (that is, $i \neq j$ in (6.12)) are in Table 6.5. The aggregate productivity estimates in Table 6.3 and Figure 6.1 were calculated by dividing ($\partial V / \partial t$) by estimated GNP, rather than by estimated profits as suggested by (6.4). This is in order to produce estimates which are comparable to results based on index number approaches. While Figures 6.1 to 6.11 do not allow the identification of each country, it is of interest to observe the common trends across the countries for each variable.

We can see from the R^2 values in Table 6.2 that the fit of the estimated equations is remarkably good, with most values being above 0.90. Only for Sweden do we get an R^2 of less than 0.5 (investment equation). On the whole, the model seems to fit the data extremely well, giving us confidence in the reliability of the results which follow.

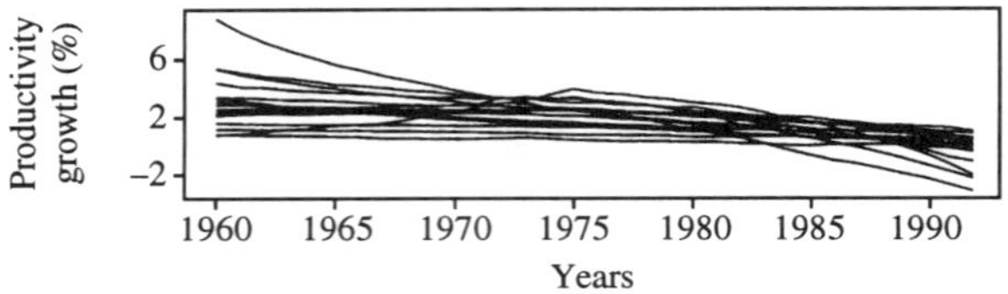

Figure 6.1 Productivity growth rates

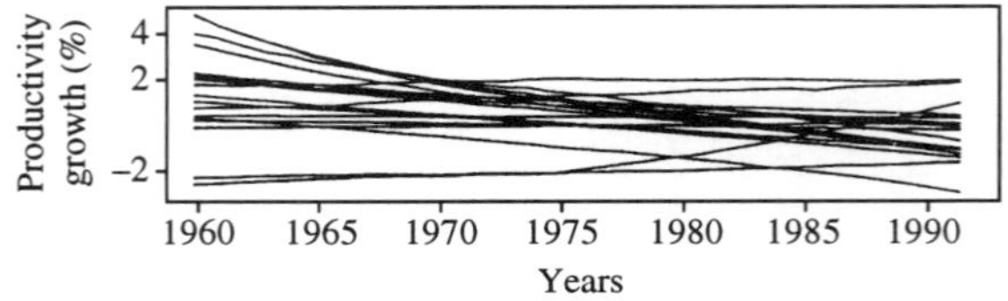

Figure 6.2 Technical progress bias: consumption

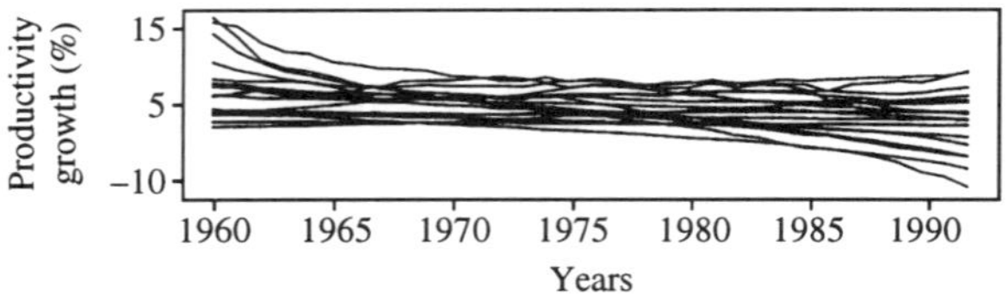

Figure 6.3 Technical progress bias: investment

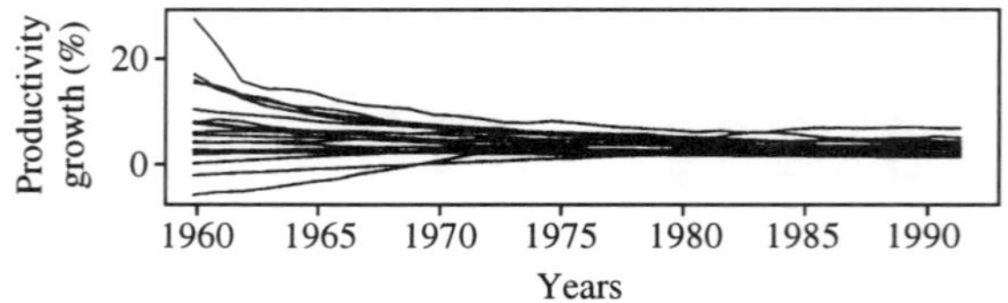

Figure 6.4 Technical progress bias: exports

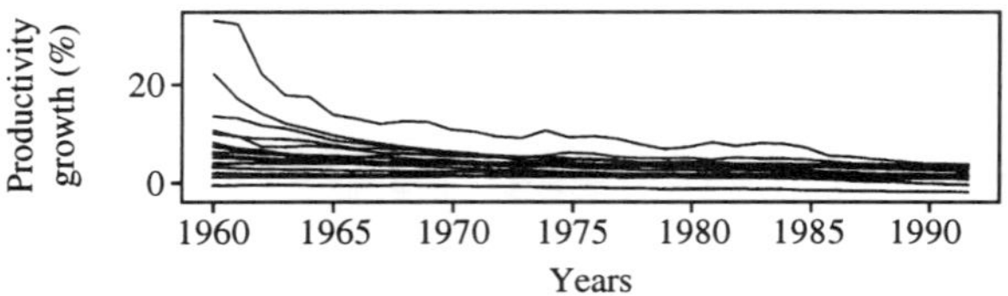

Figure 6.5 Technical progress bias: imports

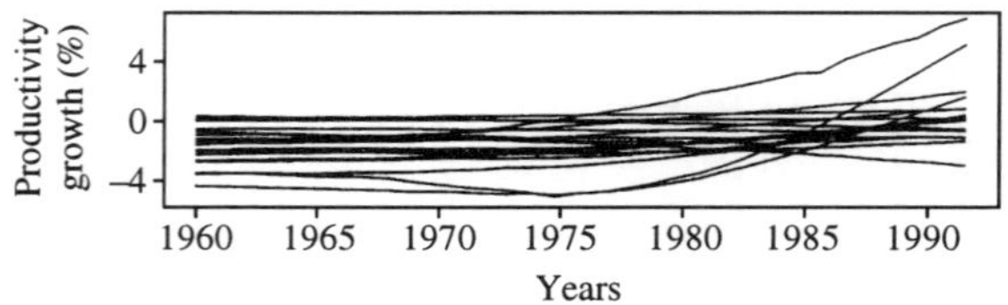

Figure 6.6 Technical progress bias: labor

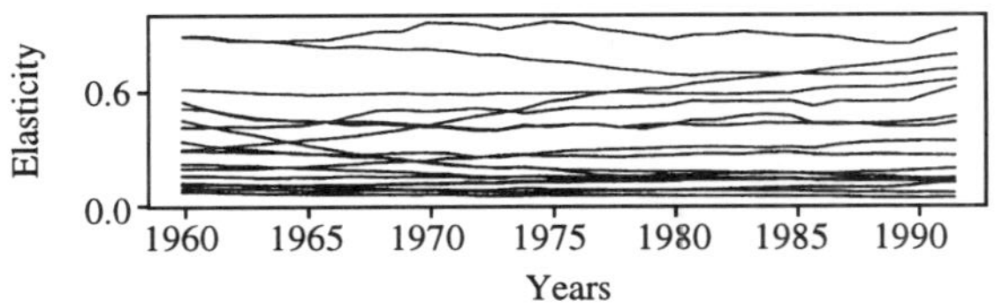

Figure 6.7 *Own price elasticity: consumption*

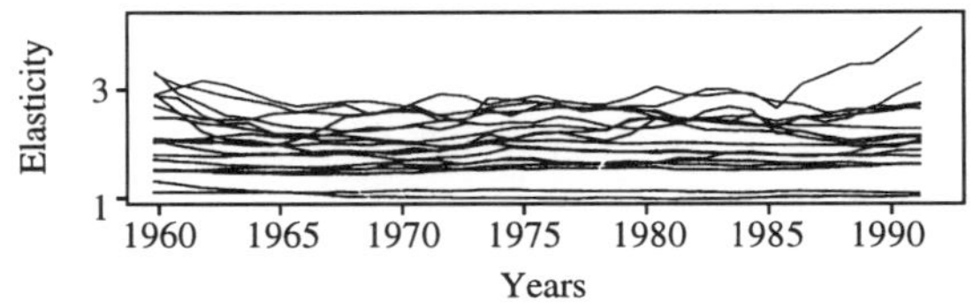

Figure 6.8 *Own price elasticity: investment*

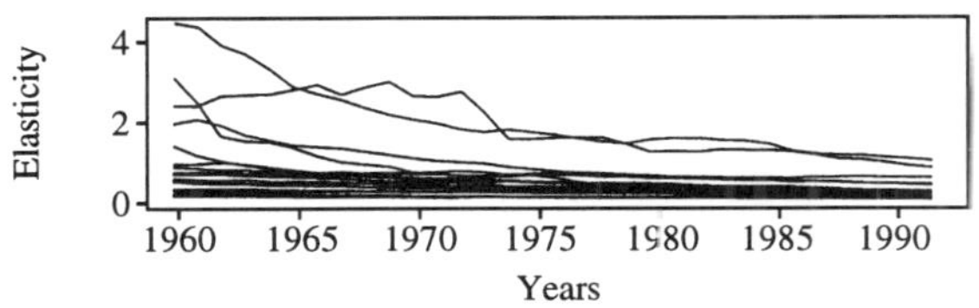

Figure 6.9 *Own price elasticity: exports*

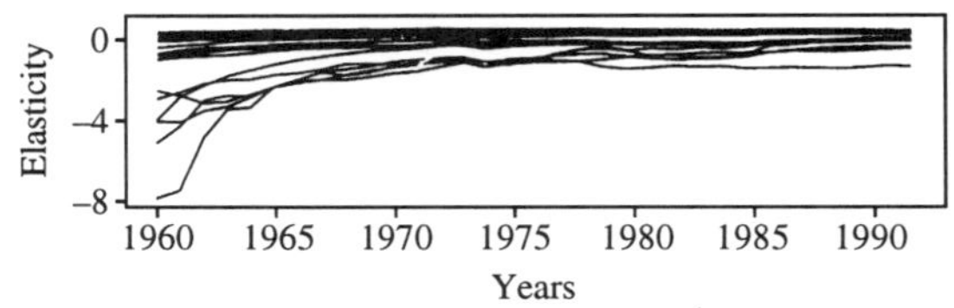

Figure 6.10 *Own price elasticity: imports*

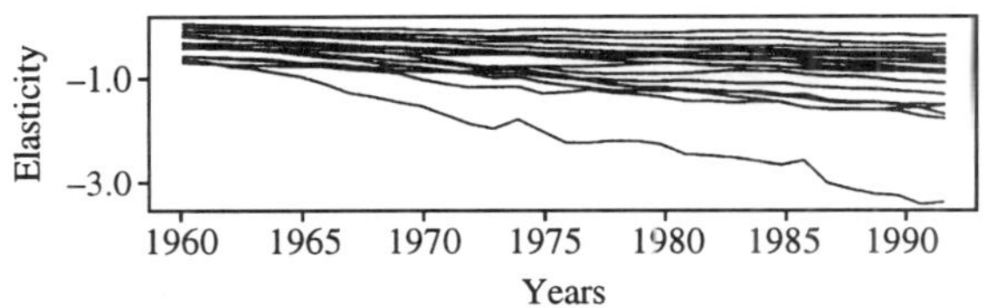

Figure 6.11 *Own price elasticity: labor*

Table 6.2 R^2 *values for each equation*

	AUS	AUT	BEL	CAN	CHE	DEU	DNK	ESP	FIN	FRA	GBR	GRC	JPN	NLD	NOR	NZL	SWE	USA
Consumption	0.999	0.998	0.997	0.996	0.989	0.997	0.995	0.995	0.992	0.999	0.988	0.998	0.999	0.989	0.993	0.969	0.995	0.997
Investment	0.917	0.802	0.846	0.983	0.854	0.795	0.731	0.941	0.643	0.935	0.726	0.800	0.939	0.619	0.887	0.582	0.470	0.910
Exports	0.982	0.994	0.991	0.987	0.994	0.975	0.992	0.993	0.980	0.991	0.992	0.987	0.997	0.974	0.989	0.991	0.987	0.956
Imports	0.984	0.987	0.985	0.991	0.981	0.979	0.983	0.984	0.954	0.985	0.973	0.981	0.921	0.964	0.967	0.949	0.945	0.988
Labor	0.977	0.805	0.966	0.996	0.927	0.695	0.616	0.915	0.623	0.939	0.907	0.784	0.640	0.851	0.946	0.979	0.768	0.991

Notes:

AUS = Australia, AUT = Austria, BEL = Belgium, CAN = Canada, CHE = Switzerland, DEU = West Germany, DNK = Denmark, ESP = Spain, FIN = Finland, FRA = France, GBR = Great Britain, GRC = Greece, JPN = Japan, NLD = Netherlands, NOR = Norway, NZL = New Zealand, SWE = Sweden

Table 6.3 TFP and technical progress biases

	Period	AUS	AUT	BEL	CAN	CHE	DEU	DNK	ESP	FIN	FRA	GBR	GRC	JPN	NLD	NOR	NZL	SWE	USA	Mean	Std. Dev
	1960-1973	2.31	2.77	3.64	2.26	1.40	2.30	2.21	4.15	2.57	3.00	2.33	5.37	1.71	3.77	2.45	0.52	2.57	0.96	2.57	1.15
TFP	1974-1992	0.89	0.93	1.84	0.63	0.96	1.51	0.97	1.84	1.15	1.63	1.22	−0.12	1.71	1.02	1.84	−0.01	0.98	0.45	1.09	0.60
	1960-1992	1.49	1.71	2.61	1.32	1.15	1.90	1.50	2.82	1.75	2.21	1.69	2.21	1.71	2.19	2.10	0.21	1.65	0.67	1.72	0.63
	1960-1973	1.58	−1.84	0.85	2.16	1.57	0.06	0.70	2.61	1.02	0.49	1.84	2.71	−1.97	2.79	1.46	−0.04	0.25	1.70	1.00	1.37
Consumption	1974-1992	0.82	−1.60	−0.27	0.03	0.51	0.14	−0.42	0.61	1.53	0.44	1.95	0.18	−0.62	0.26	0.04	−1.48	0.05	0.66	0.16	0.88
	1960-1992	1.14	−1.70	0.20	0.94	0.96	0.11	0.06	1.46	1.31	0.46	1.90	1.25	−1.19	1.33	0.64	−0.87	0.13	1.10	0.51	0.97
	1960-1973	5.53	1.23	4.94	4.69	3.36	1.48	3.87	10.02	6.13	4.42	4.11	7.10	0.02	6.96	0.68	0.24	6.24	1.74	4.04	2.75
Investment	1974-1992	−0.08	−0.69	4.35	4.76	6.58	1.70	−1.16	4.78	6.43	2.03	3.47	−2.81	2.50	−0.44	−3.41	−0.20	3.69	0.79	1.79	2.99
	1960-1992	2.30	0.13	4.60	4.73	5.22	1.61	0.98	7.00	6.30	3.04	3.74	1.39	1.45	2.70	−1.67	−0.01	4.77	1.19	2.75	2.35
	1960-1973	1.05	4.18	9.25	2.88	4.53	5.41	2.36	9.52	3.80	5.16	1.66	12.86	5.84	8.79	−1.36	1.70	7.33	−2.67	4.57	3.97
Exports	1974-1992	3.26	2.80	3.68	1.55	1.50	4.07	2.89	4.22	3.89	2.51	2.05	5.31	2.91	2.80	1.45	0.86	3.28	4.68	2.98	1.21
	1960-1992	2.33	3.39	6.04	2.11	2.78	4.64	2.66	6.47	3.85	3.63	1.83	8.51	4.15	5.34	0.26	1.22	5.00	1.56	3.66	2.09
	1960-1973	3.79	2.04	8.22	3.53	5.12	4.03	3.38	15.88	5.42	4.31	3.47	6.56	0.70	9.79	−1.07	1.18	7.11	4.73	4.90	3.81
Imports	1974-1992	2.73	1.24	3.16	3.21	2.88	2.59	0.47	6.46	2.17	1.82	3.09	4.25	0.41	2.20	−1.92	0.80	2.61	3.52	2.32	1.78
	1960-1992	3.18	1.58	5.31	3.35	3.83	3.20	1.70	10.46	3.55	2.88	3.25	5.23	0.53	5.42	−1.56	0.96	4.52	4.04	3.41	2.52
	1960-1973	−0.18	−4.46	−2.36	0.58	0.65	−2.22	−1.56	−0.89	−0.81	−1.84	−0.69	−3.22	−3.71	−0.63	−1.80	−0.65	−1.08	0.42	−1.36	1.44
Labor	1974-1992	−0.37	−2.35	−1.21	0.03	0.87	−0.86	−0.82	−1.11	3.22	−0.91	0.95	−1.44	−1.21	−0.88	−1.66	−1.86	−.05	0.42	−0.51	1.30
	1960-1992	−0.29	−3.24	−1.70	0.26	0.77	−1.44	−1.13	−1.02	1.51	−1.30	0.26	−2.19	−2.27	−0.77	−1.72	−1.35	−0.43	0.42	−0.87	1.21

Table 6.4 Own price elasticities

	Period	AUS	AUT	BEL	CAN	CHE	DEU	DNK	ESP	FIN	FRA	GBR	GRC	JPN	NLD	NOR	NZL	SWE	USA	Mean	Std. Dev
	1960-1973	0.03	0.24	0.16	0.05	0.42	0.23	0.19	0.41	0.43	0.08	0.88	0.27	0.34	0.07	0.56	0.12	0.08	0.82	0.30	0.25
Consumption	1974-1992	0.03	0.25	0.12	0.07	0.41	0.15	0.29	0.41	0.52	0.11	0.89	0.13	0.64	0.06	0.59	0.15	0.12	0.69	0.31	0.26
	1960-1992	0.03	0.24	0.13	0.06	0.41	0.18	0.25	0.41	0.48	0.10	0.88	0.19	0.52	0.06	0.57	0.13	0.10	0.74	0.31	0.25
	1960-1973	2.50	0.84	1.83	2.61	2.29	1.31	1.38	1.87	1.99	0.99	0.93	1.54	1.02	2.17	0.36	0.38	1.82	1.54	1.52	0.68
Investment	1974-1992	2.60	1.02	1.99	1.94	2.24	1.62	2.15	1.90	3.02	1.14	1.12	1.32	1.40	2.41	0.31	0.45	2.35	1.42	1.69	0.73
	1960-1992	2.56	0.94	1.92	2.23	2.26	1.49	1.82	1.89	2.58	1.08	1.04	1.41	1.24	2.31	0.33	0.42	2.13	1.47	1.62	0.68
	1960-1973	0.18	0.38	2.76	0.65	0.08	0.55	0.16	0.29	0.64	0.06	0.47	1.21	1.32	0.66	0.31	0.03	0.63	2.57	0.72	0.79
Exports	1974-1992	0.11	0.22	1.37	0.34	0.04	0.31	0.15	0.18	0.57	0.03	0.26	0.31	0.54	0.29	0.17	0.03	0.48	1.22	0.37	0.37
	1960-1992	0.14	0.29	1.96	0.47	0.05	0.41	0.16	0.22	0.60	0.04	0.35	0.69	0.87	0.45	0.23	0.03	0.55	1.79	0.52	0.55
	1960-1973	−1.07	−0.46	−2.87	−2.74	−0.94	0.36	−0.90	−3.45	−1.06	−0.67	−0.61	−2.76	−0.23	−1.92	−2.29	−0.39	−1.19	−0.49	−1.36	1.03
Imports	1974-1992	−0.69	−0.24	−1.29	−1.25	−0.37	−0.15	−0.66	−1.08	−0.69	−0.35	−0.33	−0.96	−0.10	−0.72	−1.82	−0.33	−0.76	−0.29	−0.67	0.46
	1960-1992	−0.85	−0.33	−1.96	−1.88	−0.61	−0.24	−0.76	−2.09	−0.85	−0.49	−0.45	−1.72	−0.15	−1.23	−2.02	−0.36	−0.94	−0.37	−0.96	0.68
	1960-1973	−0.45	−0.20	−0.30	−0.52	−0.74	−0.26	−0.67	−0.61	−1.19	−0.42	−0.84	−0.12	−0.49	−0.42	−0.39	−0.23	−0.60	−0.80	−0.51	0.27
Labor	1974-1992	−0.60	−0.46	−0.55	−0.68	−1.07	−0.42	1.24	−1.23	2.48	−0.76	1.40	−0.19	1.27	−0.64	−0.69	−0.31	−0.91	−0.79	−0.87	0.53
	1960-1992	−0.53	−0.35	−0.44	−0.61	−0.93	−0.35	−1.00	−0.96	−1.93	−0.61	−1.16	−0.16	−0.94	−0.54	−0.57	−0.28	−0.78	−0.79	0.72	0.41

Table 6.5 Average cross price elasticities

	AUS	AUT	BEL	CAN	CHE	DEU	DNK	ESP	FIN	FRA	GBR	GRC	JPN	NLD	NOR	NZL	SWE	USA	Mean	Std. Dev
E_{11}	0.03	0.24	0.13	0.06	0.41	0.18	0.25	0.41	0.48	0.10	0.88	0.19	0.52	0.06	0.57	0.13	0.10	0.74	0.31	0.25
E_{12}	0.05	0.18	−0.02	0.21	0.42	−0.05	0.33	0.48	0.62	0.18	0.42	−0.06	0.09	0.18	0.12	0.06	0.19	0.15	0.20	0.19
E_{13}	0.03	−0.17	0.21	0.03	−0.08	−0.17	0.13	−0.02	0.07	−0.01	−0.19	−0.06	0.03	0.06	−0.01	0.03	0.08	−0.29	−0.02	0.12
E_{14}	−0.07	−0.20	−0.33	−0.13	−0.34	−0.08	−0.24	−0.41	−0.40	−0.09	−0.28	−0.11	−0.10	−0.18	−0.24	−0.14	−0.18	−0.04	−0.20	0.11
E_{15}	−0.04	−0.05	−0.01	−0.17	−0.41	0.11	−0.46	−0.45	−0.77	−0.17	−0.83	0.04	−0.54	−0.12	−0.44	−0.09	−0.19	−0.55	−0.29	0.28
E_{21}	0.13	0.42	−0.05	0.63	1.06	−0.13	1.09	1.40	1.58	0.51	1.61	−0.18	0.18	0.54	0.27	0.19	0.64	0.57	0.58	0.56
E_{22}	2.56	0.94	1.92	2.23	2.26	1.49	1.82	1.89	2.58	1.08	1.04	1.41	1.24	2.31	0.33	0.42	2.13	1.47	1.62	0.68
E_{23}	0.01	−0.10	0.55	0.27	−0.18	0.13	0.49	0.11	0.19	−0.02	−0.13	0.67	−0.23	1.23	0.30	0.07	0.89	−0.46	0.21	0.42
E_{24}	−0.88	−0.48	−1.11	−1.35	−0.86	−0.36	−1.46	−1.35	−1.19	−0.37	−0.68	−1.30	−0.14	−2.30	−1.03	−0.15	−1.47	−0.25	−0.93	0.58
E_{25}	−1.82	−0.78	−1.31	−1.78	−2.27	−1.13	−1.94	−2.05	−3.16	−1.19	−1.84	−0.60	−1.05	−1.77	0.13	−0.53	−2.19	−1.33	−1.48	0.77
E_{31}	0.13	−0.34	0.28	0.09	−0.17	−0.46	0.28	−0.15	0.16	−0.06	−0.61	−0.39	0.16	0.09	−0.01	0.09	0.19	−3.22	−0.22	0.79
E_{32}	0.01	−0.10	0.19	0.27	−0.17	0.11	0.33	0.11	0.17	−0.05	−0.11	1.26	−0.79	0.62	0.20	0.06	0.70	−1.32	0.08	0.55
E_{33}	0.14	0.29	1.96	0.47	0.05	0.41	0.16	0.22	0.60	0.04	0.35	0.69	0.87	0.45	0.23	0.03	0.55	1.79	0.52	0.55
E_{34}	−0.26	0.26	−1.83	−0.88	0.15	0.21	−0.22	0.21	−0.01	0.14	0.18	−1.09	0.06	−0.66	−0.66	−0.10	−0.55	0.63	−0.25	0.60
E_{35}	−0.02	−0.10	−0.60	0.06	0.13	−0.27	−0.54	−0.40	−0.92	−0.07	0.20	−0.47	−0.31	−0.49	0.25	−0.09	−0.90	2.12	−0.14	0.66
E_{41}	0.27	0.35	0.41	0.36	0.68	0.22	0.46	1.83	0.93	0.31	0.75	0.34	0.49	0.26	0.34	0.33	0.43	0.44	0.51	0.38
E_{42}	1.22	0.37	0.40	1.28	0.71	0.37	0.87	2.15	1.11	0.48	0.48	1.25	0.40	1.14	0.63	0.13	1.10	0.64	0.82	0.49
E_{43}	0.23	−0.22	1.71	0.81	−0.14	−0.21	0.19	−0.16	0.01	−0.12	−0.15	0.53	−0.06	0.63	0.62	0.09	0.50	−0.58	0.20	0.53
E_{44}	−0.85	−0.33	−1.96	−1.88	−0.61	−0.24	−0.76	−2.09	−0.85	−0.49	−0.45	−1.72	−015	−1.23	−2.02	−0.36	−0.94	−0.37	−0.96	0.68
E_{45}	−0.86	−0.17	−0.56	−0.56	−0.64	−0.14	−0.77	−1.74	−1.19	−0.18	−0.63	−0.40	−0.67	−0.80	0.43	−0.19	−1.08	−0.13	−0.57	0.49
E_{51}	0.04	0.06	0.01	0.19	0.42	−0.12	0.52	0.53	0.80	0.19	0.96	−0.09	0.49	0.13	0.47	0.11	0.20	0.63	0.31	0.31
E_{52}	0.75	0.34	0.42	0.67	0.92	0.42	0.65	0.79	1.29	0.46	0.55	0.34	0.52	0.67	−0.06	0.22	0.69	0.39	0.56	0.29
E_{53}	0.01	0.05	0.55	−0.02	−0.07	0.11	0.27	0.10	0.38	0.03	−0.07	0.17	0.05	0.39	−0.17	0.04	0.37	−0.22	0.11	0.21
E_{54}	−0.26	−0.10	−0.53	−0.23	−0.33	−0.05	−0.44	−0.46	−0.54	−0.06	−0.27	−0.27	−0.13	−0.66	0.33	−0.10	−0.48	−0.01	−0.26	0.24
E_{55}	−0.53	−0.35	−0.44	−0.61	−0.93	−0.35	−1.00	−0.96	−1.93	−0.61	−1.16	−0.16	−0.94	−0.54	−0.57	−0.28	−0.78	−0.79	−0.72	0.41

Note: 1 = Consumption, 2 = Investment, 3 = Exports, 4 = Imports, 5 = Labor

Total Factor Productivity

Figure 6.1 confirms the much debated productivity slowdown (Bailey and Gorden 1988; Hulten 1992; Nordhaus 1982, 1988; Wolff 1996), with all countries having lower productivity growth in 1992 compared to 1960. From Table 6.3, the average OECD productivity growth rate for 1960-1973 was 2.57 percent, but 1.09 percent for 1974-1992. This declining productivity growth result was also found by Diewert and Fox (1997) using the same data and an index-number approach (Diewert, 1992) to generating productivity growth estimates.7 This similarity in results from alternative methods is not surprising. Kohli (1990), Diewert and Wales (1992), and Fox (1996) have noted that flexible profit function methods of obtaining technical progress estimates yield values which are smoothed versions of the estimates from the commonly used index-number approaches. From the estimates there does not appear to be a distinct regional group in terms of TFP.

Technical Progress Biases

If countries of a region are thought to be similar due to geographical location and are to be talked of as a group, then we would expect that their economies would exhibit similar characteristics, such as responding in a similar fashion to technical progress, and technical progress would be affected in a similar fashion to relative price changes. This section presents results that allow this hypothesis to be investigated.

The technical progress biases indicate that for most countries productivity growth has been output (consumption, investment, exports) augmenting, imports augmenting and labour reducing (Table 6.3, Figures 6.2 to 6.6). There are, however, a few exceptions. An interesting one is that for the USA, Switzerland, Canada (for most of the sample) and Great Britain (from 1976) technical progress has been labor augmenting. The labor reducing aspect of technical progress for most countries is of particular interest - it confirms the perception of labor being replaced through technical progress. Japan, for example, has had technical progress that was labor-reducing, until 1987.

From Table 6.3, the OECD average technical progress biases for exports and imports are clearly lower in the post-OPEC era. For Japan, the bias for imports is positive, but very low compared with other countries, indicating that technical progress has not been assisting imports to Japan much at all.

A comparison of Tables 6.1 and 6.3 allows an analysis of the effects of relative price changes on the technological biases. For example, consider a comparison between the USA, and Japan for consumption (an output). For each period considered, the technological bias is positive for the USA, but negative for Japan. From Table 6.1, we see that for Japan this means that an increase in the price of consumption leads to a decline in TFP, *ceteris paribus*. For the USA, on the other hand, an increase in the price of consumption leads to an increase in TFP. Most countries in the sample are similar to the USA in this regard, with only New Zealand and Austria exhibiting the same characteristic with regards to consumption as Japan. However, we must note that the estimates for TFP for Japan seem a lot lower than the usual estimates, indicating that there may be aspects of the Japanese economy over this period that our modeling strategy is not flexible enough to capture.

Overall, the results from Table 6.3 suggest that there is little evidence that the economies in the Asia-Pacific region are a distinct group. The variation in the signs and magnitudes of biases across the countries in the sample suggests that there are no regional characteristics which cause economies to be similar, at least in terms of the effects of technical progress.

Next we examine if there is any evidence of regional similarities from the estimates of price elasticities.

Price Elasticities

Own price elasticities (Table 6.4) indicate that labor demand has become more price-sensitive over time in every country. This perhaps reflects labor markets becoming more flexible. A partial explanation for this could be pressure on labor because of the labor-reducing technical progress in many countries, as reported in Table 6.3. Own price elasticities for exports and imports have also fallen noticeably, with elasticities being more similar across countries at the end of the sample than earlier. This could be a reflection of increased specialization due to most (perhaps all) of the countries in the sample adopting more liberal trade policies at the end of the sample than at the beginning.

The cross price elasticities reported in Table 6.5 are (arithmetic) averages for the full sample period, 1960-1992. The degree of complementarity between both the outputs and the inputs respectively is of interest. Outputs are complementary if the elasticity estimates between them are positive. In other words, an increase in the price of one output tends to increase the supply of other outputs. However, the relationship between consumption and exports is not so clear, with elasticities of different signs for different countries. From the second to last column of Table 6.5, we see that on average (across countries) these outputs are substitutes, for example, an increase in the price of consumption leads to a reduction in the supply of exports. This could be due to companies preferring to sell to markets which they know well, their domestic market being the most familiar. It may also reflect other types of uncertainty, such as exchange rate volatility. It is worth noting that relatively trade-dependent economics such as Japan, New Zealand and Australia have complementary relationships between exports and consumption. However, these elasticities of either sign are quite small for each country.

Inputs are complements if the elasticity estimates between them are negative. In other words, an increase in the price of one input tends to reduce the demand of other inputs. Imports and labor are complements in all countries except Norway. However, both of the relevant elasticities (E_{45} and E_{54}) are quite small (0.43 and 0.33, respectively).

Cross price elasticities between outputs and inputs can be analyzed in the same way, and many other observations on the results are possible, but are left to the reader with an interest in a particular aspect of recent economic history, or a particular country. However, we can note that the estimates of price elasticities again give us no evidence that membership of a regional group seems to be determining similarities between economies.

5 CONCLUSION

The results from this chapter provide a clear picture of the effects of technical progress on the economies of 18 OECD countries, 1960-1992. Own and cross price elasticties for each of the variable goods have also been reported. The approach has treated these as economies which engage in foreign trade and which have multiple outputs as well as multiple inputs. This is more realistic than the common approach of abstracting from foreign trade and assuming that only one output is produced. The approach is soundly based in economic theory, with the estimated functions satisfying the appropriate regularity conditions globally. The estimates for countries are as comparable as possible, given that the data aggregates were constructed in a consistent fashion and the same method was used for each country to estimate all of the measures of interest. The only factor stopping claims of complete comparability is that the raw data series may have been constructed using different techniques by different statistical agencies. However, give that these are all OECD countries, the techniques should be very similar.

The estimates of the effects of technical progress on the inputs and outputs shed light on how aggregate technical progress may be biased in favor of some goods and against others. The estimates allow both comparisons across countries and across time. Similarly, the price elasticities allow investigation into the differences between countries and the changes across time in the sensitivity of supply/demand to price changes.

There did not appear to be any systematic differences in the performance of economies based on regional differences. In particular, OECD member countries in the Asia-Pacific Region, a region which experienced much change in the period 1960-1992, did not exhibit any properties which seem to set them apart from the other countries as a group.

While there are many results of interest in the data, one of particular interest may be the labour reducing effect of technical progress for most countries, and the increasing sensitivity of labour demand to price changes in all countries.

APPENDIX

The variable profit function can be expressed as follows:

$$V(p, k) \equiv max_y(p'y : k = F(y)) \tag{6.13}$$

where p' denotes the transpose of the price vector, $F(y)$ is the factor requirements function and k is capital. It is assumed that (i) $p_i > 0$ for $i = 1,...,N$, where N is the number of variable goods, (ii) $k > 0$, and (iii) $y_i > 0$ if i denotes an output, and $y_i < 0$ if i denotes an input (that is, inputs are treated as negative outputs).

The conditions on the variable profit function, V, with constant returns imposed, are that it is (i) a nonnegative function, (ii) positive homogeneous of degree one in p, (iii) convex and continuous in p for every fixed k, (iv) positive homogeneous of degree one in k, (v) nondecreasing in k for every fixed p, and (vi) concave and continuous in k for every fixed p. (See Diewert, 1973, for proofs.)

The profit-maximizing supply and demand functions can then be derived by using Hotelling's Lemma - the derivative of $V(p, k)$ with respect to the price of the ith good gives the supply or demand function (alternatively 'net supply' function) for this good (see, for example, Varian, 1984: 52). The convexity of V in prices implies that the matrix of second derivatives of V with respect to prices (the first partial derivatives of the net supply functions with respect to prices) is positive semidefinite.

NOTES

1. The expressions 'technological change', 'productivity growth' and 'technical progress' are used interchangeably.
2. Diewert and Wales (1987) initially called this the Symmetric Generalized McFadden functional form.
3. A functional form is 'flexible' if it can provide a second order approximation to an arbitrary twice differentiable linearly homogeneous function at a point (Diewert, 1974: 113).
4. Kohli (1994: 11-12) discusses the identification problem that one runs into when trying to determine whether technical progress occurs because inputs become more productive or because outputs become easier to produce.
5. The OECD country codes used in the tables are as follows: AUS=Australia, AUT=Austria, BEL=Belgium, CAN=Canada, CHE=Switzerland, DEU=West Germany, DNK=Denmark, ESP=Spain, FIN=Finland, FRA=France, GBR=Great Britain, GRC=Greece, JPN=Japan, NLD=Netherlands, NOR=Norway, NZL=New Zealand, SWE=Sweden, and USA. Other countries were excluded from consideration due to the lack of appropriate data. Countries in the sample which are in the Asia Pacific region can be defined as Australia, Japan and New Zealand, although this could be extended to include Canada and the USA if the APEC definition of the Asia Pacific region is used.
6. Results for each year of the sample are available on request from the authors. All computations were performed using the econometrics computer program SHAZAM (White, 1978). The optimizing algorithm for estimating the system of nonlinear equations was SHAZAM's default, the Davidson-Fletcher-Powell algorithm.
7. See Diewert and Fox (1997) for some reasons why this measured productivity slowdown may be caused by measurement error.

REFERENCES

Bailey, M.N. and R.J. Gorden (1988), 'The productivity slowdown, measurement issues, and the explosion of computer power', *Brookings Papers on Economics Activity*, **2**, 347-420.

Diewert, W.E. (1973), 'Functional forms for profit and transformation functions', *Journal of Economic Theory*, **6**, 1393-414.

Diewert, W.E. (1974), 'Applications of duality theory', in M.D. Intriligator and D.A. Kendrick (eds), *Frontiers of Quantitative Economics*, Vol. 11, Amsterdam: North Holland, 106-71.

Diewert, W.E. (1992), 'Fisher ideal output, input and productivity indexes revisited', *Journal of Productivity Analysis*, **3**, 211-48.

Diewert, W.E. and K.J. Fox (1997), 'Can measurement error explain the productivity paradox?', manuscript.

Diewert, W.E. and T.J. Wales (1987), 'Flexible functional forms and global curvature conditions', *Econometrica*, **55**, 43-68.

Diewert, W.E. and T.J. Wales (1992), 'Quadratic spline models for producer's supply and demand functions', *International Economic Review*, **33**, 705-22.

Fox, K.J. (1996), 'Specification of functional form and the estimation of technical progress', *Applied Economics*, **28**, 947-56.

Fox, K.J. (1997), 'Open economy data sets for 18 OECD countries', 1960-1992, University of New South Wales School of Economics, discussion paper 97/26.

Hicks, J. R. (1932), *Theory of Wages*, London: Macmillan.

Hulten, C.R. (1992), 'Growth accounting when technical change is embodied in capital', *American Economic Review*, **82**, 964-80.

Jorgenson, D.W. and B.M. Fraumeni (1981), 'Relative prices and technical change', in E.R. Berndt and B.C. Field (eds), *Modeling and Measuring Natural Resource Substitution*, Cambridge, MA: MIT Press, 17-47.

Kohli, U. (1990), 'Growth accounting in the open economy: parametric and nonparametric estimates', *Journal of Economic and Social Measurement*, **16**, 125-36.

Kohli, U. (1991), *Technology, Duality and Foreign Trade*, Hertfordshire: Harvester Wheatsheaf.

Kohli, U. (1994), 'Technological biases in US aggregate production', *Journal of Productivity Analysis*, **5** (1), 5-22.

Magnus, J.R. and A.D. Woodland (1988), 'On the maximum likelihood estimation of multivariate regression models containing serially correlated error components', *International Economic Review*, **29**, 707-25.

Nordhaus, W.D. (1982), 'Economic policy in the face of declining productivity growth', *European Economic Review*, **18**, 131-57.

Nordhaus, W.D. (1988), 'Comment', *Brookings Papers on Economic Activity*, **2**, 421-25.

Solow, R.M. (1957), 'Technical change and the aggregate production function', *Review of Economics and Statistics*, **39**, 312-20.

Varian, H.R. (1984), *Microeconomic Analysis*, 2nd edn, New York: W.W. Norton and Company.

Wiley, D.E., W.H. Schmidt and W.J. Bramble (1973), 'Studies of a class of covariance structure models', *Journal of the American Statistical Association*, **68**, 317-23.

Wolff, E.N. (1996), 'The productivity slowdown: the culprit at last?

Follow-up on Hulten and Wolff', *The American Economic Review*, **86**, 1239-52.

White, K.J. (1978), 'A general computer program for econometric methods – SHAZAM', *Econometrica*, January, 239-40.

PART II

National Studies

A. Macroeconcmie Productivity Studies

7. A Tiger in the Land of the Panda: Growth Prospects for Hong Kong under Reversion to China*

James H. Gapinski and David L. Western

'We are coming now rather into the region of guess work,' said Dr. Mortimer.

'Say, rather, into the region where we balance probabilities and choose the most likely. It is the scientific use of the imagination, but we have always some material basis on which to start our speculations.'

Sherlock Holmes
The Hound of the Baskervilles

1 INTRODUCTION

Opium, an indulgence familiar to the British detective Holmes, was an evil that profiteering British traders endeavored to impose on the unwilling Chinese. After a fashion tension mounted between Britain and China leading to hostilities known as the Opium War. The Crown won handily. To the victor go the spoils, and by the Treaty of Nanking, signed in 1842, the island of Hong Kong was ceded to Britain. Fourteen years later a small craft named the *Arrow*, plying the seas under the protection of the Union Jack, was boarded by Chinese authorities at Canton. The incident sparked a Second Opium War, and again the British sailed to victory. By the resulting Convention of Peking of 1860, Britain took

*This chapter was based an a paper which had its origin in a sabbatical that Gapinski enjoyed at Curtin University during the spring of 1997. Thanks go to William Laird of Florida State University (FSU) for endorsing the leave and to Geoffrey Crockett of Curtin for providing a creative environment for conducting research. Thanks likewise go to Karen Wells and Peter Coffin of FSU for adroitly processing handscript into typescript. Gapinski and Western have made various trips to Hong Kong in recent years, one of those visits occurring only days before reversion. Both writers take full advantage of joint authorship and gladly blame each other for any statement, numerical or otherwise, that proves to be erroneous or for any assumption that, by later events, proves to be unreasonable.

possession of the tip of Kowloon peninsula thereby giving it a secure land mass to the immediate north of the fragrant harbor. But the colony of Hong Kong was to grow yet again. Concerned about the maneuverings of France and Russia in the Far East, Britain sought to further insulate Hong Kong, and to that end it leased the New Territories from China. The lease ran for 99 years starting from 1 July, 1898.

At the time of the first War, Lord Palmerston, the British Foreign Secretary, characterized Hong Kong as a 'barren island with hardly a house upon it.'[1] It would not remain barren. In fact it would become home to six million people, and in the process it would become an economic jewel in the Royal Crown. For example, during the contemporary period from 1961 to 1990, this Tiger experienced ferocious growth. Output expanded at an annual rate of 8.85 percent while labor productivity - output per worker - advanced at the rate of 6.03 percent. By comparison, the USA, a world leader, grew much more modestly at 3.28 percent and 1.54 percent, respectively. Ferocious growth by the Tiger meant almost a quadrupling of the productivity level and a remarkable shrinking of the gap between its productivity and America's. Moreover Tiger plant and equipment soared, education progressed, and, perhaps above all, trade flourished. Growth, of course, is not painless. Labor shortages developed, costs rose and businesses searched for ways to restructure their operations. Still, Hong Kong thrived under British rule that saw local government exercise loose control over economic activity, a practice known as positive nonintervention (Chiu and Liu, 1995: 85-90, 101-2).

Amid the modern triumphs of Hong Kong, Britain and China began deliberations on the reversion of the colony to Chinese sovereignty. Round upon round of negotiations ensued, and from those sometimes testy talks came the Joint Declaration of 1984. By that accord, which was forged around the concept of 'one country, two systems' envisioned by Deng Xiaoping, China's paramount leader, Britain agreed to hand over the entire colony. For its part, China agreed to a 50-year period wherein Hong Kong would have a high degree of autonomy and would maintain its capitalist orientation. Events proceeded further. In 1990 China hammered out the Basic Law, which defined the legal and constitutional framework for the new Hong Kong, formally a special administrative region. By its language, the Law laid down specifics consonant with the spirit of the Joint Declaration and, in a way, set into stone the principle of one country, two systems.[2]

Sentiment about the impending changeover was mixed. Hope and exuberance mingled with worry and fear. Deng Xiaoping's advocacy of the one-two principle struck a hopeful chord that Hong Kong would remain economically healthy under Beijing rule. Logic reinforced hope.

China needed Hong Kong to stay healthy. The Tiger served as the entry point to China, as a magnet for business ventures from the four corners of the globe, and as a center for finance and trade. Surely China had much to lose if Hong Kong's fortunes faded. Exuberance wrapped in patriotism believed that the Motherland would stick to her end of the bargain, that property rights would be honored, and that unification would build strength. As the slogan went, 'What is good for Hong Kong is good for China, and what is good for China is very good for Hong Kong.'

Yet worry could be sensed blowing in the winds of change. Business, already facing serious problems of restructuring, now would have to contend with a new political order which took a dim view of the personal freedoms that are basic to the enterprise system. And despite the aphorism of Deng, the memory of the Tiananmen Square Massacre in 1989 stirred a lingering fear that words written down by a totalitarian government may be nothing more than ink on paper. Deng's death only added to the chill.[3]

Then came 1 July, 1997. The stroke of midnight ushering in that Tuesday also ushered in the Chinese and escorted the British out. Victoria Harbour was alight with fireworks that celebrated a changing of the guard fit for the history books. Lan Kwai Fong partied, D'Aguilar Street pulsated and Nathan Road sold souvenirs as dragons danced. The revelry was intense despite the driving rain. Then came the morning after the night before. Cooler heads prevailed and wondered, What now? Would the Tiger continue its phenomenal run and keep step with the other three members of the Tiger family: Korea, Singapore and Taiwan? Would its already miraculous pace quicken? Or would the Tiger stumble and tumble?

Conjecture was easy to find. It still is. This paper attempts to place formal bounds on conjecture by using theory and empirical evidence to study the effects of reversion on the growth prospects for Hong Kong. Section 2 presents highlights of a theoretical model that features heterogeneous physical capital and that isolates determinants of growth. Section 3 sketches an economic profile of the Tiger. Section 4 quantifies the determinants of Hong Kong growth and ranks them by their importance. Section 5 then uses that information to measure the possible effects of reversion, which are summarized in a reversion matrix. Section 6 offers concluding thoughts. For expository convenience today's Hong Kong is referred to variously as a country, a nation, an economy, and, of course, the Tiger. China is the Panda.

2 A THEORETICAL FRAMEWORK

Capital goods are heterogeneous because of embodied technical progress, and consequently they must be distinguished by vintage - by date of construction. With each vintage generating output from its own production function, total output sums quantities across the separate vintages. Under restrictive conditions, that total satisfies an aggregate production function, which, for convenience, is taken to be the Cobb-Douglas:

$$Y_t = \zeta J_t^{\alpha} (E_t^{\theta} L_t)^{1-\alpha}. \tag{7.1}$$

In this aggregate function Y_t denotes the amount of homogeneous output produced at time t from all vintages in existence; namely, those having vintage numbers ranging from t back to $t-T$, T being the age of the oldest vintage. L_t designates the quantity of homogeneous labor allocated across vintages at t. Augmentation variable E_t^{θ} measures labor quality. It begins with E_t, the stock of general knowledge possessed by labor, but it adds the refinement that what counts for production is the extent to which knowledge improves performance on the shop floor. Knowledge elasticity θ captures that performance bias. J_t represents the aggregate stock of efficient capital, which can be described as

$$J_t = \int_{t-T}^{t} e^{\mu v} I_v \, e^{-\delta(t-v)} dv. \tag{7.2}$$

I_v signifies gross investment at time v. Capital goods decay at the exponential rate δ, and consequently the amount of vintage v surviving at t equals $I_v e^{-\delta(t-v)}$. The quality of that machinery is given by the capital quality index $e^{\mu v}$, where μ is the rate of embodied technical progress. The companion rate of disembodied technical progress comes from the labor quality index and equals $\theta \hat{E}$. Symbol $\hat{E}$ stands for the growth rate of E; that is, $\hat{E} = E^{-1} dE/dt$, time subscripts being ignored here and henceforth. Clearly the production process involves both embodied progress and disembodied progress. Almost just as clearly it observes the restrictions $\zeta > 0$, $1 > \alpha > 0$, $1 > \theta > 0$, $\mu \geq 0$, $\delta \geq 0$.

Output growth $\hat{Y}$ derives from equation (7.1) as

$$\hat{Y} = \hat{\zeta} + (1-\alpha)\theta \hat{E} + \alpha \hat{J} + (1-\alpha)\hat{L}. \tag{7.3}$$

Output growth depends upon input growth. Growth in ζ is included to reflect factors besides capital and labor that may govern economic activity. One such 'structural' factor is international trade. As Western (1996: 6) suggests, foreign trade can encourage a favorable reallocation of resources thereby boosting output independently of changes in capital or labor, and $\hat{\zeta}$ in equation (7.3) recognizes that possibility.[4] Expressed more precisely,

$$\hat{\zeta} = \zeta_F F. \tag{7.4}$$

F gauges the volume of foreign trade, and $\zeta_F > 0$ by hypothesis.

Labor productivity Y/L, denoted y, grows from equation (7.3) according to the schedule

$$\hat{y} = \hat{\zeta} + (1-\alpha)\theta\hat{E} + \alpha\hat{j}. \tag{7.5}$$

Letter $\hat{j}$ represents the growth of j, which signifies capital intensity J/L. Thus labor productivity growth $\hat{y}$ depends upon the rate of structural change $\hat{\zeta}$, the rate of disembodiment $\theta\hat{E}$, and the rate of capital deepening $\hat{j}$.

Growth shares measure the contribution that the separate determinants make to growth. As regards output growth, the shares line up from function (7.1) as

$$1 = (1-\alpha)\hat{L}/\hat{Y} + (1-\alpha)\theta\hat{E}/\hat{Y} + \alpha\hat{J}_K/\hat{Y} + \alpha\hat{J}_\mu/\hat{Y} + \zeta_F F/\hat{Y}. \tag{7.6}$$

In this accounting the growth of efficient capital $\hat{J}$ is understood to have two components. One component, $\hat{J}_K$, reflects efficient growth from quantity through investment level I and depreciation rate δ. The other component, $\hat{J}_\mu$, mirrors efficient growth from quality via embodiment rate μ. Hence,

$$\hat{J} = \hat{J}_K + \hat{J}_\mu. \tag{7.7}$$

From this decomposition equation (7.6) can be seen to identify the contributions to output growth due to labor quantity, labor quality, capital quantity, capital quality and foreign trade respectively. Similarly the shares for labor productivity growth appear from expression (7.5) as

$$1 = (1-\alpha)\theta\hat{E}/\hat{z} + \alpha\hat{J}_K/\hat{z} + \alpha\hat{J}_\mu/\hat{z} + \zeta_F F/\hat{z}, \tag{7.8}$$

where $\hat{z}$ indicates weighted labor productivity growth $\hat{Y} - (1-\alpha)\hat{L}$. Labor quality, capital quantity, capital quality, and trade explain labor productivity growth.

Total factor productivity (TFP) is a concept that runs through growth literature in general and through Asia-Pacific growth discussion in particular. Defined in residual fashion as the amount of output growth *not* explained by the growth in capital and labor quantities, TFP growth ($\hat{TFP}$) may be written as

$$\hat{TFP} = \hat{Y} - \alpha \hat{J}_K - (1-\alpha)\hat{L}. \tag{7.9}$$

But from expressions (7.3), (7.4), and (7.7),

$$\hat{TFP} = (1-\alpha)\theta\hat{E} + \alpha\hat{J}_\mu + \zeta_F F: \tag{7.10}$$

Total factor productivity growth depends upon the growth in labor and capital qualities and upon foreign trade. Moreover, rearranging expression (7.9) yields

$$\hat{Y} = \alpha\hat{J}_K + (1-\alpha)\hat{L} + \hat{TFP}, \tag{7.11}$$

$$1 = [\alpha\hat{J}_K + (1-\alpha)\hat{L}]/\hat{Y} + \hat{TFP}/\hat{Y}. \tag{7.12}$$

Output growth separates into the shares from quantities and TFP. Likewise, from relation (7.11)

$$1 = \alpha\hat{J}_K/\hat{z} + \hat{TFP}/\hat{z}: \tag{7.13}$$

Labor productivity growth splits into the shares from capital quantity and TFP.

Of great importance in their own right, the growth shares can be reworked to quantify the sources of TFP growth. For example, dividing the combined output share due to qualities, $(1-\alpha)\theta\hat{E}/\hat{Y} + \alpha\hat{J}_\mu/\hat{Y}$, by the output share due to TFP, $\hat{TFP}/\hat{Y}$, produces by statement (7.10) the contribution of qualities to TFP growth. Similarly dividing output's trade share, $\zeta_F F/\hat{Y}$, by its TFP share yields the contribution of trade to TFP growth. Identical magnitudes follow from the shares for labor productivity growth.

3 PROFILE OF A TIGER

Bridging from theory to practice involves data from several sources. Regardless of source, however, all data have annual frequency, and all currency magnitudes are denominated in billions of 1985 international dollars making them comparable between Hong Kong and other countries of interest.

Output Y is gauged by gross domestic product (GDP) expressed in real terms whereas labor quantity L is posited in millions of workers. Both series come from the Penn World Table Mark 5.5 (PWT) prepared by Summers and Heston (1993). Knowledge E, the anchor of labor quality, lays out as average years of schooling developed from the numbers provided by Barro and Lee (1993). Capital stock J arises from a procedure steered by specification (7.2), which requires a series on investment along with values for the rates of embodiment and depreciation. Investment evolves by backcasting the PWT real gross investment levels in a way that allows for nonstationarity. Assignments for the embodiment and depreciation rates cover a grid designed to straddle the unknown true magnitudes. The μ values run vertically from zero to about 0.06 while the δ values run horizontally from zero to about 0.15. In the end nine pairs of μ and δ settings result giving rise to nine capital stock series. Capital stock J_1 has $\mu = \delta = 0$. It neither enjoys embodied progress nor suffers daily decay and therefore can be called homogeneous-shay capital: homogeneous because vintages are identical with respect to progress and shay because they remain intact until disintegrating suddenly and fully at age T. Capital stock J_5 is the middlemost or median series with $\mu = 0.0358$ and $\delta = 0.0730$.[5]

Table 7.1 sketches the consequent economic profile of Hong Kong. It spans the 30 year history from 1961 to 1990 and segments that history into six half-decade intervals. Output, which averages 35.5 billion dollars over the three decades exhibits a neat upward trend from 9.7 billion dollars in the years 1961 to 1965 to 76.2 billion dollars in the years 1986 to 1990. Likewise exhibiting uninterrupted upward trends are labor quality - that is, education - and capital as represented either by homogeneous shays J_1 or by mean machinery J_m, which averages magnitudes across all nine capital types. Duplicating the upward movement are labor productivity and the mean capital-output ratio k_m, which averages the capital-output ratio J/Y across the nine capital models. k_1, the capital-output ratio for homogeneous shays, breaks the trend pattern by tracing out a horseshoe configuration.

Rising trends for output and inputs are impressive. More impressive, though, are the underlying growth rates. For example, the growth rate for output registers 13 percent in the 1961-1965 half-decade and 12.82 percent in the 1976-1980 segment. Moreover it never falls below 5.60 percent and, strikingly, exhibits a sustained value of 8.85 percent over the three decades. In similar fashion homogeneous-shay capital grows at rates that always exceed 6.90 percent while the mean rate 100 $\hat{J}_m$, which

Table 7.1 Economic profile of Hong Kong

	Y	L	E	J_1	J_m	y	k_1	k_m
Period	Billion Dollars	Million Workers	Years	Billion Dollars	Billion Dollars	Dollars Per Worker	Decimal	Decimal
1961-1990	35.5	2.7	6.16	98.3	1,824.3	11,896	2.81	40.25
1961-1965	9.7	1.8	5.02	29.3	209.5	5,318	3.04	21.37
1966-1970	15.1	2.0	5.06	43.3	386.0	7,441	2.87	25.48
1971-1975	22.5	2.3	5.44	62.2	703.7	9,562	2.77	31.09
1976-1980	35.8	2.9	6.29	94.7	1447.7	12,489	2.66	39.99
1981-1985	53.4	3.4	7.20	148.5	2986.6	15,884	2.77	55.56
1986-1990	76.2	3.7	7.98	211.8	5212.1	20,680	2.78	68.00
	$100\,\hat{Y}$	$100\,\hat{L}$	$100\,\hat{E}$	$100\hat{J}_1$	$100\,\hat{J}_m$	$100\,\hat{y}$	$100\,\hat{j}_1$	$100\,\hat{j}_m$
	Percent	Percent	Percent	Percent	Percent	Percent	Percent	Percent
1961-1990	8.85	2.82	1.58	8.22	11.81	6.03	5.40	8.99
1961-1965	13.00	3.21	−1.14	9.16	13.97	9.79	5.95	10.76
1966-1970	7.28	1.88	1.08	6.93	8.80	5.40	5.05	6.92
1971-1975	6.79	3.63	1.68	7.91	11.83	3.17	4.28	8.21
1976-1980	12.82	4.46	3.67	9.67	15.15	8.36	5.21	10.69
1981-1985	5.60	2.34	2.22	8.41	11.21	3.26	6.06	8.87
1986-1990	7.62	1.42	2.00	7.24	9.88	6.20	5.81	8.46
	M_1	M_m	r	$100\,s$	$100\,U$	$100\,N$	$100\,X$	$100\,W$
	Decimal	Decimal	Decimal	Percent	Percent	Percent	Percent	Percent
1961-1990	0.099	0.052		24.79	188.39	2.59	95.49	92.90
1961-1965	0.092	0.051		24.92	168.37	−1.41	83.48	84.89
1966-1970	0.097	0.053		24.27	175.30	4.72	90.01	85.29
1971-1975	0.101	0.054		24.74	169.36	3.55	86.46	82.90
1976-1980	0.105	0.053	−0.047	26.05	173.91	1.79	87.85	86.06
1981-1985	0.100	0.048	0.015	23.59	194.17	1.36	97.77	96.41
1986-1990	0.100	0.050	−0.031	25.15	249.20	5.51	127.36	121.85

Note: Each entry is an annual average over the corresponding period.

averages the growth rates across all nine kinds of capital, never drops below 8.80 percent. Labor productivity grows at ferocious rates reaching highs of 9.79 percent and 8.36 percent for 1961-1965 and 1976-1980 respectively and posting 6.03 percent overall. Along the same line homogeneous-shay capital deepens at the $100\,\hat{j}_1$ rate of 5.40 percent on balance as the average deepening rate $100\,\hat{j}_m$ computed across all capital types equals 8.99 percent on balance. Plainly the recent economic history of Hong Kong portrays phenomenal growth of output, labor productivity and physical capital. By contrast its depiction of the growth in labor quantity and labor quality is considerably more moderated.

Much of the economic life of Hong Kong revolves around international trade. Statistics from PWT confirm the point. For instance, real exports amount to 95.49 percent of real GDP generally and surpass 125 percent in the 1986-1990 half-decade. Series $100X$ has that information. Analogously series $100W$ shows that real imports represent 92.90 percent of real GDP across the board and reach beyond 120 percent in the 1986-1990 period. Net exports in relation to real GDP, the $100N$ yardstick, assume earthly magnitudes around 3 percent, but openness, the $100U$ series that sums the export and import percentages, orbits well beyond the 160 percent mark. Trade is not an economic afterthought in Hong Kong.

Other features in the profile of the Hong Kong Tiger relate to the labor intensive nature of production. Stood on its head, labor intensiveness suggests capital deficiency, which can be verified by comparing the marginal product of efficient capital against the real rate of interest. The marginal product, either M_1 for homogeneous-shays or M_m for the average across all capital types, observes the schedule $\alpha Y/J$ and uses α values estimated by the regression procedure described anon. The real rate of interest r equals the difference between the nominal rate published by the Asian Development Bank (1994) and the GDP inflation rate recorded by the International Monetary Fund (1996). Inasmuch as $M_1 > r$ and $M_m > r$ consistently over the half-decades for which r data exist, the usual optimization logic holds that Hong Kong machinery is deficient in number. In addition, given the size of the inequalities, that same logic implies that the deficiency is more than slight. From the size of the saving coefficient s, calculated via PWT in customary fashion as output net of personal and government consumption, the Tiger appears to have a sense of thrift fit to handle the situation.

4 ACCOUNTING FOR GROWTH

The growth success of Hong Kong has been truly remarkable. Explaining that success calls for an accounting of growth shares in a manner described by equations (7.6) and (7.8). Fundamental to that accounting are estimates for the underlying parameters.

Estimation proceeds by using weighted least squares to fit labor productivity equation (7.5) to a sample of 4240 observations covering 120 countries over the period 1951 to 1990. The enormously broadened scope of the inquiry is intended to improve the reliability of the estimates. However broadening coverage to encompass multiple countries, which can differ radically among themselves, recommends augmenting the productivity specification to allow for stage of development by means of dummy variables and to introduce into the $\hat{\zeta}$ term additional structural factors; namely, initial labor productivity y_o, the degree of civil liberty c, and the state of health care m. The y_o originates from PWT while c and m obtain from Barro and Wolf (1989). Coefficients of all three variables should be negative. In keeping with the notion of convergence discussed by Barro (1991: 407-9), nations with lower initial labor productivity levels should have higher productivity growth. Likewise reduced liberty, measured by higher values for the index c, and worsened health conditions, measured by increases in mortality rate m, should compromise growth. Trade volume F, the original component of $\hat{\zeta}$, is tracked by openness U to capture both dimensions of trade. By hypothesis (7.4), its coefficient should be positive.

Since there are nine kinds of capital in the data file, the augmented regression is run nine times. However the results do not vary much across types, and therefore the findings for homogeneous shays can be understood as representative. Specifically for Hong Kong

$$\underset{}{\hat{y}} = \underset{[5.089]}{0.0447} - \underset{[-2.975]}{3.2 \cdot 10^{-6}\, y_o} - \underset{[-4.962]}{0.0050\, c} - \underset{[-4.133]}{0.0169\, m} + \underset{[5.395]}{0.0835\hat{E}} + \underset{[3.173]}{0.2777\,\hat{j}_1} + \underset{[6.169]}{0.0235U}, \qquad (7.14)$$

with $R^2 = 0.074$, F = 42.45, and DW = 1.92. Brackets contain the Student-t values. Derivable from the $\hat{E}$ and $\hat{j}_1$ coefficients is an estimate for the knowledge elasticity θ, which amounts to 0.1157. Evidently, then, regression (7.14) confirms all hypotheses regarding coefficient signs and magnitudes. Further aspects of the regression work are discussed by Gapinski (1997a: 79-82).

With the parameter estimates in hand, the growth shares cascade from equations (7.6) and (7.8) after netting from output growth $\hat{Y}$ the intercept and structural terms y_o, c, and m of equation (7.14). The percentages appear in Table 7.2. To permit a sensitivity analysis, two renderings are presented, one for homogeneous-shay capital J_1 and one for mean capital J_m. The first rendering presumes that $\mu = 0$ and coincides with the view of Kim and Lau (1994: 235, 246, 249, 251) that technical progress in Hong Kong is weak at best. The second rendering averages, over all nine capital variants, shares calculated on the basis of the corresponding coefficients. It offers a more generous interpretation of capital quality.

As Table 7.2 reports, the shares for output growth under homogeneous shays typically rank trade as the most important determinant followed second by efficient capital and third by total labor. Over the 30 year period, trade accounts for 49.8 percent of output growth compared against

Table 7.2 Growth shares for Hong Kong

Period	Output Growth Share Due to							Labor Productivity Growth Share Due to				
	Labor			Capital			Foreign Trade	Labor Quality	Capital			Foreign Trade
	Total	Quantity	Quality	Efficient	Quantity	Quality			Efficient	Quantity	Quality	
	Homogeneous-Shay Capital, J_1											
1961-1990	24.5	23.0	1.5	25.7	25.7	0.0	49.8	1.9	33.4	33.4	0.0	64.7
1961-1965	25.5	26.6	−1.1	29.2	29.2	0.0	45.3	−1.5	39.8	39.8	0.0	61.7
1966-1970	19.3	18.1	1.2	25.7	25.7	0.0	55.0	1.5	31.4	31.4	0.0	67.1
1971-1975	30.9	29.3	1.6	24.6	24.6	0.0	44.5	2.2	34.8	34.8	0.0	63.0
1976-1980	34.3	31.3	3.0	26.1	26.1	0.0	39.7	4.3	38.0	38.0	0.0	57.7
1981-1985	21.4	19.3	2.1	26.6	26.6	0.0	52.0	2.6	33.0	33.0	0.0	64.4
1986-1990	13.2	11.3	1.8	22.2	22.2	0.0	64.6	2.1	25.0	25.0	0.0	72.9
	Mean Capital, J_m											
1961-1990	24.3	22.8	1.4	30.3	21.5	8.7	45.5	1.8	39.2	27.9	11.3	58.9
1961-1965	24.6	25.6	−1.0	35.4	25.8	9.6	40.1	−1.4	47.5	34.7	12.8	53.8
1966-1970	20.0	18.8	1.2	27.6	18.6	9.1	52.3	1.5	34.0	22.9	11.2	64.5
1971-1975	30.2	28.8	1.5	29.7	20.9	8.8	40.1	2.1	41.7	29.3	12.4	56.2
1976-1980	32.7	30.0	2.7	32.4	23.9	8.5	34.9	3.9	46.2	34.1	12.1	49.9
1981-1985	21.7	19.7	2.1	29.7	21.4	8.3	48.5	2.6	37.0	26.7	10.4	60.4
1986-1990	13.5	11.7	1.8	25.6	17.4	8.2	61.0	2.1	28.9	19.7	9.3	69.0

Note: Expressed as a percentage, each number represents an annual average over the appropriate period.

25.7 percent for efficient capital and 24.5 percent for labor. Its strength peaks in the last period, 1986-1990. There trade explains 64.6 percent of output growth while efficient capital explains 22.2 percent and labor, 13.2 percent. Narrowing the focus to the distinction between quantity and quality shows that quantity always dominates the corresponding quality by a substantial margin to the point where the five growth determinants tend to line up with trade first, capital quantity second, labor quantity third, labor quality a weak fourth and capital quality an inconsequential fifth.

The zero contribution by capital quality is dictated, of course, by the assumption of no embodiment. Relaxing that proviso raises the capital quality share at the expense of the others and boosts its ranking. As the entries for mean capital disclose, the capital quality share rises to 8.7 percent in the 30-year perspective and ranks fourth, a notch ahead of labor quality. Foreign trade stays first but capital and labor quantities reverse positions. In the end, the 30-year period has trade first, labor quantity second, capital quantity third, capital quality fourth and labor quality fifth. The years 1986-1990 begin with that ordering but return capital quantity to second place and move labor quantity to third. Nevertheless, for any period under either capital regime, trade leads the way followed at a distance by quantity, with capital preceding labor or labor preceding capital, and followed again at a distance by quality, with capital preceding labor in the less restrictive environment.

Labor productivity shares remove labor quantity from the determinants, and consequently the rankings, which carry over from the output shares, simplify in a logical way: trade first, capital quantity second, capital quality - when modeled - third and labor quality last. The details for the 30-year interval put the trade share at 58.9 percent, the capital quantity share at 27.9 percent, the capital quality share at 11.3 percent and the labor quality share at 1.8 percent. Respective percentages for the final half decade are roughly the same: 69.0, 19.7, 9.3 and 2.1. Thus, for either output growth or labor productivity growth, trade always matters most. Quantities always matter much less than trade but much more than qualities, and labor quality never matters much. These relationships spell out a rule of order for Hong Kong growth.

Since trade is both the leading cause of growth and, by equation (7.10), a component of TFP growth, TFP well may be a principal propellent of output and labor productivity. Table 7.2 presents the basic information. Grouping columns 3, 6 and 7 yields the share of output growth due to TFP growth whereas columns 8, 11 and 12 generate the share of labor productivity growth from that source. The results of those groupings appear in Table 7.3, which imparts numerical content to equations (7.12)

Table 7.3 Total factor productivity accounting for Hong Kong

Period	Output Growth Share Due to		Labor Productivity Growth Share Due to		Share of TFP Growth Due to	
	Quantities	TFP	Quantities	TFP	Qualities	Trade
			Homogeneous-Shay Capital, J_1			
1961-1990	48.7	51.3	33.4	66.6	2.9	97.1
1961-1965	55.8	44.2	39.8	60.2	−2.5	102.5
1966-1970	43.8	56.2	31.4	68.6	2.1	97.9
1971-1975	53.9	46.1	34.8	65.2	3.4	96.6
1976-1980	57.4	42.6	38.0	62.0	7.0	93.0
1981-1985	45.9	54.1	33.0	67.0	3.9	96.1
1986-1990	33.5	66.5	25.0	75.0	2.8	97.2
			Mean Capital, J_m			
1961-1990	44.4	55.6	27.9	72.1	18.2	81.8
1961-1965	51.4	48.6	34.7	65.3	17.6	82.4
1966-1970	37.4	62.6	22.9	77.1	16.4	83.6
1971-1975	49.6	50.4	29.3	70.7	20.5	79.5
1976-1980	53.9	46.1	34.1	65.9	24.3	75.7
1981-1985	41.1	58.9	26.7	73.3	17.6	82.4
1986-1990	29.1	70.9	19.7	80.3	14.1	85.9

Note: All magnitudes are percentages. Each indicates an annual average over the designated period.

and (7.13). Unmistakably TFP growth is a strong force even in the homogeneous-shay regime, where capital quality contributes nothing. Of the 28 entries for TFP 23 exceed 50 percent; that is, TFP customarily accounts for the majority of growth. This finding stands in sharp contrast with the assertion by Krugman (1994: 71) that TFP plays no role in Tiger growth.

Given the weak performance of capital and labor qualities, it should not be surprising to learn that the power of TFP comes from trade. Table 7.3 reports the magnitudes. In the homogeneous-shay context devoid of capital quality, trade contributes 97.1 percent to TFP growth over the 30-year horizon. Labor quality registers only 2.9 percent. When capital quality is introduced, trade's contribution drops but still remains at 81.8 percent against the 18.2 percent from qualities.

5 EFFECTS OF REVERSION

Many things matter for economic growth. By the Rule of Order, however, the determinants are not equally important, and hence an event that affects international trade probably would be more significant than would be a similarly powered occurrence that influences education. Some events are sweeping in the sense that they encompass multiple determinants simultaneously. By their nature they have the potential to alter growth greatly, and by its nature reversion falls into that category. Reversion may affect many factors. It may affect them unfavorably or favorably. It may affect them moderately or substantially. Or - perhaps - it may not affect them at all. Literally the possible outcomes of reversion are countless. Nonetheless some are much more likely than others, and the growth inquiry of the previous section can help to reduce the possibilities to manageable proportions.

Equation (7.14) of that inquiry focused on six factors: initial labor productivity y_o, civil liberty c, health çare represented by the mortality rate m, labor quality growth $\hat{E}$, capital deepening $\hat{j}_1$, and trade tracked by openness U. The first three elements y_0, c and m were givens behind the intercountry growth experiences, and hence they were appropriately netted out before calculating the growth shares for Hong Kong alone. Reversion, though, may alter even the givens bringing to five the number of factors that require attention: c, m, $\hat{E}$, $\hat{j}_1$, and U. Still five factors are hardly as formidable as 'many.' Initial labor productivity can be ignored because it is a bygone.

To deal with the magnitude of the reversion effects on the five determinants and thereby to provide a numerical reference for the notions of moderate and substantial changes, calibrations begin with the status quo, which defines the baseline situation. Through the years Hong Kong enjoyed considerable civil liberty reflected in a c value of 2.0. A value of 1.0 corresponds to free societies such as the United States, Japan, and Australia whereas a 7.0 represents the greatest infringement on rights. By that scale Hong Kong has been the freest of the Four Tigers. Taiwan's index has been 4.9 compared to 5.0 for Korea and Singapore. As regards health care, Hong Kong historically posted a mortality rate m of 0.0185, somewhat worse than the Taiwan and Singapore records of 0.0155 and 0.0175, respectively, but noticeably better than the Korea position of 0.0450. Thus baseline assignments for the growth given are $c = 2.0$ and $m = 0.0185$.

Baseline assignments for the primary determinants $\hat{E}$, $\hat{j}_1$, and U come from the 30-year period 1961-1990 in Table 7.1. Specifically baseline $\hat{E}$ equals 0.0158. That rate is the lowest among the Tigers, the highest in the family being 0.0347 for Korea. Still it is more enthusiastic than the anemic 0.0051 evidenced by Australia. The baseline rate for the deepening of homogeneous-shays $\hat{j}_1$ equals 0.0540. That figure also happens to be the lowest among the Tigers while Korea's rate of 0.1030 places near the top. Nonetheless the Hong Kong magnitude towers over the New Zealand mark of 0.0114. Rounding out the list is openness U, whose baseline rendering is 1.8839, second in the Tiger community only to the Singapore entry of 3.0741 and well above the Korea and Taiwan figures of 0.5322 and 0.7645, respectively.

The baseline marks serve as a center around which magnitudes representing the deterioration or improvement of conditions due to reversion can be established. Those bracketing values are chosen not from hypothetical musings but rather from actual accounts in the Asia-Pacific region. The logic behind such a strategy is that actuals found elsewhere in the area are likely to provide more realistic bounds for the new Hong Kong than would numbers created in a vacuum by some abstract criterion. Thus the worst case scenario for Hong Kong involves settings that rank among the least favorable conditions observed in the region. That is, c assumes the 5.0 value of Korea, m takes 0.0450 also from Korea, $\hat{E}$ uses 0.0050 as a stylized version of the Australia statistic, $\hat{j}_1$ presumes 0.0115 from New Zealand and U takes 0.7500 from Taiwan. By contrast the best case scenario draws from the most favorable circumstances in the area. More precisely, c repeats the baseline 2.0, m becomes the Taiwan 0.0155, $\hat{E}$ adopts the Korea 0.0350, $\hat{j}_1$ assumes the Korea 0.1050 and U equals 2.500 in tempered reflection of the Singapore extreme.

Averaging in stylized fashion the worst case setting against the baseline assignments produces a more modest vision of a deteriorated economic climate. Similarly averaging the best case against the baseline yields a more guarded sense of improvement. Variations on those four themes then depict other possible environments for the new Hong Kong. The reversion matrix in Table 7.4 presents 31 possibilities including the baseline to allow for perpetuation of the status quo.

Growth implications of the different environments are meted by two yardsticks, D and Q_h. Measure D is the difference in growth rates:

$$D = 100(\hat{y}_R - \hat{y}_B), \tag{7.15}$$

where $\hat{y}_R$ denotes the growth rate of labor productivity under reversion and where $\hat{y}_B$ signifies the baseline rate, which naturally presumes the absence of reversion. Both $\hat{y}_R$ and $\hat{y}_B$ derive from regression (7.14) by imposing the underlying conditions identified in the matrix. Measure Q_h is the ratio of productivity levels in the two situations h years after handover:

Table 7.4 Reversion matrix for Hong Kong under homogeneous-shay capital

	Underlying Conditions					Labor Productivity Effects			
Row	c	$100m$	$100\hat{E}$	$100\hat{j}_1$	$100U$	D	Q_h at 5 years	10 years	20 years
				Baseline					
1	2.0	1.85	1.58	5.40	188.39	0	100.00	100.00	100.00
				Moderate Deterioration					
2	2.0	1.85	1.00	3.25	125.00	−2.14	90.49	81.89	67.05
3	3.5	1.85	1.00	3.25	125.00	−2.89	87.33	76.26	58.16
4	5.0	1.85	1.00	3.25	125.00	−3.64	84.25	70.99	50.39
5	2.0	3.15	1.00	3.25	125.00	−2.35	89.59	80.27	64.44
6	3.5	3.15	1.00	3.25	125.00	−3.10	86.46	74.75	55.87
7	5.0	3.15	1.00	3.25	125.00	−3.85	83.41	69.57	48.40
				Substantial Deterioration					
8	2.0	1.85	0.50	1.15	75.00	−3.94	83.05	68.97	47.57
9	3.5	1.85	0.50	1.15	75.00	−4.69	80.10	64.16	41.16
10	5.0	1.85	0.50	1.15	75.00	−5.44	77.23	59.64	35.57
11	2.0	3.15	0.50	1.15	75.00	−4.15	82.21	67.59	45.68
12	3.5	3.15	0.50	1.15	75.00	−4.90	79.28	62.86	39.51
13	5.0	3.15	0.50	1.15	75.00	−5.65	76.44	58.43	34.14
14	2.0	4.50	0.50	1.15	75.00	−4.36	81.35	66.18	43.80
15	3.5	4.50	0.50	1.15	75.00	−5.11	78.45	61.54	37.87
16	5.0	4.50	0.50	1.15	75.00	−5.86	75.63	57.19	32.71
				Moderate Improvement					
17	2.0	1.85	2.50	8.00	220.00	1.54	107.35	115.24	132.80
18	3.5	1.85	2.50	8.00	220.00	0.79	103.72	107.58	115.74
19	5.0	1.85	2.50	8.00	220.00	0.04	100.19	100.39	100.78
20	2.0	1.70	2.50	8.00	220.00	1.57	107.47	115.50	133.39
21	3.5	1.70	2.50	8.00	220.00	0.82	103.84	107.82	116.26
22	5.0	1.70	2.50	8.00	220.00	0.07	100.31	100.61	101.23
				Substantial Improvement					
23	2.0	1.85	3.50	10.50	250.00	3.02	114.82	131.84	173.81
24	3.5	1.85	3.50	10.50	250.00	2.27	110.99	123.19	151.76
25	5.0	1.85	3.50	10.50	250.00	1.52	107.27	115.06	132.39
26	2.0	1.70	3.50	10.50	250.00	3.05	114.95	132.13	174.57
27	3.5	1.70	3.50	10.50	250.00	2.30	111.11	123.46	152.43
28	5.0	1.70	3.50	10.50	250.00	1.55	107.38	115.31	132.97
29	2.0	1.55	3.50	10.50	250.00	3.07	115.07	132.42	175.34
30	3.5	1.55	3.50	10.50	250.00	2.32	111.24	123.74	153.10
31	5.0	1.55	3.50	10.50	250.00	1.57	107.50	115.57	133.57

Notes: Apart from c, which is an index that ranges between 1.0 and 7.0, and D, which expresses growth rate differences by percentage points, the variables are denominated as percentages. Characterizations such as moderate deterioration and substantial improvement refer to the extent of change in the underlying conditions and not necessarily to the size of the resulting productivity effects.

$$Q_h = 100(\,y_R^h / y_B^h\,), \tag{7.16}$$

with y_R^h and y_B^h signifying respectively labor productivity levels under reversion and along baseline h years out. But because the productivities are identical at the moment of the event, it follows that smooth growth at the rates $\hat{y}_R$ and $\hat{y}_B$ leaves

$$Q_h = 100\,[(1+\hat{y}_R)/(1+\hat{y}_B)]^h. \tag{7.17}$$

Worsened conditions mean a D which is negative and a Q_h which lies below 100. Improvement means the exact opposite. Of course, the status quo baseline has $D = 0$ and, for any h value, $Q_h = 100$.

The reversion matrix, although founded on homogeneous-shay capital J_1, changes little by changing the capital type to median machines J_5, and hence it has general applicability. Within that general framework it shows that the worst case, Row 16, is really bad. Although the rate of productivity growth $\hat{y}_R$ remains positive, it falls 5.86 percentage points below the baseline rate. Accordingly the productivity level drops to 75.63 percent of the baseline standard five years after reversion and continues declining to 57.19 percent and to 32.71 percent at the 10- and 20-year anniversaries. Two decades after reversion, labor productivity is about a third of what it would have been had Hong Kong stayed British. By the same token the best case, Row 29, is truly a best. Now the growth rate exceeds the baseline by 3.07 points, and at the twentieth anniversary celebration, the productivity level is 175.34 percent of what British governance would have provided.

Life is neither black nor white. Economic life under reversion probably is neither as black nor as white as the worst and best cases imagine. Moderation in impact seems to be more likely. Some suppression of civil liberty is certain, but sacrifice of health care is remote. Consequently a sensible estimate for c is 3.5 or 5.0; for m it is 0.0185. As regards the primary determinants, some retrenchment might be expected. The government's philosophy of positive nonintervention that helped to make the Tiger what it had become has given way to tighter controls that may be perceived to threaten property rights. Moreover administrative efficiencies gained from decades of learning by doing have been jeopardized by arrivals who have a different attitude toward the art and science of business. In effect the learning-by-doing process has begun anew thereby subjecting Hong Kong to the inefficiencies inherent in any maiden voyage. In the wake of the changed sovereignty, the primary elements may suffer across the board. Labor quality growth $\hat{E}$ may fall from 0.0158 to 0.0100, capital deepening $\hat{j}_1$ may slow from 0.0540 to

0.0325, and openness U may close from 1.8839 to 1.2500. Under these circumstances depicted by Rows 3 and 4 of the matrix, growth loses between 2.89 and 3.64 percentage points against the status quo. Furthermore labor productivity in five years declines to 87.33 percent or to 84.25 percent of its British norm. In 20 years it erodes to 58.16 percent or to 50.39 percent. Though higher than its value at the time when Hong Kong changed hands, labor productivity amounts to roughly half of the level that would have prevailed had Britain stayed in charge.

Yet it is also credible to argue that reversion can have favorable effects on Hong Kong. Surely the Panda recognizes the economic significance of the Tiger and feels a need to nurture and promote its success. Encouraging news that China indeed has the astuteness necessary to nurture and promote comes from its own economic indicators, which according to Wu (1997: 11-13) show annual growth rates for real GDP and real physical capital of 10.3 percent and 21.5 percent respectively. Such stunning achievements cannot be lightly dismissed. In addition, by wresting control from Britain, China relegated the handover to the past and drove the hesitancy surrounding that event into the past as well. At the same time it replaced hesitancy with a reaffirmed promise that the principle of one country, two systems would preserve the basics for enabling private enterprise to flourish well into the future. In the fresh, less uncertain climate thus created, Hong Kong may see education strengthened, investment quickened, technical progress stimulated and trade intensified.

Other points bolster the argument for a positive outlook. For instance the USA has a huge economic interest in Hong Kong and would not take kindly to the prospect of having that interest compromised. The Most Favored Nation status of China is only one lever of influence that America has at its disposal. But China's management of Hong Kong should have ramifications even closer to home; that is, on the island where the Taiwan Question remains unsettled. A favorable precedent in Hong Kong might facilitate a resolution across the Taiwan Strait. And it must not be forgotten that economic unification between mainland China and Hong Kong had been under way for years and had reached a stage where the lowering and raising of flags at the midnight hour may have been much more symbolic than substantive. In a sense true handover occurred long ago, and had economic disaster been an integral part of the process, it already would have manifested itself. It did not, of course.

Optimistic thoughts such as these suggest that the primary growth determinants, if they change at all, would rise rather than fall: $\hat{E}$ from 0.0158 to 0.0250, $\hat{j}_1$ from 0.0540 to 0.0800, and U from 1.8839 to 2.2200. With c taken as either 3.5 or 5.0 and with m holding at 0.0185, Rows 18 and 19 of the matrix become operative. According to Row 18 the rate of productivity growth rises by 0.79 percentage point prompting a productivity level that runs 15.74 percent higher in 20 years. Row 19, by contrast, shows almost no increase in either the productivity rate or level. Manifestly the setback in liberty almost completely wipes out the gains from the improved performance of the primaries.[6]

6 CONCLUDING THOUGHTS

The reversion matrix implicitly supposes that the effects of reclaimed sovereignty take hold instantly and completely. That assumption obviously oversimplifies practice where delays steer events. Interviews with merchants in Hong Kong just prior to reunification suggest little noticeable change over the first few years. In that case the h clock behind the Q ratio must be adjusted appropriately although the general conclusions remain largely intact. Further the matrix quantifies alternatives that have not been discussed. Those options have merit nonetheless because they help to define reasonable bounds for the consequences of reversion and because they may enable researchers to add a numerical dimension to their own interpretations of reversion.

How the Hong Kong Tiger actually fares in the land of the China Panda is a complicated matter that admits a range of alternative outcomes. Still, in the parlance of Holmes, the scientific use of imagination through growth theory combined with a material basis from empirical evidence lead to a balance of probabilities that narrow the outcomes to the more likely. Those prospects, however, disclose an asymmetry, where the potential losses exceed the potential gains. Such an asymmetry, grounded in theory and evidence, also has intuitive appeal inasmuch as any economy enjoying the best of times near the top of the growth heap sees little room to maneuver upward but enormous room to go the other way.

NOTES

1. Authorities for the aforementioned historical matters are Endacott and Hinton (1968: 14-32), Endacott (1973: 14-25, 91-3, 109-11, 260-3), Grolier (1993), and Roberti (1994: 43-4). The Palmerston quote is provided by Endacott (1973: 18). Holmes' acquaintance with opium is recounted in *The Man with the Twisted Lip.*
2. Happenings connected with the Joint Declaration or with the Basic Law are discussed by Grolier (1993), Roberti (1994: 42, 87, 112-26, 287-92), and Sheng (1997).
3. Examples of the mixed emotions over reversion can be found in Roberti (1994: 125, 133-4, 315-8, 322), Kahn (1997), Sheng (1997), and Stockwin (1997). The

quote is attributed to Tung Chee Hwa shortly before he became chief executive of the new Hong Kong. It is found in Tung (1997: 49) and cited in Kahn (1997: All).

4. Chou (1997: 6, 12-3) supports the idea that international trade causes economic growth although he maintains that trade works through investment activity and not necessarily through resource reallocation.
5. Further facts about the capital series, including evidence supporting the plausibility of the assumptions and results, are presented by Gapinski (1997b: 152-5). Other features of the data file are found in that source as well.
6. Authorities on the deterioration or improvement of the economic situation under reversion include Brauchli (1997: A1, A12), Brauchli and Greenberger (1997: A10), Edwards (1997: 34), Patten (1997: A14), Stein (1997: A10), Thatcher (1997: A14), and Tung (1997: 48-9).

REFERENCES

Asian Development Bank, Economic and Development Resource Center (1994), *Key Indicators of Developing Asian and Pacific Countries*, vol. 25, Manila: Oxford University Press for the Asian Development Bank.

Barro, R.J. (1991), 'Economic growth in a cross section of countries', *Quarterly Journal of Economics*, **106** (5), 407-43.

Barro, R.J. and J.W. Lee (1993), 'Appendix tables to "international comparisons of educational attainment"', mimeo, Harvard University, Korea University, and National Bureau of Economic Research.

Barro, R.J. and H.C. Wolf (1989), 'Data appendix for "Economic growth in a cross section of countries"', computer materials, Harvard University and Massachusetts Institute of Technology.

Brauchli, M.W. (1997), 'Homecoming: in many ways, return of Hong Kong to China has already happened', *Wall Street Journal*, 9 June, A1, A12.

Brauchli, M.W. and R.S. Greenberger (1997), 'As Britain steps aside in Hong Kong, U.S. steps in as chief western voice', *Wall Street Journal*, 2 July, A10.

Chiu, S.W.K. and Tai-lok Liu (1995), 'Hong Kong: unorganized industrialism', in G.L. Clark and W.B. Kim, *Asian NIEs and the Global Economy: Industrial Restructuring and Corporate Strategy in the 1990s*, Baltimore: Johns Hopkins University Press, 85-112.

Chou, Ji (1997), 'The contribution of trade to economic growth - a regression analysis from cross-country data', paper presented at the Taipei International Conference on Efficiency and Productivity Growth, Taipei, Taiwan, June.

Edwards, M. (1997), 'Hong Kong: countdown to China', *National*

Geographic, March, 32-9.
Endacott, G.B. (1973), *A History of Hong Kong*, 2nd edn, Hong Kong: Oxford University Press.
Endacott, G.B. and A. Hinton (1968), *Fragrant Harbour: A Short History of Hong Kong*, Hong Kong: Oxford University Press.
Gapinski, J.H. (1997a), 'Economic growth in the Asia Pacific region', *Asia Pacific Journal of Economics and Business*, **1** (6), 68-91.
Gapinski, J.H. (1997b), 'The growth of tigers, elephants, and other metaphorical creatures under heterogeneous capital', *Southern Economic Journal*, **64** (7), 147-66.
Grolier, I. (1993), *The New Grolier Multimedia Encyclopedia*, release 6.
International Monetary Fund (1996), *International Financial Statistics Yearbook*, Washington, International Monetary Fund.
Kahn, Joseph (1997), 'The motherland: on verge of turnover to China, Hong Kong taps into patriotism', *Wall Street Journal*, 23 May, A1, A11.
Kim, J.-I. and L.J. Lau (1994), 'The sources of economic growth of the East Asian newly industrialized countries', *Journal of the Japanese and International Economies*, **8** (9), 235-71.
Krugman, P. (1994), 'The myth of Asia's miracle', *Foreign Affairs*, **73** (11/12): 62-78.
Patten, C. (1997), 'How to keep Hong Kong rich', *Wall Street Journal*, 21 May, A14.
Roberti, M. (1994), *The Fall of Hong Kong: China's Triumph and Britain's Betrayal*, New York: John Wiley and Sons, Inc.
Sheng, A. (1997), 'Hong Kong will remain a free market after 1997', *Transition*, **8** (4), 1-3.
Stein, P. (1997), 'Hong Kong business and labor unions, united under UK rule, now face rifts', *Wall Street Journal*, 2 July, A10.
Stockwin, H. (1997), 'Uniform mourning for Deng: a politically stable China?', *Jakarta Post*, **24** (2), 5.
Summers, R. and A. Heston (1993), 'The Penn World Table: Mark 5.5', computer materials, Cambridge, MA: National Bureau of Economic Research.
Thatcher, M. (1997), 'No regrets', *Wall Street Journal*, 27 June, A14.
Tung, C.H. (1997), 'Masters of our own house', *Newsweek*, special commemorative edition, May-June, 48-9.
Western, D.L. (1996), 'The reality of Asia's miracle', mimeo, Curtin University of Technology, Perth, Western Australia, September.
Wu, Y. (1997), 'Productivity growth, catch-up and convergence in China's reforming economy', paper presented at the Taipei International Conference on Efficiency and Productivity Growth, Taipei, Taiwan, June.

8. Productivity and Efficiency in China's Regional Economies[1]

Yanrui Wu

1 INTRODUCTION

China's economic reform was initiated in the late 1970s. Since then the Chinese economy has achieved an average annual growth rate of about 10 percent. This growth is unprecedented in world history with the exception of small, diamond-rich Botswana (World Bank, 1996). Economic reform was the key to the Chinese success. The reforms can boost productivity growth in two conceptually different ways. One way is by increasing the efficiency with which the existing resources are utilized in production. Due to well-known systemic reasons, centrally planned economies like the Chinese economy produce well below their best practice outputs. Economic reform aims to raise production close to the frontier (that is improvement in technical efficiency). Another way to boost productivity growth is by stimulating innovation, that is technological progress. Centrally planned economies have recorded low levels of technological progress according to international standards (Lau and Brada, 1990). An investigation of China's productivity performance, in particular the two components of productivity growth, can provide valuable insight into the understanding of that country's spectacular growth over the last 15 years, and can thus enrich the current debate on the East Asian growth model.

In this chapter, productivity growth is defined as the sum of technical efficiency change and technological progress. The former refers to catching up to the frontier and the latter to shifts in the frontier. This decomposition allows the identification of productivity growth due to either improvement in efficiency (that is, catch-up) or technological progress (that is, innovation). The original technique was popularized by Nishimizu and Page (1982) who estimated a programming model. More recent empirical work includes Lau and Brada (1990) who also applied programming models, Fecher and Pestieau (1993) who estimated an econometric model in which the rate of technological progress is constant, and Färe *et al.* (1994) who employed a nonparametric approach. This study attempts to estimate a parametric, econometric model which distinguishes technological change from efficiency improvement and which is applied to the recently released Chinese statistics.

The next section briefly reviews previous studies of productivity and economic growth. This is followed by discussion of the modeling issues as well as the empirical models in section 3. The data issues and estimation results are presented in section 4. The interpretation of the findings is illustrated in section 5. Finally the last section concludes the chapter with some summary remarks.

2 PREVIOUS STUDIES

Recent interest in productivity studies was largely triggered by the desire of economists and the general public to explain productivity slowdown in the USA over the past decades, in particular, relative to Japan. Empirical studies such as Baumol (1986), De Long (1988), Dowrick and Nguyen (1989) and Wolff (1991, 1996) focused on investigating the long-run trend of productivity growth. Especially, it is argued that the relative productivity slowdown in the USA and European countries may be due to the natural process of convergence, as countries with a low level of productivity catch up to those with a high level of productivity (see Abramovitz, 1986; Baumol, 1986; Baumol *et al.*, 1989). While the convergence view is being questioned (Baumol and Wolff, 1988; De Long, 1988), there remains empirical evidence supporting the convergence in productivity, per capita income and economic growth.

The convergence debate has recently been extended to studies of the high performing economies in East Asia. In particular empirical studies of East Asian economies have focused on examining the contribution of total factor productivity to economic growth. On the one hand, it is argued that the rate of productivity growth in the East Asian NICs is not high even though the growth of output and manufacturing exports in these countries is unprecedented (Young, 1995). This line of thinking is supported by Kim and Lau (1994) whose findings have shown that technical progress was virtually zero in the NICs during the postwar growth period. On the other hand, the World Bank (1993) and other authors have shown empirical evidence of rapid productivity growth in the high-performing Asian economies (HPAEs).[2] The existing literature covers both cross-country and industry studies. Several authors also presented empirical analyses of regional economies within countries.[3]

Empirical studies of productivity performance in the Chinese economy are more sector-oriented. There is an abundant literature on China's agricultural and industrial productivity.[4] It is now widely accepted that agricultural productivity increased considerably after the initiative of economic reform in 1979, in particular in the first half of the 1980s (McMillan *et al.*, 1989; Lin, 1992; Wu, 1995). However researchers are still uncertain about whether industrial productivity has increased since the reform. Early studies such as the World Bank (1985), Tidrick (1986), and Chow (1985) argued that industrial TFP declined in the initial years of the reform. However, more recent studies including Chen *et al.* (1988), Jefferson, Rawski and Zheng (1992, 1996) presented evidence of significant TFP growth during the reform period. Economy-wide studies are rare, with the exception of Wei (1995) and Fleisher and Chen (1997) who used regional and city-level data, respectively, and Borensztein and Ostry (1996) who employed a simple growth-accounting method. This study attempts to extend previous work and shed some light on the issues associated with productivity convergence, catch-up and growth using China regional economies as the setting.

3 ESTIMATING PRODUCTIVITY GROWTH

Conceptual Issues

The econometric model used in this study, hereafter called the frontier model, is related to the concept of output-oriented technical efficiency first proposed by Farrell (1957) and popularized by Aigner, Lovell and Schmidt (1977), and Meeusen and van den Broeck (1977).[5] The important difference between the traditional growth accounting method and the production frontier technique is that the latter allows for production below the best practice output. The panel data version of this model can be presented as follows:

$$y_{it}^F = f(x_{it}, t) \ , \ t = 1, \ldots, T \text{ and } i = 1, \ldots, N \qquad (8.1)$$

where y_{it}^F represents the frontier production level or the so-called 'best practice' output for the *i*th country or region at time t, given technology $f(\cdot)$. Then any observed output y_{it}, given input x_{it}, may be expressed as

$$y_{it} = y_{it}^F TE_{it} = f(x_{it}, t) TE_{it} \qquad (8.2)$$

where TE_{it} indicates technical efficiency, defined as the ratio of the observed output over the best practice output. Equation (8.2) can be transformed into

$$\dot{y}_{it} = f_X x_{it} + f_t + \dot{TE}_{it} \qquad (8.3)$$

where dotted variables denote time derivatives, and f_x and f_t represent, respectively, output elasticities with respect to x and t.

Solow (1957) attributed output growth to input growth and technical change. The decomposition in equation (8.3) enriches Solow's dichotomy by attributing growth in observed output to movement along a path on or beneath the production frontier (input growth), movement toward or away from the production frontier (technical efficiency change) and shifts in the production frontier (technological progress). This decomposition is graphically illustrated in Figure 8.1, following Kalirajan *et al.* (1996) and Nishimizu and Page (1982). Given technology, points a_1 and a_2 are the observed levels of output y_1 and y_2 at time 1 and 2 with corresponding frontier or potential outputs y_1^f and y_2^f at points b_1 and b_2. The difference between the observed and potential outputs in each period provides an indicator of technical inefficiency. Technical efficiency change between the two periods is then measured by the difference between TE_1 and TE_2 in Figure 8.1. Symbolically,

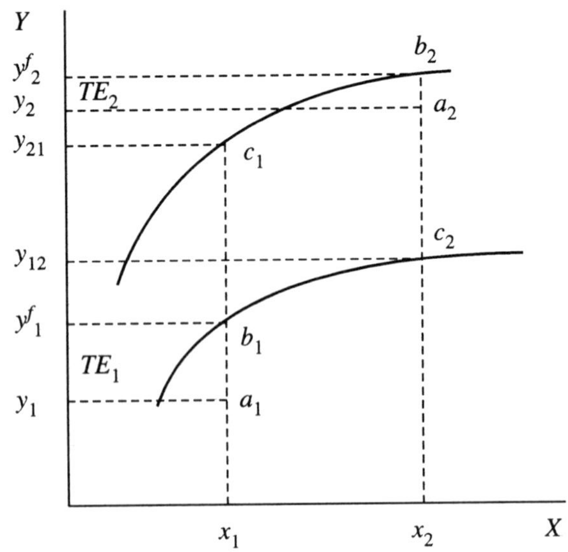

Figure 8.1 Decomposing output growth

$$\Delta y = y_2 - y_1 = (y_2^f - TE_2) - (y_1^f - TE_1) = (y_2^f - y_1^f) + (TE_1 - TE_2)$$
$$= (y_2^f - y_{12}) + (y_{12} - y_1^f) + (TE_1 - TE_2) \qquad (8.4)$$

Thus output growth $(y_2 - y_1)$ is decomposed into technological progress, $(y_2^f - y_{12})$, growth due to input changes $(y_{12} - y_1^f)$ and change in technical efficiency $(TE_1 - TE_2)$.

According to this decomposition, total factor productivity growth ($T\dot{F}P$), defined as the growth in output not explained by input growth, is the sum of technological progress and changes in technical efficiency, that is

$$T\dot{F}P_{it} = T\dot{P}_{it} + T\dot{E}_{it}, \quad t = 1,..., T, \quad i = 1,..., N. \qquad (8.5)$$

The conventional growth-accounting method cannot distinguish between technological progress and changes in technical efficiency, yet the former can be assumed to be the consequence of innovation or adoption of new technology by best practice countries or economies, and the latter due mainly to the effect of catching up. These two are analytically distinct and may have quite different policy implications, as argued by Nishimizu and Page (1982). Qualitatively this decomposition emphasizes a distinction between 'level' and 'growth' effects of economic reform on the long-run growth (Huang 1995; Lucas, 1988). On the one hand, the level effect of economic reform causes upward shifts in actual production (that is movement towards the frontier). On the other hand, the growth effect implies that economic reform not only raises the level of production in the short run but also stimulates technological progress and hence leads to sustained growth in the economy. The fundamental difference between these two effects is that level effects can be drawn out over time but not growth effects which can be large and sustainable.

Isolation of changes in efficiency and technological progress is also embodied in the Malmquist productivity approach. This approach has recently attracted a lot of interest and has been widely used in empirical analyses partly due to the fact that it typically employs linear programming models.[6] Though this approach has a number of virtues, its main drawback is that it is deterministic (Lovell, 1996). In contrast, the econometric approach employed in this chapter is stochastic, and it is capable of distinguishing the effects of statistical noise from those of inefficiency.

Empirical Model

To estimate equation (8.5), consider the following specification of a frontier production function:[7]

$$\ln Q_{it} = \alpha_0 + \alpha_1 t + \frac{1}{2}\alpha_2 t^2 + (\beta_0 + \beta_1 t)\ln L_{it} + (\gamma_0 + \gamma_1 t)\ln K_{it}$$
$$+ \frac{1}{2}(\eta_1 \ln L_{it} \ln L_{it} + 2\eta_2 \ln L_{it} \ln K_{it} + \eta_3 \ln K_{it} \ln K_{it}) + \varepsilon_{it} \quad (8.6)$$

where

$$\varepsilon_{it} = v_{it} - u_{it}, \quad (8.7)$$

$$u_{it} = \varsigma_0 + \varsigma_1 t + \omega_{it} \geq 0, \quad (8.8)$$

$$\beta_0 + \gamma_0 = 1, \beta_1 + \gamma_1 = 0, \beta\eta_1 + \eta_2 = \eta_2 + \eta_3 = 0 \quad (8.9)$$

Q, L and K represent GDP, labour and capital stock, respectively; α_i's, β_j's, γ_k's, η_1's, and ς_m's are parameters to be estimated; ε_{it} is the error term combining the white noise, v_{it}, and the term associated with technical inefficiency, u_{it}; v_{it} and u_{it} are assumed to be independently distributed, and have normal distributions with zero means and variances σ_v^2 and σ_u^2, respectively; ω_{it} is defined by the truncation of the normal distribution with zero mean and variance σ_u^2 such that the point of truncation is $(-\varsigma_0 - \varsigma_1 t)$, that is, $\omega_{it} \geq \varsigma_0 - \varsigma_1 t$; thus, u_{it}'s are non-negative and obtained by truncation at zero of the normal distribution with mean $(\varsigma_0 + \varsigma_1 t)$ and variances, σ_u^2; and equation (8.9) ensures constant returns to scale.[8]

The above specification allows the estimation of both technological progress in the stochastic frontier and time-varying technical efficiency. The distributional assumptions on the inefficiency effects, the u_{it}'s, permit the coefficients of the two t-terms to be identified in addition to the coefficients of other terms (Battese and Coelli, 1995). The model constituting equations (8.6) to (8.9) can be estimated by the maximum likelihood method using the computer program, FRONTIER 4.1.[9] Finally, given the estimates of the unknown parameters, technical efficiency rates for the ith region at the tth period are computed as the conditional expectation of $e^{-u_{it}}$ with respect to ε_{it}, that is

$$TE_{it} = E[\exp(-u_{it}) \mid \varepsilon_{it}] \text{ where } \varepsilon_{it} = v_{it} - u_{it} \quad (8.10)$$

The rate of technological progress ($\dot{T}P_{it}$) for the ith region at the tth period t is given by

$$\dot{T}P_{it} = \alpha_1 + \alpha_2 t + \beta_1 \ln L_{it} + \gamma_1 \ln K_{it} \quad (8.11)$$

Both TE_{it} and $\dot{T}P_{it}$ vary over time and across the regions.

4 DATA AND RESULTS

Data Issues

The models specified above are applied to the panel data of 27 Chinese provinces during the period 1981-1995.[10] GDP data are from the statistical yearbooks of each province. Labor statistics are from the statistical yearbooks of China for the period 1985-1995 and are estimated for the period 1981-1984 by extrapolation. The total numbers of people employed are used instead of man-hours due to the lack of data on the latter. The data of net capital stock are estimated from gross investment in each year. For this purpose, the capital stock in the first period is assumed to be the sum of all past investments and a rate of 5 per cent is allowed for capital depreciation.[11] Symbolically,

$$K(1) = \int_{-\infty}^{1} I(t)dt = \frac{I(0)e^{\theta}}{\theta} \tag{8.12}$$

where $I(t) = I(0)e^{\theta t}$, and θ and $I(0)$ are estimated by linear regressions using the investment series (1981-1995). Therefore given a depreciation rate, δ

$$K(t) = K(t-1)\delta + I(t) \qquad t = 2, ..., 15 \tag{8.13}$$

GDP and capital stock data are measured in 1980 constant prices. The price deflator is estimated from GDP data which are available in both current and constant prices. The final sample has 405 observations. Summary statistics are presented in Table 8.1. Not surprisingly, over the past 15 years, Guangdong, the province adjacent to Hong Kong, had the fastest growing economy (14 percent per annum) followed by other coastal regions such as Jiangsu (13 percent), Zhejiang (13 percent), Fujiang (13 percent) and Shandong (12 percent). At the same time, these regions also showed relatively high growth in capital stock. The regions together recorded an average annual growth of 10 per cent in GDP, 21.5 per cent in capital stock and 2.4 per cent in employment. Among the regions, Shanghai had the highest per capita income of about US$2100 in 1995.

Table 8.1 Summary statistics of Chinese provinces

Regions	Code	Population (million, 1995)	Per capita GDP (US$,1995)	Growth GDP	Growth Labor	Growth Capital
Beijing	1	12.5	1343	10.0	1.9	20.6
Tianjin	2	9.4	1177	8.6	0.6	16.4
Hebei	3	64.4	533	11.1	2.6	19.5
Shanxi	4	30.8	428	9.3	2.3	15.3
Inner Mongolia	5	22.8	439	9.7	2.1	18.9
Liaoning	6	40.9	822	8.9	1.6	19.0
Jilin	7	25.9	525	9.8	4.3	19.7
Heilongjiang	8	37.0	656	7.2	2.1	13.0
Shanghai	9	14.2	2097	9.0	0.1	22.5
Jiangsu	10	70.7	879	12.7	1.3	26.3
Zhejiang	11	43.2	983	13.0	2.0	29.1
Anhui	12	60.1	401	10.8	3.0	19.1
Fujian	13	32.4	804	13.0	3.2	29.1
Jiangxi	14	40.6	357	10.5	2.5	25.8
Shandong	15	87.1	692	12.0	2.6	22.8
Henan	16	91.0	398	10.4	2.8	19.5
Hubei	17	57.7	499	10.1	1.8	18.0
Hunan	18	63.9	414	8.8	2.7	18.3
Guangdong	19	68.7	944	14.0	2.2	26.4
Guangxi	20	45.4	426	9.9	2.8	32.7
Sichuan	21	113.3	376	9.5	2.7	20.3
Guizhou	22	35.1	216	9.0	3.5	24.4
Yunnan	23	39.9	364	10.8	2.7	22.0
Shaanxi	24	35.1	343	8.4	2.5	15.5
Gansu	25	24.4	273	9.9	2.8	30.8
Ningxia	26	5.0	399	9.2	3.2	18.1
Xinjiang	27	16.6	605	10.9	1.7	18.8
China		1211.2	580	10.3	2.4	21.5

Note: US$1 = 8.3 yuan in 1995.
Source: *Statistical Yearbook of China* (various issues) and provincial *Statistical Yearbook*.

Estimation Results

The initial estimates of the parameters in equation (8.5) are presented in Table 8.2. All coefficients are statistically significant. The negative sign of α_1 indicates the deterioration

Table 8.2 Estimation results of frontier production functions

Parameters	Estimates	Standard Errors
α_0 (intercept)	1.3224	0.0898
α_1 (t)	−0.2381	0.0189
α_2 ($\frac{1}{2}t^2$)	0.0229	0.0021
β_0 (ln$L$)	0.3160	0.0354
β_1 (tln$L$)	0.0238	0.0061
γ_0 (ln$K$)	0.6839*	n.a.
γ_1 ($t$ln$K$)	−0.0238*	n.a.
η_1 ($\frac{1}{2}\ln L \ln L$)	0.2364	0.0252
η_2 (ln$L$ln$K$)	−0.2364*	n.a.
η_3 ($\frac{1}{2}\ln K \ln K$)	0.2364*	n.a.
σ^2	0.0554	0.0038
λ	0.6159	0.0504
ς_0 (intercept)	0.7032	0.0882
ς_1 (t)	−0.1475	0.0256

Notes: * These figures are derived from the restrictions on the coefficients.

of technological progress in the initial years. This is typical of all reforming economies. At the beginning of the reform, economic restructuring can actually retard technological progress. This probably happens due to the large changes in relative prices which may adversely affect the choice of factor inputs (Färe *et al.*, 1995). In other words, economic reform may have to undertake an initial cost as argued by some observers (Portes, 1992; Reynolds, 1987a). The positive sign of α_2, however, implies the acceleration in the change of technological progress. This will be discussed further in the following section where the estimates of technical efficiency, technological progress and total factor productivity are derived by applying the above-described techniques and where interpretation of the results is also presented.

5 INTERPRETATION OF THE RESULTS

For the purpose of comparison, interpretation of the results is presented in light of the regional economies.[12] In the following sections, a brief description of the regional economies is presented first. This is followed by comparisons of productivity and efficiency performance among the regions.

China's Regional Economies

According to the conventional classification, China is geographically divided into three regional groups, that is the coastal, central and western regions. This classification is also used in the present study. In addition, three large cities, Beijing, Shanghai and Tianjin, traditionally being classified into the coastal region, are grouped together in this study. Thus there are four regional economies in China (see Figure 8.2). The three cities group consists of the above-mentioned three city-based economies. The coastal region constitutes eight provinces situated along the coast of

Figure 8.2 China's four economic regions

China, that is Hebei, Liaoning, Shandong, Zhejiang, Jiangsu, Fujian, Guangdong and Guangxi. The central region contains nine inland provinces, that is, Shanxi, Inner Mongolia, Jilin, Heilongjiang, Anhui, Jiangxi, Henan, Hunan and Hubei. Finally the western region is composed of seven border areas, namely, Sichuan, Yunnan, Guizhou, Shaanxi, Gansu, Ningxia and Xinjiang. Summary statistics about those regions are presented in Table 8.3. It is apparent that the three large cities are well ahead of the rest of China in terms of GDP per capita. All four regions have achieved significant growths in capital formation in the past 15 years. The coastal and central regions have also recorded relatively high growths in both capital formation and GDP.

Table 8.3 Summary statistics of the regions

Regions	Population (million, 1995)	Per capita GDP (US$,1995)	Growth GDP	Labour	Capital
Three cities	36.1	1595	9.2	0.9	19.8
Coastal	452.7	758	10.8	1.5	20.7
Central	429.9	445	11.1	2.3	21.3
Western	269.4	354	10.0	2.4	17.8

Efficiency and Productivity: a Comparison

Technical efficiency estimates show that, as expected, the three city economies have been the most efficient (closest to the frontier). The scatter plot of technical efficiency rates is presented in Figure 8.3. As shown in this chart, China's economic reform has brought about significant improvement in efficiency, that is, a level effect as also concluded by Borensztein and Ostry (1996). The above estimates also show the tendency of catching up among the regional economies. However the potential in efficiency improvement has been almost exhausted in the 1990s. This is clearly demonstrated in Figure 8.4 which shows the rate of efficiency changes over time. The rate of efficiency improvement has declined significantly over time. It seems that economic growth in the future will mainly rely on innovation, that is technological progress which, in contrast, may continue indefinitely.

As for technological progress, the (estimated) record for the Chinese regions is a poor one (Figure 8.5). As discussed earlier, the results show that economic reform has overshadowed technological progress in

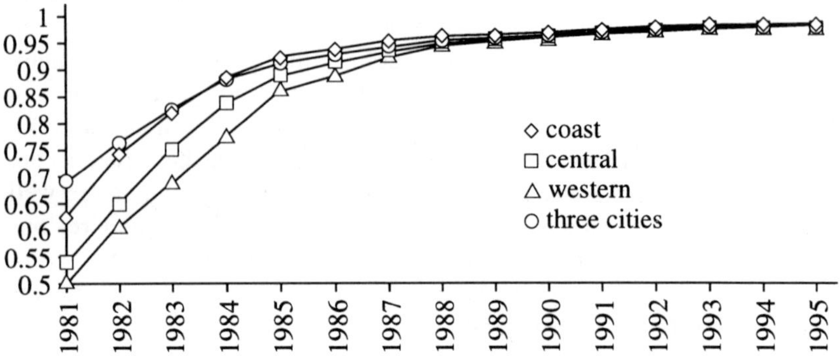

Figure 8.3 Technical efficiency in China's regional economies, 1981-1995

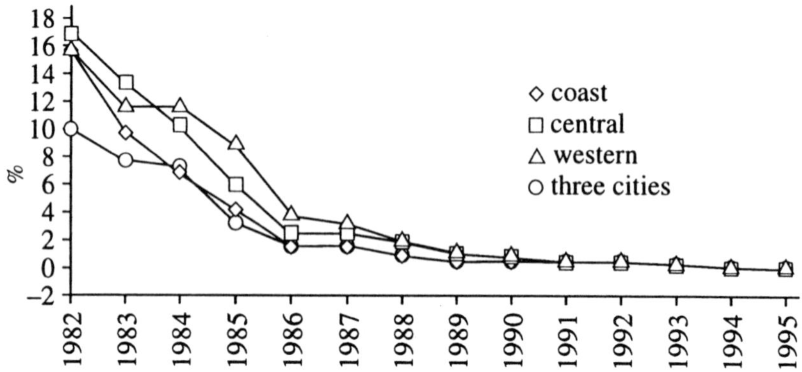

Figure 8.4 Rate of TE changes in China's regional economies, 1982-1995

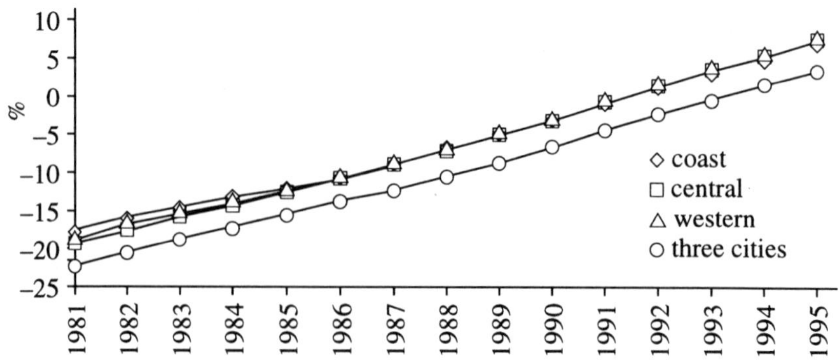

Figure 8.5 Technological progress in China's regional economies, 1981-1995

exchange for efficiency improvements. In the decade of the 1980s, all regional economies registered poor technological progress according to the estimates in this study. Significant technological progress has not been recorded until the early 1990s in all regions. This process coincided with the takeoff of the Chinese economy which recorded an average annual growth rate of 12 per cent during 1991-1995. In particular, the three city economies have the worst record of technological progress among the regions. There are three possible explanations for this. First, these city economies all have a dominant urban, state sector which has undergone the painful changes during the reform. Second, it is commonly accepted that China's rural reform in the late 1970s was successful in raising agricultural income and productivity (McMillan *et al.* 1989; Lin 1992). The three largest cities might have gained less from the rural success due to their relatively small agricultural sectors. Third, other regions have performed better in terms of technological progress perhaps because they have exploited the so-called 'advantages of backwardness'. As Abramovitz (1986) argued, backwardness may carry an opportunity for modernization in disembodied, as well as embodied, technology. Regions who are behind may have the potential to leap forward and thus to catch up with the leaders.

Due to the dominance of technological progress, TFP growth has also shown a poor record among the Chinese regions (Figure 8.6). Positive rates of TFP growth were recorded only in the 1990s. However, the pattern of productivity change among the regions does show the learning process during the period of economic reform: as shown in Figure 8.6, the

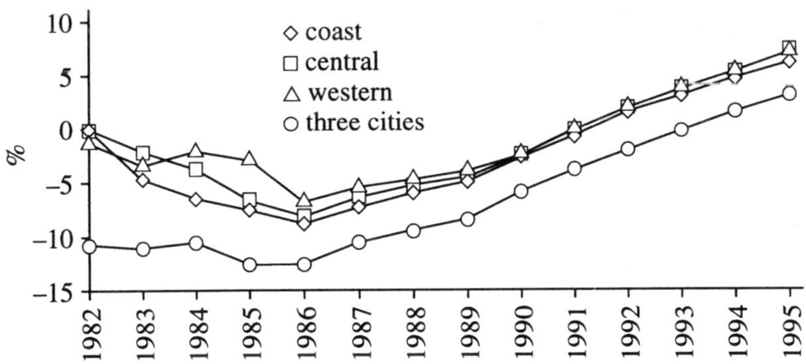

Figure 8.6 Total factor productivity growth in China's regional economies, 1982-1995

pattern of TFP growth among the regions forms a J-curve during 1982-1995. Immediately after the implementation of the reform procedures in the early 1980s, productivity performance deteriorated continuously and bottomed out in 1986 in most regions. This finding supports the view on the effects of the reform, as argued by some observers such as Lau and Brada (1990), Reynolds (1987b) and Woo *et al.* (1994). In addition, Figure 8.6 also shows that the three large cities which embody the relatively advanced economies have recorded the lowest rates of TFP growth among the regions. This again supports the argument of the so-called 'advantages of backwardness' observed in the rest of the world.

6 SUMMARY AND CONCLUSIONS

Applying a stochastic frontier technique to regional statistics, this study examines productivity growth in China's reforming economy during the period 1981-1995. In particular, the analysis focuses on the trend of technological progress and technical efficiency change among the regions. The principal findings are that, since the initiative of economic reform, the pattern of TFP growth resembles a *J*-shaped curve: productivity growth declined sharply in the initial years of the reform and recovered gradually over time. In addition, it is found that China's economic growth in the 1980s was mainly due to efficiency improvement and growth in inputs. This has however changed in the 1990s. Technological progress has now become an important factor propelling China's economic growth. This change is very favorable for sustained growth.

Specifically this study shows that technical efficiency performance in China's regional economies has converged rapidly since the early 1980s. This indicates the success of economic reform which helped stimulate the Chinese regional economies to catch up with the best practice producers. However the growth potential in efficiency was almost exhausted by the middle of the 1990s. Further growth in the regions will rely largely on improvement in innovation, that is technological progress, as has been argued by the World Bank and other China watchers. The record of technological progress among the regions is poor, especially in the 1980s. However the rate of change of technological progress has been positive. Due to this upward trend, most regions have shown a positive rate of technological progress in the early 1990s. As a result, the rate of TFP changes across the region has become positive in the 1990s.

Finally, although the findings in this study provide important insight into productivity performance in Chinese regional economies, further research is called for. Relative price changes may be an important factor influencing technological progress. Other factors may also be attributed to the rapid decline in technological progress in the early 1980s. The quality of regional statistics can be improved in the future when more detailed information is available. For example various depreciation rates could be used to estimate capital stock in different categories, and labour statistics could be based upon the employed man-hours instead of the number of employees, as is used widely in the literature at present. In terms of methodology, though the applied model has its advantages, there is still room for technical improvement. Furthermore, no matter how refined and how elaborate the analysis, 15 years of high growth in China is not sufficient to indicate high and sustained growth in the long run. Thus further theoretical and empirical work is required to obtain a better understanding of economic growth in China.

NOTES

1. Work on this chapter was supported by the Individual Grant Program, FECEL, UWA. The author thanks James Gapinski, Knox Lovell, Jacob Madsen, Michael Mcaleer and Paul Miller for their valuable comments on an early draft, and Li Shantong and Hou Yongzhi, Development Reseatch Centre, the State Council, P.R. China, for their assistance with Chinese statistics.
2. Other authors include Kawai (1994), Oshima (1995) and Sarel (1995).
3. Such as Holtz-Eakin (1993) and Evans and Karras (1994).
4. See Wu (1993) and Wu and Yang (1998) for comprehensive reviews of the literature.
5. Comprehensive surveys of efficiency measurement techniques are documented in Fried *et al.* (1993) and Lovell (1996), for instance.
6. The name of Malmquist (1953) productivity index was introduced by Caves *et al.* (1982). This approach has become popular largely due to Färe et al. (1989, 1992).
7. This function form was proposed by Christensen, *et al.* (1971), and Griliches and Ringstad (1971), and applied to productivity studies by, for instance, Nishimizu and Page (1982), Lau and Brada (1990), and Young (1995).
8. The original model was proposed by Battese and Coelli (1995). Other similar models include, for example, Reifschneider and Stevenson (1991), and Huang and Liu (1994).
9. Readers may refer to Coelli (1992) for further details about the FRONTIER program.
10. China is divided into 30 provinces. Data for Tibet are incomplete in the original source. Hainan Island became a province in 1988 and has been listed independently only since 1989. An initial plot of all variables against time indicates that there are serious problems with statistics from Qinghai Province. As a result, all three regions are dropped from the final estimation.
11. The same technique was also used in Chou (1995).

12. More detailed analysis is documented in Wu (1998).

REFERENCES

Abramovitz, M. (1986), 'Catching up, forging ahead, and falling behind', *Journal of Economic History*, **46** (2), 385-406.

Aigner, D.J., C.A.K. Lovell and P.J. Schmidt (1977), 'Formulation and estimation of stochastic frontier models', *Journal of Econometrics*, **6** (1), 21-37.

Battese, G. and T. Coelli (1995), 'A model for technical inefficiency effects in a stochastic frontier production function', *Empirical Economics*, **20**, 325-32.

Baumol, William (1986), 'Productivity growth, convergence and welfare: what the long-run data show', *American Economic Review*, **76** (5), 1072-85.

Baumol, W. and E. Wolff (1988), 'Productivity growth, convergence and welfare: reply', *American Economic Review*, **78** (5), 1155-59.

Baumol, W., S.A.B. Blackman and E. Wolff (1989), *Productivity and American Leadership: the Long View*, Cambridge, MA: MIT Press.

Borensztein, E. and J.D. Ostry (1996), 'Accounting for China's growth performance', *American Economic Review* (*Papers and Proceedings*), **86**, 225-28.

Caves, D.W., L.R. Christensen and W.E. Diewert (1982), 'Multilateral comparisons of output, input and productivity using superlative index numbers', *Economic Journal*, **92**, 73-86.

Chen, K., H.C. Wang, Y.X. Zheng, G.H. Jefferson and T.G. Rawski (1988), 'Productivity change in Chinese industry, 1953-85', *Journal of Comparative Economics*, **12**, 570-91.

Chou, J. (1995), 'Old and new development models: the Taiwan experience', in T. Ito and Anne O. Krueger (eds), *Growth Theories in Light of the East Asian Experience*, Chicago and London: University of Chicago Press, 105-28.

Chow, G. (1985), *The Chinese Economy*, New York: Harper and Row.

Christensen, L.R., D.W. Jorgensen and L.J. Lau (1971), 'Conjugate duality and the transcendental logarithmic production function', *Econometrica*, **39**, 255-56.

Coelli, T.J. (1992), 'A computer program for frontier production function estimation: FRONTIER, version 2.0', *Economics Letters*, **39**, 29-32.

De Long, J. Bradford (1988), 'Productivity growth, convergence and welfare: comment', *American Economic Review*, **78** (5), 1138-54.

Dowrick, S. and D.-T. Nguyen (1989), 'OECD comparative economic growth 1950-85: catch-up and convergence', *American Economic Review*, **79** (5), 1010-30.

Evans, P. and G. Karras (1994), 'Are government activities productive: evidence from a panel of US states', *Review of Economics and Statistics*, **76**, 1-11.

Färe, R., S. Grosskopf and W. Lee (1995), 'Productivity in Taiwanese manufacturing industries', *Applied Economics*, **27**, 259-65.

Färe, R., S. Grosskopf, B. Lindgren and P. Roos (1989), 'Productivity developments in Swedish hospitals: a Malmquist output index approach', discussion paper 89/3, Southern Illinois University.

Färe, R., S. Grosskopf, B. Lindgren and P. Roos (1992), 'Productivity changes in Swedish pharmacies 1980-1989: a nonparametric Malmquist approach', *Journal of Productivity Analysis*, **3**, 85-101.

Färe, R., S. Grosskopf, M. Norris and Z. Zhang (1994), 'Productivity growth, technical progress and efficiency change in industrialised countries', *American Economic Review*, **84** (1), 66-83.

Farrell, M.J. (1957), 'The measurement of productive efficiency', *Journal of the Royal Statistical Society*, series A, general 120, 253-82.

Fecher, F. and P. Pestieau (1993), 'Efficiency and competition in OECD financial services', in H. Fried, C.A.K. Lovell and S. Schmidt (eds), *The measurement of productive efficiency*, Oxford: Oxford University Press, 374-85.

Fleisher, B.M. and J. Chen (1997), 'The coast-noncoast income gap, productivity and regional economic policy in China', *Journal of Comparative Economics*, **25** (2), 220-36.

Fried, H., C.A.K. Lovell and S. Schmidt (eds) (1993), *The Measurement of Productive Efficiency*, Oxford: Oxford University Press.

Griliches, Z. and V. Ringstad (1971), *Economies of Scale and the Form of the Production Function*, Amsterdam: North-Holland Publishing Company.

Holtz-Eakin, D. (1993), 'Solow and the states: capital accumulation, productivity and economic growth', *National Tax Journal*, **46**, 425-39.

Huang, C.J. and J.T. Liu (1994), 'Estimation of a non-neutral stochastic frontier production function', *Journal of Productivity Analysis*, **5**, 171-80.

Huang, Y. (1995), 'Can institutional transition stimulate long-run growth?', Economics Division working papers 95/8, Australian National University.

Jefferson, G.H., T.G. Rawski and Y. Zheng (1992), 'Growth, efficiency and convergence in China's state and collective industry', *Economic Development and Cultural Change*, **40** (1), 239-66.

Jefferson, G.H., T.G. Rawski and Y. Zheng (1996), 'Chinese industrial productivity: trends, measurement issues and recent developments', *Journal of Comparative Economics*, **23**, 146-80.

Kalirajan, K.P, M.B. Obwona and S. Zhao (1996), 'A decomposition of total factor productivity growth: the case of Chinese agricultural growth before and after reforms', *American Journal of Agricultural Economics*, **78**, 331-38.

Kawai, H. (1994), 'International comparative analysis of economic growth: trade liberalisation and productivity', *Developing Economies*, **17** (4), 373-97.

Kim, J.-I. and L. Lau (1994), 'The sources of economic growth in the East Asian newly industrialised countries', *Journal of the Japanese and International Economies*, **8**, 235-71.

Lau, K. and J.C. Brada (1990), 'Technological progress and technical efficiency in Chinese industrial growth: a frontier production function approach', *China Economic Review*, **1**, 113-24.

Lin, J.Y. (1992), 'Rural reforms and agricultural growth in China', *American Economic Review*, **82**, 34-51.

Lovell, C.A. Knox (1996), 'Applying efficiency measurement techniques to the measurement of productivity change', *Journal of Productivity Analysis*, 7, 329-40.

Lucas, R.E. (1988), 'On the mechanics of economic development', *Journal of Monetary Economics*, **22**, 3-42.

Malmquist, S. (1953), 'Index numbers and indifference curves', *Trabajos de Estatistica*, **4**, 209-42.

McMillan, J., J. Whalley and L. Zhu (1989), 'The impact of China's economic reforms on agricultural productivity growth', *Journal of Political Economy*, **97** (4), 781-807.

Meeusen, W. and J. van den Broeck (1977), 'Efficiency estimation from Cobb-Douglas production functions with composed error', *International Economic Review*, **18** (2), 435-44.

Nishimizu, M. and J.M. Page (1982), 'Total factor productivity growth, technological progress and technical efficiency change: dimensions of productivity change in Yugoslavia, 1965-78', *Economic Journal*, **92**, 920-36.

Oshima, M. (1995), 'Trends in productivity growth in the economic transition of Asia and long-term prospects for the 1990s', *Asian Economic Journal*, **9** (21), 89-111.

Portes, R. (1992), 'Structural reform in Central and Eastern Europe', *European Economic Review*, **36**, 661-9.

Reifschneider, D. and R. Stevenson (1991), 'Systematic departures from the frontier: a framework for analysis of farm inefficiency', *International Economic Review*, **32**, 715-23.

Reynolds, B.L. (ed.) (1987a), *Reform in China: Challenges and Choices*, New York, M.E. Sharpe.

Reynolds, B.L. (1987b), 'Introduction', *Journal of Comparative Economics*, **11**, 291-4.

Sarel, M. (1995), 'Growth in East Asia: what we can and what we cannot infer from it', in P. Andersen, J. Dwyer and D. Gruen (eds), *Productivity and Growth*, proceedings of a conference, Reserve Bank of Australia.

Solow, R.M. (1957), 'Technical change and the aggregate production function', *Review of Economics and Statistics*, **39** (3), 312-20.

State Statistical Bureau, *Statistical Yearbook of China*, various issues, Beijing: Statistical Publishing House of China.

Tidrick, G. (1986), 'Productivity growth and technological change in Chinese industry', World Bank working papers No. 761, Washington, DC: World Bank.

Wei, S.-J. (1995), 'The open door policy and China's rapid growth: evidence from city-level data', in T. Ito and A.O. Krueger (eds), *Growth Theories in Light of the East Asian Experience*, Chicago and London: University of Chicago Press, 73-104.

Wolff, E.N. (1991), 'Capital formation and productivity convergence over the long term', *American Economic Review*, **81**, 565-79.

Wolff, E.N. (1996), 'The productivity slowdown: the culprit at last? follow-up on Hulten and Wolff', *American Economic Review*, **86**, 1239-52.

Woo, W.T., W. Hai, Y. Jin and G. Fan (1994), 'How successful has Chinese enterprise reform been? Pitfalls in opposite biases and focus', *Journal of Comparative Economics*, **18**, 410-37.

World Bank (1985), *China: Long-Term Development Issues and Options*, Baltimore: Johns Hopkins University Press.

World Bank (1993), 'The East Asian miracle', a World Bank policy research report, Oxford University Press.

World Bank (1996), 'From plan to market', world development report, Oxford University Press.

Wu, Y. (1993), 'Productive efficiency in Chinese industry: a review', *Asia-Pacific Economic Literature*, **7** (2), 58-66.

Wu, Y. (1995), 'Productive growth, technological progress and technical efficiency change in China: a three-sector analysis', *Journal of Comparative Economics*, **21**, 207-29.

Wu, Y. (1998), 'Is China's economic growth sustainable? A productivity analysis', working paper series, China Centre for Economic Research (CCER), Peking University.

Wu, Y. and H. Yang (1998), 'Productivity and growth: a review', in K.P.

Kalirajan and Yanrui Wu (eds), *Productivity and Growth in Chinese Agriculture*, London: Macmillan, (forthcoming).

Young, A. (1992), 'A tale of two cities: factor accumulation and technical change in Hong Kong and Singapore', *NBER Macroeconomic Annual*, NRT Press.

9. Total Factor Productivity and Outward Orientation in Taiwan: What is the Nature of the Relationship?

Sébastien Dessus*

1 INTRODUCTION

Recent econometric literature generally supports the view that outward orientation enhances total factor productivity (TFP) growth.[1] More uncertain is the question of how exactly imports and exports affect productivity. Much attention has been paid on this issue to East Asian countries' experience (mainly South Korea and Taiwan), conciliating increasing outward orientation and exemplary growth performances, but there is still disagreement about the link between the two. In a famous report, the World Bank (1993) supported the view that the promotion of exports had been a significant source of rapid productivity change, through greater access to best practice technologies. In turn, non-exporting firms could benefit from such information-related externalities. This proposition has been strongly criticized by Rodrik (1995) and others, on the basis of the empirical work by Young (1995) who concluded that productivity performance has been respectable in both countries, but hardly spectacular. These results were hence sufficient to reject the view that export promotion could have generated positive externalities, since substantial TFP growth was not observed.

While exaggerated,[2] these criticisms rightly emphasize the weakness of the theoretical background and the lack of robust empirical evidence on the relationship between exports and TFP growth. The hypothesis of

* OECD Development Centre, 94, rue Chardon-Lagache, 75016, Paris, France. The author is indebted to J.C. Berthelemy, S. Demurger, Y.S. Hong, D. van der Mensbrugghe, I. Nadiri, and the participants of the Taipei International Conference on Efficiency and Productivity Growth for their fruitful comments. The views expressed in this chapter are not necessarily those of the OECD. Usual disclaimers apply.

economies of scale is questioned for Taiwan, considering its small average size of firms in comparison with foreign competitors (Pack, 1992). If competitive pressures in export markets forced firms to purchase new technology contained in imported inputs, then the variable of interest should be the imports of technology - rather than exports - to explain TFP growth. Access to new technologies should depend on the technological gap between the leader and its follower. The question of the causality between exports and TFP must be carefully explored to identify a mechanism of spillovers from exports to TFP growth.[3] Finally, cross-section analysis, which has been widely used to assess the correlation between growth and openness, is now considered as a weak tool of characterization of dynamic processes and causal relationships. Indeed it does not allow controlling for unobserved country-specific effects, which necessarily biases the results (Caselli, Esquivel and Lefort, 1996).

This chapter aims at examining what consideration of the temporal information available since 1950 can contribute to current thinking about these issues for Taiwan, and especially about the role of outward orientation on TFP growth.[4] In order to do so, we first identify a cointegrated relationship between growth of value added and inputs - labor, physical and human capital stocks. This first step makes it possible to assess the significant contribution of TFP growth to GDP growth. Second, we explore econometrically three channels through which outward orientation could have encouraged such TFP growth:

1. through a learning by exporting effect
2. through an increasing use of imported technology, in a context of decreasing returns to imitation;
3. through an improvement of the allocative efficiency of factor markets, due to the progressive removal of external barriers and increased competition.

These three channels have very different policy implications, so that it is useful to distinguish the contribution of each to TFP growth; they are also very different in nature, thus econometric specifications must be adapted to each hypothesis in order to test its validity.

The econometric results strongly suggest that imports of technology and the removal of domestic distortions have played a major role in Taiwan's TFP growth. Conversely, export promotion, *per se*, did not affect TFP growth significantly, but it did have an indirect effect through its contribution to financing imports. We conclude that, although outward orientation policies indeed played a major role in TFP growth, the benefit of the latecomer advantage has been conditional on the design of adaptive educational policies within a highly atomized and flexible economy, and not the result of economies of scale, nor of external economies, due to the rapid growth of exports.

This chapter is organized as follows. Section 2 presents the results of the error-correction estimation of a Solow-augmented production function, and deals with the hypothesis of information-related externalities due to the growth of exports. In section 3, we report estimates of the determinants of the speed of convergence in productivity with respect to the USA. Section 4 assesses the impact of the removal of domestic barriers on factors' sectoral allocation. Section 5 synthesizes the overall effect of outward orientation on TFP and concludes.

2 ESTIMATING THE TFP GROWTH IN TAIWAN

Since Young's study the debate on the role of productivity in GDP growth, and its tacit policy implications, has been largely reactivated. It was, however, in a sense somehow biased by a strange conception of what an exceptional TFP growth rate should be. This is especially the case for Taiwan, for which, despite its rapid rate of accumulation and the most minimalist definition of TFP, Young estimates the annual growth rate of TFP to be equal to 2.1 percent over the period 1966-1990, which can hardly be considered as marginal.[5]

As discussed below, our results are close to Young's estimates, using a different methodology and other data. We estimate a Solow-augmented production function (Mankiw, Romer and Weil, 1992), employing the data set proposed by Summers and Heston (1991). Using purchasing power parity (PPP) variables makes it possible to compare countries' levels of TFP, in order to assess productivity convergence phenomena. Unfortunately the most recent version of their Penn World Tables (PWT 5.6) only covers Taiwan until 1990, so that recent years are not considered. The general augmented production function takes the form:

$$Y_t = AK_t^{\alpha} L_t^{\beta} h_t^{\gamma} e^{gt} \qquad (9.1)$$

where Y denotes GDP, K physical capital stock, L labor, h human capital stock, and g the average annual growth rate of TFP. The two first variables are measured in 1985 international dollars; L is measured in hours of work, while h is the average number of years of schooling of the working age population. K is computed using the perpetual inventory method with an annual depreciation rate of 4 percent. A level of physical capital stock is chosen for 1962, following Fry's (1990) application of

Harberger's (1978) method of estimation for the capital stock at the steady state. Sensitivity analysis on the depreciation rate and the choice of the capital stock level within reasonable confidence intervals confirms the robustness of the results. All the variables considered in this section are integrated of order 1, so that a linear combination of them is a candidate for a cointegrated relationship.[6] Sources for the different variables and methodological issues are annexed.

Table 9.1 reports different estimates of the production function. With respect to equation (9.1), we add two variables. The first one, *d*8890, is a dummy variable for the years posterior to 1987. This year most likely corresponds to a radical change of the institutional framework in which economic agents have been evolving. 1987 is the year of abolishment of martial law and of the starting phase of the democratization process. It also corresponds to significant improvements in financial liberalization, and marks a serious change in monetary, exchange rate and budgetary policies (Roemer and Ji, 1996). Whatever the reason, standard econometric tests of stability suggest considering this structural break. The second variable, *Yus*, is the GDP of the USA, measured in international dollars. There are at least two reasons to introduce this

Table 9.1 Estimates of the production function (1951-1990) (Dependent variable: Ln(Y))

	(1)	(2)	(3)	(4)	(5)
Intercept	−0.257 (0.17)	−6.454 (5.67)	−6.837 (4.08)	−7.473 (7.32)	0.013 (0.97)
Ln(*K*)	0.331 (4.05)	0.310 (4.45)	0.324 (4.05)	0.295 (4.61)	0.315 (2.57)
Ln(*L*)	0.526 (2.38)	0.575 (4.30)	0.620 (3.13)	0.705 (11.0)	0.557 (6.39)
Ln(*h*)	0.254 (2.36)	0.251 (2.83)	0.278 (3.07)	0.295 (4.03)	0.398 (3.50)
Trend	0.024 (3.08)	0.011 (1.42)	0.007 (1.02)	0.008 (1.09)	
d8890	0.089 (3.69)	0.093 (3.82)	0.100 (4.26)	0.096 (4.08)	0.063 (8.30)
Ln(*Yus*)		0.469 (6.06)	0.468 (6.00)	0.472 (6.01)	0.292 (2.50)
Ec(−1)					−0.767 (5.40)
Adj. R^2	0.9991	0.9995	0.9995	0.9995	0.5780
DW	0.7846	1.5932	1.6516	1.6563	1.7228
ADF	0.0169	0.0005	0.0003	0.0001	0.0075

Notes: Columns (1), (2) (4) and (5) are estimated with OLS. Column (3) is estimated using instrumental variables (IV) for *K*, *L*. Instruments are: hours worked in the USA; physical capital stock in the USA; world price of crude petroleum and total value of world exports. In column (4) we impose constant returns to scale. Column (5) is an error-correction model, for which variables are first differentiated, but Ec(−1), which is the lagged residual of column (4). Statistics in parentheses are t-Student, corrected for heteroskedasticity using White's method. ADF is the p-value of the augmented Dickey-Fuller test of unit roots for residuals.

variable. First it captures short-term external shocks that faced Taiwan (for which the US was the principal trading partner over the period), and may be considered as an adjustment capacity utilization variable. Second it can be viewed as a proxy for the exogenous rate of technological progress, if we assume the USA to be the technological leader over the period.

Columns (1) and (2) report OLS estimates of the production function. Column (3) reports the estimate with instrumental variables for the two inputs, in order to check for the exogeneity of the latter. The Hausman test of specification cannot reject the null hypothesis of exogeneity of the inputs at the 10 percent level.[7] Column (4) imposes constant returns to scale on capital and labor. The Wald test cannot reject the null hypothesis of constant returns at the 10 percent level. Conversely it rejects at the one percent level the hypothesis of constant returns to scale on accumulated factors (K and h), thus repudiating hypotheses of self-sustained growth.[8] All the four first estimates can be considered as relationships of cointegration, since the residuals are all stationary at the one percent level. Column (5) reports the error-correction estimates of the long-term relationship described in Column (4). It appears that the GDP adjusts rapidly to supply conditions, since three- guarters of an external shock is absorbed within a year. It also confirms the robustness of the long-term relationship described in Columns (1) to (4).

Estimated inputs' elasticities are highly significant and present plausible values. If it is difficult to appreciate the value of the human capital parameter, its significance and estimated contribution to growth confirms previous econometric works by Tallman and Wang (1994) at the macro-level, and Jiang (1992) at the micro-level. Labor and physical capital parameters can be more easily judged, since they correspond theoretically to the factor shares remuneration in GDP in a situation of perfect competition.[9] National accounts report an average share of 0.4 for physical capital for the period 1951-1990. Following Fry (1990) and Young (1995), we believe that this measure overestimates the real contribution of capital to GDP, since it includes invisible labor remuneration, such as the implicit labor income of employers, unpaid family workers and self employed workers, which is sizable in agriculture and services. The factor share of capital is probably much closer to 0.3 than 0.4, as suggested by our estimates and supported by previously cited econometric and accounting studies.

The verified assumption of constant returns to scale and our estimates makes it possible to define the TFP index, X, as follows:

$$X_t = Y_t / K_t^{0.3} L_t^{0.7} \tag{9.2}$$

Over the period 1951-1990, TFP has grown at an average rate of 3.16 percent.[10] Once the human capital accumulation is removed, 2.33 percentage points of growth still remain to be explained, or 2.26 for the 1966-1990 period, which is comparable to Young's estimate, or to the 2.0 percentage points found by Bosworth and Collins (1996) for the 1960-1994 period.

The question we address is to know to what extent TFP growth was due to an increase in external trade and its possible derived externalities. We first deal with simple hypotheses on the nature of the relationship between trade and TFP growth. We consider in the analysis the usual definition of TFP, rather than its definition net of human capital. This allows testing the interactions between greater access to international best-practice technology and the domestic endowment in skills. Table 9.2 reports simple attempts to capture the relationship between trade and TFP growth.

We tested several specifications, with two new variables, exports and imports over GDP, to explain TFP. It appears that these variables are not robust to the introduction of the activity variable of the USA. This would

Table 9.2 Estimates of the relation between external trade flows and TFP (1951-1990)(Dependent variable: Ln(X))

	(1)	(2)	(3)	(4)
Intercept	−1.015 (5.34)	−1.149 (9.53)	−8.263 (5.92)	−6.766 (5.71)
Ln(*h*)	0.395 (4.19)	0.396 (5.13)	0.272 (3.32)	0.323 (4.08)
Trend	0.015 (3.73)	0.016 (5.69)	0.008 (2.42)	0.007 (2.39)
d8890	0.125 (5.54)	0.106 (6.43)	0.090 (4.06)	0.101 (6.02)
Ln(*Yus*)			0.528 (5.40)	0.427 (4.79)
Ln(*EY*)	0.074 (2.67)		−0.019 (0.56)	
Ln(*MY*)		0.077 (3.12)		0.022 (0.98)
Adj. R^2	0.9953	0.9953	0.9969	0.9970
DW	1.2484	0.8984	1.6194	1.5975
ADF	0.0150	0.0087	0.0002	0.0004
χ^2	7.93 (0.16)	1.52 (0.91)	3.61 (0.73)	0.07 (0.99)

Notes: *EY*: Exports over GDP. *MY*: imports over GDP. Statistics in parentheses (except for the last row) are *t*-Student, corrected for heteroskedasticity using White's method. ADF is the *p*-value of the augmented Dickey-Fuller test of unit roots for residuals. χ^2 is the statistic of the Hausman test of specification, used to check for the exogeneity of external trade flows. In parentheses are the corresponding *p*-values for this test. All equations are estimated with OLS.

actually suggest that these two trade variables are good proxies for capturing the increasing sensitivity of Taiwan's economy to external shocks, but not *per se* responsible for an increase in TFP for structural reasons. The issue of exogeneity of these variables is also addressed. One can observe in column (1) that the hypothesis of exogeneity of exports with respect to TFP is almost rejected at the 15 percent level, while the introduction of the share of imports over GDP - does not seem to produce simultaneity bias. In Columns (3) and (4), trade variables are not significant in explaining TFP, so that their status of exogenous/endogenous variables is not anymore a sensitive issue.

These preliminary results indicate that external shocks and trends affect TFP, but equally that the channels through which it occurs are probably more complex than generally reported in the applied literature. Indeed, on the basis of our tests, we can reject the simple hypotheses of learning by exporting and importing. Other hypotheses, inducing more precise specifications, are to be explored for a better understanding of the nature of the relationship between TFP growth and outward orientation.

3 TFP GROWTH AND TRADE IN A LEADER-FOLLOWER MODEL FRAMEWORK

Convergence phenomena have been at the heart of empirical research on growth in recent years. It analyzes transitional growth toward the steady state, defined by human and physical capital stocks accumulated in a context of decreasing returns to scale. Less systematically explored have been the convergence phenomena in productivity. The theoretical principle is similar, since it assumes diminishing returns to imitation and adaptation of foreign technologies, which tends to generate a pattern of convergence: follower countries tend to grow faster the greater the technological gap from the leaders.

However it is most likely that being backward does not itself guarantee that the economy will catch up. This process is probably conditional, for a given technological gap, on the domestic capacity to import, use and diffuse advanced technologies. One can illustrate it with:

$$\dot{X}/X = Z\,\phi(X^*/X),\ \phi'>0,\ \phi''<0,\ \phi(1)=1 \qquad (9.3)$$

Where Z stands for the domestic conditions and policies which affect the speed of convergence in productivity, while X^* denotes the TFP level in the most advanced countries. In line with the literature, one can suggest that human capital availability (Pissarides, 1997) and significant trade activity with advanced countries (Coe *et al.*, 1997) are necessary conditions to catch up in productivity. The more the country trades with advanced countries, the more it is aware of the variety of suited technologies. Moreover importing technological inputs makes it possible to initiate the imitation process.

We test here several specifications of the determinants of the convergence speed, to assess the role of trade expansion in the productivity catch-up phenomenon. In order to do so we consider the TFP level in the USA as being the one of the most advanced country over the period of analysis. The TFP level in the USA, X^*, is computed the same way we did for Taiwan.[11] It is measured in the same units, so that levels of productivity are directly comparable. In 1951, TFP in the USA was approximately four times higher than in Taiwan. In 1990, TFP in the USA was only 50 percent higher than in Taiwan. One cannot therefore seriously contest the existence of a catch-up phenomenon in productivity between the two economies. Using traditional convergence equations (Mankiw *et al.*, 1992), we can define the speed of convergence in productivity, λ_t, writing the catch-up phenomenon as:

$$\ln(X_t) - \ln(X_{t-1}) = \lambda_t[\ln(X^*_{t-1}) - \ln(X_{t-1})] \tag{9.4}$$

The speed of convergence is stationary until 1986, averaging 0.032, but increases dramatically after, underlining the fact that the structural change observed in Taiwan after 1987 was not due to a significant increase in TFP of advanced countries. Table 9.3 reports several attempts to estimate the determinants of the speed of convergence, once first differentiated.

Among the set of structural variables tested,[12] only the variables related with imports are significant and robust to specification changes. Neither the share of exports over GDP, nor the human capital stock is significant in explaining the speed of convergence. The latter is surprising, and fails to corroborate previous results by Benhabib and Spiegel (1994). This could be due to the fact that the availability of human capital has never been a binding constraint on technological diffusion, if we assume that the availability of imported inputs and human capital were complement in the catch-up process.

The share of imports over GDP is a very significant variable to explain the speed of convergence (column 1, Table 9.3). It captures the positive impact of trade inflows on TFP. This measure is further decomposed in columns 2 and 3, where we introduce successively the share of imported intermediate inputs over total intermediate consumption, *CI*, and the share

Table 9.3 The determinants of the speed of convergence in productivity (1953-1990) (Dependent variable: $\Delta\lambda$)

	(1)	(2)	(3)	(4)	(5)
Intercept	−0.005 (0.94)	−0.001 (0.20)	0.000 (0.01)	0.013 (1.70)	0.029 (4.19)
Δ Ln (*MY*)	0.198 (2.72)				
Δ Ln (*CI*)		0.178 (4.50)		0.131 (3.36)	0.081 (2.25)
Δ Ln (*CA*)			0.091 (2.72)	0.059 (2.25)	0.038 (2.03)
$\lambda(-1)$				−0.345 (2.25)	−0.931 (6.34)
*d*8790					0.087 (5.81)
Adj. R^2	0.1611	0.2262	0.2336	0.4709	0.6924
DW	2.7101	2.6660	2.6884	2.1450	1.8473

Notes: Δ is the first-difference operator. *CI*: share of imported intermediate inputs over total intermediate consumption. *CA*: share of imported capital goods over total investment. Statistics in parentheses are *t*-student, corrected for heteroskedasticity using White's method. All equations are estimated with OLS.

of imported capital goods over total investment, *CA*. These two variables are also highly significant and very robust to specification changes. It is likely that the share of imports over GDP is a proxy for the two other variables. When the three vectors of transmission are introduced jointly to explain the speed of convergence, this variable drops out.

Our results suggest that the import of intermediate inputs was the main vector of technological transfers, since it combines a greater marginal impact on the speed of convergence with a more rapid growth than the imports of capital goods.[13] The impact of imported inputs to the catch-up in productivity may be explained as follows. First, the product mix changed to the extent that there was an increase in imported inputs. The proportion of agricultural and textile raw materials decreased in relation to inputs incorporating a more advanced technology, such as electric or electronic components and chemical products. In general, the share of imported manufactured inputs increased in relation to raw materials. The second possible explanation arises from the fact that the growing access of domestic producers to foreign markets increased the range of available intermediate inputs, enabling the set of constraints in which the factors' demand is optimized to be relaxed. Third, this significant contribution of imported intermediate inputs to TFP growth could reflect the fact that copying and 'reverse engineering' of a broad range of foreign products was a valuable source of technological learning and improvement during the earlier period of Taiwan's industrialization. When a Taiwanese firm copied the design of a foreign product, it had to rely on foreign suppliers for many key technology-intensive components. For instance, a typical computer made in Taiwan uses a foreign microprocessor. The processor, which represents the bulk of the technology embodied in the computer, is an imported intermediate input, but the computer is considered as a local capital good.

Imports of capital goods constitute another important vector of imported technology. This is not the case of foreign direct investment (FDI), which cannot be distinguished from domestic investment with regard to their respective productivity. The share of FDI over total investment does not influence significantly the speed of convergence. It is most likely that it did not constitute a major source of technological transfers. Foreign investors generally leant toward highly labor-intensive industry, which uses less advanced technology and whose products were mainly intended for export (Liang and Hou Liang, 1984). To illustrate this point, the share of imported capital goods in foreign investment dropped from 50 per cent in 1965 to 2 per cent in 1980.[14]

On the basis of these results, we can assess to what extent technological transfers played a role in TFP growth. In columns 4 and 5 of Table 9.4, we estimate dynamic equations of the determinants of the speed of convergence, enabling a predictor of the speed of convergence in level to be identified. The contribution of the imported technology to overall TFP, *Z*, is then obtained by comparing the actual evolution of TFP

Table 9.4 TFP, human capital and the imported technology over the long run (1953-1990)(Dependent variable: Ln(X))

	(1)	(2)	(3)	(4)*
Intercept	−1.104 (11.0)	−0.934 (10.3)	−6.052 (6.84)	−0.853 (5.87)
Ln (*Z*)	0.782 (5.93)	1.018 (8.10)	0.962 (13.7)	1.174 (4.56)*
Ln (*h*)		0.301 (3.19)	0.253 (3.19)	0.292 (2.89)
Trend	0.023 (13.5)	0.012 (3.45)	0.001 (0.51)	0.011 (2.78)
Ln (*Yus*)			0.405 (5.84)	
d8790				0.072 (3.68)
Adj. R^2	0.9942	0.9952	0.9976	0.9944
DW	0.4925	0.5696	1.0726	0.620
ADF	0.0086	0.0070	0.0012	0.0110

Notes: Statistics in parentheses are *t*-student, corrected for heteroskedasticity using White's method. ADF is the *p*-value of the augmented Dickey-Fuller test of unit roots for residuals. All equations are estimated with OLS. *: in equation (9.4), Ln(*Z*) is modified with respect to equations (9.1),(9.2),and (9.3). In this case, the dummy variable *d*8790 is not considered for the calculus of the effect of imported technology.

to what would have prevailed if TFP in the USA and the shares of imported inputs had remained unchanged from their 1951 levels:

$$\ln Z_t = \ln\{\hat{X}_t[\hat{\lambda}_t(M_t), X^*_{t-1}]\} - \ln\{\hat{X}_t[\hat{\lambda}(M_0), X^*_0]\} \tag{9.5}$$

where $\ln\{\hat{X}_t[\hat{\lambda}_t(M_t), X^*_{t-1}]\}$ is the predictor of the TFP calculated using equation (9.5) in Table 9.3, with X^* the TFP in USA and M the share of imported inputs (capital goods and intermediate inputs) for the period t. The variable Z therefore measures the dynamic gain in TFP resulting from an increase in the US's TFP and in the share of imported inputs over total inputs. This variable grew at the average annual rate of 1.08 percent over the 1953-1990 period, and is integrated of order 1.

We can now reintroduce the effect of imported technology in the log-linear framework of analysis previously developed, to control for the impact of thc others variables in the long run, such as human capital. Table 9.4 reports econometric estimates of the long-run relationship between the TFP and its major determinants. All the relations are cointegrated. The estimates of short-term adjustments towards the long-term relationship will be presented in section 6.

One can observe the significant impact of imported technology on TFP. Introducing this variable does not reduce the significance or the value of the elasticity of the TFP with respect to human capital. Adding the contemporaneous GDP in the USA reduces the residuals' autocorrelation, without affecting other variables. This probably suggests once again that this variable captures short-term external shocks faced by Taiwan. Finally we modify the calculus' mode for the variable Z, using equation (9.4) in Table 9.3, rather than equation (9.5). We can therefore test whether the correlation between the TFP and the imported technology variables is overestimated by the presence of the dummy variable $d8790$ in the latter. This appears not to be the case, since we obtain very similar results, assuming that the dramatic increase of the late 1980s is independent of the convergence phenomenon. Part of the explanation of this important increase could lie in the strong effort provided in the late 1980s by the country to develop its own capacity of innovation, as illustrated with the success of the Hinschu Science-Based Industrial Park in promoting high technology industries. The lack of sufficient statistical information makes it however impossible to test formally this hypothesis.[15]

On the basis of the results presented in Table 9.4, one can estimate that the increase in imported technology has accounted for approximately one-third of total TFP growth.[16] This decomposition is somewhat artificial (like any exercise of growth accounting), since this effect is presumably not independent from the others' sources of TFP, like human capital. One can also think that a high capacity of adjustment to the permanent shift in the production frontier - and its induced changes in sectoral factor demands - was a necessary condition to reap the benefits of access to best practice technologies and develop new comparative advantages. This is precisely the object of the next section, whose aim is to assess the role of factor reallocation in TFP, and to observe to what extent outward orientation may have reinforced the allocative efficiency of Taiwan's economy.

4 TFP GROWTH, FACTOR ALLOCATION AND OUTWARD ORIENTATION

Efficient allocation of labor and capital is a major ingredient of increased total factor productivity. The reallocation of rural labor in Taiwan toward industry during the early phases of development was probably a major source of increased average labor productivity. If these gains of allocation are *per se* theoretically static, or in other words, without influence on long-term TFP growth, it is most likely that they largely reinforce the impacts of the long-term determinants of TFP previously analyzed. Having identified the empirical impact of such gains on TFP, we try here to assess the role of increasing outward orientation on factor reallocation. Indeed the progressive removal of distortions theoretically increases the economy's allocative efficiency, by helping to identify sectoral comparative advantages.

It is possible to estimate the contribution of the sectoral reallocation of factors to the increase of TFP by using a method developed by Syrquin (1986). The theoretical framework is developed with a single factor of production (labor). Next it is shown that an extension to two factors follows from the same reasoning. The relationship between aggregate growth of the gross domestic product and the N sectoral products is derived from the definitions of value added, Y, and of average labor productivity, y:

$$Y = \sum_i^N Y_i \quad \text{and} \quad y = \sum_i^N y_i \gamma_i \tag{9.6}$$

with γ_i the share of employment of sector i (or L_i/L), Y_i the value added in sector i and y_i the average labor productivity in the same sector i (or L_i/L). Using growth rates gives, after some algebra:

$$\frac{\dot{Y}}{Y} = \sum_i^N \rho_i \frac{\dot{Y}_i}{Y_i} \quad \text{and} \quad \frac{\dot{Y}}{Y} = \sum_i^N \rho_i \frac{\dot{Y}_i}{Y_i} + \sum_i^N \rho_i \frac{\dot{\gamma}_i}{\dot{\gamma}_i} \tag{9.7}$$

The growth rate of value added, $\dot{Y}/Y$, equals the sum of the sectoral growth rates weighted by the sectoral share of total value added, ρ_i (or Y_i / Y). The growth rate of labor productivity, $\dot{y}/y$, is the sum of two components. The first term is the average of sectoral productivity growth rates, weighted by the sectoral share of total value added. The second term measures the contribution of labor mobility to the growth rate of labor productivity. This derives from the reallocation of this factor. If productivity in two production sectors is different, the greater the importance of labor in the sector with the higher productivity, the greater will be the aggregate productivity. A shift of labor towards the sector with the highest productivity will automatically increase the growth rate of average labor productivity, $\dot{y}/y$.

In a Cobb-Douglas production function with constant returns to scale, the total factor productivity can be written in logarithmic form as follows:

$$\ln(X) = \alpha \ln(Y/K) + (1-\alpha)\ln(Y/L) \tag{9.8}$$

where (Y/K) and (Y/L) are the average productivity of capital and labor respectively. Writing equation (9.8) in first-differences gives:

$$\ln(X_t / X_{t-1}) = \alpha \ln\left(\frac{Y_t / K_t}{Y_{t-1} / K_{t-1}}\right) + (1-\alpha)\ln\left(\frac{Y_t / L_t}{Y_{t-1} / L_{t-1}}\right) \tag{9.9}$$

Thus the theoretical framework developed by Syrquin can be generalized to a multi-factor production function. The total effect of reallocating capital and labor, r, is the sum of the reallocation effect of each factor, r_K and r_L, weighted by the respective elasticities of value added with respect to each factor:

$$r = \underbrace{\alpha \sum_i^N \rho_{i,t-1} \ln(\mu_{i,t} / \mu_{i,t-1})}_{r_K} + \underbrace{(1-\alpha) \sum_i^N \rho_{i,t-1} \ln(\gamma_{i,t} / \gamma_{i,t-1})}_{r_L} \tag{9.10}$$

where $\mu_{i,t}$ and $\gamma_{i,t}$ are respectively the share of capital of sector i in total capital and the share of labor of sector i in total labor at the period t. $\rho_{i,t-1}$ is the share of value added of sector i in total value added at the period $t-1$.

We compute the two effects of reallocation, dividing the economy in nine sectors.[17] The overall effect of labor reallocation was a 28 percent increase in average labor productivity (from 1951 to 1990), while the capital reallocation had virtually no impact (a gain of 0.03 points of percentage of annual growth of TFP) on its average productivity (from 1961 to 1990).[18] This last result supports the criticism that the overall efficiency of financial institutions in allocating funds has been far from satisfactory in Taiwan. It is believed that governmental intervention in the financial system created inefficiencies in the allocation of funds. The authorities controlled the major part of the financial system and adopted various price and nonprice interventions to accommodate the financial needs of certain industries or economic activities. In short, it appears that the two main criteria used by financial institutions for allocating credit were the enterprise's size and whether it belonged to the export sector, rather than anticipated capital productivity (Dessus *et al.*, 1995).

In what follows, we thus focus on the analysis of the determinants of labor reallocation, r_L. We test the impact of outward orientation on labor reallocation, once having controlled for the effect of human capital. It is known that education was one of the main factors influencing mobility and reducing the disparity of wages (Jiang, 1992). Access to information about the labor market and its opportunities, as well as adaptability to new tasks, on the whole, are favored by a higher educational level. The human capital variable, h, will therefore be introduced as an explanatory variable in the equation of labor reallocation effect.

The objective measure of increased outward orientation, understood here as a more intensive exposure of domestic markets to international competitiveness, is trickier. We retain two indicators. The first one, *MY*, is the classical import penetration rate, measured by the ratio of imports over GDP. The second one, *Dist*, is an estimated indicator of the domestic market protection inspired by Dollar (1992). It assumes that the real exchange rate (RER) is determined by factor endowments and trade policy. If all the goods were exchangeable and in the absence of distortions, the real exchange rate will always be equal to unity. However, the existence of nontradable goods should be taken into account, and their prices depend on the factor endowments necessary for their production. Thus, the method consists in estimating the RER of Taiwan (with respect to the USA) depending on its relative endowments (the ratio of GDP per capita in Taiwan over the GDP per capita in the USA).[19] The residual of the estimate represents the level of distortion.

Table 9.5 reports estimates of the role of increased outward orientation and human capital on labor reallocation, r_L, for the 1952-1990 period.[20]

Table 9.5 Labor reallocation, human capital and outward orientation (1952-1990) (Dependent variable: r_L)

	(1)	(2)	(3)	(4)
Intercept	0.010 (3.66)	0.008 (3.18)	0.009 (2.99)	0.005 (1.60)
Δ Ln (*h*)	0.190 (3.25)	0.202 (3.65)	0.195 (2.46)	0.214 (3.36)
Δ Ln (*MY*)		0.052 (2.51)		0.067 (4.06)
Δ Ln (*Dist*)			−0.026 (1.98)	−0.046 (3.12)
Adj. R^2	0.1482	0.3395	0.2031	0.4431
DW	1.4451	1.5569	1.9249	1.5481

Notes: Δ is the first-difference operator. Statistics in parentheses are *t*-student, corrected for heteroskedasticity using White's method. Equations (9.1), (9.2) and (9.4) are estimated with OLS. In equation (9.3), the autocorrelation of residuals is corrected in *MA*(1). The Hausman test of specification cannot reject the null hypothesis of exogeneity for the variable Ln(*MY*), at the 10 percent level. The corresponding χ^2 equals 0.55.

Estimates clearly suggest that education has favored labor movement toward the most productive sectors. Increased outward orientation itself has also favored this movement, as shown in equations (9.2) and (9.3) in Table 9.5. The share of trade inflows in GDP, *MY*, is certainly an imperfect measure of what it aims to capture, since it reflects basically what should be the outcome of the removal of distortions. Its status of exogeneity must also be questioned, but we could not identify a significant bias of simultaneity. Estimating the same specification with instrumental variables provides comparable results, and incites to consider that progressive import liberalization has positively affected labor reallocation. This appraisal is reinforced by the estimate of the same relationship, using the indicator of domestic protection, *Dist*, which bears the expected negative sign and is statistically different from zero at the 10 percent level. The combination of the two measures of outward orientation improves the general fitness of the model. This last equation also suggests that these two measures are not capturing the same information, and are probably complementary, since both are imperfect.

Conversely, export promotion (measured by the ratio of exports over GDP, *EY*) had no significant impact on labor reallocation towards the most productive sectors (results not reported). Once again, the observed correlation between trade flows and TFP reflects actually a relationship between imports and TFP, rather than between exports and TFP.

5 SYNTHESIS AND CONCLUDING REMARKS

In the previous sections, we have econometrically identified the contributions of what we think are the major determinants of long-run TFP growth. Of course, this is not an exhaustive identification, but it is most likely that human capital and technological catch-up have constituted the principal sources of increased productivity. Potential increases in TFP have in turn been maximized by a very high capacity of adjustment of labor markets to technological changes, itself enhanced by skills' endowment and the progressive removal of external barriers. One can synthesize in a general framework the two manners in which increased outward orientation favored productivity growth in Taiwan between 1951 and 1990.

In order to do so, we combine in an error-correction model, short-term allocation phenomena with the long-term determinants of TFP. Formally, we can write:

$$\ln(X_t / X_{t-1}) = \eta \ln(W_t / W_{t-1}) + \mu r_L + \varphi \ln(X_{t-1} / W_{t-1}) \qquad (9.11)$$

where W represents the set of factors affecting TFP in the long run, while r_L is the short-term labor market adjustment factor towards the long-term relationship. The error correction process only applies for the relation between X and W. The long-term relationship is defined by the estimate of the TFP level depending on human capital accumulation, imported technology and a linear trend (see equation (9.2) in Table 9.4). Table 9.6 reports several estimates of Equation (9.11).

Table 9.6 Short-term adjustment to the long-run determinants of TFP (1954-1990) (Dependent variable: $\Delta Ln(X)$)

	(1)	(2)	(3)
Intercept	0.001 (0.13)	−0.007 (0.72)	−0.011 (1.41)
$\text{Ln}(W_t / W_{t-1})$	0.977 (5.74)	0.916 (6.51)	0.940 (7.43)
r_L		0.639 (2.12)	0.510 (1.76)
$\text{Ln}(Yus_t / Yus_{t-1})$			0.183 (2.20)
$\text{Ln}(X_{t-1} / W_{t-1})$	−0.290 (2.45)	−0.377 (3.34)	−0.335 (2.83)
Adj. R^2	0.4999	0.5531	0.5909
DW	1.5781	1.8355	1.9009

Notes: Δ is the first-difference operator. Statistics in parentheses are t-student, corrected for heteroskedasticity using White's method. All equations are estimated with OLS. W is the predictor of the TFP in the long run: defined by: $\text{Ln}(W) = -0.340 + 1.018\ \text{Ln}(Z) + 0.301\ \text{Ln}(h) + 0.012\ t$ (see equation (9.2) in Table 9.4).

Introducing short-term corrections in the labor market significantly improves the global fitness of the model, and is in conformity with the theory, since the coefficient associated with r_L is not statistically different from the elasticity of GDP with respect to labor (around 0.7). Adding the activity variable in the USA allows for capturing short-term external shocks and real business cycles. In total, these estimates are econometrically satisfying, for their robustness and their high coefficients of determination. They permit the gathering of the different factors of TFP growth which have been identified in previous sections.

Among those factors it is clear that increased outward orientation has favored TFP growth, but the nature of the relationship is certainly more complex than widely stated. Using adapted specifications of the links between TFP and openness makes it possible to identify it more precisely. Our results provide econometric support for the view that imports of technology have constituted the main channel through which trade flows affected productivity. Conversely, we cannot find empirical evidence of the existence of any export externality. It does not mean that export growth had no impact on TFP growth, but that it must be viewed as a necessary but not a sufficient condition to enhance productivity. Indeed, export promotion has relaxed the foreign exchange constraint, encouraging a progressive removal of external barriers and the increased imports of technology (Esfahani, 1991). If one assumes that export growth was in part due to increased productivity, then one can imagine a virtuous circle between export and import promotion. This movement reaches a limit when the external sources of TFP growth are exhausted, which is the case when the technological gap with respect to advanced countries is filled.

Free trade and greater integration in world markets is assuredly a positive factor of development. But to maximize growth opportunities, it requires sufficient domestic capacities, which are not provided by export promotion policies. In Taiwan, the benefits of increased outward orientation have been conditional on the design of adaptive policies in the fields of education and labor market organization, but also probably in the fields of provision of infrastructure, financial intermediation, and research and development among others (Dessus *et al.*, 1995).

APPENDIX: DATA SOURCES

GDP and investment data for Taiwan and the USA are taken from the Penn World Tables (PWT 5.6) and measured in 1985 international dollars. Physical capital stocks are built using the perpetual inventory method, that is, $K_t = (1 - \delta)K_{t-1} + I_t$, with K_t the physical capital stock at the end of period t, I_t the gross domestic fixed investment and δ a constant 4 percent depreciation rate. The ratios of physical capital stock over GDP in 1990 equal 2.33 in Taiwan and 3.50 in the USA. Middle of period capital stocks, that is $(K_t + K_{t-1})/2$, are employed for the econometric analysis. Human capital stock (h) is taken from Chang (1991), who reports mean years of educational attainment of the civilian population aged 15 and over. The labor variable, L, is measured in number of hours worked. Labor data are taken from the Taiwan Statistical Data Book (DGBAS, various issues) for Taiwan and from the International Labor Office for the USA. Exports and imports variables are taken from the National Income (DGBAS, 1992), and are measured in NT$ 1986. In this case, the corresponding denominator is expressed in the same units. Sectoral data required to compute the reallocation effects are taken from the Taiwan Statistical Data Book for the GDP and labor, and from the 'Trends in multifactor productivity' (DGBAS, 1993) for the physical capital stocks. Sectoral GDP and physical capital stocks are measured in NT$ 1986 and sectoral labor in number of people employed.

NOTES

1. See Havrylyshyn (1990) and Harrison (1996) for a general presentation of such empirical work.
2. In a recent paper, Rodrik (1997) recognizes that one cannot rule out the possibility that East Asia has in fact experienced a tremendous amount of technological progress. One can also argue that technical change and accumulation are not independent. On the one hand, part of the technological progress is embodied in capital stocks. On the other hand, high rates of returns to capital stocks, due to TFP growth, certainly encourage capital accumulation (Fry, 1990).
3. Granger causality tests on macroeconomic variables (generally GDP and exports) have been largely used for this purpose (Xu, 1996), but suffer from major shortcomings: (i) they focus on short-term dynamics, and cointegrated relationships are rarely identified; (ii) they generally do not address the endogeneity issue and (iii) they deal with poorly defined theoretical specification, possibly generating omission bias. The treatment of microeconomic panel data is probably more adapted to address the question. In a recent paper, Bernard and Wagner (1996) found strong econometric support for the view that exporters in Germany were already more productive than nonexporters before they actually became exporters, but not for the reverse proposition that would claim that entry into the export market generates productivity gains.
4. The question of the impact of increased openness on capital accumulation is not

addressed in this chapter. It is most likely that the promotion of exports has encouraged investment (Pack, 1992), giving the opportunity for investors to expand their markets, but this phenomenon is by definition orthogonal to productivity changes.

5. Young's definition of TFP is minimalist in the sense that he considers human capital as a regular input that must be subtracted from value added to compute TFP. Young also adjusts for public sector output growth, and includes military personnel in labor, reducing *de facto* TFP growth.
6. We follow the sequential strategy of unit root tests proposed by Jobert (1993) to identify the order of integration for each variable.
7. The χ^2 statistic test equals 2.69, for 7 degrees of freedom. Its *p*-value exceeds 91 percent.
8. The Fisher statistic for the test of returns to scale on capital and labor ($\alpha + \beta = 1$) equals 1.47 (or a *p*-value exceeding 23 percent); the Fisher statistic for the test of self-sustained growth ($\alpha + \gamma = 1$) equals 13.28 (or a *p*-value lower than 0.1 percent).
9. One can admit this statement on the basis of the work by Hou and Wu (1985). They show that the dispersion of wages largely reflects the dispersion of marginal productivities among workers.
10. Average growth rates are computed by the regression of the logarithm of the variable considered over an intercept and a linear trend, so as to take into account all the statistical information.
11. We use a Cobb-Douglas production function with constant returns, with an elasticity of 0.3 for capital and 0.7 for labor. The GDP and investment data are from the PWT 5.6 database. The series for labor and hours worked came from the International Labor Office (ILO). The capital stock is estimated using the perpetual inventory method. Its average annual growth rate is 3.1 percent per annum, or the same order of magnitude as several other studies using different data: Nehru and Dhareshwar (1993) obtained an annual average of 3.2 percent for 1950 to 1990; Meyer-zu-Schlochtern (1988) found an annual average of 3.1 percent for 1960 to 1990 (updated); the OECD (1991) estimated that private fixed capital stock (excluding residential) grew 3.2 percent per annum from 1955 to 1989. The annual average growth rate of total factor productivity in the USA during the 1970-1985 period corresponds to the estimates of Englander (1988). An average of 0.16 per cent was found in this study for the same period (1970-1985). Englander estimated the growth rate at between 0.1 and 0.2 percent. Our estimate (an average annual growth rate of 0.88 percent from 1951 to 1990) is also comparable to the one provided by Maddison (1995), who estimates the TFP in USA to have grown at the average rate of 1.02 percent a year.
12. We tested the following variables, in level, logarithm and growth rates, for the period 1951-1986 and 1951-1990 to explain the first difference of λ : the ratio of imported capital goods over total investment; the ratio of imported intermediate inputs over total intermediate consumption, the human capital stock of total population, the human capital stock per capita (*h*), the share of working-age population educated abroad, the share of imports over GDP, the share of exports over GDP, the share of foreign direct investment over total investment. For each

variable, we tested several lag patterns and statistical distributions for the residuals. The ratio of the stock of imported physical capital stock over total capital stock was also tested, but the results were not convincing, since they were highly sensitive to the choice of the initial imported capital stock.

13. The share of imported intermediate inputs over total intermediate consumption grew at the rhythm of 1.8 percent a year from 1951 to 1990, while the share of imported capital goods over total investment grew at a rhythm of 0.9 percent a year. These growth rates are econometrically estimated.
14. Foreign investors prefer to buy used equipment on the domestic market, which is less advanced, the least expensive, easy to maintain, and the best adapted to the skills of the domestic labor supply (Schive, 1988).
15. Statistical information on R&D activity has only been available since 1970. One can refer to Dessus *et al.* (1995) for a more in-depth description of the research activity in Taiwan since 1950.
16. The contribution is computed assuming that the elasticity of TFP with respect to the imported technology is equal to one. The contribution is therefore equal to 1.08/3.16.
17. The nine sectors are: agriculture (1), mining (2), manufactured goods (3), electricity, gas and water (4), construction (5), commerce (6), transportation and communications (7), finance, insurance and real estate (8), and other services (9). The last sector includes governmental services. Sectoral deflators of GDP are only available beginning with 1961, but labor data are available from 1951. Rather than lose the first ten years of the sample, the same deflator has been used for all the sectors. A comparison of results for the two samples for the 1961-1990 period does not show any significant difference in the estimate of the contribution of the reallocation effect on increased labor productivity (23.8 percent with the sectoral deflators and 24.1 percent with the GDP deflator). The data came from the national accounts and are expressed in 1986 Taiwan dollars. For capital stocks, sectoral data is only available beginning in 1961 (DGBAS, 1993). The analysis only concerns eight sectors, due to the lack of information on the capital stock in agriculture.
18. The relevance of these calculations is confirmed by the regression of the growth rate of total factor productivity with respect to the reallocation of capital and labor for the 1961-1990 period. The results are coherent with the theoretical framework. The estimated coefficient for the capital (respectively labor) reallocation effect is 0.317 (respectively 0.643). The Wald test cannot reject the null hypothesis of constant returns to scale.
19. The RER variable is directly available in the PWT 5.6 database, as well as the GDP per capita of Taiwan and the USA measured in purchasing power parity. Detailed results of this estimation are available from the author.
20. Other factors have certainly favored the labor reallocation in Taiwan towards the most productive sectors, such as rural policy (Ranis, 1993) or the flexibility of production based on the large number of small and medium-sized firms. It is, however, difficult to assess their respective contribution within a time series analysis framework.

REFERENCES

Bernard, A. and J. Wagner (1996), 'Exports and success in German manufacturing', paper presented at the Eleventh Annual Congress of the European Economic Association, Istanbul, 21-24 August.

Benhabib, J. and M. Spiegel (1994), 'The role of human capital in economic development evidence for aggregate cross-country data', *Journal of Monetary Economics*, **34**, 143-73.

Bosworth B.P. and S.M. Collins (1996), 'Economic growth in East Asia: accumulation versus assimilation', *Brookings Papers on Economic Activity, Macroeconomics*, **2**, 135-203.

Caselli, F., G. Esquivel and F. Lefort (1996), 'Reopening the convergence debate: a new look at cross-country growth empirics', *Journal of Economic Growth*, **1** (3), 363-89.

Chang, C.C. (1991), 'The nine-year compulsory education policy and the development of human resources in Taiwan (1950-1990)', PhD dissertation, Maryland University.

Coe, D.T., E. Helpman and A.W. Hoffmaister (1997), 'North-south R&D spillovers', *The Economic Journal*, **107** (440), 134-49.

Dessus, S., J.D. Shea and M.S. Shi (1995), *Chinese Taipei: the origins of the economic 'miracle'*, Development Center Studies, Paris: OECD.

DaBAS, *Taiwan Statistical Data Book, various issues*, Taipei.

DaBAS (1992), *National Income in Taiwan Area of the Republic of China 1992,* Taipei.

DaBAS. (1993), *The Trends In Multifactor Productivity*, Taipei.

Dollar, D. (1992), 'Outward-oriented developing economies really do grow more rapidly: evidence from 95 LDCs, 1976-1985', *Economic Development and Cultural Change*, **40** (3), 523-44.

Englander, A.S. (1988), 'Tests of total factor productivity measurement', Economics Department working paper no. 54, OECD, Paris.

Esfahani, H.S. (1991), 'Exports, imports and economic growth in semi-industrialized countries', *Journal of Development Economics*, **35** (1), 93-116.

Fry, M.J. (1990), 'Current macroeconomic policy issues in Taiwan', *Tamkang Chair Lecture series*, vol. 80, Taipei.

Harberger, A. (1978), 'Perspectives on capital and technology in less-developed countries', in M.J Artis and A.R. Nobay (eds), *Contemporary Economic Analysis,* 42-72, Croom Helm.

Harrison, A. (1996), 'Openness and growth: a time-series, cross-country analysis for developing countries', *Journal of Development Economics*, **48** (2), 419-47.

Havrylyshyn, O. (1990), 'Trade policy and productivity gains in developing countries: a survey of the literature', *The World Bank Research Observer*, **5** (1), 1-24.

Henin, P.Y. and T. Jobert (1993), 'Annexe méethodologique', in P.Y. Hénin (ed.), *La persistence du chômage*, 259-89, Paris: Economica.

Hou, C.M. and H.L. Wu (1985), 'Wages and labor productivity in Taiwan', *Industry of Free China*, Taipei, May and June.

Jiang, F.F. (1992), 'The role of educational expansion in Taiwan's economic development', *Industry of Free China*, April.

Liang K.S. and C.I. Hou Liang (1984), 'Trade, technology transfers, and the risks of protectionism: the experience of the Republic of China', *Industry of Free China*, January.

Maddison, A. (1995), *Monitoring the World Economy 1820-1992*, Development Center Studies, Paris: OECD.

Mankiw, N.G., D. Romer and D. Weil (1992), 'A contribution to the empirics of economic growth', *Quarterly Journal of Economics*, **107** (5) 407-37.

Meyer-Zu-Schlochtern, F.J.M. (1988), 'An international sectoral data base for thirteen OECD countries', Economics Department working paper no. 57, Paris: OECD.

Nehru, W. and A. Dhareshwar (1993), 'A new database on physical capital stock: sources, methodology and results', *Revistas de Análisas Económico*, **8** (1), 37-59.

OECD (1991), *Flows and Stocks of Fixed Capital*, Paris: OECD.

Pack, H. (1992), 'New perspectives on industrial growth', in G. Ranis, (ed.), *Taiwan from Developing to Mature Economy*, 73-120, Westview Press, Boulder, CO.

Pissarides, C.A. (1997), 'Learning by trading and the returns to human capital in developing countries', *The World Bank Economic Review*, **11** (1), 17-32.

Ranis, G. (1993), 'Labor markets, human capital and development performance in East-Asia', Center discussion paper no. 697, Economic Growth Center, Yale University, New Haven.

Rodrik, D. (1995), 'Getting interventions right: how South Korea and Taiwan grew rich', *Economic Policy*, **20**, 55-107.

Rodrik, D. (1997), 'TFPG controversies, institutions, and economic performance in East Asia', NBER working paper no. 5914, Cambridge, MA.

Roemer, M., C. Ji (1996), 'The economic development of Taiwan, 1980 to 1993, macroeconomic policy: overzealous or inflexible?', Development discussion papers no. 546, Harvard Institute for International Development, Harvard University.

Schive, C. (1988), 'Foreign investment and technology transfers in

Taiwan: past experience and future potential', *Industry of Free China* August.

Summers, R. and A. Heston (1991), 'The Penn World Table (Mark 5): an expanded set of international comparison', *Quarterly Journal of Economics*, **106** (5), 327-68.

Syrquin, M. (1986), 'Productivity growth and factor reallocation', in H. Chenery, S. Robinson and M. Syrquin (eds), *Industrialization and Growth: A Comparative Study*, 229-62, Oxford: Oxford University Press.

Tallman, E.W. and P. Wang (1994), 'Human capital and endogenous growth: evidence from Taiwan', *Journal of Monetary Economics*, **34**, 101-24.

World Bank (1993), *The East Asian Miracle: Economic Growth and Public Policy*, Oxford University Press for the World Bank.

Xu, Z. (1996), 'On the causality between export growth and GDP growth: an empirical reinvestigation', *Review of International Economics*, **4** (6), 172-84.

Young, A. (1995), 'The tyranny of numbers: confronting the statistical realities of the East Asian experience', *Quarterly Journal of Economics*, **110** (8), 641-79.

10. Technology Adoption and Technical Efficiency in Taiwan: Foreign Investment Led versus Export Performance Promoted*

Been-Lon Chen, Mei Hsu and Jing-Yi Chen

1 INTRODUCTION

The experience of economic development after World War II witnesses only few developing economies having caught up with developed countries and having become prosperous and wealthy, while most developing economies have lagged behind and have remained stagnant and poor. The issue pertaining to elimination of persistent scarcity and poverty of developing countries and to catching up with developed countries has thus been one of the most widely discussed topics in economics. Many policies have been proposed to escape poverty, aiming to raise the rate of economic growth. In this perspective, increasing technical efficiency becomes one of the important targets. To achieve this end, importation and absorption of technology seem to be a first move.

An explicit incorporation of technology adoption in theoretical models has been pioneered by Findlay (1978) and extended by Wang (1990). Recently the works by Romer (1993, 1994) have also emphasized the importance of technology adoption towards closing the gap between the level of technology in developing economies and that of developed economies. It follows that there seems to be little doubt concerning the

*The first version of this chapter was completed while Jing-Yi Chen was research assistant at Academia Sinica. The authors are grateful to Wen Chern, Bernard Yeung, especially Wim Vijerberg, a referee, and workshop participants at National Chung-Cheng University, the Productivity and Efficiency Conference held in June 1997 at Academia Sinica in Taipei and the 1997 Far Eastern Econometrics Society Meeting held in Hong Kong for valuable and helpful comments and suggestions. The authors certainly declare the remaining errors. Been-Lon Chen is grateful to Su-Min Liaw for assistance and to the National Science Council for financial support.

significance of technology adoption for a developing economy.[1] The issue of more relevance is through which way to adopt technology as there are various channels and some of them are more effective than others. The studies on this point, however, have not yet offered a clear answer.

Many existing works contend foreign direct investment to be a vital instrument in adopting technology. Koizumi and Kopecky (1980), Wang and Blomstrom (1992), and Malley and Moutos (1994), among many others, pursued their works along this line. Wang and Blomstrom (1992), for example, have asserted that multinational corporations have become the most important actors in the generation, application and international transfer of modern technology. Recently, building on the models of Caves (1974) and Globerman (1979), Blomstrom and Persson (1983), Blomstrom (1989) and Kokko (1994) use census data in manufacturing at the four-digit level in Mexico and found that labor productivity of domestically owned private plants is positively associated with the share of foreign-owned firms in the same industry, controlling for other important determinants of labor productivity. That is, there exists an intraindustry spillover effect of foreign direct investment in the Mexican manufacturing. Based on a similar model, Haddad and Harrison (1993) used panel data in Morocco's manufacturing industry and also found evidence of intraindustry spillover from foreign direct investment. These studies therefore support the hypothesis that increasing foreign direct investment can enhance labor productivity of domestically-owned private plants. Employing an identical method of constructing the variables as used in Blomstrom (1989) to the 1986 and 1991 Taiwan Manufacturing Survey data, we find, however, that the simple correlation coefficient between average labor productivity of domestically-owned plants in an industry and the share of foreign direct investment is -0.05 in 1986 and -0.01 in 1991.[2] Although the simple correlation coefficients may not be very informative, they seem to cast doubt on the conclusion that Blomstrom (1989) and others have reached. Intuitively multinationals affect the host country through the generation of backward and forward linkages and other effects. The impact of multinationals on the host country depends on the linkages they generated compared to the linkages that would be generated by domestic firms they displaced. To the extent that multinationals have fewer linkages than domestic firms, increasing foreign direct investment reduces rather than raises labor productivity of domestic firms.[3]

There is another channel to raise labor productivity. This is via international trade, with exports in particular. Conventional wisdom holds that countries with superior export performance have superior growth accomplishment (Bhagwati and Srinivason, 1979; Krueger, 1980).

Important mechanisms of technology adoption via better export performance include: greater horizontal specialization; greater learning-by-doing; improvement in production-scheduling, sale-promotion, and after-sale services in remote locations and in the world markets; and the stimulative effects of the need to achieve international competitive prices and quality (Grossman and Helpman, 1991; World Bank, 1991, chapter 5). All these mechanisms serve to increase familiarity with and facilitate absorption of better technology and management, consequently generating a higher level of productivity. The advocation of an export-oriented strategy in enhancing productivity growth is now a convergent point even for economists who are either free-market advocates (World Bank, 1993) or government-intervention proponents (Amsden, 1989).

Although export performance seems to assist technology adoption and thereby ameliorates technology efficiency, the existing empirical works documenting the positive influence of foreign direct investment in Australia, Canada, Mexico and Morocco, however, do not examine at the same time whether export performance is positively correlated with labor productivity of local plants. This omission could be due to a lack of data in exports in these countries, or due to the fact that Mexico and Morocco were not open to international trade in the years under study. In this chapter we attempt to conduct an empirical study of the association between labor productivity and both the aforementioned channels of technology adoption while controlling for other factors of labor productivity. A consideration of these two competing channels of technology adoption is important as they have been and remain employed in an important manner by successful developing countries, especially East Asian NIEs, in their course of economic development. We use Taiwan as a case study for investigating whether Taiwan's labor productivity in manufacturing is more foreign investment led or more export performance promoted.

The reasons for choosing Taiwan are at least fourfold. First, Taiwan is a successful developing economy which started from having no modern industry to its current high level of industrialization via adopting technology from the West. This fact facilitates the study of technology adoption. Second, Taiwan has survey data for both foreign direct investment and exports in 1986 and 1991. This makes investigating the effects of both channels possible. Third, Taiwan has maintained an open attitude toward both foreign direct investment and international trade. As a source of capital formation in the manufacturing sector, foreign direct investment has accounted for more than 10 percent in the 1950s and 1960s, and about 6 percent in the 1970s and the 1980s (Council for Economic Planning and Development, 1994). The figure in the latter two decades is in line with Brazil and Mexico, although it is less than those of Southeast Asian economies. As for exporting, Taiwan's record is well known; its share in GDP rose from 30 percent on average in the 1960s and 1970s to 50 percent in the 1980s. These numbers are surely larger than those of Mexico and many other countries in the world. Fourth, there has been a surge in foreign direct investment in the world since the mid-1980s (Graham and Krugman, 1993), while at the same time the world economy has become more open toward international trade. Taiwan has been a role model of economic success that enjoyed rapid economic growth even after the 1980s when its economy became more mature.

Our main findings are as follows. Export performance always enhances statistically significantly labor productivity of a firm and an industry, whereas foreign direct investment never statistically significantly enhances labor productivity of indigenous plants in the same industry and in most cases it discourages labor productivity of local plants. The results are robust no matter whether the individual year data in 1986 and 1991, the pooled data, the industry-level data or the firm-level data are used.

This study contributes to the existing literatures in at least two aspects. First, earlier studies have found positive and statistically significant effects of foreign direct investment on (i) the level of labor productivity of local manufacturing industry for countries including Canada (Caves, 1974), Australia (Globerman, 1979), Mexico (Blomstrom, 1989; Kokko, 1994), and Morocco (Haddad and Harrison, 1993), (ii) the growth rate of labor productivity of local manufacturing in Mexico (Blomstrom and Wolff, 1994), and (iii) the growth rate of GDP per capita across developing countries (Borensztein *et al.*, 1995). Our finding of a negative intraindustry spillover of foreign direct investment stands in sharp contrast to this line of existing works. Second, our finding that the labor productivity is closely associated with the capability of an industry's export performance (i) is supportive of the conventional wisdom in trade and development (Bhagwati and Srinivason, 1979; Krueger, 1980), (ii) complements and generalizes the work of Aw and Hwang (1995) in which, using data in Taiwan's electronics industry from the 1986 Manufacturing Census, they find technical efficiency of exporters to be larger than nonexporters, and (iii), moreover, to the extent that exports and imports are complements, also provides evidence to support the recent call for a move towards international trade liberalization (Sachs and Warner, 1995).

This chapter is organized as follows. In section 2 we specify the model and in section 3 we illustrate the source of the data and the construction of variables. Section 4 reports the summary statistics of the data and the regression results, whereas section 5 conducts tests of robustness. Section 6 provides the conclusion.

2 THE SPECIFICATION OF MODEL

The basic empirical model is used to test whether, other things being equal, there exists a positive relationship between the productivity level of local plants (denoted as y_d) and two channels of technology adoption, namely, foreign direct investment (denoted as FDI) and export performance (denoted as X_d/L_d), in four-digit industries in Taiwan. While ideally the productivity measure is calculated as the ratio of total value added to a summary index of factor inputs, available data did not permit this. We therefore follow Caves (1974), Globerman (1979) and Blomstrom (1989) to employ a partial productivity index, namely, value added per employee. While we expect export performance to raise value added per employee, foreign direct investment may raise or reduce it depending on the linkages it generates compared to those that would be generated by the domestic firms they replaced.

In order to isolate the effects of foreign direct investment and export performance, it is necessary to control other factors influencing value added per employee. There are four variables: quantity of inputs, quality of inputs, market condition and technology scale.[4] The first is the capital intensity in domestically-owned plants (denoted as K_d/L_d). Other things being equal, a larger capital intensity is expected to lead to a greater value added per employee as capital is an important input. The second factor that may influence value added per employee is the quality of the employees (denoted as QUA_L). In general, for a given number of labor, a laborer with higher quality produces larger value added per employee. We therefore expect both K_d/L_d and QUA_L to enlarge technology efficiency.

Since the labor productivity is expressed in terms of market values, the market structure condition of an industry may affect the values. Intuitively, two otherwise identical industries may obtain different value added per employee because of different degrees of monopoly. To capture the degree of monopoly, an industrial concentration ratio is incorporated. The Herfindahl index (denoted as H_L) has been shown to be the best measure of industrial concentration among 11 different measures (Vanlommel *et al.*, 1977). Finally technical efficiency may differ across plants simply because of scale economies. A variable that represents scale economy (denoted as $SCALE_d$) therefore influences productivity. It is well known, however, that Taiwan's industrial structure is characterized by small- and medium-sized enterprises (Lau, 1990). These small- and medium-sized firms normally perform very well because they are nimble and are quick in responding to profit opportunities (Wade, 1990). It follows that a smaller scale (smaller $SCALE_d$) may encourage or discourage productivity depending on whether the flexibility dominates or is dominated by the scale effect. Furthermore the market structure in Taiwan featured by small- and medium-sized firms may reflect the fact that these firms are competitive rather than monopolistic. As a consequence, the market power (H_L) may not be large enough to raise the value added per employee.

We summarize the preceding discussion in the following function,

$$y_d = f(FDI, X_d/L_d; K_d/L_d, QUA_L, H_L, SCALE_d). \qquad (10.1)$$

This function is better viewed as a reduced form that is generated from production technology, and supply and demand conditions. Following conventional wisdom, we employ a single-equation model although there could be a simultaneous effect of local productivity on foreign direct investment and export performance.[5] Using this model permits us to compare with conventional wisdom. Our primary interest is to inquire whether, other things being controlled, differences in technical efficiency in Taiwan's manufacturing can be explained by foreign direct investment and/or export performance.

3 SOURCE OF DATA AND CONSTRUCTION OF VARIABLES

The data for this study comes from the *Manufacturing Survey, 1986 and 1991 Industrial and Commercial Censuses in Taiwan*. The Directorate-General of Budget, Accounting and Statistics (DGBAS) in Taiwan has conducted an industrial and commercial census at a frequency of every five years since 1956, among which is the survey of the manufacturing sector. Although the survey started in the 1950s, only those in 1986 and 1991 included the data of foreign capitals. In these two years, all plants with annual sales above 50 million New Taiwan dollars are surveyed, whereas those below are divided into five classes based on sales and a random sampling method is applied to each class. The surveyed data set contains 8 421 plants and is classified into 176 four-digit industries in 1986, and consists of 13 330 plants and is sorted into 243 four-digit industries in 1991. However nine industries in 1986 and six in 1991 have no data. Moreover 529 plants in 1986 and 588 in 1991 are owned by multinationals (to be defined), and some domestically owned plants have either no output, no capital or no labor input. We therefore obtain the data of 167 industries in 1986 which were aggregated from 7 221 domestically owned plants and 237 industries in 1991 which were grouped from 12 247 domestically owned plants (see Table 10.2).

We now construct the variables. We define the labor productivity (y_d) as the ratio of total value added (thousands of Taiwan dollars) to total number of employees of a domestically owned plant or of local plants in a four-digit industry, depending on whether the data at a plant level or an industry level is employed. Unlike Blomstrom we do not exclude state-owned plants as there are only 46 state-owned plants and we do not have an evidence a priori that the objects and efficiencies of state-owned enterprises in Taiwan differ significantly from those of local privately owned firms.[6] Following Blomstrom (1989) those plants of which at least 15 percent of capital shares are owned by foreigners are defined as foreign.[7] The foreign direct investment (FDI) is then constructed as the foreign share of employment in each four-digit industry. For export performance (X_d/L_d), it is defined as the ratio of total export to total number of employees of an indigenous plant or of local plants in a four-digit industry (thousands of Taiwan dollars).

We define the capital intensity (X_d/L_d) as the ratio of the book value of total fixed assets (thousands of Taiwan dollars) to total number of employees of a domestically owned plant or of domestically owned plants in a four-digit industry. As for the measure of labor quality (QUA_L), a better measure is the educational level and years of working experience, but there is no such data in the survey. We use as a proxy the ratio of staff to workers in a four-digit industry as there is a distinction in the survey between staff and workers.[8] Staff usually works with managerial and administrative posts or have higher skill, whereas workers take part in assembling or manufacturing activity. Staff therefore require a quality level of education or experience that is higher than workers.

The Herfindahl concentration index of an industry is constructed as $H_L = \sum_{i=1}^{n} (l_i/l)^2$, where l_i is the employment of one of n individual plants and l denotes the total employment of a four-digit industry. We use (labor) input rather than output to construct H_L because the dependent variable under study is measured using output. Finally we construct the variable for the scale economies ($SCALE_d$). Since a direct measure for scale economies is difficult in the absence of specific engineering data, an indirect measure is usually employed (Cory, 1981). The basic assumption for this indirect measure is that the unit production cost curves are (approximately) J-shaped over a significant range of output levels beyond a minimum efficient scale (*MES*). The measure of *MES* is usually constructed as the average gross output of the largest plants that accounts for 50 percent of an industry's gross output (Cory, 1981; Blomstrom and Persson, 1983). Although the cut-off point of 50 percent is not indisputable, we nevertheless follow existing wisdom. Once a measure of

MES is constructed, the scale variable ($SCALE_d$) is then defined as the ratio of the average gross production in local plants to the measure of *MES* plants. For a better illustration, the variables employed and the methods for constructing the variables are summarized in Table 10.1.

Table 10.1 Variables and construction of the data

Variables	Method of Construction
y_d	The ratio of total value added to total number of employees of domestically owned plants in a four-digit industry or of a domestically owned plant (in thousands of Taiwan dollars)
FDI	The ratio of number of employees in foreign plants of a four-digit industry to total number of employees of a domestically and foreign owned plants in the same industry (%)
X_d/L_d	The ratio of total exports to total number of employees of domestically owned plants in a four-digit industry or of a domestically owned plant (in thousands of Taiwan dollars)
K_d/L_d	The ratio of book value assets to total number of employees of domestically owned plants in a four-digit industry or of a domestically owned plant (in thousands of Taiwan dollars)
QUA_L	The ratio of staffs to workers of domestically owned plants in a four-digit industry (%)
H_L	$H_L=\sum_{i=1}^{n}(l_i/l)^2$ where l_i = the numbers of employees of ith plants in a four-digit industry, l = the total number of employees of domestically and foreign owned plants in the four-digit industry (%)
MES	Average gross output of the largest plants in a four-digit industry that accounts for 50% of the industry s output (in thousands of Taiwan dollars)
$SCALE_d$	The ratio of average output of domestically owned plants in a four-digit industry to the *MES* measure in the industry (%)

4 SUMMARY STATISTICS AND REGRESSION RESULTS

Summary Statistics

Before proceeding to regression analysis, we report in Table 10.2 the summary statistics of variables employed. Figures in 1986 in the table are converted to 1991 prices using the industry wholesale price index. In 1986, 8 421 plants classified into 176 four-digit industries were under survey, in which 7 221 domestic plants belonging to 167 industries and 529 multinational plants belonging to 114 industries were employed in this work. The number of multinationals accounted for about 7 percent of all plants in this study. As can be seen from the table, the multinationals on average were more capital-intensive and had a larger labor productivity than their local counterparts. The real capital per employee and the real value added per employee for multinationals were respectively 35 and 45 percent larger than that of local plants. The labor quality index is on average 0.693, meaning that for every ten blue-collar workers employed, a four-digit manufacturing industry on average hires about seven white-collar workers. The Herfindahl index is 0.0802, whereas the scale index is 0.1976. Both indexes are small, reflecting possibly the industrial structure of small- and medium-sized firms in Taiwan. Employment share of foreign firms on average accounts for 13.57 percent in an industry, whereas a plant exports on average 540.86 thousand dollars per employee.

For 13 330 plants in 243 four-digit industries under survey in 1991, 12 247 local plants belonging to 237 industries and 588 multinationals belonging to 147 industries were employed in this study. In this year, although both real capital per employee and real value added per employee are still larger for multinationals than for local counterparts, the gap was smaller than in 1986. The labor quality index is 0.4496, being only 50 percent of its counterpart in 1986. The Herfindahl index is 0.0788 and the scale index is 0.1436, both being similar to those in 1986. The employment share of foreign firms in an industry was on average 10.99 percent, being lower than that in 1986. Export per employee is on average 403.88 thousand dollars, being smaller than its counterpart in 1986.

In Table 10.2 we also include the simple correlation coefficients between value added per employee and all explanatory variables in the model. Some points deserve mentioned. As is clear, K_d/L_d has the largest correlation coefficient with y_d, regardless of the year. The simple correlation coefficients between FDI and y_d and between X_d/L_d and y_d in both years are low. As will be seen, however, the situation changes in regressions when other variables are controlled: while the relation between FDI and yd is significantly negative in most cases, the relation between X_d/L_d and y_d is significantly positive. The regressions are conducted using both firm-level data and industry-level data respectively.

Empirical Results using Firm-level Data

For the regressions using firm-level data, we start by illustrating the estimates of 1986 data, and then the outcomes of 1991 data and of pooled data. Since the heteroskedasticity happens often in cross-sectional data, the Glejser tests are employed to examine the existence of heteroskedasticty by testing various forms of relationships between the residuals generated from the ordinary least square (OLS) and the

Table 10.2 Summary statistics of four-digit manufacturing plants in Taiwan[a]

	1986		1991	
	Mean (Standard Deviation)	Correlation Coefficient with y_d	Mean (Standard Deviation)	Correlation Coefficient with y_d
Number of Industries Surveyed	176	n.a.[b]	243	n.a.
Number of Plants Surveyed	8421	n.a.	13 330	n.a.
Number of Industries used in this Study	167	n.a.	237	n.a.
Number of Domestic Plant used in this Study	7221	n.a.	12 247	n.a.
Industries with Multinationals[c]	114	n.a.	147	n.a.
Number of Multinationals	529	n.a.	588	n.a.
y_d (thousand NT$)[d]	309.42 (297.9)[e]	1.00	440.0183 (384.8)	1.00
y_f (thousand NT$)	575.29 (1379.9)	n.a.	729.32 (610.43)	n.a.
K_d/L_d (thousand NT$)	547.5338 (1256.8)	0.328	1355.417 (2628.4)	0.256
K_f/L_f (thousand NT$)	876.4 (2975.9)	n.a.	1643.8 (2452.5)	n.a.
QUA_L (%)	0.6932 (3.846)	0.0312	0.4496 (0.5434)	0.0945
H_L (%)	0.0802 (0.102)	0.1077	0.0788 (0.0998)	0.0869
$SCALE_d$ (%)	0.1976 (0.111)	0.0091	0.1436 (0.0952)	0.0026
FDI (%)	0.1357 (0.158)	−0.0789	0.1099 (0.1322)	0.0073
X_d/L_d (thousand NT$)	540.8571 (1071.2)	0.1749	403.8777 (1089.6)	0.1762

Notes:
a. All figures are in 1991 value.
b. n.a. means not applicable.
c. Multinationally owned plant is one that at least 15 percent of capital shares are owned by foreigners.
d. NT$ means New Taiwan dollars.
e. Number in parentheses is standard deviation.

explanatory variables.[9] We find that the square residuals of OLS regressions are highly related to the square K_d/L_d. This situation is reasonable given the usual case that the variation of value added per employee tends to change with the intensity of capital. To get consistent and more efficient estimators, we follow the estimation suggestion proposed by Greene (1997: 567-9). Specifically the weighted least square (WLS) estimation method is employed with the weight K_d/L_d, and the White estimator is used to correct the variances of estimators. The reason for the choice is that the White variance estimators are consistent, and employing WLS with White estimators is more efficient than simply using OLS with White estimators. We focus on the effects of foreign direct investment and export performance with the four other variables controlled. The results are illustrated in Table 10.3.

Table 10.3 Labor productivity regressions using plant-level data (1986, 1991 and pooled)

Equation	(1)[a]	(2)[a]	(3)[b]	(4)[b]	(5)[c]	(6)[c]
Numbers of Observation	7221	7221	12247	12247	19468	19468
Constant	121.36***	122.23***	174.62***	176.55***	126.42***	127.80***
	(9.2778)	(9.3363)	(6.4792)	(6.5870)	(5.7100)	(5.7701)
K_d/L_d	0.4328***	0.4314***	0.2569***	0.2561***	0.3303***	0.3285***
	(0.0930)	(0.0929)	(0.0355)	(0.0354)	(0.0515)	(0.0513)
QUA_L	0.5063#	0.5093#	22.105***	22.447***	0.7447**	0.7450**
	(0.3438)	(0.3385)	(5.5096)	(5.5480)	(0.3363)	(0.3298)
H_L	17.199	14.202	66.646***	−70.361***	−18.336*	−22.181**
	(17.439)	(17.371)	(10.936)	(11.158)	(9.7406)	(9.8833)
$SCALE_d$	−19.986	−17.740	26.026*	25.701*	−12.049	−10.650
	(18.618)	(18.448)	(14.185)	(14.191)	(11.453)	(11.402)
FDI	−109.72***	−114.75***	0.4080	−20.815	−106.26***	−114.51***
	(10.987)	(11.664)	(11.529)	(15.411)	(6.5344)	(7.3268)
X_d/L_d	0.0611***	0.0547***	0.0583***	0.053***	0.0633***	0.0555***
	(0.0077)	(0.0082)	(0.0052)	(0.0063)	(0.0049)	(0.0057)
$FDI{*}X_d/L_d$	--	0.0414	--	0.0667#	--	0.0604**
		(0.0304)		(0.0419)		(0.0243)
Dummy	--	--	--	--	53.481***	53.513***
					(4.3698)	(4.3473)
Adj. R^2	0.3661	0.3670	0.2896	0.2910	0.3943	0.3960

Notes:
a. 1986 survey data; b. 1991 survey data; c. Pooled data.
Dependent variable is value added per employee. The weighted least squares estimation method is employed in all regressions. White standard error estimates are in parentheses.
***,**,* and # represent statistical singificance at the 1 percent, 5 percent, 10 percent and 15 percent level, respectively.

The estimated result for 1986 are illustrated in equations (10.1)-(10.2) in Table 10.3. As can be clearly seen from equation (10.1), the estimated coefficients of K_d/L_d, FDI and X_d/L_d are statistically significant at less than the 1 percent level. For the controlled variable, the estimated coefficient indicates that, holding in control other relevant variables, value added per employee is raised by 439 dollars if capital intensity (K_d/L_d) is increased by one standard deviation (1 256.8 dollars according to Table 10.2). For the labor quality (QUA_L), the estimated coefficient is positive and weakly statistically significant, indicating that a laborer with a higher quality enhances labor productivity. For the remaining two controlled variables (H_L and $SCALE_d$), their estimated coefficients are statistically insignificant.[10] This indicates that on average market power and scale do not enhance the labor productivity of a plant statistically significantly in 1986. This result is related to Taiwan's small- and medium-sized market structure as emphasized in section 2.

For the two variables of our focus, the estimated coefficient of FDI is negative and statistically significant at the 1 percent level, whereas the estimated coefficient of X_d/L_d is positive and statistically significant at the 1 percent level. The estimated coefficient of FDI indicates that an increase in the share of multinationals in a four-digit industry by one standard deviation (0.158 percentage points according to Table 10.2) reduces the labor productivity of the local plants in the same industry by 17 336 dollars, other things being equal. The estimated coefficient of X_d/L_d indicates that, other things being equal, an increase in exports per employee by one standard deviation (1 071.2 thousand dollars according to Table 10.2) raises value added per employee by 65.5 thousand dollars.

The evidence for the effect of X_d/L_d and FDI seems to indicate the aftermath that export performance promotes labor productivity in Taiwan, whereas foreign direct investment lowers labor productivity of indigenous plants. In particular the finding of significantly negative spillovers of foreign direct investment on labor productivity of local firms stands in sharp contrast to the existing works which finds evidence of positive spillovers on the level of labor productivity for manufacturing in various countries at both an aggregate (industry) level (Caves, 1974; Globerman, 1979; Blomstrom, 1989; Kokko, 1994) and a firm level (Haddad and Harrison, 1993). This result is nevertheless consistent with the negative spillover effect of foreign direct investment on economic growth (i) across developing countries (Saltz, 1992) and (ii) across manufacturing industries in Taiwan (Chen *et al.*, 1997).

Is it possible that the direct effect of FDI works to enhance the labor productivity of local firms after controlling its interaction with export performance as multinationals take advantage of cheaper labor in Taiwan and use it as an export platform for some advanced markets as emphasized, for example, by Hiemenz (1987)? To answer this question we encompass the interaction term of foreign direct investment and exports per employee ($FDI*X_d/L_d$) in equation (10.2) in Table 10.3. As the results show the estimated coefficient of $FDI*X_d/L_d$ is positive but statistically insignificant at the 10 percent level, indicating that foreign direct investment could possibly raise labor productivity of a local plant in the same industry through its interaction with exports. Nevertheless the direct effect of FDI and X_d/L_d remain the same and this result is maintained without changing the magnitude of and the significance of the estimated coefficients of controlled variables. According to the estimates, the coefficient of FDI is significantly negative and its magnitude is even larger than in equation (10.1) in Table 10.3, whereas the effect of X_d/L_d remains significantly positive at the 1 percent level although its magnitude is smaller than in equation (10.1). The indirect effect of FDI through its interaction with X_d/L_d is small. To see the net effect of foreign direct investment, suppose that both FDI and X_d/L_d are increased by one standard deviation. The indirect effect of foreign direct investment is then to increase the value added per employee by 849.9 dollars whereas the direct effect is to reduce the value added per employee by 18 131 dollars. The difference is more than 2.5 times and the net effect of FDI is thus negative.

We next investigate whether the results using the 1986 survey data remain carried over if either the 1991 survey data or the pooled data of 1986 survey and 1991 survey are employed. The resulting outcomes using 1991 data are listed in equations (10.3)-(10.4) of Table 10.3, whereas those using pooled data are in equations (10.5)-(10.6). By looking at equations (10.3)-(10.4) we see that, holding in control other independent variables, the direct effect of foreign direct investment remains to be nowhere statistically significantly positive regardless of whether its interaction with X_d/L_d is controlled. The estimated coefficients of export performance continue to be positive and statistically significant at the 1 percent level. We next examine equations (10.5)-(10.6) where the pooled survey data in 1991 and 1986 is employed.[11] The results are unchanged: the estimated coefficients of FDI remain not to reveal any statistically significantly positive effect on labor productivity, whereas those of X_d/L_d show a positive and statistically significant influence.

Empirical Results Using Industry-Level Data

So far our results are obtained using firm-level data. To provide rigorous and convincing evidence it is necessary to document the results using industry-level data. We focus on the two independent variables of our major concerns holding constant other independent variables and therefore only estimated results of these two variables are reported in Table 10.4. The effects of controlled variables are as expected as mentioned in section 2.

Table 10.4 Labor productivity regressions using industry-level data (1986, 1991 and pooled)

Equation	(1)[a]	(2)[a]	(3)[b]	(4)[b]	(5)[c]	(6)[c]	(7)[d]	(8)[d]
Number of Observations	167	167	237	237	404	404	75	75
FDI	51.567	80.829	−100.92	−32.549	3.8293	35.754	--	--
	(87.811)	(121.68)	(73.577)	(108.27)	(55.950)	(77.026)		
X_d/L_d	0.0197	0.0250	0.0488***	0.0585***	0.0322**	0.0380**	0.0481***	--
	(0.0220)	(0.0257)	(0.0183)	(0.0171)	(0.0141)	(0.0162)	(0.0164)	
$FDI * X_d/L_d$	--	−0.0401	--	−0.0669	--	−0.0405	--	--
		(0.0717)		(0.0750)		(0.0525)		
FDI_{-1}	--	--	--	--	--	--	−32.111	−16.283
							(87.830)	(84.352)
$(X_d/L_d)_{-1}$	--	--	--	--	--	--	--	0.046***
								(0.0251)
Adj. R^2	0.4777	0.4753	0.5601	0.5601	0.5710	0.5706	0.7293	0.7166

Notes:
a. 1986 data; b. 1991 data; c. 1986 and 1991 pooled data; d. 1991 data except for FDI which uses 1986 data.
Dependent variable is value added per employee. All equaitons control K_d/L_d, QUA_L, H_L and $SCALE_d$ and include an intercept term. For the regressions using pooled data, an additional time dummy is controlled. The weighted least square estimation method is employed in all regressions. White standard error estimates are in parentheses. ***, ** and * represent statistical significance at the 1 percent, 5 percent and 10 percent level, respectively.

Equations (10.1)-(10.2) in Table 10.4 are the results for 1986, whereas equations (10.3)-(10.4) and equations (10.5)-(10.6) are the results for 1991 and for pooled data, respectively. According to these six equations, although the spillovers of foreign direct investment are not as significantly negative as using firm-level data, we find no significantly positive spillover of FDI as documented in existing wisdom. On the other hand the estimated coefficients of X_d/L_d continue to be positive and statistically significant at the 1 percent level in most cases, meaning that the export performance of an industry enhances its labor productivity.

Is it likely that it takes time for the spillover effect of foreign direct investment to become effective? This lag effect of FDI has been documented in Caves (1974) and Globerman (1979). Since the 1986 survey data is available, we can test the hypothesis. To restrict to the same industries in both 1986 and 1991, some industries have to be abandoned due to changes in categorization between the survey years. As a consequence we obtained for each survey year 75 industries which are respectively assorted from 8 949 plants in the 1991 survey data and from 5 701 plants in 1986 survey data, so still more than 70 percent of plants are involved. We entail the effect of foreign direct investment in 1986 (FDI_{-1}) on the labor productivity of local firms in the same industry in 1991 in equations (10.7) and (10.8) in which either the contemporary effect or lag effect of X_d/L_d is included. As the results clearly show, in contrast to the finding of a statistically lag positive spillover on labor productivity of foreign direct investment obtained in Caves (1974) and Globerman (1979), the estimated coefficients here indicate a negative, although statistically insignificant, lag spillover effect. Export performance remains to have positive and statistically significant effect no matter whether it is the current exports or it was the exports five years ago.

5 TESTS FOR ROBUSTNESS

In this section we assure that our previous results are robust and are therefore not sensitive to variations in the specification of the empirical model. It is, however, impossible to examine all kinds of combinations. Since our emphasis is on the effect of foreign direct investment and export performance, we will modify the environment in this direction. The situation most relevant to the current work is how the variables foreign direct investment and export performance are constructed and whether the inclusion of state-owned enterprises dominates the results.[12]

Various Ways of Constructing Foreign Direct Investment

The cut-off point at 15 percent of capital shares in defining a foreign plant could be controversial. In a usual practice a plant is defined as foreign if foreigners possess 50 percent or more of its capital shares because foreigners accordingly control the plant fully. In contrast it may be contended that a small fraction of foreign capital shares is enough in generating spillover since foreign skills and managerial practices may then be transferred. We have examined whether our previous results are robust when the cut-off point is set at 50 percent and when it is set at 10 percent and above 0 percent. These figures are chosen so that one accords with the common notion of foreign control and the remaining two reflect the situation where only a small fraction is necessary in bringing technology. As our empirical results show, the conclusions in Tables 10.3 and 10.4 of a significantly positive effect of export performance and of a nonpositive or even negative effect of foreign direct investment stay unchanged, no matter which cut-off point is employed.

Different Method of Constructing Export Performance

In the previous regressions, we use exports per employee to construct the variable of export performance. We now use the exports as a proportion of sales as an alternative way to construct this variable. As our empirical results at an industry level reveal, the outcomes for FDI are consistent with Table 10.4, whereas the estimated coefficients for export performance ($X_d / Sale_d$) is positive but not statistically significant. The latter result is obtained probably because value added and sales are positively correlated, but value added appears in the dependent variable whereas sales appear in the denominator of the independent variable. As a result, the parameter of the exports/sales ratio is negatively biased.[13] Nevertheless, when the data at a plant level is employed, a larger exports/sales ratio of a plant clearly enhances the plant's labor productivity statistically significantly.

Excluding State-Owned Enterprises

Our regressions so far are conducted using the data that include domestic plants of both private and public enterprises. It has been argued that the state-owned plants should be excluded from the labor productivity analysis of local plants for reasons that public plants have other goals than private plants or they have lower productivity because of the purpose of increasing employment or decreasing geographic centralization (for example, Blomstrom, 1989). Although there is no evidence a priori showing that these different goals are important for public enterprises in Taiwan, we provide tests to confirm that our previous results continue to hold even when state-owned plants are excluded from the analysis.[14] As our empirical results show, we continue to obtain the same outcomes as those in the previous section.

Other Tests

We also conduct other tests of robustness. We change the way FDI is constructed by using total gross output share of multinationals in an industry. We also estimate a loglinear model. Specifically we estimate a model where logarithmic values of y_d, K_d/L_d and X_d/L_d and original values of other variables are employed.[15] The results remain the same as in Tables 10.3 and 10.4 when data at both a firm level and an industry level are used respectively.

6 CONCLUDING REMARKS

Using Taiwan's survey data, we investigate the relationship between technical efficiency and the two channels of technology adoption, namely, both foreign direct investment and export performance. To facilitate comparisons with those of conventional wisdom, we employ the same model used in Blomstrom (1989) and others. We find that foreign direct investment not only has insignificantly positive intraindustry spillovers on technical efficiency of local firms in a four-digit manufacturing industry, but the effects are significantly negative in most cases under study, other things being controlled. On the contrary, export performance always has a positive and statistically significant effect on technical efficiency. These results are obtained no matter whether one uses survey data of an individual year, pooled data, industry-level data or plant-level data. The outcomes are robust under variations in the specification of the empirical model, including different ways of constructing foreign direct investment and export performance, with or without public enterprises included, and employing linear or loglinear models.

The nonpositive and even detrimental intraindustry spillover effect of foreign direct investment stands in sharp contrast to one strand of conventional wisdom which finds evidence of significantly positive spillovers using similar models (Caves, 1974; Globerman, 1979; Blomstrom, 1989; Haddad and Harrison, 1993; Kokko, 1994) and different models (Blomstrom and Wolff, 1994; Borensztein *et al.*, 1995). This result also casts doubt on the positive extenality assumption of multinational firms usually made in theoretical works (Ethier and Markusen, 1996, among others). Our second finding that export performance enhances labor productivity, on the other hand, supports one line of the conventional wisdom in trade and economic development (Krueger, 1980; Grossman and Helpman, 1991). This finding also complements and generalizes that of Aw and Hwang (1995) in a case study of Taiwan's electronics industry. Moreover, to the extent that exports and imports are complements, our evidence lends supports to the recent call for international trade liberalization (Sachs and Warner, 1995).

Since the intraindustry spillover effect of foreign direct investment is nonpositive and even detrimental and differs from conventional results, we provide some possible explanations. Intuitively, although foreign direct investment could generate intraindustry spillovers on domestic plants, the net effect depends on whether this effect dominates the linkages that would be generated by domestic plants it replaced. To the extent that the latter effect dominates, foreign direct investment tends to harm domestically owned plants. In general, the multinationals in Taiwan have a large ratio of intra-firm transactions and a low share of local procurement according to the Investment Commission (1993), indicating small backward and forward linkages with domestic firms.[16] Moreover many multinationals manage to retard the inflows of technology using various methods. For example, a study by Liu (1987), concerning the electronics industry in Taiwan and Japanese direct foreign investment, found that the inflow of technology with Japanese multinationals was usually accompanied by restrictions on key components or product market constraints in order to hinder dissemination of their technologies. In effect the effect of foreign subsidiaries may be purely to inject additional competitions into domestic market destroying rents that otherwise count in domestic firms' productivity levels. All these factors make possible the nonpositive spillovers of foreign direct investment.

Our study has useful policy implications. The result of nonpositive and even detrimental intraindustry spillover of FDI may cast doubt on the conventional preferential policies for stimulating foreign direct investment. Indeed foreign direct investment may be just a particular form of capital. It follows that state intervention in inducing foreign direct investment through subsidies, tax breaks or other distortionary incentives, should be kept to a minimum. Indeed there is no need for special treatment of foreign investors. In this regard our implication is similar to some principles in obtaining foreign investment set out by Graham (1996). Alternatively the government may instead concentrate its effort on opening its economy and in encouraging exports. To the extent imports and exports are complements, knowledge of new products, improving production and quality control, after-sale services and other kinds of information could be learned and assimilated through international trading activity. All knowledge of these kinds helps improve productivity.

We must point out that we only find evidence of detrimental *intra*industry spillover of foreign direct investment. It remains open whether there is a positive *inter*industry spillover on a firm or an industry at a four-digit level from a one-digit or two-digit level *à la* Caballero and Lyons (1992) and Chan *et al.* (1995). Moreover, our evidence is obtained using the data in 1986 and 1991 when Taiwan became more mature. The results may change if the data are used from the period when Taiwan was less developed. Intuitively, the technology gap between domestic and foreign plants is larger in a less developed than a more developed economy, so the potential of spillover may exist. The survey data that we employed, however, constrains the analysis in this direction. Other data sources could be used for further evidence. Furthermore our measure of foreign direct investment is in terms of employment share and gross output share. More research with other measures of foreign direct investment should be done before the finding is conclusive. This suggests avenues for subsequent research.

NOTES

1. See also Chen and Shimomura (1998) for the role of technology adoption in industrialization, takeoff and economic growth.
2. A detailed description regarding the source of the data and the construction of the variables is left to section 3.
3. See Rodriguez-Clare (1996) for a theoretical formulation of similar points.
4. We utilize the same independent variables incorporated in Blomstrom and Persson (1983) and Blomstrom (1989). The reasons for following their model is not only that these variables are appropriate for Taiwan and the data is available, but also these two studies had a more complete set of controlled variables than others. This facilitates comparisons across studies.
5. For a documentation of the causality between foreign direct investment and economic performance, see Karikari (1992), and of that between export and economic performance, see Chow (1987).
6. See section 5 for an analysis excluding state-owned plants.
7. See section 5 for the results using different critical points of capital share in defining FDI.
8. According to the survey, staff includes managers, engineers, technicians and accountants, whereas workers consist of mechanics, assembly-line workers, drivers and coolies.
9. For a detailed procedure of Glejser tests, see Greene (1997).
10. In Blomstrom (1989), the estimated coefficients of H_L and $SCALE_d$ are statistically insignificant.
11. We include a year dummy (denoted as Dummy) in Table 10.3 to capture the time effect when pooled data is used, assigning 1 for a firm in 1991 and 0 otherwise. The results without including a year dummy are the same (not reported).
12. In order to save space, we will not report the empirical results of robust tests in tables. For readers who are interested in these tables, they are available from the first author of this chapter upon request.
13. We thank a referee for contributing the explanation.
14. A plant is defined as public if the local and state governments hold 50 percent or more of capital shares.
15. Since a number of firms have no exports, we assign 1 to X_d/L_d for these firms.

16. A survey conducted by the Investment Commission (1993) in Taiwan reveals that foreign subsidiaries have on average 60 percent of imports in materials and thus have a small share of local procurement.

REFERENCES

Amsden, A.H. (1989), *Asia's Next Giant: South Korea and Late Industrialization*, New York: Oxford University Press.

Aw, B.-Y. and A.R. Hwang (1995), 'Productivity and the export market: a firm-level analysis', *Journal of Development Economics*, **47** (2), 319-32.

Bhagwati, J. and T.N. Srinivasan (1979), 'Trade and development', in R. Dornbush and J.A. Frankel (eds), *International Economic Policy*, Baltimore: Johns Hopkins University Press, 1-35.

Blomstrom, M. (1989), *Foreign Investment and Spillovers*, London: Routledge.

Blomstrom, M. and H. Persson (1983), 'Foreign investment and spillover efficiency in an underdeveloped economy: evidence from the Mexican manufacturing industry', *World Development*, **11** (6), 493-50.

Blomstrom, M. and E.N. Wolff (1994), 'Multinational corporations and productivity convergence in Mexico', in, W. Baumol, R. Nelson and E. Wolff (eds), *Convergence of Productivity: Cross-National Studies and Historical Evidence*, New York: Oxford University Press, 264-84.

Borensztein, E.J. De Gregorio and J.-Wha Lee (1995), 'How does foreign direct investment affect economic growth?', NBER working paper 5057.

Caballero, R.J. and R.K. Lyons (1992), 'External effects in U.S. procyclical productivity', *Journal of Monetary Economics*, **29**, 209-25.

Caves, R.E. (1974), 'Multinational firms, competition, and productivity in host-country markets', *Economica*, **41**, 176-93.

Chan, V.-Lin, B.-L. Chen and K.-N. Cheung (1995), 'External economies in Taiwan's manufacturing industries', *Contemporary Economic Policy*, **13** (4), 118-30.

Chen, B.-L., M. Hsu and K.-Y. Shi (1997), 'Growth and catch-up in a cross section of local manufacturing industries', in G. Ranis, S. Hu and Y. Chu (eds), *The Economics and Political Economy of Development in Taiwan into the 21st Century*, London: Edward Elgar, 51-77.

Chen, B.-L. and K. Shimomura (1998), 'Self-fulfilling expectations and economic growth: a model of technology adoption and industrialization', *International Economic Review*, **39** (1), 151-70.

Chow, P.C.Y. (1987), 'Causality between export growth and industrial development: empirical evidence from NICs', *Journal of Development Economics*, **26**, 55-63.

Cory, P.F. (1981), 'A technique for obtaining improved proxy estimates of minimum optimal scale', *Review of Economics and Statistics*, **63** (1), 96-106.

Council for Economic Planning and Development (1994), *Taiwan Statistical Data Book*, Taipei.

Ethier, W. and J. Markusen (1996), 'Multinational firms, technology diffusion and trades', *Journal of International Economics*, **41** (1-2), 1-28.

Findlay, R. (1978), 'Relative backwardness, direct foreign investment and technology transfer: a simple dynamic model', *Quarterly Journal of Economics*, **81**, 1-38.

Globerman, S. (1979), 'Foreign direct investment and spillover efficiency benefits in Canadian manufacturing industrics', *Canadian Journal of Economics*, **12** (1), 42-56.

Graham, E.M. (1996), *Global Corporations and National Governments*, Washington, DC: Institute for International Economics.

Graham, E.M. and P.R. Krugman (1993), 'The surge in foreign direct investment in the 1980s', in K. Froot (ed.), *Foreign Direct Investment*, Chicago: University of Chicago Press, 13-36.

Greene, W.H. (1997), *Econometric Analysis*, 3rd edn., New Jersey: Prentice-Hall.

Grossman, G. and E. Helpman (1991), *Innovation and Growth in the Global Economy*, Cambridge, MA: MIT Press.

Haddad, M. and A. Harisson (1993), 'Are there positive spillovers from direct foreign investment? Evidence from panel data for Morocco', *Journal of Development Economics*, **42**, 51-74.

Hiemenz, U. (1987), 'Foreign direct investment and industrialization in ASEAN countries', *Weltwirtschaftliches Archiv*, **123** (1), 121-39.

Investment Commission (1993), *Statistics on Overseas Chinese & Foreign Investment, Outward Investment, Outward Technical Cooperation, and Indirect Mainland Investment*, Taipei: Ministry of Economic Affairs.

Karikari, J.A. (1992), 'Causality between foreign investment and economic output in Ghana', *Journal of Economic Development*, **17** (1), 7-17.

Koizumi, T. and K. Kopecky (1980), 'Direct foreign investment, technology transfer and domestic employment effects', *Journal of International Economics*, **10** (1), 1-20.

Kokko, A. (1994), 'Technology, market characteristics, and spillovers', *Journal of Development Economics*, **3**, 279-93.

Krueger, A. (1980), 'Trade as an input to development', *American Economic Review, Paper and Proceedings*, **70**, 288-92.

Lau, L. (1990), *Models of Development: A Comparative Study of Economic Growth in South Korea and Taiwan*, San Francisco: ICS Press.

Liu, C.C. (1987), 'Taiwan's electronics industry and Japanese direct investment', in T. Sasaki (ed.), *Foreign Direct Investment of Japanese Electronics Industry*, Tokyo: Hosei University Press, 79-100.

Malley, J. and T. Moutos (1994), 'A prototype of macroeconomic model of foreign direct investment', *Journal of Development Economics*, **43** (2), 295-315.

Rodriguez-Clare, A. (1996), 'Multinationals, linkages and economic development', *American Economic Review*, **86** (4), 852-73.

Romer, P. (1993), 'Two strategies for economic development: using ideas and producing ideas', Proceedings of the World Bank Annual Conference on Development Economics 1992, supplement to the *World Bank Economic Review*.

Romer, P. (1994), 'Idea gaps and object gaps in economic development', *Journal of Monetary Economics*, **32**, 543-73.

Sachs, J. and A. Warner (1995), 'Economic reform and the process of global integration', *Brookings Paper on Economic Activity*, **1**, 1-118.

Saltz, I.S. (1992), 'The negative correlation between foreign direct investment and economic growth in the third world: theory and evidence', *Revista Internazionale di Economiche e Commerciali*, **39** (7), 617-33.

Vanlommel, E., B. de Brabander and B. Liebaers (1977), 'Industrial concentration in Belgium: Empirical comparison of alternative seller concentration measures', *Journal of Industrial Economics*, **26** (1), 1-20.

Wade, R. (1990), *Governing the Market: Economic Theory and the Role of Government in East Asian Industrialization*, New Jersey: Princeton University Press.

Wang, J.-Ye (1990), 'Growth, technology transfer, and the long-run theory of international capital movements', *Journal of International Economics*, **29**, 255-71.

Wang, J.-Ye and M. Blomstrom (1992), 'Foreign investment and technology transfer: a simple model', *European Economic Review*, **36**, 137-55.

World Bank (1991), *World Development Report*, New York: Oxford University Press.

World Bank (1993), *The East Asian Miracle: Economic Growth and Public Policy*, Washington, DC: Oxford University Press.

11. Measurement of Total Factor Productivity in Japan: How to Evaluate Impacts of New Technologies on TFP Growth*

Masahiro Kuroda and Koji Nomura

1 INTRODUCTION

Recent statistics in OECD countries suggested that productivity growth at the macro level has been in a downward trend since the second half of the 1970s. In fact there has been observed a sort of paradoxical movement in the relationship between the trend of real investment and productivity growth during the period of recent economic recovery. Intuitively, this situation implies that expected productivity growth has not been realized in spite of the sizable increases of real investment along with the new development of technology including high-tech and information instruments in the economic recovery of OECD countries. It seems that the so-called 'conceptualization problem' comes from these intuitive questions.[1] Although they are naive and intuitive questions initially, however, they include various important issues to be clarified from the viewpoints of properties of new technologies as well as the measurement of productivity growth. In other words 'conceptualization problems' finally come to the conclusion that impacts of the new technologies on the economy should be clarified or conceptualized by analyzing the structural changes related to those technologies from the standpoint of productivity growth. Analysis of these objectives seems to be divided into various stages. First of all we should begin with the problems of measurement of productivity, where our productivity measures are confined to the concept of 'total factor productivity (TFP) '. It is often pointed out that TFP growth measures have various possibilities of measurement errors

*This chapter was based on a paper prepared for the Taipei International Conference on Efficiency and Productivity Growth, 20-21 June, 1997.

because of their definitions, where they are defined by differences between observed growth rates of inputs and outputs. It might be one of the most important issues how to evaluate the quality changes of inputs and outputs in terms of their quantity and price measures. Experiments in the revisions of the price and quantity index numbers including a hedonic approach suggested that considerations regarding quality measures of inputs and outputs could be expected to give a sizable change in the results of TFP growth measures. Although this type of measurement error is important, we do not refer to this issue in this chapter. A second source of the measurement errors in TFP growth measures comes from an aggregation bias. Measures of inputs and outputs in the estimation of TFP growth are defined by an aggregate measure of various heterogeneous types of inputs and outputs at the industry level as well as at the macro level. We can observe at in the composition of the inputs and outputs in our historical statistics. In the simple aggregate procedures, which ignored these changes of the composition, there might be a sort of aggregation bias. We discussed these aggregation bias problems in TFP growth measures in Kuroda and Shimpo (1992). As we mentioned in the paper we have to consider carefully these changes of the compositions as an index number problem in aggregate measures of inputs and outputs. Since these changes of the composition in inputs and outputs reflect the market structures of the economy, there are some possibilities of aggregation biases in TFP growth measures even if we could solve the abovementioned measurement errors in terms of quality changes in inputs and outputs.

In this chapter we would like to focus on the basic problem of the conceptualization from the viewpoints of the properties of the recent new technologies, where we try to analyze the impacts of new technologies on productivity growth and evaluate quantitatively the implication of the spillover effect of TFP growth on the structural change of the Japanese economy. Our analytical framework is based upon the dynamic inverse approach of the input-output analysis. In the dynamic inverse approach, a structure of the economy is composed of linear equations described by input coefficients of intermediate and labor as well as capital inputs as structural parameters. Structural changes of the economy are described by the changes of structural parameters. We assume here that the development of new technologies could be embodied on changes of capital input coefficients as structural parameters and it would have the spillover effect on the whole economy through the productivity growth. The development of new technologies assume to be realized by the changes of composition among capital goods in capital formation and observed by the changes of the capital coefficients in capital stock by sector. We begin with the development of the measures of capital input in current and constant prices for each of the 43 industrial sectors in Japan for the period 1955-1992. We estimate capital formation in terms of flow and stock in order to evaluate the impact of the structural changes in capital coefficients on the economy, where new technologies have been expected to be embodied. The methodological framework for the measurement of capital input and capital stock is discussed with some fact findings on estimated results in section 2. Estimated capital stocks by sectors are extended to the capital stock matrices consistently with the input-output flow matrices in each year. We can estimate capital coefficients matrices classified by commodities and industrial sectors. Our capital stock matrices are divided into matrices for private and government enterprises, and social overhead capital. We discuss our estimated results from the viewpoints of structural changes in terms of changes of capital coefficients. Section 3 presents the methodological framework for the evaluation of structural changes based upon the theory of the dynamic inverse approach, where we try to propose the measurement of production efficiency in terms of the static and dynamic measures of the total factor productivity. Our concept of the measurement of the total factor productivity is an extension of the concept of the ordinary TFP measures by sector analysis from the viewpoints of technological properties of commodity production and spillover effect of the technology as a system. Section 4 presents the estimated results on the pattern of structural changes in terms of capital coefficients including private capital and infrastructure in Japan during the period 1955-1992. Furthermore, we will evaluate the impacts of the major changes of capital coefficients including private and social overhead capital formation, where the development of new technologies is embodied, on TFP growth.

2 CAPITAL FORMATION IN JAPAN DURING THE PERIOD 1955-1992

2.1 Capital Input and Capital Stock: Measurement

We assume that all of the new development of technologies are originally embodied in the new investment and changes of compositions of capital stock might have impacts on the substitution of factor inputs and TFP growth. In order to analyze quantitatively the impacts of the structural changes of capital formation which embodied new technologies on TFP growth, we should begin with the estimation of capital flow and stock matrices, which are divided into private and government enterprises owned capital classified by industry and social overhead capital unclassified by industry. We choose the perpetual inventory method as the methodological framework to estimate the stocks of depreciable capital assets.[2]

Capital formation except social overhead capital is divided into the formation by private and government enterprises. Both private and government enterprises are classified by 43 industrial sectors as shown in Table 11.1. Social overhead capital is not classified into sectors, but divided into 13 broad categories.[3] On the other hand, capital formation in each industrial sector is classified by 78 types of capital good as types of asset, which are corresponding to the commodity classification in the input-output table.[4] We can show the framework of our capital formation matrices in Figure 11.1. In this figure, the lower part of matrix, I_{lj},

Table 11.1 Industry classification

No. of Sector	Industry name	No. of Sector	Industry name
1	Agri. forestry and fishery	2	Coal mining
3	Other mining	4	Construction
5	Foods manufacturing	6	Textile
7	Apparel	8	Woods and related products
9	Furniture and fixture	10	Paper and pulp
11	Publishing and printing	12	Chemical products
13	Petroleum and refinery	14	Coal products
15	Rubber products	16	Leather products
17	Stone and clay	18	Iron and steel
19	Non-ferrous metal	20	Metal products
21	Machinery	22	Electric machinery
23	Motor vehicle	24	Other transp. machinery
25	Precision instruments	26	Other manufacturing product
27	Railroad transport	28	Road transport
29	Water transport	30	Air transport
31	Storage facility service	32	Communication
33	Electricity	34	Gas supply
35	Water supply	36	Trade
37	Finance and insurance	38	Real estate
39	Education	40	Research
41	Medical service	42	Other service
43	Public admin.		

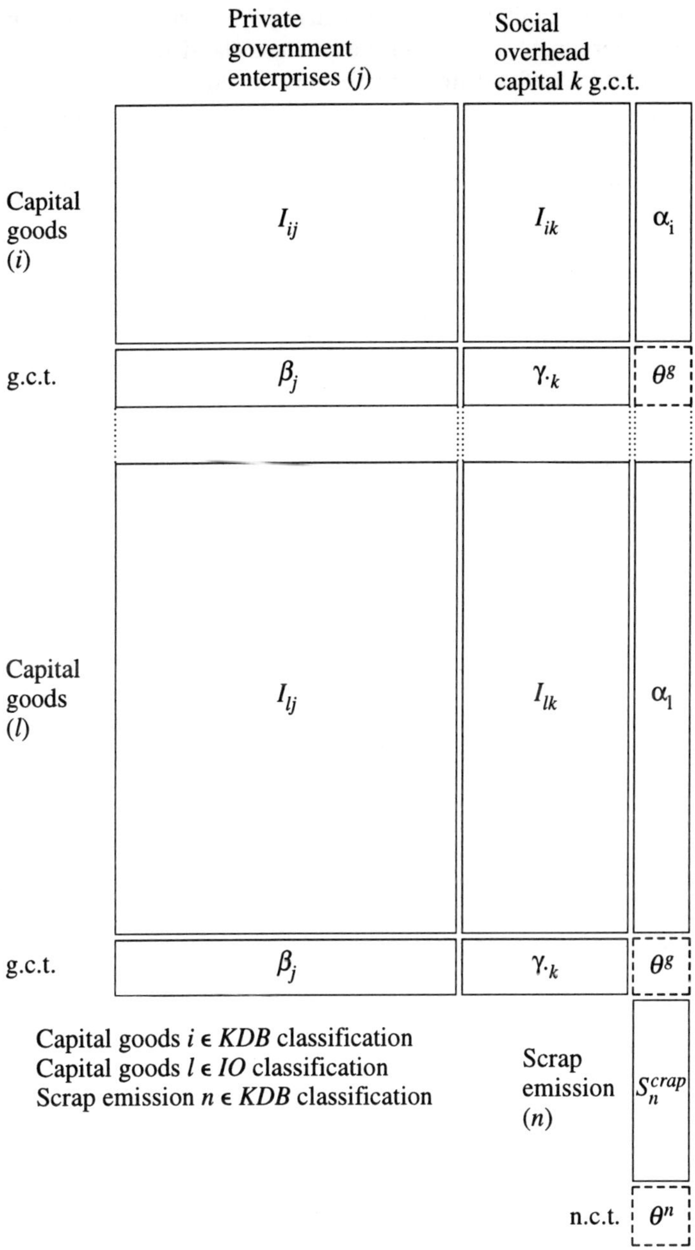

Figure 11.1 Framework of KDB-FCFM

corresponds to the capital formation matrix by private and government enterprises, where capital goods in the row are classified into 78 capital goods and industries of private and government enterprises in the column are classified into 43 industrial sectors. The lower part of the matrix, I_{lk}, corresponds to the capital formation matrix of social overhead capital, where capital goods in the row are classified into 78 capital goods and categories of social overhead capital in the column are classified into 13 categories. The upper part of the matrices, I_{ij} and I_{lk}, represent the consolidated matrices of the lower part of the matrices, I_{ij} and I_{lk}, where 78 capital goods are aggregated into 43 industrial classifications. Vectors of the sum of columns, α_i and α_l equally correspond to the capital formation vector in the input-output table. Furthermore, the total sum of the capital formation by commodity, θ^g is equal to the domestic capital formation of the aggregate in the System of National Accounts after some adjustment of the differences in the concept of scrap. We tried to estimate capital stock matrices in the same framework which are consistent with the flow matrices of the capital formation.

Let us summarize fact findings in the trends of the capital formation in Japan during the period 1955-1992. Table 11.2 represents average annual rates of growth in capital stock of private enterprises by industry during the period 1955-1990, where the period is divided into the following seven subperiods; 1955-1960, 1960-1965, 1965-1970, 1970-1975, 1975-1980, 1980-1985 and 1985-1990, in order to clarify the features on the capital accumulation in the Japanese economy. According to results in this table growth rates of the private capital accumulation in all sectors except water supply since 1975 were clearly slowed down in comparison with the rapid growth until 1975, while those in the 1980s were gradually recovered in some sectors such as electric machinery, motor vehicle, precision instrument, communication and education. Annual growth rates of capital stock during the three subperiods since 1960 were significantly higher than those of labor input by sector in the same periods.[5] Especially during the second subperiod, 1960-1965, 28 sectors of 43 sectors accomplished high growth of capital stock at more than 10 percent annually. This trend continued during the next two terms until 1975. After the oil crisis almost all industries except electricity, gas, medical and other service experienced dramatic slowdown of the growth in terms of capital stock.[6] During the fifth subperiod, 1975-1980, the growth rate of capital stock deteriorated by less than half of the growth rate in the previous subperiods by sectors. During the period 1955-1975 capital input by sector has grown rapidly in the high-growth rate, more than the historical standard of the Japanese economy. Since 1980 capital formation by sector has gradually recovered. Annual growth rate of capital stock

Table 11.2 Annual growth rate of private capital stock (unit: %)

	1955-1960	1960-1965	1965-1970	1970-1975	1975-1980	1980-1985	1985-1990
1. Agriculture	0.31	7.11	13.90	12.72	4.79	1.76	1.72
2. Coal mining	−6.21	0.62	−1.31	9.89	6.24	1.27	−1.55
3. Other mining	1.24	13.01	9.75	10.57	−0.04	0.48	1.23
4. Construction	9.40	23.56	18.18	19.54	7.78	4.23	6.09
5. Foods	2.15	17.11	12.62	14.48	5.69	5.19	5.46
6. Textile	−0.29	5.93	9.06	8.34	0.01	1.99	3.30
7. Apparel	8.55	16.92	16.67	9.81	4.58	3.38	5.29
8. Woods	−4.99	10.94	11.38	14.18	0.15	−1.26	2.46
9. Furniture	−3.58	17.17	14.67	14.39	3.11	1.06	4.91
10. Paper and pulp	14.60	10.41	12.88	18.60	5.39	3.39	5.33
11. Publishing	7.57	20.80	14.90	12.73	5.77	7.01	8.34
12. Chemical	13.64	14.64	12.11	14.03	4.68	4.18	5.02
13. Petroleum	3.47	14.06	18.29	16.63	4.45	3.78	2.82
14. Coal products	11.31	20.66	20.20	14.18	4.26	−0.24	2.01
15. Rubber products	7.58	13.97	17.03	17.82	5.61	6.35	6.38
16. Leather products	5.15	9.59	10.17	6.96	3.92	3.32	5.42
17. Stone and clay	13.34	15.79	13.63	14.47	3.46	4.92	4.81
18. Iron and steel	15.84	11.00	15.52	13.97	5.47	2.36	2.02
19. Non-ferrous	3.13	13.41	17.06	13.50	3.65	5.50	5.88
20. Metal products	18.09	17.95	22.18	18.50	7.05	6.76	6.64
21. Machinery	16.63	18.26	20.25	16.13	4.34	6.23	6.45
22. Elec. mach.	25.20	8.12	14.29	12.93	6.35	10.85	10.68
23. Motor vehicle	21.58	19.15	16.44	14.81	5.20	8.20	7.87
24. Other transp. mach.	2.78	10.48	15.56	23.35	−2.12	−0.23	0.61
25. Precision instruments	7.90	14.59	20.27	20.67	2.63	10.86	8.96
26. Other mfg prod.	18.89	23.39	16.83	19.68	4.90	7.31	8.05
27. Railroad transport	11.79	6.11	3.58	12.04	2.66	2.80	15.85
28. Road transport	42.11	1.30	7.96	17.52	8.78	7.20	3.60
29. Water transport	8.90	6.10	10.51	7.52	0.88	3.75	1.05
30. Air transport	40.93	21.51	14.57	11.91	3.22	3.90	4.97
31. Storage	5.91	6.40	8.99	11.11	2.92	2.36	9.65
32. Communication	3.72	17.24	4.27	22.89	6.50	22.74	32.76
33. Electricity	7.81	4.41	6.72	14.14	9.59	5.29	3.86
34. Gas supply	10.66	6.77	12.50	15.18	10.60	4.40	1.87
35. Water supply	−14.18	14.05	13.11	12.15	16.54	11.84	15.44
36. Trade	3.18	11.42	9.83	14.02	7.86	3.95	5.93
37. Finance	12.49	15.09	9.61	7.06	3.52	4.10	8.98
38. Real estate	3.47	25.13	15.46	20.02	6.20	5.88	10.98
39. Education	−5.90	6.95	5.77	7.49	5.68	4.68	4.51
40. Research	−0.17	−0.54	2.94	14.50	4.18	17.22	9.38
41. Medical service	−26.07	12.58	14.07	28.13	17.43	11.02	9.15
42. Other service	−1.17	4.56	5.41	12.98	10.98	13.18	12.62
Total	6.09	10.02	11.80	14.16	6.22	5.52	6.78

was increased in the 16 industries during the period, 1980-1985, and in the 26 industries after 1985. It is one of the interesting characteristics that the capital formations in the specific industries such as electric machinery, precision machinery and communication were increased rapidly after 1985.[7]

Table 11.3 represents a series of estimated capital stock by government enterprises. Annual growth rates of capital accumulation in government enterprise show constantly rapid growth such as 6.00 percent, 10.90 percent, 9.77 percent, 13.37 percent, 8.18 percent, 4.55 percent, 2.28 percent during every five years since 1955 respectively. We have to note that values after 1989 in the table are not adjusted by the trends of privatization of government enterprises.

Trends of social overhead capital are shown in Table 11.4. The

Table 11.3 Estimated capital stock: government enterprises (unit: 1 billion yen at 1985 price)

	1955	1960	1965	1970	1975	1980	1985	1990
1. Agriculture	730	1 246	2 231	3 979	8 392	13 921	19 406	24 860
3. Other mining	0	0	0	6	9	8	6	10
4. Construction	90	127	226	358	486	490	499	506
5. Foods	176	96	129	145	215	276	218	154
11. Publishing	2	3	27	27	25	26	31	38
12. Chemical	1	1	1	3	4	5	10	13
20. Metal products	0	1	5	7	8	8	8	9
27. Railroad transport	153	189	421	703	1 192	1 704	1 699	1 505
28. Road transport	1	14	92	196	398	490	645	742
29. Water transport	4	13	35	67	130	158	200	322
30. Air transport	0	0	1	6	19	30	34	59
32. Communication	891	1 572	3 541	6 531	12 751	17 094	18 285	13 881
33. Electricity	1 087	1 467	1 491	1 159	1 172	1 350	1 507	1 273
34. Gas supply	6	9	15	18	46	77	111	147
35. Water supply	0	451	1 286	2 757	6 359	9 599	12 070	14 548
36. Trade	5	18	50	123	403	570	629	717
37. Finance	18	19	46	54	75	204	204	522
38. Real estate	1	0	1	2	25	60	148	207
39. Education	1 178	1 630	2 850	4 411	8 448	13 597	16 926	19 758
40. Research	27	110	191	324	747	1 169	1 466	1 956
41. Medical service	94	225	585	1 463	3 105	4 848	6 670	8 484
42. Other service	16	59	269	601	1 690	2 742	3 566	4 627
43. Public admin.	2 906	2 726	3 710	5 095	9 017	13 941	19 071	21 560
Total	7 388	9 975	17 204	28 036	54 716	82 366	103 410	115 898

Table 11.4 Social overhead capital by asset categories (upper: 1 billion yen at 1985 price, lower: annual growth rate %)

	Housing	Railway	Toll Road	Road	Harbor	Airport	Park
1955	1 143	7 340	42	4 687	1 939	16	620
1960	1 559	7 316	208	6 452	1 961	24	523
1965	2 585	8 822	1 036	11 649	2 497	63	509
1970	4 778	11 496	2 756	20 017	3 411	181	676
1975	8 438	14 947	5 683	30 281	4 777	421	1 055
1980	10 633	18 778	8 670	39 763	6 146	528	1 716
1985	11 107	20 230	12 176	47 878	7 295	548	2 691
1990	11 121	18 782	18 120	60 206	8 813	846	4 754
1955-1960	6.21	−0.07	31.95	6.39	0.23	8.92	−3.39
1960-1965	10.11	3.75	32.16	11.82	4.83	19.05	−0.56
1965-1970	12.29	5.29	19.56	10.83	6.24	20.98	5.69
1970-1975	11.37	5.25	14.48	8.28	6.74	16.89	8.89
1975-1980	4.62	4.56	8.45	5.45	5.04	4.50	9.74
1980-1985	0.87	1.49	6.79	3.71	3.43	0.76	9.00
1985-1990	0.03	−1.49	7.95	4.58	3.78	8.67	11.38
	Sewage	Forestry	Rivers	Erosion	Seashore	Land Import	Total
1955	1 302	652	3 465	332	423	6	21 967
1960	1 070	705	3 539	485	496	150	24 488
1965	1 444	884	4 260	764	747	1 056	36 317
1970	2 843	1 188	5 694	1 228	934	2 879	58 080
1975	6 315	1 662	7 938	1 915	1 204	5 878	90 513
1980	11 443	2 278	11 125	2 860	1 536	7 966	123 442
1985	16 055	2 728	14 266	3 740	1 835	9 694	150 244
1990	22 039	3 356	18 146	4 748	2 235	11 282	184 450
1955-1960	−3.93	1.56	0.42	7.62	3.17	63.16	2.17
1960-1965	6.00	4.51	3.71	9.08	8.22	39.07	7.88
1965-1970	13.55	5.91	5.80	9.48	4.47	20.06	9.39
1970-1975	15.96	6.73	6.65	8.89	5.08	14.27	8.87
1975-1980	11.89	6.30	6.75	8.03	4.87	6.08	6.21
1980-1985	6.77	3.61	4.97	5.36	3.55	3.93	3.93
1985-1990	6.34	4.15	4.81	4.77	3.95	3.03	4.10

accumulation of social overhead capital has been almost stable since 1955, although its growth rate was slightly less than that of private and government capital accumulation. Since 1965 the growth rate of the accumulation in toll road, road, airport, park and sewage has increased rapidly. The term of maximum growth rate of each social overhead capital is different: Road (1960-1965), Harbor (1970-1975), Airport (1965-1970), Park (1985-1990), Sewage (1970-1975), Forestry (1970-1975), Rivers (1975-1980), Erosion (1965-1970) and Seashore (1960-1965). We also have to note that the share of toll road to general road increased rapidly from 0.090 percent in 1965 to 23.14 percent in 1990.

2.2 Structural Changes in Capital Coefficients

Capital stock matrices for private and government enterprises at 1985 constant prices, where a matrix is classified by 43 commodities in column and 43 industries in row, are estimated every year during the period 1955-1992. Forty-three commodities are aggregated into 12 types of assets: 1. Animal and Plants, 2. Construction, 3. Apparel, 4. Wood products, 5. furniture, 6. Metal products, 7. Machinery, 8. Electric machinery, 9. Motor vehicle, 10. Other transportation equipment, 11. Precision instruments and, 12. Miscellaneous products. Capital coefficients are defined as follows:

$$b_{ij}=K_{ij}/X_j, \quad (i=1,...,12, j=1,...,43). \tag{11.1}$$

We can know structural changes from trends of capital coefficients by industry, where the volume of coefficients designates the degree of capital intensity in industry and the trend or change of coefficients during the periods represents the patterns of the structural changes in terms of capital intensity or capital productivity, where K_{ij} includes capital stock both for private and government enterprises. From the viewpoints of the structural changes in terms of changes of the technology, we have to focus on both changes of the set of intermediate input coefficients, a_{ij} and capital coefficients, b_{ij}. In the next section we will return to these points by using the dynamic inverse approach. Here we will investigate the changes of capital coefficients preliminary. Figure 11.2 represents change of capital coefficients at the macro-level during the period 1955-1992, where poll in the figure stands for the level of capital coefficient and the number in each poll corresponds to the asset types classified into 12 categories. We can observe that capital coefficients at the macro level increased from 1.5 in 1955 to 2.5 in 1992 and moreover compositions of machinery and electric machinery among assets have gradually increased instead of building and construction. The figure also shows the relationship between real value added and volume of capital stock by a solid line (*) during the period 1960-1992. This also represents a rapid increase of capital-output ratio in terms of value added base.

When it comes to the development of technologies, we should focus on observations at the industry level instead of macro level. We will pick up certain typical changes of coefficients by industries: 1. Agriculture, 4. Construction, 6. Textile, 18. Iron, 21. Machinery, 22. Electric machinery, 23.

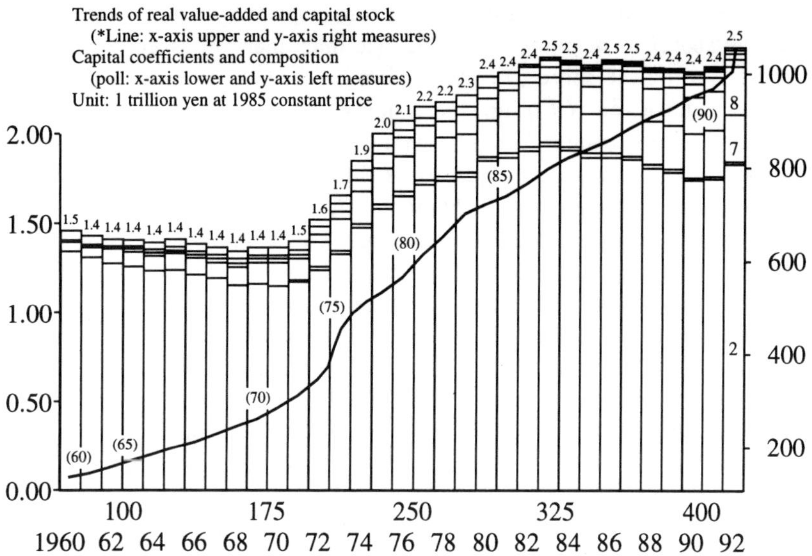

Classification of capital goods: 1. Animals/plants, 2. Construction, 3. Apparel, 4. Wood products, 5. Furniture, 6. Metal products, 7. Machinery, 8. Electrical machinery, 9. Vehicle, 10. Other transport, 11. Precision instruments, 12. Miscellaneous products.

Figure 11.2 Trends of capital coefficients and changes of capital composition

Motor vehicle and 33. Electricity. Capital coefficients in agriculture increased rapidly from 0.3 in 1960 to 3.0 in 1992 in terms of the sum of coefficients, which implies that capital productivity has been declining historically. Growth rate slightly decreased in the first half of the 1980s, but it recovered in the last half . Although capital coefficient of machinery has been increasing rapidly, more than 70 percent of the assets is shared by construction. We have to note in the agricultural sector that capital accumulation, especially for construction, owed mainly to that in government enterprises. Capital productivity in the construction sector also has been declining gradually and almost all of the assets are shared by the own products. In the textile industry changes of coefficients were more characteristic, where they were fairly stable in the 1960s and shifted higher in the 1970s and continued to increase gradually in the 1980s. Volume of coefficients changes from 0.2 in 1960 to 0.7 in 1992. Recently we can observe rapid increases of capital coefficients in machinery and electric machinery in the textile industry. In the iron and steel industry, capital coefficients increased from 0.2 in 1960 to 1.0 in 1992 totally, where the trend to increase slowed down, especially after 1985. Here again the shares of machinery and electric machinery in assets have been increased, while the share of construction has been declining recently. In machinery the level of capital coefficients in total capital stock shifted after the oil shock from 0.3 to 0.5, where decreases of capital coefficients for construction instead of increases of those in electric machinery after 1975 are one of the specific characteristics. Electric machinery is an exceptional example where the capital coefficients had a decreasing trend from the beginning of the 1960s. It means that in the electric machinery sector its capital productivity increased rapidly. After 1975, capital coefficients of input for construction in the electric machinery sector were decreasing gradually, while those from electric machinery by itself were increasing rapidly. Capital coefficients of the motor vehicle industry were relatively stable, although after 1975 they represent trends of gradual decreasing. While total volume of capital coefficients in motor vehicle were stable, the composition of capital coefficients have been remarkably changed, where coefficients of construction have been decreasing and coefficients of machinery and electric machinery increased rapidly in recent years. Finally, in electricity, trends in its capital coefficients completely changed at the beginning of the 1970s. They might represent changes in the source of electric power where nuclear power station was introduced in the late 1960s in Japan.

3 UNIT STRUCTURE AND DYNAMIC INVERSE

As we mentioned in the previous section, capital coefficients for private and government capital including social overhead capital have been changing since 1960. Especially capital asset shares of machinery and electric machinery instead of those of construction have been increasing rapidly in almost all sectors recently. Simultaneously we have to note that capital productivity in the machinery and electric machinery sectors has improved historically and such trends of capital productivity in these sectors were really rare exceptions among 43 industries. It seems to be one of the important characteristics in the recent movement of capital formation. In the economy changes of capital coefficients have impacts on the changes of input coefficients in intermediate and labor inputs as a system of the economy and finally the production efficiency in terms of TFP growth measure. The purpose of this section is to clarify the meanings of the characteristics in the movement of capital coefficients from viewpoints of the structural change of input coefficients, A_t, and capital coefficients, B_t, by using the concept of 'unit structure' and an approach on the 'dynamic inverse' which was proposed by Leontief (1970). Before the explanation of the framework of the dynamic inverse approach, we try to propose the concept of the 'unit structure', in which we can clarify the interdependent relationships among commodities as characteristics of the specific commodity production technology.[8] A unit structure of the specific commodity represents the internal linkages among production directly and indirectly, which is described by intermediate input coefficients, A_t, and factor input coefficients such as labor and capital, l_t, and k_t. In this concept, we can define the static measure of the production efficiency for a specific commodity, where the measure defined here is closely related to the traditional measure of TFP. In the dynamic inverse approach we can extend above the concept of 'unit structure' into the dynamic concept of the unit structure. Finally we can extend the static TFP measure into the corresponding measures of the dynamic production efficiency. By using the measures of the dynamic production efficiency, we would like to evaluate the contribution of the capital accumulation embodied by new technologies in the recent developing process of the Japanese economy by private and government enterprises to the economic growth.

We begin with the explanation of the concept of 'unit structure'. In the static input-output framework, the system of production can be described in terms of input coefficient matrix, A_t, vector of final demand, F_t, vector of output, X_t, vector of value added, V_t and unit vector, i, as follows:

$$A_t X_t + F_t = X_t \tag{11.2}$$

$$i' V_t = F_t i \tag{11.3}$$

If A_t is a nonsingular matrix, we obtain the following equation system.

$$X_t = (I - A_t)^{-1} F_t = B_t F_t \tag{11.4}$$

We will call the following equation the 'unit system' of the j commodity production.

$$A_t \hat{B}_j i + f_j^* = B_j, \tag{11.5}$$

and

$$i' v^* = f_j^* i, \tag{11.6}$$

where $\hat{B}_j$ represents a diagonal matrix with the j column vector of inverse matrix $(I - A_t)^{-1}$ as elements, f_j^* stands for the final demand vector with unity as j element and zero as other elements and v^* is a row vector of the unit value added. In the system of the equation (11.5), the following matrix,

$$U^{(j)} = u_{ik}^{(j)} = A_t \hat{B}_j \tag{11.7}$$

is referred to as the 'static unit structure' peculiar to the j commodity. The technology of the economy is described by the compound system of the 'unit structure' of the various commodities. Each unit structure of the j commodity represents the characteristics of the technology of the production. If we can define factor input coefficients such as labor and capital, l_t and k_t, we can define the vectors of labor and capital inputs corresponding to the unit structure L_t and K_t, which represent the direct and indirect input requirements of labor and capital by sectors in the production of the final demand f_j^*.

We can understand that a 'unit structure' for the j commodity represents the direct and indirect input requirements in terms of intermediate inputs, labor and capital inputs which are needed to supply one unit of final demand of j commodity. We can define a measure of the production efficiency of any k, (k = 1,..., n) sector in the production system based upon 'unit structure' for the j commodity production as follows:

$$v_{TK}^{t} = \frac{\dot{X}_k}{X_k} - \sum_i v_{xik} \frac{\dot{X}_{ik}}{X_{ik}} - v_{Lk} \frac{\dot{L}_k}{L_k} - v_{Kk} \frac{\dot{K}_k}{K_k}, \ (k=1,\ldots, n), \tag{11.8}$$

where X_k, X_{ik}, L_k, K_k represent output, intermediate inputs, labor and capital inputs of the k commodity which is needed to supply one unit of j final demand, directly and indirectly, and v_{xik}, v_{Lk}, v_{Kk} stand for the cost share of each input respectively. We should note that TFP measure defined by equation (11.8) exactly corresponds to an ordinary measure of sectoral TFP. Furthermore we can define an aggregate measure of the production efficiency in the framework of unit structure as follows:

$$v_{Tj}^{t} = \sum_k \frac{p_k X_k}{P_v V} v_{Tk}^{t} \tag{11.9}$$

where p_k represents output price of the k commodity and $p_v V$ stands for aggregate nominal value added, which is defined by the sum of sectoral labor and capital compensations, $\Sigma_k L_k\, p_{Lk}$ and $\Sigma_k K_k\, p_{Kk}$. v_{Tj}^{t} is an aggregate measure of the production efficiency in term of the unit structure of the j commodity. This measure designates the production efficiency of the j commodity production, where the production efficiency is evaluated as a measure of the total factor productivity as a system which is needed to supply one unit of j commodity as final demand.[9] We will refer a measure, v^t_{Tj}, to 'static unit TFP' on the j commodity as its 'unit structure'.

The above concepts of 'unit structure' and 'static unit TFP' correspond to a measure of the production efficiency of the j commodity in the specific time period t. In the production of the j commodity at year t, capital stock in the production has been already accumulated in the past period as a result of the investment in every sector. When we focus on the historical perspective of the capital accumulation, we can define another concept of 'dynamic unit structure' and 'dynamic unit TFP' in order to evaluate the production efficiency of the j commodity production at the year t as a dynamic process including the capital accumulation. Here we have to begin an explanation of a 'dynamic inverse', which was proposed by Leontief.

The framework of dynamic inverse is summarized below. We begin with the following n-commodity balance equations:

$$A_t x_t + I_t^P + I_t^G + c_t = x_t \tag{11.10}$$

where I_t^P is the capital formation matrix of private and government enterprises, I_t^G the infrastructure formation matrix as social overhead capital like toll road and c_t the other final demand except investment. I_t^P is defined by perpetual inventory method using depreciation rate δ^P and capital stock matrix K_t^P $(n \times n)$,

$$I_t^P = K_{t+1}^P - (I - \widehat{\delta^P}) K_t^P. \tag{11.11}$$

And the infrastructure formation matrix is defined similarly,

$$I_t^G = K_{t+1}^G \Phi^{GP} - (I - \widehat{\delta^G}) K_t^G \Phi^{GP}, \tag{11.12}$$

where the scale of K_t^G is the n(commodity)$\times m$(infrastructure) matrix and the converter from one infrastructure to one industry is defined by Φ^{GP} $(m \times n)$. We assume that some infrastructure services are imputed by only one particular industry and that some more general infrastructures, for example park, sewage and so on, are ignored and treated as the other final demand c_t. Substituting the equations (11.11) and (11.12) into (11.10), we can obtain the following equation using capital coefficient B_t,

$$G_t x_t - B_{t+1} x_{t+1} = c_t, \tag{11.13}$$

where

$$G_t = I - A_t + (I - \widehat{\delta^P})B_t^P + (I - \widehat{\delta^G})B_t^G, \tag{11.14}$$

$$B_t = B_t^P + B_t^G. \tag{11.15}$$

The equation (11.13) is realized from the distant past. When we can look back on them from the present base year t, these equations in the past different years are written as follows.

$$\begin{pmatrix} G_{t-\infty} & -B_{t-\infty} & & & & \\ & \ddots & \ddots & & & \\ & & G_{t-2} & -B_{t-1} & & \\ & & & G_{t-1} & -B_t & \\ & & & & G_t & \end{pmatrix} \begin{pmatrix} x_{t-\infty} \\ \vdots \\ x_{t-2} \\ x_{t-1} \\ x_t \end{pmatrix} = \begin{pmatrix} c_{t-\infty} \\ \vdots \\ c_{t-2} \\ c_{t-1} \\ c_t \end{pmatrix} \tag{11.16}$$

where G_t is $I - A_t$. For the achievement of the present consumption c_t, the equations (11.16) give us a series of production which is needed to supply one unit of final demand at the year t directly and indirectly in the static and dynamic process. In the production they should require the commodity production not only as direct and indirect transactions in the static linkages, but also as direct and indirect requirement of the capital goods in the dynamic linkages, where the capital stock must have been produced in the previous year or earlier. The long continuous production chain can make it possible that present consumption is realized. Then equation (11.16) represents 'dynamic unit structure' on the j commodity production, which corresponds to the concept of 'static unit structure', as mentioned above.

By using our estimated intermediate input coefficients matrices and capital coefficient matrices during the period 1960-1992, we can evaluate direct and indirect production requirements in each industrial sector, which are dynamically induced by a certain volume of final demands, one unit (1 million yen at the 1985) constant prices as consumption in certain period. Technology in a certain period should be evaluated by a set of A_{ij} and B_{ij} at that time. Changes of the coefficients represent the structural changes. Observed changes of coefficients represent the trends of structural changes reflected by technological changes. Also we can estimate dynamic changes of labor requirements, which were required for the direct and indirect production in each sector, induced by increases of final demand. By using the concept of the dynamic unit structure, we can define a measure of the production efficiency on the production of the j

commodity which is consistent with the supply of one unit of the j commodity as final demand at the year t, where the direct and indirect requirement of intermediate inputs and labor input are evaluated dynamically. At first we can define a measure of the production efficiency of the k, (k = 1,..., n) sector and any $t-m$, (m = 1,..., ∞) time specific point as follows:

$$v_{Tk}^{t-m} = (\frac{\dot{X}_k}{X_k})^{t-m} - \sum_i v_{xik}(\frac{\dot{X}_{ik}}{X_{ik}})^{t-m} - v_{Lk}(\frac{\dot{L}_{ik}}{L_k})^{t-m} \tag{11.17}$$

Sectoral and time-specific TFP measure defined above could be aggregated to ($t-m$) time-specific aggregate TFP as follows:

$$v_T^{t-m} = \sum_k (\frac{p_k X_k}{p_v v})^{t-m} - v_{Tk}^{t-m} \tag{11.18}$$

Time-specific TFP measure defined in equation (11.18) could be also aggregated to dynamic unit TFP, in which we can evaluate dynamically total efficiency of the production which are directly and indirectly required to supply one unit of the j commodity final demand at the year t as follows:

$$v_{TT}^t = \sum_m \sum_k (\frac{(p_k X_k)^{t-m}}{\Sigma_m p_v v}) v_{Tk}^{t-m} \tag{11.19}$$

We refer to this measure v_{TT}^t as growth rate of 'dynamic unit TFP'. By using the concept of 'dynamic unit TFP', we can recognize the impact of the structural changes in the intermediate input coefficients, labor coefficients and capital coefficients on certain specific commodity production as a production system as a whole in the economy. As we mentioned above, the recent trend of capital coefficients represents that the share of machinery and electric machinery, where the characteristics of the new developed technology is expected to be embodied, has increased rapidly. Productivity changes in these industries which were realized by the new developed technology are expected to have impacts on the productivity changes in all of other sectors directly and indirectly through the dynamic process of the capital formation in each sector.

4 STRUCTURAL CHANGE AND TRENDS OF EFFICIENCY IN JAPAN

We begin with the comparison between ordinary measures of growth rate of sectoral TFP and growth rate of static unit TFP as unit structure of *j* commodity shown in Tables 11.5 and 11.6 respectively. As mentioned previously while an ordinary measure of sectoral TFP represents the efficiency of the *j* commodity production of its own, the static unit TFP based upon unit structure implies the total efficiency in the *j* commodity production, where we can evaluate the efficiency of direct and indirect linkages of the technology as a system of the *j* commodity production. According to the results shown in Table 11.5, high growth of TFP in the 1960s rapidly deteriorated in the first half of the 1970s in almost all industries. After the slight recovery in the second half of the 1970s could be observed in some sectors, growth of TFP turned to be lower again in the second half of the 1980s. It should be noted, however, that there were some exceptional sectors such as chemical, rubber products, metal products, machinery, electric machinery, precision instruments, communication and trade, where TFP has grown continuously and been stable during these periods. On the other hand, according to the results shown in Table 11.6, efficiency based upon unit structure seems to be exaggerated by the interdependency of the production linkages. In the first half of the 1970s, when TFP growth in almost all of the sectors deteriorated, growth rates of 'static unit TFP' worsened in comparison with those of ordinary TFP in almost all the industries except rubber products. Adversely, in the 1980s, growth rates of static unit TFP represent a smooth recovery of the production efficiency in many sectors. It implies that efficiency gains in the sectors where the efficiency of their own technology has been improved could compensate for efficiency loss in the other sectors where the efficiency of their own technology has deteriorated. Especially it might be expected that there were some leading sectors where the production efficiency in those sectors increased rapidly in recent years. For example, in the agricultural sector, its growth rates of static unit TFP have been compensated by the technology linkages to other sectors during all periods except the first half of the 1970s, while its own efficiency has been deteriorating during the whole period except the period 1980-1985. In machinery and electric machinery, the efficiency gain increased in the unit measures rather than in the own measure during the whole periods.

Let us turn to the dynamic approach. By using the framework of the dynamic inverse we can estimate sectoral output requirements in the past which are needed to supply the certain amount of final demand at the reference year. Dynamic output requirements for the final demand of one dollar's worth of all commodities in the past has been diminishing for the past eight or ten years. We can observe that the values of the dynamic multiplier are fairly high in the sectors producing capital goods as well as

Table 11.5 Annual growth rate of ordinary TFP

	1960-1965	1965-1970	1970-1975	1975-1980	1980-1985	1985-1990
1. Agriculture	−1.3077	−4.3221	−3.3016	−2.4688	1.5785	−0.1974
2. Coal mining	3.8811	−0.3878	1.2771	−0.2889	−1.6105	−1.7632
3. Other mining	4.4893	8.8258	−4.7350	3.3521	−1.3112	0.7910
4. Building and const.	−0.6095	0.8505	−0.4919	−1.6646	0.6742	1.3549
5. Foods	0.0113	0.3943	−1.6787	2.1207	0.4095	−0.7967
6. Textile	0.7578	1.1515	0.5108	1.8962	0.0621	1.2304
7. Apparel	−0.0427	1.7720	0.8461	0.7811	−0.0379	−0.6712
8. Woods	1.8399	1.2007	1.0502	−2.7758	4.6759	−0.6181
9. Furniture	0.0496	1.8068	1.1657	1.2556	0.3766	1.4214
10. Paper and pulp	2.4421	2.2873	−1.4226	0.7936	1.5967	2.1654
11. Publishing	−4.1313	-3.1734	−1.9146	0.0544	0.6344	1.0549
12. Chemical	2.7707	4.9361	−1.8884	1.4397	2.6167	1.6342
13. Petroleum	4.0592	0.3054	−5.8485	−1.3468	0.2224	7.4601
14. Coal products	−0.6847	2.1301	−5.0960	−6.6112	−0.8756	2.4796
15. Rubber products	2.8239	2.7447	−2.0794	0.7218	1.3812	3.4169
16. Leather products	3.7839	0.4059	3.6165	−2.6481	1.1115	−0.6034
17. Stone and clay	2.6059	0.7939	−1.9768	1.4394	1.1999	1.6556
18. Iron and steel	−0.0154	1.9992	0.1969	0.9408	−0.3389	0.3613
19. Non-ferrous	−0.1351	0.7294	2.7689	2.4247	2.0591	0.2801
20. Metal products	2.8911	2.1074	-0.7550	2.1963	0.7989	1.4219
21. Machinery	−0.1367	2.6666	-0.7238	2.8382	1.7006	1.0546
22. Elec.mach.	1.8461	6.1067	1.9931	5.7103	2.1493	3.4755
23. Motor vehicle	0.9089	5.0628	2.0070	3.3043	0.7801	0.7465
24. Oth.Transp.mach.	5.1026	0.4876	−5.0888	1.3701	1.7506	1.4038
25. Precision instruments	4.4876	4.6906	0.3390	6.8586	1.6426	0.6412
26. Oth. mng. prod.	3.1183	4.0118	1.1778	1.6722	1.2636	0.5820
27. Tailroad transport	1.2072	0.0707	0.2298	−6.9686	2.8033	1.9171
28. Road transport	1.3181	4.5826	−9.3917	1.2409	−0.8960	0.7901
29. Water transport	0.2880	7.9355	−1.6750	1.1446	2.4544	−2.9659
30. Air transport	9.0226	4.1891	9.0837	2.3454	2.7712	0.8766
31. Storage	2.9782	5.7793	−3.7156	6.1078	0.5425	0.1161
32. Communication	4.5557	3.6786	−0.6545	4.9151	5.4584	4.7433
33. Electricity	3.8477	5.9104	−2.9874	−1.4776	2.2659	2.0111
34. Gas Supply	3.8952	1.8433	−1.2478	0.7191	1.5502	3.7512
35. Water Supply	−3.5270	1.2446	−5.4244	−3.3220	−2.8816	−0.7331
36. Trade	7.1881	5.3540	−0.2659	3.0210	0.0949	3.8118
37. Finance	5.5362	0.4879	−0.3705	−0.1567	4.0564	1.0889
38. Real estate	5.6265	−0.1291	−2.8262	−0.6861	0.7860	−0.3331
39. Education	2.8088	3.2496	3.6762	−2.9407	−1.8137	−0.8030
40. Research	6.6442	4.7453	−1.8705	1.9826	−5.2463	−0.4816
41. Medical service	2.5538	0.3339	5.9443	−2.2433	−1.0273	−3.8555
42. Other service	−6.0195	1.6479	−3.9797	0.9994	−1.4490	−2.3343
43. Public admin.	4.6701	5.8536	8.7946	−3.6579	0.1032	1.8943

Table 11.6 Annual growth rate of static unit TFP

	1960-1965	1965-1970	1970-1975	1975-1980	1980-1985	1985-1990
1. Agriculture	−0.8710	−4.2143	−5.0595	−2.2520	2.5838	0.4224
2. Coal mining	4.5011	1.4707	−0.7413	−0.0010	−0.8582	−1.1111
3. Other mining	5.7886	10.2580	−6.2949	4.1796	−0.5575	2.2040
4. Build. and const.	1.9016	4.6281	−2.5073	−0.3961	1.6776	2.5185
5. Foods	0.1293	−0.4985	−4.9516	1.9850	1.7522	−0.2096
6. Textile	2.7263	4.2506	−1.5260	3.6467	1.6602	3.1541
7. Apparel	2.6538	5.3501	−0.7186	2.8242	0.9636	1.1687
8. Woods	2.2025	0.0658	−2.0414	−3.7326	6.9270	0.0796
9. Furniture	2.3977	4.5308	−0.6667	1.5541	2.3813	2.4512
10. Paper and pulp	5.1786	5.5148	−4.5933	1.3326	3.9843	4.3944
11. Publishing	−2.3612	−0.8895	−4.1974	0.8446	2.0993	2.4585
12. Chemical	6.0342	9.6538	−5.2038	2.6686	4.6474	3.4405
13. Petroleum	4.2628	0.6153	−6.6108	−1.2135	0.4678	8.1491
14. Coal products	1.6046	4.2602	−7.0153	−7.1860	−0.9367	3.0802
15. Rubber products	5.1842	6.5512	−4.1788	1.9194	3.0948	5.0464
16. Leather products	8.5287	3.3193	4.3431	−2.3608	2.8968	0.1552
17. Stone and clay	5.0320	5.0088	−5.2366	2.7080	1.9606	3.0699
18. Iron and steel	1.6058	7.7867	−1.7826	1.4190	−0.0727	1.7919
19. Non-ferrous	3.7721	8.7168	0.9332	5.4914	4.3779	1.5926
20. Metal products	4.3685	5.9150	−2.0795	3.3919	1.4112	2.4789
21. Machinery	1.3060	7.3788	−1.9518	5.7575	3.2430	2.5937
22. Elec. mach.	4.0548	11.8970	1.3414	9.0530	3.8494	5.9231
23. Motor vehicle	3.2606	10.8287	1.5521	6.6313	2.2809	2.7389
24. Oth. trasp. mach.	7.6626	4.8338	−7.0837	3.3813	3.2480	3.0030
25. Precision instruments	7.0828	8.9303	−0.3720	9.5766	3.1281	1.8736
26. Oth. mng. prod.	5.9031	8.1545	−3.8291	3.0055	3.3720	2.1203
27. Railroad transp.	3.0243	1.6352	−1.9731	−6.1998	3.5238	2.2419
28. Road transport	2.3333	6.1912	−10.2870	1.8285	−0.4865	1.4815
29. Water trasport	1.5071	10.9124	−3.0295	1.8525	4.2648	−2.7567
30. Air transport	11.3572	6.1315	7.9388	3.5064	4.0744	2.0325
31. Storage	3.4205	6.8405	−5.6140	6.4616	1.0566	0.2052
32. Commuinication	4.7596	4.1355	−1.4277	5.1463	5.2896	4.9797
33. Electricity	4.5203	6.6429	−4.8534	−1.6834	2.4658	2.5643
34. Gas Supply	4.9419	2.7329	−2.1905	3.9083	2.0216	3.9044
35. Water Supply	−3.1095	2.3160	−7.3048	−3.6003	−1.7915	0.0616
36. Trade	8.2365	6.7221	−1.4032	3.4770	0.7190	4.2479
37. Finance	5.4298	1.3509	−1.5342	0.2614	4.5193	1.0451
38. Real estate	5.8691	0.4185	−3.1804	−0.6926	1.0732	−0.2453
39. Education	2.6103	4.1838	3.2145	−2.8556	−1.6433	−0.6086
40. Research	6.1856	5.7750	−3.0835	2.2919	−5.0097	−0.2791
41. Medical service	4.2327	2.8539	4.1853	−1.4248	0.0906	−2.7871
42. Other service	−4.6120	3.5857	−5.7576	1.7402	−0.4889	−1.4768
43. Public admin.	5.6705	7.1161	7.6592	−3.3134	0.4751	2.2577

in services.

We can estimate a measure of dynamic unit TFP defined in equation (11.19), in which we can evaluate dynamically total efficiency of the production which is directly and indirectly required to supply one unit of j commodity final demand at the year t. Table 11.7 shows the results. Since dynamic impacts of production chains for one unit of production of j commodity of final demand seem to diminish until ten years ago as we mentioned above, our estimates of dynamic aggregate TFP can be evaluated after the period 1970. In Table 11.7 we can show annual growth rate of this measure for every five years since 1970 in each sector. As previously stated, structural changes in the economy are designated by the changes of structural parameters, A_t, B_t, and l_t in our input-output framework. Capital coefficients, B_t include both parameters of capital coefficients of private and government capital and social overhead capital, B_t^P and B_t^G. Social overhead capital is divided into eleven categories: 1. Housing, 2. Railway construction, 3. Toll road, 4. Road, 5. Harbor, 6. Airport, 7. Forestry protection, 8. River improvement, 9. Erosion, 10. Seashore erosion and 11. Land improvement. Each social overhead capital corresponds to specific industries. Social overhead capital including 7, 8, 9 and 10 correspond to the agricultural sector. Social overhead capital 2 (railway) corresponds to the railway industry. Social overhead capitals 3 and 4 correspond to the road transportation industry. Social overhead capitals 5 and 6 correspond to water transportation, air transportation and finally 1 and 11 are imputed to real estate industry, respectively. These parameters should be considered to designate the structure of the economy as a compound set.[10]

The structure of the economy is assumed to be designated by a set of above structural parameters, A_t, B_t^P, B_t^G and l_t in each year t. During the period 1960-1992 these structural parameters have been changing gradually. We are considering that impacts of the structural changes on productivity growth could be identified by changes of the dynamic unit TFP measures in equation (11.19). Results are shown in Table 11.7. Each entry in the table represents average annual growth rate of dynamic unit TFP as measures of the impact of structural change during each subperiod, where the growth rate is evaluated by the difference per year between the dynamic unit TFP corresponding to the structure of the beginning year and that of the ending year in each subperiod. Then each value in the table implies the degree of the annual impact by the structural changes during each subperiod. According to our results, impacts of the structural changes were fairly high in every sector. We focus on the recent impact of new technology on TFP growth during the period 1985-1990. As we mentioned above, coefficients of machinery and electric machinery have

Table 11.7 Annual growth rate of dynamic unit TFP

	1970-1975	1975-1980	1980-1985	1985-1990
1. Agriculture	−2.2790	−2.6317	1.5333	0.6850
2. Coal mining	−4.4393	−0.7217	−1.1370	−6.3471
3. Other mining	−1.8268	5.6029	1.3169	4.1859
4. Build. and const.	1.4701	0.6559	2.3198	4.2201
5. Foods	−2.8898	2.3760	1.8281	1.3313
6. Textile	0.8058	4.7147	3.1124	4.7031
7. Apparel	1.6113	3.3548	2.0228	2.6532
8. Woods	1.0999	−4.4979	7.9188	0.6123
9. Furniture	2.5372	1.2530	3.4254	3.3402
10. Papre and pulp	−1.7425	2.4998	4.7308	6.3626
11. Publishing	−1.5909	1.3973	2.9004	4.0175
12. Chemical	−2.2657	3.5825	5.2407	5.6562
13. Petroleum	−5.8090	−0.0148	0.6832	10.6335
14. Coal products	−6.4876	−5.6901	0.0908	1.4124
15. Rubber products	−2.6921	3.1247	3.6483	6.3996
16. Leather products	7.9675	−0.3172	2.5801	1.2962
17. Stone and clay	−2.3030	3.2118	2.1039	4.9658
18. Iron and steel	0.6999	2.6810	0.4330	3.8527
19. Non-ferrous	3.2777	7.5830	3.4984	4.5632
20. Metal products	0.6366	3.6701	0.9555	3.9991
21. Machinery	0.6198	6.5612	4.5068	5.0387
22. Elec. mach.	5.0818	9.8984	5.0155	7.9444
23. Motor vehicle	3.6990	8.7458	3.0192	4.1987
24. Oth. Transp. mach.	−4.9727	4.9327	3.4767	4.6106
25. Precision Instruments	2.2844	11.3045	2.7687	3.3155
26. Oth. mng. prod.	−0.8597	3.6117	4.3360	3.5126
27. Railroad Transport	−0.2211	−3.9472	1.8763	5.5564
28. Road Transport	−5.3017	0.6071	0.5630	4.0326
29. Water Transport	2.1123	0.9871	3.6442	−2.0024
30. Air Transport	7.4987	7.3549	4.3717	5.1771
31. Storage	−1.6223	6.4430	1.7181	1.9357
32. Communication	5.6489	0.1968	6.5992	8.2108
33. Electricity	−0.5969	−0.5920	1.9297	5.5362
34. Gas Supply	3.3754	4.6903	0.6797	6.8394
35. Water Supply	−5.3636	−1.8461	1.7057	2.2770
36. Trade	2.0026	4.2955	1.6125	5.5408
37. Finance	1.7724	1.7513	5.5082	2.6388
38. Real estate	−1.9181	0.7078	0.4283	−0.2783
39. Education	2.9225	−3.7591	−2.4127	0.5217
40. Research	−2.5443	1.7445	−3.0759	1.0413
41. Medical service	6.8286	−0.3763	0.4396	−1.3107
42. Other service	−2.7600	1.8008	0.7127	0.1916
43. Public admin.	8.6809	−4.2797	0.2824	3.1698

rapidly increased in almost all sectors in which these changes of composition in capital coefficients are expected to embody recent new development of technologies in production. In spite of the hypothesis it is highly difficult to see the impacts on productivity growth in the results of ordinary measures of TFP growth as shown in the last column of Table 11.5. In 23 of 43 sectors annual growth rate of TFP in the ordinary measures deteriorated in the period 1985-1990 rather than that in the previous subperiod. It might suggest that there are initial intuitive questions, the so-called 'productivity paradox' in the recent years. When it comes to focus upon the measures defined by the static unit TFP as shown in Table 11.6, a number of industries with the deterioration of TFP growth during the period 1985-1990 decreased from 23 in the ordinary measures to 20 in the static unit TFP measures. On the other hand, if we try to measure TFP growth in the dynamic unit TFP concept as shown in Table 11.7, the deterioration of TFP growth can be observed only in 11 of 43 sectors. In comparison with the static unit TFP, the dynamic unit TFP represents the improvement of the production efficiency in almost all sectors except coal mining, coal products and real estate. We can conclude that there were fairly dominant impacts of the new technologies on TFP growth even in these sectors. It would be verified by changes of capital coefficients, especially capital coefficients of machinery and electric machinery which are expected to embody new technologies in the recent years.

5 CONCLUSION

In this chapter, we try to evaluate the impacts of the recent new technology on the TFP growth. We started from the intuitive observation of TFP growth in the recent OECD countries. Statistics of macro-TFP measures in OECD countries designate the so-called 'productivity paradox', where the TFP growth has been deteriorating recently in spite of the increases of real investment. 'Productivity paradox' should finally come to a conclusion to evaluate the real impacts of the recent new technology on the productivity growth. Concerning the evaluation of the impacts, we have to clarify the problems of measurement of TFP growth at first. Broadly speaking, the measurement errors are divided into two sources. One is that measurement errors come from the evaluation of the quality changes in inputs and output measures. The other is the aggregation bias in the measurement of inputs and outputs. We focused on the latter error of the measurement in Kuroda and Shimpo (1992). We could conclude the aggregation bias in the measurement of aggregate TFP growth should not be ignored. Especially during the periods where the new technological progress has been continuing positively, the aggregation bias should not be ignored, because there are expected sizable changes of allocation of resources among sectors.

'Productivity paradox' suggests that there are more important issues in the evaluation of the new technology from the viewpoints of TFP growth. Even if the above problems of measurement errors of TFP growth were solved, it still remains to clarify the impacts of the new technology on the TFP growth or the economic growth as one of the basic issues. In this chapter, we assume that such new technology might be embodied in the new investment and the changes of capital stock along with the new investment should have impacts on the TFP growth. We try to measure the changes of compositions of the capital stock by new technology from changes of trends in capital coefficients in each industrial sector. We can observe remarkable changes of the capital coefficients, where the capital coefficients of machinery and electric machinery as capital goods in each sectors have increased rapidly instead of the decreases of construction as capital goods in almost all of sectors recently. In order to evaluate the impacts of the changes of the composition in capital coefficients, we proposed new measures of TFP growth, where TFP growth in specific commodity production is evaluated by a unit system in which the spillover effect of the productivity is taken into account directly and indirectly. It is an extension of ordinary TFP growth measures. New measurement of TFP growth is divided into two concepts, 'static unit TFP' and 'dynamic unit TFP'. While in the measure of static unit TFP direct and indirect spillover effects of TFP growth among sectors are taken into account in the static input-output framework, dynamic unit TFP growth measures try to evaluate direct and indirect spillover effects of TFP growth dynamically. Analysis of dynamic unit TFP approach is based upon the framework of dynamic inverse, where we can evaluate the impacts of the changes of capital coefficients embodied new development of technologies on TFP growth. Dynamic unit TFP growth represents the reasonable impacts of the recent new development of technology. It implies that there are no paradoxical movements in the recent years from viewpoints of the relationships between TFP growth and new investment.

Although we try to give one implication concerning 'productivity paradox' in recent years, the analysis of the conceptualization in productivity growth still has several remaining issues. One is the evaluation of the impacts of the new technologies on the labor market. In our context of the analysis, we can extend our analysis to the evaluation of changes of labor coefficients related to those of capital coefficients. These might have impacts on the substitutability among labor and capital from new technology. It might be expected to have some time-lag in the changes of labor coefficients in the adjustment process to the new technologies. The other issue remaining here is the effect of the externality of the new technologies. In partiular new information technology might be expected to have some impact on the externality along with the network in the society.

NOTES

1. Greenspan (1995, 1996).
2. The perpetual inventory method is briefly described as the following: Let I_m^j be the quantity of gross investment made in the m asset in the j industry, and u_m^j the rate of replacement of the m asset utilized in the j industry ($0 < u_m^j < 1$). The method relates changes in the level of capital stock to current acquisitions of capital goods and replacement requirements; or, to put it in a different perspective, it links current level of capital stock to past acquisitions of capital goods as follows:

$$\begin{aligned} A_m^j(T) &= I_m^j(T) + (1-u_m^j)\,A_m^j(T-1) \\ &= \sum_{S=1}^{T}(1-u_m^j)^{T-S}\mathrm{I}_m^j(S) \\ &\quad + (1-u_m^j)^T A_m^j(0), \quad (m=1,\ldots,M;\, j=1,\ldots,J), \end{aligned} \tag{11.20}$$

   where $A_m^j(0)$ is the benchmark capital stock for the j industry's m asset.
3. Social overhead capital is divided into the following 13 categories: 1. housing, 2. railway construction, 3. Toll road, 4. Road, 5. Harbor, 6. Airport, 7. Forestry protection, 8. River improvement, 9. Erosion, 10. Seashore erosion, 11. Land improvement, 12. Park and 13. Sewage. They can subdivided into 52 categories in detail.
4. Commodity classification of capital goods corresponds to the commodity in the Basic Japanese Input-Output Table classified by 541 commodities and capital goods are divided into 78 commodities in the table.
5. According to our estimation, average annual growth rates of labor input were 2.929 percent, 2.201 percent, and −0.097 percent in 1960-1965, 1965-1970 and 1970-1975 at the macro level respectively. See Kuroda and Shimpo (1993).
6. In Japan where more than 90 percent of the energy sources were imported, impacts of the oil crisis were unexpectedly serious. Trends of capital formation in almost all of the industries were kinked downward. Few exceptions like electricity, gas, medical and other services were due to the investment promotion policy in utility sectors supported by government in order to avoid serious deterioration of the economy.
7. Japan National Railway and National Telecommunication Company were privatized in 1987 and 1885. Growth rates of both industries in Table 11.2 include their impacts.
8. Ozaki and Shimuzu (1984).

9. Aggregate measure of TFP growth defined by equation (11.9) has to be distinguished from growth rate of TFP in the ordinary measure at the macro level. The measure defined here corresponds to an aggregate measure of the production efficiency in term of the unit structure of the j commodity.
10. Park and sewage classified into social overhead capital in Table 11.4 are ignored here, because it is difficult to correspond to industry.

REFERENCES

Ackerman, S.R. (1973), 'Used cars as a depreciating asset', *Western Economic Journal*, **11**, 463-74.

Akerlof, G.A. (1970), 'The market for lemons: quality uncertainty and the market mechanism', *Western Economic Journal*, **84** , 488-500.

Arrow, K.J. and M.A. Kurz, *Public Investment, the Rate of Return, and Optimal Fiscal Policy*, Baltimore: Johns Hopkins University Press.

Arrow, K., H. Chenery, B. Minhas and R. Solow (1961), 'Capital-labor substitution and economic efficiency', *The Review of Economics and Statistics*, 43.

Biorn, E. (1989), *Taxation, Technology and the User Cost of Capital*, Amsterdam: North-Holland.

Coen, R. (1975), 'Investment behavior, the measurement of depreciation, and tax policy', *American Economic Review*, **65**, 59-74.

Diewert, W.E. (1986), *The Measurement of the Economic Benefits of Infrastructure Services*, Berlin Heidelberg, Springer-Verlag, 278.

Feldstein, M.S. and M. Rothschild (1974), 'Towards an economic theory of replacement investment', *Econometrica*, **42**, 393-423.

Greenspan, Alan (1995), Speech at the Economic Club of Chicago.

Greenspan, Alan (1996), Keynote Speech at the Conference held by the Federal Reserve Bank of Kansas.

Hall, R.E. (1968), 'Technical change and capital from the point of view of the dual', *The Review of Economic Studies*, **35**, 35-46.

Hall, R.E. (1971), 'The measurement of quality change from vintage price data', in Z. Griliches (ed.), *Price Indexes and Quality Change: Studies in New Methods of Measurement*, Cambridge, MA: Harvard University Press, 240-71.

Hall, R.E. and D.W. Jorgenson (1967), 'Tax policy and investment behavior', *American Economic Review*, **57**, 391-414.

Hulten, C.R. (1990), 'The measurement of capital', in E.R. Berndt and J.E. Triplett (eds), *Fifty Years of Economic Measurement: The Jubilee of the Conference on Research in Income and Wealth*, Chicago: The University of Chicago Press, 119-58.

Hulten, C.R. and G.E. Peterson (1984), 'The public capital stock, trends, and performance', *American Economic Review*, **74**, 166-73.

Hulten, C.R. and F.C. Wykoff (1981a), 'Economic depreciation and accelerated depreciation: an evaluation of the Conable-Jones 10-5-3 Proposal', *National Tax Journal*, **34**, 45-60.

Hulten, C.R. and F.C. Wykoff (1981b), 'The estimation of economic depreciation using vintage asset prices: an application of the Box-Cox power transformation', *Journal of Econometrics*, **15**, 367-96.

Hulten, C.R. and F.C. Wykoff (1981c), 'The Measurement of economic depreciation', in C.R. Hulten (ed.), *Depreciation, Inflation, and the Taxation of Income from Capital*, Washington: The Urban Institute Press, 81-125.

Jorgenson, D.W. (1963), 'Capital theory and investment behaviors', *American Economic Review*, **53**, 247-74.

Jorgenson, D.W. (1974), 'The economic theory of replacement and depreciation', in W. Sellekaerts (ed.), *Econometrics and Economic Theory; Essays in Honour of Jan Tinbergen*, New York: Macmillan, 189-221.

Jorgenson, D.W. (1989), 'Capital as a factor of production', in D.W. Jorgenson, and R. Landau (eds), *Technology and Capital Formation*, Canbridge: The MIT Press, 1-35.

Jorgenson, D.W. and Z. Griliches (1967), 'The explanation of productivity change', *The Review of Economic Studies*, **34**, 249-83.

Kuroda, M. (1988), 'A method of estimation for updating transaction matrix in the input-output relationships', in K. Uno and S. Shishido (eds), *Statistical Data Bank Systems, Socio-Economic Database and Model Building in Japan*, Amsterdam: North-Holland, 128-48.

Kuroda, M. and K. Shimpo (1992), 'Sources of aggregate economic growth in Japan during the period 1960-85', *Journal of Applied Input-Output Analysis*, **1**, 55-70.

Lee, B.S. (1978), 'Measurement of capital depreciation within the Japanese fishing fleets', *The Review of Economics and Statistics*, **60**, 255-73.

Leontief, W.W. (1970), 'The dynamic inverse', in A.P. Carter, and A. Brody (eds), *Contributions to Input-Output Analysis*, Amsterdam: North-Holland Publishing, 17-46.

Musgrave, J.C. (1980), 'Government-owned fixed capital in the United States, 1925-79', *Survey of Current Business*, **60**, 33-43.

Nadiri, I.M. and T.P. Mamuneas (1994), 'The effect of public infrastructure and R&D capital on the cost structure and performance of U.S. manufacturing industries', *The Review of Economics and Statistics*, **76**, 22-37.

Ohta, M. and Z. Griliches (1975), 'Automobile prices revisited: extensions of the hedonic price hypothesis', in N.E. Terleckyj (ed.), *Household Production and Consumption*, New York: Columbia University Press, 325-90.

Ozaki, I. and M. Shimuzu (1984), 'Technological change and the pattern of economic development', *Proceedings of the Seventh International Input-Output Techniques*, New York: United Nations.

Shah, A. (1992), 'Dynamics of public infrastructure, industrial productivity and profitability', *The Review of Economics and Statistics*, **74**, 28-36.

Solow, R.M. (1955), 'The production function and the theory of capital', *The Review of Economic Studies*, **23**, 101-8.

Solow, R.M. (1962), 'Substitution and fixed proportions in the theory of capital', *The Review of Economic Studies*, **29**, 207-18.

Solow, R.M. (1963), 'Heterogeneous capital and smooth production function: an experimental study', *Econometrica*, **31**, 623-45.

12. Productivity Growth in Taiwan's Manufacturing Industry, 1961-1993

Chi-yuan Liang and Dale W. Jorgenson [1]

1 INTRODUCTION

The economic miracle of the four Asian newly industrialized economies (NIEs), that is, Hong Kong, Korea, Singapore and Taiwan in the past three decades has attracted many economists' attention. The focus is mainly on the causes which lead to the economic success of the Asian NIEs.

Basically relevant researches, whether industry broken-down or aggregate, can be classified into either demand-side or supply-side. Those from demand-side analysis attribute NIEs' economic growth to the growth of both domestic and foreign demand. The studies from the supply-side approach, using production functions, generally allocate the growth of the economy or an industry to the growth of factor inputs and total factor productivity (TFP), or technical change.

Many interesting studies have been done from the supply-side approach. For country studies, there is Tsao (1982) on Singapore; Kim and Park (1985) on Korea; Hsing (1985) and Liang (1989,1992) on Taiwan, and Kim and Lau (1994), Lau (1994) and Young (1994) for international comparison.

According to Kim and Lau (1994) and Young (1994), the secret of the economic miracle in Singapore, Hong Kong, Korea and Taiwan during the past three decades has little to do with TFP or technological change, and much to do with the rapid increase in factor inputs. They also maintained that the growth rate of TFP in the four Asian NIES is less than for developed countries.

Liang (1995b) found that the argument proposed by Krugman (1994), Kim and Lau (1994) and Young (1994) - that the fast growth of NIEs has little to do with TFP improvement - is valid over a long period (1961-1993) but invalid for 1982-1993, and that the other hypothesis proposed by Kim and Lau (1994) and Young (1994) that the growth rate of the TFP in the NIEs is less than for developed countries, such as Japan and the

USA, is valid during 1961-1973 and 1973-1982 but not during 1982-1987. If the same situation can be found in other NIEs, the future of economic growth in NIEs and the Asian New Tigers might be much brighter than the Krugman forecast. Since Liang (1995b) focuses on the whole economy only, it might be interesting to examine the trend of TFP growth in individual industry such as manufacturing.

Kim and Lau (1994), Lau (1994), Young (1994) and Krugman (1994) do not take into account the heterogeneous characteristics of the input, which might lead to a measurement error on TFP changes. For example the nature of labor input is different for various occupations: skilled labor, unskilled labor, manager, clerk, engineer and technician. As for capital input, the nature of buildings, machinery, transportation equipment, land and inventories also vary. For an accurate measurement of the contribution factor inputs to the growth of output and changes in productivity, every factor input should be further decomposed before being summed up by using an appropriate weight such as the translog index.

Jorgenson and his associates (Christensen and Jorgenson, 1970; Gollop and Jorgenson, 1980; Jorgenson, Gollop and Fraumeni, 1987) have conducted research in this area. However they ignore the heterogeneous characteristics of inputs related to different sectors.

The quality changes of inputs caused by industrial structural changes should be taken into account in calculating the TFP of the economy as a whole. We extend Jorgenson and his associates' approach by incorporating the quality changes of inputs caused by industrial structural change, taking them as another heterogeneous characteristic of inputs in TFP calculation.

In addition these papers discuss only the relationship between value added and factor inputs such as labor and capital. In fact the intermediate input accounts for a greater portion of total cost than do capital and labor. The substitutability and complementarity between intermediate input and capital, and between intermediate input and labor, are so important that it is inappropriate to ignore them. Besides, since the oil price shocks the relationship between energy input and other factor input has become a worldwide concern. Consequently the value added model should be replaced with a model in which the change in total output can be explained by the changes in factor input, including capital, labor, energy and intermediate input, as well as change in TFP or technical change.

The objective of this chapter is to employ a new method to measure the growth of TFP and to analyze the causes of growth in output in Taiwan's twenty manufacturing sectors. Finally policy implications are drawn from the findings. A translog production function, which is more general than the conventional Cobb-Douglas and constant elasticity of substitution (CES) production function, is employed for this.

In addition to the introduction, the outline of the rest of this chapter is as follows: section 2, methodology; section 3, data compilation; section 4, empirical results; section 5, conclusions and implications.

2 METHODOLOGY

Following Gollop and Jorgenson (1980), we measure sectoral productivity by using translog production function: [2]

Output (Q) is a function of the logarithms of capital (K), labor (L), energy (E), intermediate input (M) and time (T) which indexes the level of technology. The production function is assumed to be constant returns to scale, so that a proportional change in all inputs results in a proportional change in output.[3]

If we consider data at any two discrete points of time, say T and $T-1$, the average rate of technical change can be expressed as the difference between successive logarithms of output and inputs, including capital, labor, energy and intermediate input with weights given by average value shares:[4]

$$\begin{aligned}\overline{R_T} &= \ln Q(T) - \ln Q(T-1) - \overline{S_K}[\ln K(T) - \ln K(T-1)] \\ &\quad - \overline{S_L}[\ln L(T) - \ln L(T-1)] - \overline{S_E}[\ln E(T) - \ln E(T-1)] \\ &\quad - \overline{S_M}[\ln M(T) - \ln M(T-1)],\end{aligned} \tag{12.1}$$

where

$$\overline{S_i} = \frac{1}{2}[S_i(T) + S_i(T-1)],\ i = K, L, E, M$$

We refer to this expression for the average rate of technical change, R_T, as the translog index of rate of technical change or the translog index of rate of total factor productivity change. The translog index is sometimes called the discrete version of the Divisia index or the Tornqvist index.[5] Diewert has shown that if the production function is a homogeneous translog, then the translog index will be exact. This provides a theoretical foundation for using the translog index in productivity analysis.

Furthermore, we can consider specific forms for the functions defining industry aggregate capital (K), labor (L), energy (E) and intermediate input (M). For example the intermediate input aggregate can be expressed as a translog function of m individual intermediate inputs.

Analogically, considering the data at discrete points of time, the difference between successive logarithms of intermediate input is a weighted average of differences between successive logarithms of individual intermediate inputs and the weights are given by average value shares:

$$\ln M(T) - \ln M(T-1) = \sum_{j=1}^{m} \overline{S_{M_i}} [\ln M_i(T) - \ln M_i(T-1)], \qquad (12.2)$$

where

$$\overline{S_{M_i}} = \frac{1}{2}[S_{M_i}(T) + S_{M_i}(T-1)], \; (i = 1, 2, \ldots, m) \qquad (12.3)$$

Similarly, if aggregate capital, labor and energy inputs are translog of their components, we can express them as the weighted average difference between successive logarithms of their component inputs in the following form

$$\ln K(T) - \ln K(T-1) = \sum_{i=1}^{k} \overline{S_{K_i}} [\ln K_i(T) - \ln K_i(T-1)], \qquad (12.4)$$

$$\ln L(T) - \ln L(T-1) = \sum_{i=1}^{l} \overline{S_{L_i}} [\ln L_i(T) - \ln L_i(T-1)], \qquad (12.5)$$

$$\ln E(T) - \ln E(T-1) = \sum_{i=1}^{e} \overline{S_{E_i}} [\ln E_i(T) - \ln E_i(T-1)], \qquad (12.6)$$

where

$$\overline{S_{K_i}} = \frac{1}{2}[S_{K_i}(T) + S_{K_i}(T-1)], \quad (i = 1, 2, \ldots, k) \qquad (12.7)$$

$$\overline{S_{L_i}} = \frac{1}{2}[S_{L_i}(T) + S_{L_i}(T-1)], \quad (i = 1, 2, \ldots, l) \qquad (12.8)$$

$$\overline{S_{E_i}} = \frac{1}{2}[S_{E_i}(T) + S_{E_i}(T-1)], \quad (i = 1, 2, \ldots, e) \qquad (12.9)$$

Furthermore, in order to measure the changes in TFP of broader categories, such as the manufacturing sector or the economy as a whole, aggregating the above sectoral inputs is necessary.

The methodology we employed to aggregate the sectoral intermediate inputs is as follows:

$$\ln M^A(T) - \ln M^A(T-1) = \sum_{j=1} \overline{S^{M_j}}(T)[\ln M^j(T) - \ln M^j(T-1)]$$

$$(j=1,\ldots,2) \tag{12.10}$$

where

$M^A(T)$: the translog index of the intermediate input in the aggregate sector,
$M^J(T)$: the translog index of the intermediate input in subsector j,
$S^M{}_j(T)$: the intermediate input value share of subsector j in the aggregate sector.

$$\overline{S^{M_j}} = \frac{1}{2}[S^{M_j}(T) + S^{M_j}(T-1)],\ (j=1, 2,\ldots) \tag{12.11}$$

Analogically the translog index of the capital, labor and energy inputs of the aggregate sector, is calculated respectively by the following:

$$\ln K^A(T) - \ln K^A(T-1) = \sum_{j=1} \overline{S^{K_j}}(T)[\ln K^j(T) - \ln K^j(T-1)] \tag{12.12}$$

$$\ln E^A(T) - \ln E^A(T-1) = \sum_{j=1} \overline{S^{E_j}}(T)[\ln E^j(T) - \ln E^j(T-1)] \tag{12.13}$$

$$\ln L^A(T) - \ln L^A(T-1) = \sum_{j=1} \overline{S^{L_j}}(T)[\ln L^j(T) - \ln L^j(T-1)]. \tag{12.14}$$

where
$K^A(T)$: the translog index of the capital input in the aggregate sector,
$K^j(T)$: the translog index of the capital input in subsector j,
$S^{K_j}(T)$: the capital value share of subsector j in the aggregate sector,
$E^A(T)$: the translog index of the energy index in the aggregate sector,
$E^j(T)$: the translog index of the energy input in subsector j,
$S^{E_j}(T)$: the energy value share of subsector j in the aggregate sector,
$L^A(T)$: the translog index of the labor input in the aggregate sector,
$L^j(T)$: the translog index of the labor input in subsector j,
$S^{L_j}(T)$: the labor value share of subsector j in the aggregate sector.

Finally, the average rate of technical change of the aggregate sector at any two discrete points of time ($\overline{R_T^A}$) can be calculated as:

$$\overline{R_T^A} = \ln Q^A(T) - \ln Q^A(T-1) - \overline{S_K^A}[\ln K^A(T) - (T-1) - \ln K^A(T-1)]$$
$$- \overline{S_L^A}[\ln L^A(T) - (T-1) - \ln L^A(T-1)] - \overline{S_E^A}[\ln E^A(T) - (T-1) \tag{12.15}$$

$$- \ln E^{A}(T-1)] - \overline{S^{A}_{M}}[\ln M^{A}(T) - (T-1) - \ln M^{A}(T-1)] \, ,$$

where $\overline{S^{A}_{K}}$, $\overline{S^{A}_{L}}$, $\overline{S^{A}_{E}}$ and $\overline{S^{A}_{M}}$ are the moving averages of the value share of the capital, labor, energy and intermediate inputs of subsector j in the aggregate sector at any two discrete points of time, respectively.

3 THE DATA COMPILATION METHOD AND SOURCES

The observation period runs from 1961 to 1993. The manufacturing sector is decomposed into the following 20 sectors: food processing, beverage and tobacco, textiles, clothes and wearing apparel, leather and leather products, wood and furniture products, paper and printing, chemical and plastic (decomposed into chemical materials, chemical products and plastic products), rubber products, oil refinery, nonmetallic minerals, basic metals, metal products, machinery and equipment, electric machinery and electronics, transportation equipments and miscellaneous manufacturing.

3.1 Capital Input

Capital input is decomposed into six categories:

(1) construction (K_1), (2) other construction (K_2), (3) transportation equipment (K_3), (4) machineries (K_4), (5) inventory (K_5) and (6) land (K_6).

Various types of capital stock come from the National Wealth Censor, Industry and Commercial Censor and the Directorate General of Budget, Accounting and Statistics (DGBAS), Executive Yuan. Except for land (K_6), all types of capital are calculated by adding up the corresponding net capital formation, which is the difference of gross capital formation and depreciation, starting from 1951. The gross capital formation during 1951-1989 comes from the DGBAS, while the types of depreciation are compiled by employing the constant rate depreciation method and year of depreciation listed in the National Wealth Censor (1988). The time series capital stock during 1961-1989 is then calculated by adding up the net capital formation starting from 1951 - the beginning year of the National Income Account in Taiwan. This method implicitly assumes that there was no net capital stock existing before 1951. The land data comes from the Industrial and Commercial Censor in various years. Finally we adjust the series data of capital stock by employing the National Wealth Censor (1988) except for land and inventory.

The types of capital service prices are compiled by using the following equation of Christensen and Jorgenson (1970):

$$P_{K_i} = \frac{1-\mu(T)\cdot Z_i(T)}{1-\mu(T)}[P_{I_i}(T-1)\cdot(1-\mu(T))\cdot R_r(T)+\delta_i\cdot P_{I_i}(T)-(P_{I_i}(T)-P_{I_i}(T-1))]$$
$$+P_{I_i}(T)\cdot\tau_i(T), \quad (i=1,2,3,4,5,6) \qquad (12.16)$$

Where

- $\mu(T)$: the effective business income tax rate,
- $Z_i(T)$: the present value of depreciation deduction on one dollar of investment,
- $P_{I_i}(T)$: the price index of gross investment of type I,
- δ_i: the depreciation rate,
- $\tau_i(T)$: the property tax rate of capital of type I,
- $R_r(T)$: the nominal rate of return.

The effective business income tax rate is the ratio of the business income tax divided by total profit of all sectors. The data on business income tax comes from the yearbook of the Ministry of Finance. The total profit of all sectors (excluding interest and rent) is taken from the National Income Account.

Employing the constant rate of depreciation method, the present value of deduction on dollar of investment is calculated by the following equations:

$$Z_i(T) = \sum\left[\frac{(1-\delta)^{\omega-1}\cdot\delta}{(1+r)^{\omega}}\right] \qquad (12.17)$$

$$\delta = 1-\left(\frac{s}{c}\right)^{\frac{1}{N}} \quad \text{(given } s=0.1c\text{)}$$

where

- N: the time span of investment goods,
- δ: the constant rate of depreciation,
- r: one year primary interest rate,
- c: cost of investment goods,
- S: remaining value of investment goods.

The data on N and r come from the National Wealth Censor (1988) and *Financial Statistics Monthly*, respectively.

The deflator of type I for each sector capital is the quotient of the gross capital formation at current prices and the gross capital formation at constant (1986) prices. Both of them are provided by the Statistics Bureau of DGBAS.

Based on the corresponding tax code, property tax ($Z_i(T)$), construction (K_1) and Miscellaneous construction (K_2) are assumed as 3 percent. That of land (K_6) is assumed as 1.5 percent. There is no property tax on the machineries (K_4) and inventory (K_5).

The property tax rate on the transportation equipment (K_3) is calculated as:

$$K_3 = \frac{\text{The license revenue of mobile cars}}{K_3 \text{ at current price} + \text{the value of the transportation equipment of all residents}}. \quad (12.18)$$

The internal rate of return ($R_r(T)$) is calculated by:

$$R_r(T) = \frac{PC - \sum_{i=1}^{6} [\frac{1-\mu(T)\cdot Z_i(T)}{1-\mu(T)}(\delta \cdot P_{I_i}(T) - P_{I_i}(T)]}{\sum_{i=1}^{6} [1-\mu(T)\cdot Z_i(T)] P_{I_i}(T-1) K_i(T)}, \quad (12.19)$$

where PC denotes the property compensation, which is the sum of rent, interest, profit depreciation, and which equals the summation of the products of K_i and P_{k_i}:

$$PC = \sum_{i=1}^{6} P_{K_i} K_i(T-1) \quad (12.20)$$

The data of property compensation (PC) as well as the share of capital (S_K) by sector comes from the gross domestic product and factor income by sector, as released by the Statistics Bureau, DGBAS.

3.2 Labor Input

Labor is classified into four groups: (1) managers and clerks; (2) engineers and technicians; (3) skilled labor; and (4) nonskilled labor. The data for aggregate quantity of labor input is provided by the DGBAS. The structure of labor input, classified by the four types, is derived by interpolating the *Industrial and Commercial Census* data in 1961, 1966, 1971, 1976, 1981, 1986, and 1991.

The data for the breakdown of labor compensation before 1976 were compiled by: (1) interpolating the census data in 1961, 1966, 1971, and 1976, and the data of *Labor Statistics Monthly* in 1981 to get a preliminary estimate of four types of wages P_{L_i}; (2) adjusting P_{L_i} with information from *Adjustment of the Manufacturing Wage Statistics in Taiwan Area* to obtain P_{L_i}'; (3) multiplying L_i by P_{L_i}' to get the labor compensation L_i P_{L_i}'; (4) adjusting the labor compensation L_i P_{L_i}' with information from the *National Income Account* to get the adjusted labor compensation; and (5) using the adjusted labor compensation and L_i to get the wage rate P_{L_i}. The breakdown of labor compensation data after 1976 is from DGBAS.

The value and the value share of labor compensation in total output comes from the *National Income Account.*

3.3 Intermediate Inputs

The intermediate inputs are split into five categories: agricultural, industrial, transportation, services and imports' intermediate input. The data on value shares of each intermediate input during 1961-1993 is then obtained by interpolating and extrapolating the input-output table in 1961, 1966, 1969, 1971, 1976, 1981, 1986 and 1989.

The value and value share of intermediate inputs as a whole comes from the *National Income Account.* Since the data on intermediate input in the *National Income Account* includes the energy input, we subtract the value of the energy input (see next section) from the value of the intermediate input; the value of each detailed intermediate input (at current prices) is the product of multiplying value share of the intermediate input S_{M_i} by the value of total intermediate input M_i. Finally the value of each intermediate input at constant prices is produced by deflating the value of each intermediate input with the corresponding deflator. The sources for those deflators are: (1) agricultural intermediate input: *Statistical Yearbook*, DGBAS; (2) industrial intermediate input: *Commodity Price Statistics Monthly*, DGBAS; (3) service intermediate input: *GDP deflator for service sector in National Income Account*; (4) transportation intermediate input: *GDP deflator for transportation sector in National Income Account*; (5) import intermediate input: *Monthly Statistics of Exports and Imports*, Ministry of Finance.

3.4 Energy Input

Energy input consists of coal, oil products, natural gas and electricity. We calculated the translog index of energy by using equation (12.6). The quantities of energy consumed are available in *Energy Balance in Taiwan, ROC*, issued by the Energy Commission, MOEA. The energy consumption data for the utility sector need special treatment. Electricity consumption contains the electricity consumption on power generation, pumping storage and transmission loss. Cost shares of the types of energy are calculated by using the energy consumption data mentioned above and the data on prices of types of energy. The price of coal products consists of three types of coal price that is, domestic coal, import coal, coke and coal gas. The price data of domestic coal and coke come from *Commodity Price Monthly*, DGBAS, and *Import-Export Trade Monthly*, MOF. The price of coal gas is 5/9 the price of natural gas. The price of electricity varies with its usage. For most of the sectors, the price for industrial usage is applied. For the service sector, the unweighted average of the price of residential use and commercial use is adopted. The data on prices of natural gas and oil products is obtained from the Chinese Petroleum Corporation and *Energy Yearbook*, Energy Commission.

3.5 Real Total Output and Value Added

Total output is defined as the sum of capital compensation (including depreciation allowance and profit) labor compensation and intermediate input (including energy and nonenergy intermediate inputs). Value added is the difference between total output and intermediate input. The time series total output and value added at constant price (1986 price) in the manufacturing sector as a whole during 1961-1993 come from DGBAS.

However the time series for two-digit sectors are available from DGBAS starting from 1977. Therefore we employ the 1961-1977 time series output and value added data of Liang (1995a) instead. According to Liang (1987), the total output at constant price (1986 price) was compiled by multiplying the sectoral industrial production index with the corresponding 1986 sectoral total output value, published in *National Income Account*. The value added at constant price comes out as a product of total output at constant prices (1986 prices) and the sum of value added shares of capital input and labor input. We then use the value added at constant prices (1986 prices) data of manufacturing sectors as a whole, published by DGBAS, to control the sum of the corresponding value added (at 1986 prices) of two digit sectors, such as food processing, textiles and so on.

4 EMPIRICAL RESULTS

4.1 The Growth of Real Total Output and Value Added

4.1.1 The growth in sectoral real total output

Column 1 in Table 12.1 presents the growth of real total output by sector during 1961-1993. From this table we conclude that:

Table 12.1 The growth of real total output and value added in Taiwan's manufacturing by sector during 1961-1993 (*unit: %*)

Item	Total Output			Value Added		
	1961-1993	1961-1982	1982-1993	1961-1993	1961-1982	1982-1993
Manufacturing	11.46	13.93	6.75	10.67	12.76	6.68
Food processing	9.41	11.87	4.72	8.31	9.77	5.52
Beverage and tobacco	5.13	4.27	6.76	8.18	8.89	6.83
Textiles	10.33	14.44	2.48	11.45	15.90	2.96
Clothes and wearing Apparel	11.47	18.91	−2.73	9.09	15.21	−2.58
Leather and leather Products	9.48	13.16	2.47	9.97	13.68	2.89
Wood and furniture Products	4.26	7.29	−1.52	4.06	6.29	−0.20
Paper and printing	8.57	9.52	6.75	9.36	11.01	6.22
Chemical and plastics	15.01	17.96	9.37	15.44	18.59	9.44
Chemical materials	—	—	10.34	—	—	10.76
Chemical products	—	—	10.98	—	—	11.50
Plastic products	—	—	7.75	—		7.10
Rubber products	12.07	16.43	3.76	12.79	17.40	3.98
Oil refinery	8.51	11.44	2.91	6.95	8.28	4.41
Nonmetallic mineral	9.26	10.98	5.98	10.21	12.49	5.86
Basic metal	10.70	12.17	7.90	10.52	10.89	9.80
Metal products	13.87	16.58	8.68	14.03	16.72	8.90
Machinery and equipment	12.49	13.79	10.02	11.47	12.44	9.61
Elect. Mach. and electronics	21.21	25.73	12.59	20.57	25.32	11.50
Transportation equipment	15.31	19.56	7.18	15.37	20.16	6.21
Miscellaneous	15.52	21.32	4.46	15.22	21.14	3.93

1. The real total output (at 1986 prices) of manufacturing as a whole grew with a pace of 13.93 percent per annum during 1961-1982. It dropped to 6.75 percent during 1982-1993 owing to the second oil crises and the huge appreciation of the New Taiwan dollar, and the remarked increase of wage and real estate prices, which weakened Taiwan's export competitiveness during 1987-1993. For the whole observation period (1961-1993), the manufacturing sector grew at a pace of 11.46 percent per annum.
2. Comparing the sectoral real output growth rate during 1961-1982, we found that except for beverage and tobacco, all sectors' real output growth rate decreased during 1982-1993.

4.1.2 The growth in sectoral real value added

Column 2 in Table 12.1 gives the growth rate of sectoral real value added (at 1986 prices) during 1961-1993. We conclude from this table that:

1. The real value added of the whole manufacturing sector registered a 12.76 percent per annum growth rate during 1961-1982. It fell to 6.68 percent per annum during 1982-1993. The growth rate average was 10.67 percent per annum during the whole observation period (1961-1993).
2. Compared with that of 1961-1982, the real value added growth rate decreased in all sectors during 1982-1993.
3. In the case of manufacturing as a whole, according to Young (1994), the value added TFP grew with a pace of 2.4 percent in Taiwan, which was greater than that of Singapore (−1.1 percent) but smaller than that of Korea (2.95 percent). In contrast, the manufacturing value added TFP growth rate was estimated by this study as 6.68 percent per annum in Taiwan during 1982-1993, which was greater than that estimated by Young (1994). Taiwan turned out to be the value added TFP growth champion in the manufacturing sector among Singapore, Korea and Taiwan during 1982-1993.

4.2 The Changes in Total Factor Productivity

4.2.1 The growth of total output TFP

Column 1 in Table 12.2 presents the growth of total output TFP during 1961-1993. From this, the following important conclusions emerged:

1. The total output TFP growth rate of the manufacturing sector as a whole increased from 0.2 percent per annum during 1961-1982 to 0.55 percent per annum during 1982-1993. It averaged 0.32 percent per

Table 12.2 The growth of total factor productivity in Taiwan's manufacturing sector during 1961-1993 (unit: %)

Item	Total output TFP			Value Added TFP		
	1961-1993	1961-1982	1982-1993	1961-1993	1961-1982	1982-1993
Manufacturing	0.32	0.2	0.55	2.46	2.33	2.72
Food processing	2.89	3.68	1.37	4.02	4.51	3.09
Beverage and tobacco	0	−2.16	4.1	4.02	3.69	4.67
Textiles	3.22	3.88	1.96	5.56	6.9	3
Clothes and wearing apparel	0.88	1.05	0.53	4.24	6.67	−0.41
Leather and leather products	−3.08	−4.12	−1.11	3.7	5.75	−0.22
Wood and furniture products	−9.09	−12.35	−2.86	−0.32	−0.79	0.57
Paper and printing	−5.57	−8.66	0.34	2.18	2.88	0.85
Chemical and plastics	3.12	3.01	3.33	6.41	6.1	7
Chemical materials	–	–	4.59	–	–	10.75
Chemical products	–	–	1.75	–	–	3.32
Plastic products	–	–	0.89	–	–	−1.7
Rubber products	2.66	3.38	1.28	5.35	7.09	2.01
Oil refinery	−2.15	−4.27	1.88	−2.58	−4.29	0.68
Nonmetallic minerals	1.24	1.36	1.02	3.58	3.09	4.51
Basic metals	−0.93	−2.67	2.41	1.36	−2.43	8.58
Metal products	0.46	0.3	0.78	4.01	5.35	1.45
Machinery and equipment	0.31	−0.47	1.81	2.88	1.9	4.75
Elect. mach. and electronics	4.05	5.44	1.4	7.46	9.04	4.44
Transportation equipments	2.38	3.5	0.22	6.64	8.7	2.71
Miscellaneous	2.59	3.54	0.76	7.29	10.41	1.33

annum during the whole observation period 1961-1993.

2. The electrical machinery and electronics sector marked the greatest growth in total output TFP at 5.44 percent per annum during 1961-1982. The textiles sector (3.88 percent) and food (3.68 percent) ranked second and third, respectively. In contrast, the laggards were wood and furniture products (−12.35 percent), paper and printing (−8.66 percent), oil refinery (−4.27 percent) and leather and leather products (−4.12 percent)
3. The leading manufacturing sectors during 1982-1993 were chemical materials, 4.59 percent; beverage and tobacco, 4.1 percent; chemical and plastics 3.33 percent; basic material, 2.41 percent and textile, 1.96 percent. Conversely, the laggards were wood and furniture products (−2.86 percent), leather and leather products (−1.11 percent) and transportation equipments (0.22 percent).

4.2.2 The growth of value added TFP

For calculating TFP changes, conventionally the value added is used as depend variable instead of total output. For comparison, we calculate value added TFP growth as well.

Column 2 in Table 12.2 gives the growth of value added TFP during 1961-1993. From them, we conclude:

1. For the manufacturing sector as a whole, the value added TFP growth rate increased from 2.33 percent per annum during 1961-1982 to 2.72 percent per annum during 1982-1993.
2. Among the 19 manufacturing sectors, miscellaneous marked the greatest growth rate in value added TFP - a 10.34 percent per annum growth during 1961-1982. The transportation equipment sector with a 9.41 percent annual growth rate ranked second. The electrical machinery and electronics sector (9.07 percent) ranked third. Conversely, the laggards were oil refinery (−4.26 percent), basic metals (−2.29 percent) and wood and furniture products (−1.08 percent).
3. During 1982-1993 chemical materials, growing by 8.62 percent per annum in value added TFP, ranked first. The other leading manufacturing sectors contained chemical products, 8.06 percent; chemical material, 7.0 percent and machinery and equipment, 4.67 percent. In contrast, the laggards included clothes and wearing apparel (−0.75 percent), leather and leather products (−0.26 percent), wood and furniture products (0.20 percent) and paper and printing (0.87 percent).

4.2.3 Comparison of this study and Jorgenson-Gollop-Fraumeni's method in measuring the TFP growth in manufacturing sector

We employ equation (12.15) to calculate the TFP changes in manufacturing as a whole. For comparison, we also calculate the TFP growth in the manufacturing sector as a whole by using Jorgenson-Gollop-Fraumeni's method as stated in equation (12.1), which is indifferent with subsector of manufacturing sector, such as food processing and so on.

The difference between this study and Jorgenson-Gollop-Fraumeni's method in TFP measurement of manufacturing as a whole is tabulated in Table 12.3. We conclude that:

Table 12.3 Two measurement differences of added TFP growth in Taiwan's manufacturing sector, 1961-1993 (unit: %)

Period	(1) Liang's Study	(2) Jorgenson-Gollop-Fraumeni's Method	$\frac{(2)-(1)}{(2)}$
1961-1993	2.46	2.85	12.63
1961-1982	2.33	2.51	6.77
1982-1993	2.72	3.36	20.24
1961-1973	3.69	3.69	0.27
1973-1982	0.5	0.84	44.05
1982-1987	4.85	5.41	10.54
1987-1993	0.95	1.76	43.75

1. All of the TFP growth rates estimated by Jorgenson-Gollop-Fraumeni's method (employing equation (12.1)) in the six subperiods during 1961-1993 are greater than that calculated by employing equation (12.15) in this study. The magnitude of the relative difference varied from a low of 0.27 percent during 1961-1973 to a high of 44.05 percent during 1973-1982.
2. Conversely, during the whole observation period (1961-1993), the value added TFP growth of Taiwan's manufacturing sector as a whole was estimated as 2.46 percent per annum in this study (employing equation (12.15)), while it was estimated as 2.85 percent by Jorgenson-Gollop-Fraumeni's method. The measurement difference between the two is 12.63 percent [= (2.85 − 2.46)/2.85].
3. From (1) and (2), we conclude that when measuring an aggregate sector such as a manufacturing sector as a whole or an economy, Jorgenson's method should be modified so that not only the quality changes caused by heterogeneous characteristics of the inputs but also

those caused by the industrial structural changes should be taken into account.

4.3 The Contribution of TFP to the Growth of Total Output and Value Added

The relative contribution rate of TFP toward the growth of total output and value added is tabulated in Table 12.4 and from this table we conclude that:

Table 12.4 The relative contribution of TFP toward total output and value added growth in Taiwan's manufacturing sector, 1961-1993 (unit: %)

Item	Total output			Value added		
	1961-1993	1961-1982	1982-1993	1961-1993	1961-1982	1982-1993
Manufacturing	2.8	1.43	8.17	23.06	18.22	40.7
Food processing	30.7	31.03	29.12	48.35	46.11	55.95
Beverage and tobacco	−0.09	−50.47	60.67	49.18	41.45	68.41
Textiles	31.18	26.86	79.18	48.52	43.38	101.18
Clothes and wearing apparel	7.63	5.57	−19.59	46.57	43.85	16
Leather and leather products	−32.5	−31.27	−45.01	37.09	42.05	−7.73
Wood and furniture products	−213.49	−169.52	187.74	−7.94	−12.54	−286.46
Paper and printing	−65.04	−91.04	4.97	23.31	26.17	13.62
Chemical and plastics	20.78	16.74	35.57	41.49	32.81	74.13
Chemical materials	–	–	44.36	–	–	99.83
Chemical products	–	–	15.91	–	–	28.86
Plastic products	–	–	11.51	–	–	−23.97
Rubber products	22.04	20.59	34.09	41.82	40.78	50.51
Oil refinery	−25.3	−37.29	64.71	−37.14	−51.79	15.36
Nonmetallic minerals	13.41	12.36	17.07	35.03	24.74	76.87
Basic metals	−8.65	−21.98	30.56	12.89	−22.3	87.57
Metal products	3.33	1.8	8.94	28.6	32.02	16.33
Machinery and equipment	2.52	−3.41	18.08	25.11	15.28	49.4
Elect. mach. and electronics	19.1	21.15	11.13	36.27	35.71	38.6
Transportation equipment	15.53	17.91	3.13	43.21	43.15	43.61
Miscellaneous	16.66	16.6	17.16	47.91	49.27	33.91

1. The relative contribution ratio of value added TFP toward value added growth in the manufacturing sector increased from 18.22 percent during 1961-1982 to 40.70 percent during 1982-1993.
2. Compared with that of 1961-1982, the relative contribution of both total output TFP and value added TFP toward output during 1982-1993 increased in all sectors except five.
3. Based on (1) and (2), we conclude that the TFP played an increasingly important, even dominant role in explaining the value added growth of Taiwan's manufacturing industry, during 1982-1993. This industry-level finding reinforces the argument of Liang (1995b) that Krugman's hypothesis - the fast growth of NIEs has little to do with TFP growth - is invalid for the last decade (1982-1993). We believe that the important role of TFP growth in the last decade reveals the future trend of TFP in Taiwan's economic growth.

According to Liang (1995b) the acceleration of TFP growth during 1982-1993 can be attributed to industrial structural change, education improvement in employment, R&D and inbound brain drain.

5 CONCLUSIONS AND IMPLICATIONS

The objective of this chapter is to employ a new method to measure the growth of TFP and to analyze the causes of growth in output and TFP in Taiwan's twenty manufacturing sectors. Finally, policy implications are drawn from the findings. For this, a translog production function, which is more general than the conventional Cobb-Douglas and constant elasticity of substitution (CES) production function is employed.

The major findings of this chapter are as follows:

1. All of the TFP growth rates in Taiwan's aggregate manufacturing sector estimated by Jorgenson-Gollop-Fraumeni's method in the employing equation (12.1) six subperiods during 1961-1993 are greater than that calculated by employing equation (12.15) in this study. The magnitude of the relative difference varied from a low of 0.27 percent during 1961-1973 to a high of 44.05 percent during 1973-1982.
2. Conversely, during the whole observation period (1961-1993), the value added TFP growth of Taiwan's manufacturing sector as a whole was estimated as 2.46 percent per annum in this study by employing equation (12.15), while it was estimated as 2.85 percent by Jorgenson-Gollop-Fraumeni's method. The measurement difference between the two is 12.63 percent [=(285 − 246)/285].

3. Comparing (1) and (2), we conclude that when measuring an aggregate sector such as a manufacturing sector as a whole or an economy as a whole Jorgenson's method should be modified so that not only the quality changes caused by heterogeneous characteristics of the inputs but also the industrial structural changes should be taken into account.
4. For the manufacturing sector as a whole, the value added TFP growth rate increased from 2.33 percent per annum during 1961-1982 to 2.72 percent per annum during 1982-1993. The contribution ratio of TFP toward value added growth in the manufacturing sector jumped from 18.2 percent during 1961-1982 to 40.7 percent during 1982-1993.
5. We conclude that the TFP played an increasingly important, even dominant role in explaining the value added growth of Taiwan's manufacturing industry, during 1982-1993. This industry-level finding reinforces the argument of Liang (1995b) that Krugman's hypothesis - the fast growth of NIEs has little to do with TFP growth - is invalid for the last decade (1982-1993). We believe that the important role of TFP growth in the last decade reveals the future trend of TFP in Taiwan's economic growth.

NOTES

1. Chi-yuan Liang is Research Fellow of the Institute of Economics, Academia Sinica. Dale W. Jorgenson is Frederic E. Abbe Professor of Economics, Harvard University. The authors would like to express their sincerest gratitude to three editors and one anonymous referee for their valuable advice. They are also indebted to Professors Mo-huan Hsing and Sheng-cheng Hu of Academia Sinica, Professor Chen Sun of National Taiwan University, Chang-yaon Shea, Shi-ming Hwang, and Tien-shih Liu of DGBAS, Yih-chi Chuang of Cheng-Chi University, Jun-hsiung Wu of CEPD, and Mun-sing Ho of Harvard University for their assistance with advice and data collection. He would also like to thank his painstaking and capable assistants, Hwei-lin Chu, Polly Lien, Jason Chen, Shin-chiu Lin, Ing-jei Chang, Shao-Yun Sun and Shr-Chian Chiou. Special thanks are given to Jin-Yung Chang of National Taiwan University for her help in computer programming. Finally, the authors would like to express their greatest gratitude to the financial support of Chiang Ching-Kuo Foundation for International Scholarly Exchanges.
2. Christensen and Jorgenson (1970) introduced the translog function which is a much more generalized functional form than the Cobb-Douglas and CES. It is a second-order approximation constant elasticity of substitution like the Cobb-Douglas and CES.
3. See Gollop and Jorgenson (1980).
4. See Gollop and Jorgenson (1980). For proof, see Diewert (1976).
5. See Berndt (1980) and Diewert (1976).

REFERENCES

Berndt, E.R. (1980), 'Comment: U.S. productivity growth by industry, 1947-73 (by F. Gollop and D. Jorgenson)', in J.W. Kendrick and B. Vaccara (eds), *New Development in Productivity Measurement and Analysis*, Chicago: University of Chicago Press, 124-136.

Chirstensen, L.R. and D.W. Jorgenson (1970), 'U.S. Real Product and Real Factor Input, 1929-67', *Review of Income and Wealth*, Series **16** (1) March, 1-50.

Department of Statistics, Central Bank, *Financial Statistics Monthly*, (various years).

Diewart, W.E. (1976), 'Exact and superlative index numbers', *Journal of Economics*, **4** (2), 115-45.

Directorate General of Budget, Accounting and Statistics, Executive Yuan (1988), *National Wealth Censor in 1986*.

Gollop, F.M. and D.W. Jorgenson (1980), 'U.S. productivity growth by industry, 1947-1973', in J.W. Kendrick and B. Vaccara (eds), *New Development in Productivity Measurement and Analysis*, Chicago: University of Chicago Press.

Jorgenson, D.W. and C.-Y. Liang, (1996), 'The industry-level output growth and total factor productivity change in Taiwan, 1961-1993', Project report submitted to the Chiang Ching-Kuo Foundation for International Scholarly Exchange, April.

Jorgenson D.W., F. Gollop and B. Fraumeni (1987), Productivity and U.S. Economic Growth, Chapter 9, 301-22, Harvard University Press.

Kim, J.I. and L.J. Lau (1994), 'The sources of economic growth in the East Asian newly industrialized countries', *Journal of the Japanese and International Economics*, **8** (3), September, 235-71.

Krugman, P. (1994), 'The myth of Asian's miracle', *Foreign Affairs*, **73**, (6), 62-78.

Lau, L.J. (1994), 'Sources of long-term economic growth: empirical evidence from developed and developing countries', Stanford University, Mimeographed.

Liang, C.Y. (1995a), 'Overview of productivity performance in Taiwan's industrial sector', in K.-Y. Tsui, T.-T. Hsueh and T.G. Rawski (eds), *Productivity, Efficiency and Reform in China's Economy*, Hong Kong Institute of Asian-Pacific Studies, The Chinese University of Hong Kong.

Liang, C.Y. (1995b), 'Productivity growth in Asian NIEs: a case study of the Republic of China, 1961-93', *APO Productivity Journal*, Asian Productivity Organization, Tokyo, Japan, winter.

Young, A. (1994), 'The tyranny of numbers: confronting the statistical realities of East Asian growth experience', NBER working paper no. 4680, Cambridge, MA: Cambridge University Press.

B. Microeconomic Efficiency Studies

13. The Achilles' Heel of Thailand's Financial Market*

Jonathan E. Leightner

1 INTRODUCTION

According to Greek mythology, Achilles' mother wanted to make her new born son, Achilles, invincible, so she dipped Achilles in the river Styx which flows between the worlds of the living and dead. However, she had to keep a hold of him in order to prevent his being washed away, and she chose to hold his heel. The only vulnerable part on Achilles body was his heel and an arrow through it is what destroyed Achilles.

Several years ago, Thailand looked invincible. 'The World Bank reported that the Thai economy, for a decade, had grown faster than any other in the world' (Butler, 1997). The International Monetary Fund (IMF) 'predicted that by the year 2020 Thailand's economy would grow to be the eighth largest in the world, surpassing France' ('Anand', *Bangkok Post*, 1997). But Thailand had an Achilles heel - its 91 finance and securities companies. It is debatable what exactly was the arrow which pierced Thailand's financial heel; some argue that the Bank of Thailand (Thailand's central bank) failed to properly supervise these companies, others blame it on greed, others on financial liberalization and others on a speculative bubble. The wound, however, centers on Thailand s finance and securities companies.

Between March and August of 1997, 64 percent of Thailand's 91 finance and securities companies were forced to shut down by government edict. These shutdowns led to problems for Thailand's stock market and currency (the baht).[1] Thailand's problems predate, by only a few months, similar problems throughout Asia, especially in Indonesia

*I appreciate the advice and help of C.A. Knox Lovell in preparing this chapter, assistance with the data given by Huon Le and Charles Lockett and the acquisition of the data made possible by Chetthavee Charoenpitaks. I also appreciate the comments and suggestions of the referee and the excellent conference hosted by Tsu-Tan Fu and Cliff Huang.

and South Korea. This chapter analyzes Thailand's finance and securities companies between 1990 and 1995, the period just prior to the current financial crisis. During the time period analyzed, the Thai government took major steps to liberalize its financial market and tried to establish Thailand as a major international financial center of Southeast Asia. These government steps would ultimately increase competition for Thailand's finance and securities companies from both Thai and foreign banks. Thailand's finance and securities companies were too small to effectively compete with these future rivals which were much bigger and more efficient. Between 1990 and 1995 the average Thai finance and securities company more than quadrupled in size and part of this growth was driven by a desire to become big enough to survive in a liberalized market. However, much of that growth was based on unwise speculation in Thailand's property market, which began to collapse in 1996, which led to their current problems.[2]

The major finding of this chapter is that, in spite of quadrupling in size, Thailand's finance and securities companies remained noticeably smaller than optimal throughout the entire time period studied, 1990 to 1995. Thus my findings are consistent with current efforts to reduce the number of Thai finance and securities companies by shutting many of the weakest ones down and forcing many of the others to merge. The remainder of the chapter is organized as follows. Section 2 describes the linear programming techniques used. Section 3 describes the data and the model. Section 4 presents the empirical results and section 5 concludes.

2 ANALYTIC TECHNIQUES

Because linear programming techniques can easily handle multiple outputs and are relatively independent from an assumed functional form (Berger and Humphrey, 1997: 177), these techniques[3] are used to construct a best-practice production frontier between outputs and inputs. This frontier tightly envelops the data from above for all outputs and from below for all inputs. The distance each observation is from the frontier is a measure of the performance, or efficiency, of that observation. Distance from the frontier is measured along rays from the origin such that all outputs are increased proportionately. An output orientation was used because the recent history of Thailand s finance and securities companies suggests an emphasis more on increasing outputs than on constraining inputs. The ratio of maximally expanded output production to actual output production (Φ) provides an output-oriented measure of the technical efficiency of each observation, or its ability to increase outputs given its current level of inputs. Denote the outputs of an observation by y_{jm}, $j = 1,..., J$, $m = 1,..., M$ and the inputs of an observation by x_{jn}, $j = 1,..., J$, $n = 1,..., N$. Consider the following linear programming problem:

$$
\begin{aligned}
&\max \quad \Phi \\
&\text{subject to} \quad \Sigma_j \lambda_j x_{nj} \leq x_n^{\text{o}}, \qquad n = 1,..., N \\
&\qquad \Phi y_m^{\text{o}} \leq \Sigma_j \lambda_j y_{mj}, \qquad m = 1,..., M \\
&\qquad \Sigma_j \lambda_j = 1 \\
&\qquad \lambda_j \geq 0, \quad j = 1,..., J.
\end{aligned}
$$

This problem is solved J times, once for each observation in the sample. For observation o under evaluation, the problem seeks the maximum radial expansion in all outputs y_m^{o} consistent with best practice observed in the sample, that is, subject to the constraints in the problem.

The dual to the above linear programming problem is

$$
\begin{aligned}
&\min \quad \Sigma_n \pi_n x_n^{\text{o}} + \pi \\
&\text{subject to:} \quad \Sigma_m \pi_m y_m^{\text{o}} = 1 \\
&\qquad \Sigma_n \pi_n x_{nj} - \Sigma_m \pi_m y_{mj} + \pi \geq 0, \quad j = 1, ..., J \\
&\qquad \pi_n \geq 0, \quad n = 1, ..., N; \quad \pi_m \geq 0, \quad m = 1, ..., M; \quad \pi \text{ free}
\end{aligned}
$$

This problem seeks a set of nonnegative weights π_m and π_n which, when attached to its output and its inputs, minimize the shadow value of inputs for observation o under evaluation. The dual variables which emerge out of the dual linear programming problem can be used to calculate the marginal products and marginal rate of product transformation each firm would face if it eliminated its technical inefficiencies and, thus, were on the best practice frontier.

The optimal values of the dual shadow values (π_m^*, π_n^*) show the effect on the optimal value of the primal objective Φ^* of a slight relaxation in the respective primal constraint. In other words, π_m^* (π_n^*) shows the change in efficiency from a change in output m (input n). Consequently, the ratio of the dual variables for two outputs provides a measure of the shadow marginal rate of product transformation between those outputs - the amount of one output that must be given up to increase the other output by one unit, holding everything else constant. The marginal rate of product transformation (MRPT) of the output called 'net interest income' (r) to the output called 'fee income' (f) is calculated as the ratio of (π_f^*/π_r^*), for those observations in which both π_f^* and $\pi_r^* > 0$. If either π_f^* or π_r^* equals 0, then MRPT is considered undefined for that observation.

Likewise, the ratio of the dual variables for input *n* and output *m* (π_n^*/π_m^*) provides a measure of the shadow marginal product of input *n* for producing output *m* - the amount of *m* output that can be gained by increasing *n* input by one unit, *ceteris paribus* (if $\pi_m^* = 0$, then the shadow MP is not defined for that observation; if, however, $\pi_n^* = 0$, then the MP = 0). The marginal product of the output 'net interest income' (*r*) to labor (*l*) can be converted into the following elasticity $(\pi_l^*/\pi_r^*)(Q_l / \Phi Q_r)$ where Q = quantity. Returns to scale is calculated using Forsund's (1996) equation $\Sigma_n \pi_n^* Q_n / \Sigma_m \pi_m^* \Phi Q_m$.

Finally a return to growth measure can be calculated for a given output by (1) transforming the marginal products of all inputs with respect to that output into elasticities, (2) adding the elasticities calculated in step one in order to find the percent change in that output from a 1-percent simultaneous increase in all inputs, (3) multiplying the result of step 2 by the price (or per unit value) of that output to find the percent increase in the value of that output resulting from a 1-percent increase in all inputs, (4) multiplying the results of step 3 by the ratio of the value of that output to the value of all outputs summed in order to find the percent increase in the value of total production due to a 1-percent increase in all inputs when only the output considered is increased (all other outputs are held constant). Mathematically, returns to growth for the output 'net interest income' (*r*) is equal to $[\Sigma_n(\pi_n^*/\pi_r^*)(Q_n/\Phi Q_r)](P_r)(P_rQ_r / \Sigma_m P_m Q_m)$ where P is price and Q is quantity. Returns to growth can be calculated for each output. The output with the largest returns to growth is the output that is most profitable for the company to expand, and the returns to growth associated with that output are called the firm's returns to 'strongest' growth. Mathematically returns to strongest growth is max $\{[\Sigma_n(\pi_n^*/\pi_m^*)(Q_n/\Phi Q_m)](P_m)(P_mQ_m / \Sigma_m P_m Q_m)\}$ for $m = 1,\ldots, M$.

Clearly 'returns to strongest growth' is an alternative to 'returns to scale'. Returns to scale considers a simultaneous increase in all outputs; in contrast, returns to strongest growth considers the effects (on the value of total production) of increasing only the optimal output. Since the marginal rate of product transformation found in this study is not equivalent to one, I believe that returns to strongest growth provides a more meaningful measure for management than returns to scale.

3 DATA AND MODEL

Most studies of financial institutions focus on banks. When Berger and Humphrey (1997) surveyed 130 studies of the efficiency of financial institutions, they cite only two studies of credit unions, one study of financial services, and eight studies of insurance companies. The remaining 119 studies were of banks, savings and loans, or bank branches. I know of no studies of just finance and securities companies, and thus of no efficiency models designed explicitly for them. Furthermore directly borrowing an efficiency model for a bank is problematic because there is longstanding disagreement over what banks produce (Berger and Humphrey, 1992: 246). There is also disagreement over what banks consume in order to produce. Berger and Humphrey identify three approaches to bank efficiency: the production (or value added) approach, the user cost approach, and the intermediation (or asset) approach. None of these approaches perfectly fit Thai finance and securities companies. Therefore I devise my own model based upon the short and long-run objectives of Thai finance and securities companies.

Finance and securities companies in Thailand focus on distinctly different short-run and long-run goals. Like most firms, they wish to maximize profits in the short run. In the long run, they wish to acquire a banking licence because banks can earn more profits than finance and securities companies because banks (1) are less constrained, (2) enjoy higher demand for their products due to their better reputations, and (3) face lower risks than finance and securities companies. The Bank of Thailand has fostered this long-run goal by repeatedly saying that future banking licences may be available for finance and securities companies which are big enough and managed well enough. In order to get big enough, mergers and acquisitions in Thailand's finance and securities market have been common. In spite of these mergers and acquisitions, the number of finance and securities companies did not drop below 91 from 1991 to 1996 because the Bank of Thailand maintained a steady number of licences in this sector.

The outputs behind finance and securities companies short-run goal can be captured by net interest income and noninterest (or fee) income.[4] Net interest income consists of interest earned from loans and leasing, plus dividends paid on securities, minus interest paid for deposits and borrowing fees. Noninterest income consists of brokerage fees, profits from buying and selling securities, other fees, gains from exchange and all other sources of revenue. All of this data come from the revenue and expense statements of these firms. Indeed, my analysis of finance and securities companies' short-run goals incorporate all items used to calculate firm profits except for taxes and miscellaneous expenses.

The outputs behind finance and securities companies' long-run goal can be captured by credits (or loans) and securities, and data on credits and securities come from the asset accounts of these companies. These outputs also capture the Bank of Thailand's goal of financing economic growth. However more than just regulator encouragement lies behind the long-run goals of Thailand's finance and securities companies. These firms also wish to gain market share, diversify and grow in order to increase their chances of profitable survival. The returns to growth results, which emerge from both my short- and long-run analyses, are indicative of the 'need to grow in order to survive in the long run' which drives many of Thailand's finance and securities companies.

For both the long- and short-run analyses I use the same three inputs: expenses due to labor, building and equipment and the provision for bad debt. The provision for bad debt is used as a proxy for risk-taking. Risk-taking is included in the model because of its major importance in the market analyzed. It is included as an input because firms wish to minimize risk at any given level of output, or maximize output at any given level of risk, which makes risk act like an input. For similar reasons, other authors have included nonperforming loans in the analysis of banks (Berger and DeYoung, 1997). Whether nonperforming loans or the provision for bad debt is a better measure of risk taking is a mute point here since data on nonperforming loans is still not available for Thai financial institutions.[5]

All input and output data are given in millions of baht, and from 1990 to 1996 the exchange rate was fixed at 25 baht to one US dollar. I did not correct for inflation because (1) the choice of which price index (or indices) to use would affect the results and (2) not all outputs and inputs should be divided by the same price index, but dividing different inputs and outputs by different price indices would obscure the results, especially the calculations of returns to strongest growth. Although I did not directly correct for inflation, I compare the results to the inflation rate where appropriate.

My data spans from 1990 to 1995. I have all the data required by both of my models for 100 percent of Thailand's finance and securities companies for 1991, 1992 and 1993. Additionally I have all the required data to analyze just the short-run objectives of Thailand's finance and securities companies in 1995. Tables 13.1 and 13.3 (panel 1, row 3) show the percent of Thailand's finance and securities companies represented in my data. I choose to present the results for years in which I do not have data for all firms because (1) the results are still meaningful and they add to the analysis, (2) I always have at least 69 percent of all Thai finance and securities companies represented in my analysis, and (3) I clearly label what percent of the market lies behind each result so the reader can decide how to adjust their interpretation of the results.

Table 13.1 Results for all firms using firms' short-run objectives

	1990	1991	1992	1993	1994	1995
1. Data						
Firms in Sample	82	91	92	91	66	91
Firms in Thailand	94	91	92	91	91	91
Percent of Population used in Non-DEA	87	100	100	100	73	100
Number with Negative Net Interest	12	8	7	6	0	3
Number with Negative Fee Income	2	1	1	1	1	5
Percent population used in DEA results	72	90	91	92	71	91
Mean Net Interest Income	86	113	186	234	395	386
Mean Fee Income	104	114	222	300	364	271
Mean Labor	29	36	55	78	108	117
Mean Capital	10	16	27	40	55	64
Mean Risk	17	20	39	37	33	30
Outputs/Inputs	3.25	3.04	3.54	3.17	4.29	4.97
2. Output Results						
Mean Efficiency Scores	71	72	70	71	55	64
Percent with Slack Interest Income	29	22	13	24	25	20
Percent with Slack Fee Income	26	25	30	19	28	39
MRPT: △Interest/△Fees	3.43	1.23	2.76	2.39	3.65	3.18
3. Maximum Marginal Product						
Labor	11.25	6.64	8.38	8.33	7.84	12.16
Capital	25.05	20.69	21.79	11.89	11.14	13.68
Risk	10.05	74.40	13.28	37.91	81.92	13.27
4. Returns to Growth (RTG)						
RTG wrt Net Interest Income	1.13	0.80	1.15	1.09	1.09	1.29
RTG wrt Fee Income	1.25	1.22	0.81	0.76	0.59	1.60
Maximum RTG	2.03	1.59	1.62	1.45	1.45	2.57
Returns to Scale	1.00	0.89	0.84	0.95	1.12	1.03

Table 13.2 Results for top ten firms using firms' short-run objectives

	1990	1991	1992	1993	1994	1995
1. Data						
Percent of Net Interest in Market		57	52	50		46
Percent of Fee Income in Market		47	42	43		38
Percent of Labor in Market		41	39	37		31
Percent of Capital in Market		37	37	34		30
Mean Net Interest Income	404	583	900	1 061	1 438	1 608
Mean Fee Income	400	484	863	1 184	1 368	937
Mean Labor	99	135	195	263	328	331
Mean Capital	31	53	93	124	148	173
Mean Risk	30	62	120	138	122	119
Outputs/Inputs	5.22	4.36	4.42	4.37	4.69	4.13
2. Output Results						
Mean Efficiency Scores	93	98	99	94	92	88
Percent with Slack Interest Income	20	20	20	20	30	10
Percent with Slack Fee Income	0	0	10	10	20	20
MRPT: △Interest/△Fees	9.52	1.90	1.51	6.71	1.10	2.30
3. Maximum Marginal Product						
Labor	29.99	7.89	6.85	18.62	4.60	10.36
Capital	10.03	6.01	6.66	3.67	4.51	4.47
Risk	23.24	5.23	85.60	5.32	32.11	10.01
4. Returns to Growth (RTG)						
RTG wrt Interest Income	3.46	0.96	0.93	1.69	0.43	0.86
RTG wrt Fee Income	1.24	0.85	0.87	0.27	1.24	1.61
Maximum RTG	4.25	1.28	1.27	1.92	1.41	2.09
Returns to Scale	0.73	0.80	0.75	0.47	0.63	0.72

Tables 13.1 and 13.2 present means for the data and the empirical results when short-run objective outputs are used. Table 13.1 presents the means for all firms in my sample and Table 13.2 presents means for the largest 10 finance and securities companies. Tables 13.3 and 13.4 are the counterparts for Tables 13.1 and 13.2 when long-run objective outputs are

Table 13.3 Results for all firms using firms' long-run objectives

	1990	1991	1992	1993	1994	1995
1. Data						
Firms in Sample	82	91	92	91	66	63
Firms in Thailand	94	91	92	91	91	91
Percent of Population	87	100	100	100	73	69
Mean Credits	3 420	4 184	5 697	7 742	11 454	16 246
Mean Securities	413	461	722	1 065	1 660	2 454
Mean Labor	29	36	55	78	108	126
Mean Capital	10	16	27	40	55	70
Mean Risk	16	20	39	37	33	37
Outputs/Inputs	66	66	59	65	72	86
2. Output Results						
Mean Efficiency Scores	67	59	58	64	67	64
percent with Slack Credits	4	5	13	19	6	14
percent with Slack Securities	41	41	35	20	33	13
MRPT: △Credits/△Securities	11.74	9.96	13.32	8.19	4.30	16.84
3. Maximum Marginal Product						
Labor	150	164	215	109	83	266
Capital	619	437	357	268	314	478
Risk	181	65	140	801	95	653
4. Returns to Growth (RTG)						
RTG wrt Credits	2.02	1.53	1.43	1.26	1.23	1.82
RTG wrt Securities	0.39	0.22	0.53	0.26	0.24	0.28
Maximum RTG	2.12	1.59	1.79	1.32	1.25	1.96
Returns to Scale	1.12	0.95	0.91	0.78	0.86	0.99

used. For 1990 through 1995, I have all the required data for the largest ten finance and securities companies in Thailand for both models. Here large is measured as the sum of credits plus securities. In 1990 the average large Thai finance and securities company produced more than 4.0 times as much income while using less than 3.0 times as much inputs as the average finance and security company in Thailand (Table 13.1 and 13.2, panel 1). Similar disparities exist for every year in my sample. The

Table 13.4 Results for top ten firms using firms' long-run objectives

	1990	1991	1992	1993	1994	1995
1. Data						
Percent of Credits in Market		49	47	44		
Percent of Securities in Market		49	50	46		
Percent of Labor in Market		41	39	37		
Percent of Capital in Market		37	37	34		
Mean Credits	14 114	18 562	24 814	30 844	38 508	45 593
Mean Securities	1 532	2 061	3 303	4 425	6 154	8 634
Mean Labor	99	135	195	263	328	331
Mean Capital	31	53	93	124	148	173
Mean Risk	29	62	120	138	122	119
Outputs/Inputs	104	90	72	70	77	91
2. Output Results						
Mean Efficiency Scores	89	87	90	83	94	93
Percent with Slack Credits	0	20	10	20	10	30
Percent with Slack Securities	30	40	10	10	10	0
MRPT:△Credits/△Securities	14.51	9.74	7.13	2.99	2.90	9.36
3. Maximum Marginal Product						
Labor	189	92	142	50	52	94
Capital	164	145	99	66	60	78
Risk	193	96	120	66	159	196
4. Returns to Growth (RTG)						
RTG wrt Credits	1.47	0.79	1.25	0.58	0.73	0.82
RTG wrt Securities	0.16	0.11	0.17	0.18	0.30	0.16
Maximum RTG	1.47	0.80	1.39	0.67	0.78	0.89
Returns to Scale	0.76	0.60	0.80	0.66	0.65	0.73

year with the smallest gap between the average firm and the average large firm was 1994 when the average large firm produced 3.7 times as much income as the average firm and used only 3.1 times as much inputs.

The ten largest Thai finance and securities companies are always the same firms, and they capture a noticeable percent of the entire market. Panel 1 (rows 1-4) of Tables 13.2 and 13.4 show the percentage of the entire market captured by the ten largest Thai finance and security companies in each year for which I have data on all firms in the market. In 1991 when there were 91 firms in the market, the ten largest firms captured 57 percent of the net interest income, 47 percent of the noninterest income, 49 percent of the credits and 49 percent of the securities in the market. In contrast, they used only 41 percent of the labor and 37 percent of the capital. The percentage of outputs produced being noticeably greater than the percentage of inputs used by the ten largest firms is an empirical indication that largeness is associated with greater efficiency and success. However notice also that the percentage of the market captured by these largest finance and securities companies appears to be declining through time - between 1991 and 1995, their share of net interest in the market declines from 57 percent to 46 percent and their share of fee income declines from 47 percent to 38 percent.

From 1990 to 1995, the ten largest Thai finance and security companies never reported negative amounts of net interest income or negative amounts of fee income. However, a noticeable number of the smaller firms in the market posted negative amounts of either net interest or fee income (Table 13.1, panel 1, rows 4 and 5). Since the analytical techniques described in section 2 do not handle negative outputs well, these firms were eliminated when the short-run objective model was calculated. No firms were eliminated when the long-run objective model was calculated since none of the firms ever had negative long-run objective outputs.

Eliminating firms with negative outputs has a minimal effect on the linear programming results because (1) these firms would not define the frontier for firms associated with positive outputs and, thus, (2) the only observations affected by this elimination are observations for other firms with negative outputs, which are also eliminated. However, eliminating these firms probably leads to higher mean efficiency scores. Table 13.1, panel 1, row 6 shows the percentage of Thai finance and securities companies used for the linear programming problems after firms with negative outputs are eliminated. This percent never falls below 69 percent of the entire number of firms in the market.

The number of firms with negative outputs (Table 13.1, panel 1, rows 4 and 5) declines from 1990 to 1993, drops drastically in 1994 and shoots up again in 1995. A related pattern is seen in mean net interest income and mean noninterest (fee) income (Table 13.1, panel 1, rows 7 and 8). For all firms in the market mean net interest income and non-interest income increased from 1990 to 1994 and then fell in 1995. Even the ten largest firms (Table 13.2, panel 13.1, rows 5 and 6) mirror this pattern with the exception that net interest income continued to climb in 1995 for the ten largest Thai finance and securities companies. In contrast, mean long-run objective outputs grew during the entire time period (1990-1995) for both the entire market and for the 10 largest firms (Tables 13.3 and 13.4, panel 1).

4 EMPIRICAL RESULTS

The discussion of empirical results will focus on four things: (1) measures of growth, (2) evidence of productivity change, (3) indicators of efficiency (net of economies of strongest growth effects) and (4) evidence of economies of strongest growth.

4.1 Growth

Both the short-run and long-run objective outputs for Thai finance and securities companies grew at a relatively rapid rate, especially when compared to the rate of inflation. From 1990 to 1994 consumer prices increased by 1.3 times, but mean net interest income increased by 4.6 times, fee income increased by 3.5 times, credits increased 3.3 times and securities increased 4.0 times for the entire market (Tables 13.1 and 13.3, panel 1). When just the ten largest firms are considered for the 1990 to 1994 time period, net interest income increased by 3.6 times, fee income increased by 3.4 times, credits increased by 2.7 times, and securities increase by 4.0 times (Table 13.2 and 13.4, panel 1). Although the output growth rates for the ten largest firms are less than that for the entire market, the output of these largest firms grew at more than double the rate of inflation.

The noticeably-greater-than-inflation growth rates of Thai finance and securities outputs for 1990 to 1994 contrast with the 1994 to 1995 growth rates. From 1994 to 1995, consumer prices increased by 5.8 percent but mean net interest income for all firms decreased by 2 percent, mean fee income for all firms fell by 26 percent, mean net interest income for the ten largest firms increased by 12 percent, and mean net fee income for the ten largest firms decreased by 32 percent.

In contrast to outputs, the use of both labor and capital grew for the entire time period (1990-1995). Labor expense increased for all firms by 4.0 times and capital increased by 6.4 times between 1990 and 1995 (Table 13.1, panel 1, rows 9 and 10). For the ten largest firms, labor increased by 3.3 times and capital increased by 5.6 times between 1990 to 1995 (Table 13.2, panel 1, rows 7 and 8). No clear-cut conclusions about total factor productivity can be drawn by comparing the growth rates of outputs and inputs since not all outputs grew at a rate greater or less than the growth rates of all inputs.

4.2 Productivity Change

Since all the data is given in baht, it is possible to calculate an output-input ratio by dividing the sum of all outputs by the sum of all inputs for each firm and then finding the mean of these ratios. This mean of output-input ratios provides a measure of mean productivity change and is reported in the last row of panel 1 of each table. These ratios also provide a measure of profitability since they are equal to the value of outputs divided by the cost of inputs.

When short-run objective outputs are used for all firms, mean productivity fluctuates from 1990 to 1993, and then climbs from 1993 to 1995. The increase in mean productivity between 1994 and 1995 is puzzling because both short-run objective outputs fell between 1994 and 1995 and the use of capital and labor increased (Table 13.1, panel 1, rows 7-10). This puzzle is solved by realizing (1) that the productivity of one small firm, Erawan Trust, was 211 in 1995 and (2) that without this one outlier the mean output-input ratio would be 2.68, which (3) is consistent with the expected fall in productivity between 1994 and 1995. The climb in the average firm's short-run output-input ratio from 3.17 in 1993 to 4.29 in 1994 is a 35 percent increase, but the fall from 4.29 to 2.68 (eliminating Erawan Trust) is a 38 percent decline. These productivity changes are large.

When considering long-run objective outputs for all firms (Table 13.3, panel 1, last row), productivity is practically the same for 1990, 1991 and 1993, falls by 11 percent in 1992 and rises from 1993 to 1995 by 32 percent. Productivity for the 10 largest firms for producing long-run objective outputs follows a U pattern - falling from 1990 to 1993 by 33 percent and then rising from 1993 to 1995 by 30 percent. When the outlier, Erawan Trust, is eliminated from 1995's short-run results, then the productivity of the average large firm is always noticeably higher than that of the average firm when both short- and long-run objective outputs are used. This implies that largeness in this market is associated with greater efficiency and higher profit rates.

The magnitudes of the output-input ratios are significant. The mean output-input ratio for short-run objective outputs of 3.04 in 1991 implies that the average baht of input generated 3.04 baht of output (income) in that year. Furthermore, 3.04 is the smallest output-input ratio in all the tables. This implies that the average revenue from an unit of inputs is at least 3.0 times the average cost of those inputs.

4.3 Efficiency

Row 1 of panel 2 of each table shows the efficiency scores. The 1990 mean efficiency score of 71 for all firms using short-run objective outputs (Table 13.1, panel 2, row 1) implies that the average 1990 firm produced 71 percent of the short-run objective outputs of a best-practice firm which used the same amounts of inputs. Whether these efficiency scores represent a maximum level of efficiency or the actual level of efficiency depends on how slack variables are interpreted. Slacks occur when the dual problem discussed in section 2 produces weights of 0 for one or more of the inputs and/or outputs. The percent of my observations which produced slack outputs are given in panel 2, rows 2 and 3, of each table. When all firms are considered, between 27 percent and 59 percent of my observations generated a dual value of 0 for one of the outputs. Slacks among the inputs were also common. According to one school of thought, a slack value for an input means that input could be reduced without increasing the use of other inputs or sacrificing output. Likewise, a slack value for an output implies that output could be increased without using additional inputs or sacrificing other outputs. Thus, according to this school, slacks imply that actual efficiency is less than the efficiency score. An alternative school of thought interprets slacks as just an inconsequential effect of linear programming. This school argues that if the piecewise constructed frontier devised by the linear programming problem was replaced by a smooth frontier, then slacks would not exist. Thus this school would say that the efficiency scores reported in my tables are close to the actual scores (how close depends on how the smoothing is done).

No matter how slacks are interpreted, the mean efficiency scores found in this study for all firms are consistent with the results of nonparametric studies of financial institutions in the USA. The efficiency scores for both short-run objective outputs (Table 13.1, panel 2) and for long-run objective outputs (Table 13.3, panel 2) are all at or below the mean of 72 percent, and are within the standard deviation of 17, found for the 78 nonparametric studies of financial institutions in the USA which were surveyed by Berger and Humphrey (1997: 185). Changes in annually determined efficiency scores (like those in this paper) do not indicate changes in productivity, instead they indicate whether the average firm is catching up or falling further behind best-practice. A fall in annually determined efficiency scores, like the one seen in Table 13.1, panel 2 for 1994, could be because (1) best-practice firms are gaining productivity faster than the average firm is or (2) because the average firm is losing productivity faster than best-practice is losing productivity.

Therefore, the gap between best practice and the average firm in producing short-run objective outputs stayed relatively constant from 1990 to 1993, increased in 1994 and then partially closed in 1995 (Table 13.1, panel 2, row 1). The gap between best practice and the average firm was bigger for long-run objective outputs than it was for short-run objective outputs for every year except for 1994 (Tables 13.1 and 13.3, panel 2, row 1); this pattern also holds for the ten largest firms (Tables 13.2 and 13.4, panel 2, row 1). Finally, the average efficiency of the ten largest firms ranged from 19 percent to 37 percent higher than the average firm for both short- and long-run objective outputs. This means that the gap between the average large firm and best practice is noticeably less than the gap between the average firm and best practice.[6]

The short-run objective output empirical results of this study indicate inefficiency in at least two additional ways: (1) the marginal rate of product transformations (MRPT) differ from 1 and the maximum marginal products (MP) of all inputs are not equal to each other and to 1. In the context of the linear programming techniques described in section 2, both MRPT and MP are 'frontier' concepts - each observation is projected to the frontier and the corresponding slope of the frontier in output-output space is the MRPT and the slope of the frontier in output-input space is the MP of that input.

Since the outputs used in the short-run analysis are types of income (net interest income and non-interest income), the 1995 MRPT of 3.18 for the average firm implies that, by reducing fee income by one baht, net interest income could have been increased by 3.18 baht without using additional inputs (and thus without increasing costs). Tables 13.1 and 13.2 (panel 2, row 4) show that reducing fee income in order to increase net interest income would have profited the average firm and the average large firm in every year between 1990 and 1995. However, the amount of increase in profits due to switching a dollar from fee income into net interest income varied noticeably from year to year and between the average firm and the average large firm.

The maximum marginal products given in panel 3 of Tables 13.1 and 13.2 also indicate inefficiency. In order to calculate the maximum marginal product for each input, the input's marginal product with respect to net interest income was compared to its marginal product with respect to fee income. Since an efficient firm would want to place additional inputs where they would be most productive, the maximum of the two marginal products was selected.[7] Finally these maximum marginal products were averaged across all firms in order to construct panel 3 of Tables 13.1 and 13.2.

A maximum marginal product for short-run objective outputs of 11.25

for labor for the average firm in 1990 implies that 11.25 baht of income could have been generated by hiring an additional baht of labor. Clearly, the maximum marginal products being greater than 1 for every single year, for every single input, and for both the average and the average large firm, implies that this market is extremely inefficient.[8] Perhaps Thailand's finance and securities companies did not add additional inputs because they were constrained by cash flow problems. However even if that was the case, the maximum short-run marginal products of the three inputs differing from each other indicates inefficiency. For example, the average firm in 1992 moving a baht from labor would have cost that firm 8.38 baht of income, but that freed up baht used to purchase capital would have generated 21.79 baht of output for a net gain of 13.41 baht. These firms are not maximizing profits.

4.4 Returns to Strongest Growth

A firm faces increasing returns to scale if doubling all inputs more than doubles all outputs. However, given the marginal rate of product transformation results reported above, the manager of the average Thai finance and security company would be foolish to increase all outputs by the same amount. Therefore I develop a new measure, 'returns to strongest growth', which involves only the best output increasing, and then I compare this new measure to the more standard 'returns to scale'.

Returns to strongest growth is the percentage increase in the value of all outputs if all inputs are increased by 1 percent, if the optimally chosen output is increased and all other outputs are held constant. Increasing (decreasing) returns to strongest growth occur if the value of outputs increases by greater than (less than) the 1 percent increase in all the inputs. In this study, I will assume that the value of a baht of net interest income is equal to a baht of fee income and that a baht of credits is worth a baht of securities. How both 'returns to growth' and 'returns to strongest growth' are calculated is explained in section 2. The results of these calculations are reported in panel 4 of each table.

For every year between 1990 and 1995, and for both short- and long-run objective output analyses, the average Thai finance and security company faced increasing returns to strongest growth (penultimate row of Tables 13.1 and 13.3), which implies that the average firm in this market would gain by increasing their production of their best output. Furthermore, the magnitude of the returns to strongest growth for the average firm are relatively large. The smallest returns to strongest growth for short-run objective outputs for the average firm is 1.45 in 1993 and this number implies that a 10 percent increase in all inputs (which are then used to produce the best output) would have increased the value of outputs by 14.5 percent. In other words, this result means that, by increasing all inputs by 10 percent, the value of output/cost of inputs ratio of 3.17 for the average firm in 1993 (see last row of panel 1 for Table 13.1) would have increased to 3.30 (or $3.17 \times 1.145/1.1$). When long-run objective outputs are used, the lowest returns to strongest growth for the average Thai finance and security company was 1.25 in 1994 which means that a 10 percent increase in all inputs would have increased the output-input ratio of 72 to 74.

Like the average firm, the average large firm also faced increasing returns to strongest growth when short-run objective outputs are used in every year between 1990 and 1995 (Table 13.2, penultimate row). In contrast, the average large firm faced decreasing returns to strongest growth when long-run objective outputs are used in 1991, 1993, 1994 and 1995 (Table 13.4, penultimate row). This result, however, does not imply that the average large firm ought not to expand its holdings of long-run objective outputs. It only means that the value of outputs will increase by a smaller percentage than the increase in all inputs, but since the ratio of long run outputs to inputs remains above 70 for 1990 to 1995 (Table 13.4, panel 1, last row), it may still be profitable to expand. For example, the smallest returns to strongest growth (of 0.67) for long-run objective outputs for the average large firm occurs in 1993 which also is the year of the lowest output-input ratio (of 70); thus a 10 percent increase in all inputs in 1993 for the average large firm would have decreased that firm's long-run objective output-input ratio of 70 to 68. Sixty-eight baht of additional credits and securities from an additional baht of inputs could be quite profitable.[9]

Credits were associated with much larger returns to growth than securities for both the average firm and the average large firm in every year of my analysis (Tables 13.3 and 13.4, panel 4, rows 1 and 2). This result reinforces the marginal rate of product transformation results discussed above (Tables 13.3 and 13.4, panel 2, row 4).[10]

As expected, returns to strongest growth (penultimate line of all tables) is greater than returns to scale (last line of all tables). However, the magnitude of the difference between these two measures is large. Indeed under short- and long-run analyses for the average firm, returns to strongest growth is always between 2.49 and 1.29 times as large as returns to scale. Furthermore, the average firm always enjoyed 'increasing' returns to strongest growth from 1990 to 1995 under both short- and long-run objective analyses. In contrast, the average firm faced decreasing returns to scale for 50 percent of the time for short run outputs and for 83 percent of the time for long run outputs. The increasing returns to strongest growth results are much more consistent with the marginal rate of product transformation and marginal product results discussed above than the returns to scale results are.

5 CONCLUSION

From 1990 to 1995, Thailand's finance and securities companies enjoyed (1) tremendous profitability as shown by large 'value of output/cost of input' ratios, (2) rapid growth as seen by long-run objective outputs increasing by a factor of 4.9 times and (3) large potential returns for future growth. This chapter has also documented large inefficiencies in this market in that profits could have been increased even more by (1) changing the output mix, (2) increasing the use of inputs, (3) adjusting the input mix and (4) growing more.

Even Thailand's ten largest finance and securities companies were smaller than optimal. Financial liberalization, and the threat that came with it that in the future Thailand's finance and securities companies would have to increasingly compete with the much larger Thai banks, must have scared Thailand's finance and securities companies. Increasing this fear is the fact that the playing field between banks and finance and securities companies is not level; for example, the opening of finance and securities company branches have been forbidden, but Thailand's 15 domestic banks have over 3000 branches. Given their current smaller than optimal size and their future outlook, Thailand's finance and securities companies' best prospects lie in becoming big enough to convince the Bank of Thailand to give them one of the few new banking licenses planned for the near future. This combination of motivating forces caused Thailand's finance and securities companies to take unwise risks in order to grow faster than all the other finance and securities companies. The usually cited aspects which contribute to financial crises were also evident - like insufficient supervision, a belief that the government would always bail out all financial institutions, greed and spillover effects like runs on sound financial institutions due to uncertainty created by problem financial institutions. In this chapter, I have contributed to the literature by providing evidence that (in addition to the usually cited reasons) the structure of Thailand's finance and securities market played an important role in the financial crisis now facing Thailand. The structure of this market was of too many firms, which were too small, and too constrained in comparison to their partial competitors - the banks.

NOTES

1. After Thailand suspended the operations of the first 16 finance and securities companies, foreign banks became concerned that they would not get their money back if Thailand suffered a financial meltdown. Therefore, dollar inflows into Thailand slowed to a trickle, the Bank of Thailand tried to defend the Baht for awhile, but the baht was ultimately floated on 2 July, 1997 when it promptly fell in value by 20 percent which was only the beginning of its fall. See Pandey and Sivasomboon (1997) and Ingsrisawang and Bunyamanee (1997) for more information.
2. About 755 000 housing units were built in Bangkok between 1992 and 1996, compared with the estimate of 382 240 needed under the seventh National Economic and Social Development Plan (Parnsoonthorn, 1997). A study conducted by the Government Housing Bank showed that 40.4 percent of the houses built in Bangkok during this time period remained unoccupied. The total supply of empty property is now estimated at about 350 000 units in Bangkok and 850 000 units nationwide. Furthermore, 24 percent of finance and securities company loans were to the property market when the speculative bubble burst in early 1997, in comparison to only 9 percent of commercial bank loans to the property market (Nivatpumin and Sivasomboon, 1997).
3. These techniques are based upon Shephard (1970), Debreu (1951), Farrell (1957), Charnes *et al.* (1978), and Banker, et al. (1984).
4. Rogers (1996) provides an empirical illustration of the importance of incorporating noninterest income in analyses of bank performance.
5. If the provision for bad debt works as it was designed to work, then it would be an excellent proxy for risks due to granting credits. It however would not capture the risk of buying securities. Auditors, who examine the quality of a financial institution's loans, recommend a minimum level for the provision for bad debt to the Bank of Thailand who then requires the financial institution (except in the rare case of a waiver) to set aside at least the recommended amount. Financial institutions are allowed to set aside even more than the Bank of Thailand requires if they think that is prudent. However, having said all the above, I doubt that the provision for bad debt worked as designed for finance and securities companies after 1992 because the provision for bad debt declined after 1992 while the amount of credits skyrocketed (Table 13.3, panel 1, rows 4 and 8). Furthermore, events in 1997 have revealed that many of the credits granted by Thai finance and securities companies after 1992 were based on speculation in the property market.

   A few finance and securities companies actually reported negative provisions for bad debt during the time period studied. This can occur if the auditors in a given year believe that the finance and security company's quality of loans has improved enough that it can safely reduce its provision for bad debt. However, since negative inputs are theoretically questionable and the analytic techniques used do not like negative inputs, negative risk was changed to zero for the 4 percent of my observations involved.
6. It is important to realize that the efficiency measures, given in panel 2 of each table, ignore economies of scale - firms with very few inputs are compared to

other firms with very few inputs and firms with large amounts of inputs are compared to other firms with comparable amounts of inputs. These efficiency scores do not indicate what size (small, large or medium) is optimal.

7. For each firm, the maximum marginal product of labor, capital and risk (all inputs) will correspond to the same output. This occurs as a mathematical result of the linear programming techniques described in section 2.
8. For short-run objective outputs, the maximum marginal product of labor is sometimes greater for the average firm and sometimes greater for the average large firm. In contrast, the maximum marginal product of capital is greater for the average firm than it is for the average large firm for the entire time period studied. This implies that the average large firm is more efficient in the use of capital than the average firm when short run objective outputs are used. When long-run objective outputs are considered, the maximum marginal product of both capital and labor for the ten largest firms is always less than the maximum marginal product for the average firm, except for the marginal product of labor in 1990.
9. It is also interesting to note that the average Thai finance and security company always faced larger returns to strongest growth than the average large company from 1990 to 1995 (as expected) when long-run objective outputs are used (last row of Tables 13.3 and 13.4), but not when short-run objective outputs are used (last row of Tables 13.1 and 13.2).
10. In contrast, returns to growth for fee income exceeded returns to growth of net interest income for the average firm in 1990, 1991 and 1995 and for the average large firm in 1994 and 1995 (Tables 13.1 and 13.2, panel 4, rows 1 and 2). This result appears to conflict with the marginal rate of product transformation results (Tables 13.1 and 13.2, panel 2, row 4). This apparent inconsistency could be due to one of two things (1) the different ways observations with slacks were handled when calculating the marginal rate of product transformation and the returns to growth, and/or (2) the different meanings behind the marginal rate of product transformation and returns to growth. When the marginal rate of product transformation was calculated, all observations with slack outputs were eliminated, but when returns to growth were calculated, observations with slack were not eliminated, instead they entered the mean calculations as zeros. Remember that the number of observations with slack outputs was noticeable (all Tables, panel 2, rows 2 and 3). An alternative explanation is based on the different meanings of marginal rate of product transformation and returns to strongest growth. The marginal rate of product transformation assumes all inputs are held constant, but returns to strongest growth is based on all inputs being increased by the same percent.

REFERENCES

Bangkok Post: Internet Edition (1997), 'Anand: Govt must follow IMF rules', 7 August.

Banker, R.D., A. Charnes and W.W. Cooper (1984), 'Some models for estimating technical and scale efficiencies in data envelopment analysis', *Management Science*, **30**, 1078-92.

Berger, A.N. and D.B. Humphrey (1997), 'Efficiency of financial institutions: international survey and review', *European Journal of Operational Research*, **98** (2), 175-212.

Berger, A.N. and D.B. Humphrey (1992), 'Measurement and efficiency issues in commercial banking', in Z. Griliches (ed.), *Output Measurement in the Service Sectors,* National Bureau of Economic Research Studies in Income and Wealth, vol. 56, Chicago and London: The University of Chicago Press.

Berger, A.N. and R. DeYoung (1997), 'Problem loans and cost efficiency in commercial banks', *Journal of Banking and Finance*, **21**, 849-70.

Butler, S. (1997), ' "It was too easy to make money" and now the Thai economy is barely afloat', *U.S. News and World Report,* 28 July.

Charnes, A., W.W. Cooper and E. Rhodes (1978), 'Measuring the efficiency of decision making units', *European Journal of Operational Research*, **2**, 429-44.

Debreu, G. (1951), 'The coefficient of resource utilization', *Econometrica*, **19** (3), 273-92.

Farrell, M.J. (1957), 'The measurement of productive efficiency', *Journal of the Royal Statistical Society*, Series A, general, **120**, 253-81.

Forsund, F.R. (1996), 'On the calculation of the scale elasticity in DEA models', *Journal of Productivity Analysis*, **7**, 283-302.

Ingsrisawang, Cholada and Soonruth Bunyamanee (1997), 'Foreign banks restrict loans', *Bangkok Post: Internet Edition*, 10 July, 1997.

Nivatpumin, C. and B. Sivasomboon (1997), 'Post-boom reality calls for new rules', *Bangkok Post: Internet Edition*, 10 March.

Pandey, U. and B. Sivasomboon (1997), 'Foreign bank chief offers help to ride out slump, *Bangkok Post: Internet Edition*, 6 August.

Parnsoonthorn, K. (1997), 'Greed reaps grim reward', *Bangkok Post: Economic Review: Year-End 1996*, January, 62-3.

Rogers, K.E. (1996), 'The recent expansion of nontraditional banking activities: a theoretical and empirical analysis', unpublished PhD dissertation, University of Georgia, Athens, GA 30602, USA.

Shephard, R.W. (1970), *The Theory of Cost and Production Functions*, Princeton: Princeton University Press.

14. Cost Efficiency of the Farmers' Credit Unions in Taiwan

Cliff J. Huang, Tsu-Tan Fu and Mei-Ying Huang

1 INTRODUCTION

The Farmers' Credit Unions (FCUs), or the Credit Department of Farmers' Associations, have been regarded as the most important financial institution in rural communities in Taiwan. An FCU is more often than not the only banking facility in a township that provides banking services to its members on accepting deposits, making loans, handling remittance services and acting as a custodian for township treasury. In 1995 as many as 285 out of 305 Farmers' Associations (FAs) had their own credit unions or credit department, with an island-wide network of 854 branches located in every town and rural village. In 1994 the FCUs as a whole had a 12 percent share of total deposits and an 8 percent share of total outstanding loans in the entire financial system in Taiwan. These shares were much higher in the rural community, where its shares were 30 percent for deposits and 25 percent for outstanding loans. In the same year FCUs provided more than NT$400 billion of agricultural loans to their members, which accounted for more than 50 percent of the total agricultural loans in Taiwan. Furthermore, to promote certain agricultural and rural development projects, the Taiwan government frequently appropriates or subsidizes farm loans to be processed through FCUs at rates well beneath prevailing market rates.

The FCU banking services have increased significantly in recent years, despite the deregulation and liberalization of the financial system. Average annual growth rates during the period from 1990 to 1994 were 20.5 percent and 24.3 percent for FCU savings and loans, respectively, as compared to 17.8 percent and 20.8 percent for other financial institutions in Taiwan. However the dominant position of FCUs has continuously been challenged by other financial institutions trying to extend their banking services into the rural community. And the rapid growth of FCU banking services has frequently come at the expense of bank efficiency and the financial integrity of FCUs. The ratio of the overall defaults/arrears to loan outstanding in FCUs was 2.6 percent in 1994, which is lower than that in other financial institutions. However, the ratio has been increasing steadily; it rose to 5.07 percent at the end of 1995 and to 7.25 percent in July 1996. Since 1995 over 30 FCUs have experienced cash-run crises after the concern of huge problem loans were made public. Since cost-inefficient credit unions tend to have loan performance problems due to ineffectiveness in credit screening and loan monitoring, the measurement of the relationship between loan quality and efficiency among FCUs has become an important policy issue.[1]

The Farmers' Associations in Taiwan are a federated system of farmers' cooperative type organizations which are at three levels, namely, the provincial, county and township FA. However, only township FAs are authorized to operate credit unions and to provide banking services to their members and families. The township FAs are governed by a board of directors and supervisors who are elected by their members. A general manager appointed by the directors is responsible for the operation of the township FCU. However, local politics and elections often exert pressure and interference on the business of the credit department, which supposedly is financially and operationally an independent administrative unit. Fraudulent practice, loose internal control and lack of managerial efficiency contributed to the failure of many FCUs in 1995.

Under the current Farmers' Association Law and arrangement, all FCUs operate their business independently, without any vertical (with provincial or county FAs) or horizontal (with other township FCUs) link between them. Since FCUs are mutual form organizations, as opposed to the stock form for most financial institutions, by law the FCUs are not allowed to extend banking services to nonmembers or to engage in financial investments other than loans to their own members. Any FCU surplus loanable funds are thus routinely redeposited with the three government-owned agricultural banks, the Farmers' Bank of China, the Land Bank of Taiwan, and the Cooperative Bank of Taiwan. Although the ratio of redeposits to total FCU deposits has been declining from a peak of 53 percent in 1986, the ratio was still more than 30 percent in 1995. The lack of expertise, inadequate staff training in credit operations in township FCUs and the conservative practice of putting security/safety first on loans, all contribute to the huge surplus funds. This redeposit arrangement amounts to a risk-free disposition of the loanable funds, and a risk-averse manager has no incentive to accept a normal risk in making loans to members. Over a quarter of FCU income was generated from redeposit at the three agricultural banks in 1994. Although there is no regulation governing loan policy to members, FCUs place heavy emphasis on credit ratings and loan guarantors. Unsecured loans accounted for only 7 percent of total outstanding loans in 1994, and the ratio has been declining since then. This restriction and the practice on the utilization of loanable funds places a severe constraint on the efficiency of operation and management of township FCUs.

This chapter examines the cost efficiency of FCUs by using a stochastic shadow cost frontier. There is a voluminous literature concerning bank cost efficiency. Berger *et al.* (1993) and Berger and Humphrey (1997) provided a critical review and a survey of 130 studies that apply frontier efficiency analysis to financial institutions in 21 countries. Jang *et al.* (1997) investigate the cost efficiency of six small- to medium-size banks in Taiwan, and Chang (1997) and Chang and Hsieh (1997) study the efficiency of FCUs in Taiwan. The point of departure for this study from the traditional frontier approach is the concept of shadow outputs and shadow prices. In the context of a cost frontier, it recognizes that production inefficiency and allocative distortions are both output- and input-specific. The traditional stochastic frontier approach measures cost inefficiency as the distance between observed cost and the minimum cost frontier, and so inefficiency simply shifts the observed cost upward. However, this procedure does not take into consideration the possibility that cost inefficiency due to loan quality and the FCUs' loan practices causes both output- and input-specific distortions. The loan output shall be measured as quality-adjusted output or shadow output. The lower quality loans are likely to entail high administrative cost and use of labor input in attempting to collect and resolve the bad loans. It raises the marginal cost of output and possibly input prices as well. For example, based on the 304 US banks, Hughes and Mester (1993) found evidence that lower quality assets increase interest cost, which contains a risk premium.

In this chapter the FCU production possibility frontiers are assumed to be union-specific, and explicitly account for loan quality differentials among FCUs. The shadow cost frontier approach assumes that all FCUs have the same underlying production frontier that measures the loan output in terms of quality-adjusted units. Furthermore, union-specific input allocative inefficiency in cost minimization is reflected in input shadow prices, which are a function of such variables as the percentage of unsecured loans and the percentage of loanable funds redeposited at the three agricultural banks.

The rest of the chapter is organized as follows. Section 2 presents the formulation of a stochastic shadow cost frontier that explicitly takes into consideration the quality-adjusted output and the allocative distortion factors in cost minimization. Section 3 discusses the empirical implementation of the model to estimate the cost efficiency of the 283 FCUs from a two-year panel. The cost of distortions in output and in input allocations are estimated, as are economies of scale and scope. Section 4 provides a conclusion.

2 A STOCHASTIC SHADOW COST FRONTIER

Consider an FCU producing a vector of m outputs $Q = (Q_1,\ldots, Q_m)$ using a vector of n inputs $X = (X_1,\ldots, X_n)$. The shadow cost approach postulates that various union-specific production possibility frontier, $F_t(Q, X) = 0$, can be pooled together and be represented by a single common frontier that applies to the 'quality-adjusted' outputs Q^*. That is, $F(Q^*, X) = 0$. This formulation is based on the hypothesis that there exists an array of production processes that describe the production of various degree of loan quality. At a given point in time, each FCU makes a rational decision according to its own risk preferences, available credit reference on borrowers and the extent of market competition in choosing its own production possibility frontier, $F_t(Q, X) = 0$.

The unobserved 'quality-adjusted', or shadow, outputs Q^* are assumed to be related to the observed outputs Q and a set of quality indicator Z_Q. That is, $Q^* = Q^*(Q, Z_Q)$. The output quality indicator Z_Q might be the loan defaults/arrears rate. We assume that credit unions are price-takers in the input markets, so that the corresponding input price vector $P = (P_1,\ldots, P_n)$ is exogenously determined. The cost minimization behavior can then be stated as

$$\text{Minimize C} = \sum_{j=1}^{n} P_j X_j \ \text{ subject to } F(Q^*, X) = 0. \qquad (14.1)$$

The first-order conditions for cost minimization can be arranged to obtain

$$\frac{\partial F / \partial X_j}{\partial F / \partial X_1} = \frac{F_j}{F_1} = \frac{P_j \theta_j}{P_1} = \frac{P_j^*}{P_1^*},\ j = 2, \ldots, n. \qquad (14.2)$$

where P_1 is the normalizing input price and hence $P_1 = P_1^*$. The parameter $\theta_j \neq 1$, represents allocative distortion associated with the input pair (j, 1). Since the prices in the first-order conditions are the ratio of P_j^*, and not the observed input prices P_j, the relevant prices in cost minimization are P_j^*, the shadow prices. Following Atkinson and Halvorsen (1986), the unobserved allocative distortion parameter θ_j is a function of the observed price P_j and the allocative distortion factor Z_P, $\theta_j = \theta_j(P_j, Z_P)$. The distortion parameter θ_j is neither constant nor independent to the input prices as generally assumed in the literature. Thus the shadow price is $P_j^* = P_j^*(P_j, Z_P)$. The allocative distortion factors might be the percentages of unsecured loans and FCU's redeposit at the three agricultural banks. Most unsecured loans made by the township FCUs are small and short-term in nature, and carry a much higher implicit transaction cost in credit investigation, monitoring and bookkeeping than do secured loans. The transaction cost incurs higher shadow prices in labor and capital inputs relative to the FCU's interest cost. Conversely, the implicit transaction cost of the FCU's redeposit is minimal, as it only involves a transfer of loanable funds to the three agricultural banks.

The above first-order conditions and quality-adjusted production frontier $F(Q^*, X) = 0$ can be used to solve for the conditional input demands, $X_j = X_j^*(P^*, Q^*)$. The corresponding shadow cost frontier is then

$$C^* = C^*(P^*, Q^*) = \sum_{j=1}^{n} P_j^* X_j^*(P^*, Q^*) \tag{14.3}$$

The cost share equations are obtained from the partial derivatives

$$S_j = \frac{\partial \ln C^*}{\partial \ln P_j^*}, \quad j = 1, \ldots, n. \tag{14.4}$$

The overall economies of scale (SCALE) measures the elasticity of total cost with respect to the m outputs. Assuming the output proportions remain unchanged, the SCALE is defined as

$$\text{SCALE} = \left(\sum_j \frac{\partial \ln C^*}{\partial \ln Q_j^*}\right)^{-1} \tag{14.5}$$

There are overall economies of scale if SCALE > 1, and overall diseconomies of scale if SCALE < 1, and constant overall economies of scale if SCALE = 1.[2]

In addition to economies of scale, a multi-product cost frontier allows the measure of economies of scope (SCOPE). Economies of scope exist between outputs if the total cost of joint production is less than the cost of separate production. For an FCU producing both farm loans Q_F and non-farm loans Q_C, the conventional measure of a within-sample economies of scope (SCOPE) is defined as

$$\text{SCOPE} = \frac{C^*(P^*, Q_F - Q_F^m, Q_C^m) + C^*(P^*, Q_F^m, Q_C - Q_C^m) - C^*(P^*, Q_F, Q_C)}{C^*(P^*, Q_F, Q_C)}$$

where Q_F^m and Q_C^m are the minimum values of Q_F and Q_C in the sample.

Economies of scope entail cost complementarity and hence SCOPE > 0. Similarly, SCOPE < 0 implies diseconomies of scope. Large FCUs may be exposed to diseconomies of scope and scale due to the layers of management structure or the hierarchical diseconomies (Mester, 1993).

The shadow cost frontier is derived with Z_Q and Z_P as output- and input-specific distortion factors, respectively. Other distortions in cost minimization may not be output- and/or input-specific but are nevertheless cost-augmenting. Following the spirit of the stochastic frontier approach, a stochastic shadow cost frontier, C_V^*, is defined as

$$C_V^* = C^* + V,$$

where V is a two-sided random error representing statistical noise. The neutral cost-augmenting inefficiency, U, is specified as

$$U = C - C_V^* \geq 0,$$

where C is observed cost.[3]

The stochastic shadow cost frontier with neutral cost-augmenting inefficiency is then

$$C = C^*(P^*, Q^*) + U + V,$$

The regression estimation is then a matter of assuming distributions of the random variables U and V. Usually it is assumed that V is normally distributed with mean 0 and variances σ_V^2 and the distribution of U is truncated from below at zero from a normal distribution with mean 0 and variance σ_U^2. The U is distributed independently of the random noise V. Following Jondrow *et al.* (1982), the union-specific neutral cost-augmenting inefficiency can be estimated by the conditional mean of U given the composite error $\varepsilon = U + V$,

$$E(U \mid \varepsilon) = \frac{\sigma\lambda}{1+\lambda^2}\left(\frac{\phi(\varepsilon\lambda/\sigma)}{1-\Phi(\varepsilon\lambda/\sigma)} - \frac{\varepsilon\lambda}{\sigma}\right). \tag{14.6}$$

where $\phi(.)$ and $\Phi(.)$ are the standard normal density and distribution functions, respectively. The σ^2 is defined as $\sigma^2 = \sigma_U^2 + \sigma_V^2$ and $\lambda = \sigma_U/\sigma_V$

3 EMPIRICAL IMPLEMENTATION

The data in this study were taken from a 1994-1995 two-year panel data of 283 farmers' credit unions of all sizes obtained from the Farmers' Association *Yearbook*. The data were collected at the township level. Since FCUs are not permitted to make any securities or other investments except loans to their own township FCU members, only two output variables are used in the cost function:

Q_F = total farm loans,
Q_C = total nonfarm loans.

The distinction in output is to recognize the primary function of an FCU in serving its farm members and farming related activities. However, due to low profitability in farming relative to other investments, the FAs in recent years have encouraged and made nonfarm loans to their members engaging in nonfarming activities. The total cost C of an FCU includes interest payment on deposits, wages and salaries, payment for real capital services and other operating expenses. The interest payment on deposits excludes the payment on the portion of deposits that are redeposited at the three agricultural banks. This is the loanable funds approach. Only costs that are attributable to the production of these two outputs are included.

Two normalized inputs prices are used with the price of loanable funds (or deposits) being the normalization factor:

P_K = (price of capital)/(price of loanable funds)
P_L = (wage rate)/(price of loanable funds).

The price of capital is calculated by dividing the total rental cost on building, equipment, depreciation and maintenance by the net book value of capital assets. The wage rate is calculated by dividing total wages and salaries by the total annual employee hours. Since the predominant source of loanable funds comes from members' savings and deposits, the price of loanable funds is defined as the average interest rate paid on deposits and is calculated by dividing the total interest payments on all deposits by the total deposits.

Three Z-variables, the loan quality indicator, Z_Q, and the allocative distortion factors, Z_U and Z_R, are used to obtain the quality-adjusted outputs and the input shadow prices. These three Z-variables are defined as:

Z_Q = loan quality, measured as the percentage of overdue loans in defaults/arrears for 90 days or more
Z_U = percentage of unsecured loans
Z_R = percentage of loanable funds redeposited at the three agricultural banks.

Three other explanatory variables are also included in the cost function. There are defined as:

Rural = a dummy variable that takes on a value of unity if an FCU is located in a rural district, and zero otherwise
Branch = number of branch offices
Other = remittances and special project loans handled as a percentage of total loans ($Q_F + Q_C$).

The rural dummy variable is included to account for location differential in operating costs. A rural township is defined as having population of no more than 50 000 and more than 40 percent of the residents being farmers. Almost all credit unions in the sample have multiple branch offices. To shed some light on how the multiple branches affect the total cost, the number of branches is added as an explanatory variable. Two other activities and services are also rendered by township FCUs. Handling remittance service and acting as a custody for township treasury are one of them. Channeling government special project loans and receiving a handling charge is another. Since these two activities are service to the members, they are expected to be positively correlated with the total cost.

Table 14.1 tabulates the sample statistics of the defined variables. It

Table 14.1 Description of the data

Variable	mean	standard deviation	maximum	minimum
Total asset	4 619 562	4 481 795	31 959 200	245 784
C: Total cost	218 112	233 418	2 123 454	10 862
Q_F: Total farm-loans	424 071	684 938	3 525 190	0
Q_C: Total nonfarm-loans	2 047 522	2 571 724	19 209 100	0
Price of capital	0.7524	0.8748	8.8639	0.0013
Price of labor	0.5005	0.1581	1.2732	0.1222
Price of deposit	0.0529	0.0065	0.0845	0.0056
Z_Q: percentage of overdue loans	2.1976	3.1533	32.1300	0
Z_U: percentage of unsecured loans	10.2876	19.9213	100.0000	0
Z_R: percentage of redeposit	30.9956	11.4690	78.8774	11.3475
Rural: percent of rural FCUs	47.3500			
Branch: Number of branch	2.8400		13.0000	0
Other: percentage other services	1.8671	0.2214	0.9999	0.0006

Note: Assets, cost, and loans are measured in thousands of NT$. The relative price of capital and the relative price of labor are obtained by divisions, P_K = (price of capital)/(price of deposit), P_L = (price of labor)/(price of deposit).

presents the maximum and minimum values and shows a considerable variation among FCUs. Some FCUs are relatively small in terms of asset size, and others concentrate either entirely on making farm loans or entirely on making nonfarm loans. The total farm loans account for only 24 percent of the total loans compared to almost 76 percent in 1970. The decline reflects the low profitability in farming relative to other investments in recent years. The quality of loans, measured in the percentage of loans in defaults/arrears for 90 days or more, ranges from zero to over 32 percent of the total outstanding loans. Considerable ranges are also observed in the activity of transferring the loanable funds at the three agricultural banks, ranging from 11.35 percent to a high of almost 79 percent and with an average of 31 percent. Nearly half (47 percent) of the FCUs are located in rural areas. The wide range of these FCUs' characteristics makes it more crucial to formulate a shadow cost frontier in the quality-adjusted outputs and the input shadow prices.

To empirically estimate the cost function we approximate the underlying shadow cost frontier by a translog form. The stochastic shadow cost frontier is specified as

$$\begin{aligned}\ln C = {} & \alpha_0 + \alpha_1 \ln Q_F + \alpha_2 \ln Q_C^* + \beta_1 \ln P_K^* + \beta_2 \ln P_L^* \\ & + \tfrac{1}{2}\alpha_{11} (\ln Q_F)^2 + \alpha_{12} (\ln Q_F)(\ln Q_C^*) + \tfrac{1}{2}\alpha_{22} (\ln Q_C^*)^2 \\ & + \tfrac{1}{2}\beta_{11} (\ln P_K^*)^2 + \beta_{12} (\ln P_K^*)(\ln P_L^*) + \tfrac{1}{2}\beta_{22} (\ln P_L^*)^2 \\ & + \gamma_{11} (\ln Q_F)(\ln P_K^*) + \gamma_{12} (\ln Q_F)(\ln P_L^*) \\ & + \gamma_{21} (\ln Q_C^*)(\ln P_K^*) + \gamma_{22} (\ln Q_C^*)(\ln P_L^*) \\ & + \varphi_1 (\text{Rural}) + \varphi_2 (\text{Branch}) + \varphi_3 (\text{Other}) + U + V\end{aligned}$$

The associated cost share equations for capital and labor are

$$S_K = \beta_1 + \beta_{11} \ln P_K^* + \beta_{12} \ln P_L^* + \gamma_{11} \ln Q_F + \gamma_{21} \ln Q_C^* + W_K$$

$$S_L = \beta_2 + \beta_{12} \ln P_K^* + \beta_{22} \ln P_L^* + \gamma_{12} \ln Q_F + \gamma_{22} \ln Q_C^* + W_L$$

where W_K and W_L are random error terms. The quality-adjusted nonfarm loans and the shadow prices are defined as

$$\ln Q_C^* = (1 + \delta_{11} Z_Q) \ln Q_C$$

$$\ln P_K^* = (1 + \delta_{21} Z_U + \delta_{22} Z_R) \ln P_K$$

$$\ln P_L^* = (1 + \delta_{31} Z_U + \delta_{32} Z_R) \ln P_L$$

where δ are parameters to be estimated. The coefficient δ_{11} is expected to be positive. The cost associated with making one dollar of bad loan is equivalent to making more than one dollar's worth of good loan.[4] Thus $Q_C^* > Q_C$. Since the total farm loans are small and most of the defaults/arrears were due to nonfarm loans, the farm loans are not subject to the quality adjustment. It is assumed that $Q_F^* = Q_F$. Both normalized shadow prices are a function of the percentage of unsecured loan Z_U and the percentage of redeposit Z_R. Since the quality-adjusted loans and the shadow prices are specified in logarithmic form, the adjustment factor, Q_C^* / Q_C, P_K^*/P_K, and P_L^*/P_L are neither constant nor exogenous to the observed loan quantity Q_C and prices, P_K and P_L.[5]

We follow the two-step procedure of Bhattacharyya *et al.* (1996) to estimate the above cost and cost share system. Since the neutral inefficiency term U is restricted to be nonnegative, the mean of U is added to the constant ($\alpha_0 + E(U)$), so that a new composite error, ($U + V - E(U)$), has a zero mean. Thus, in the first- step, the iterative nonlinear seeming unrelated method is used to simultaneously estimate the cost and the cost share system with cross equation restrictions on coefficients. In the second- step, the estimated constant of the cost equation is 'corrected' by subtracting $E(U)$ to obtain the estimate of α_0. With the appropriate distribution assumption on U, the neutral cost inefficiency is then estimated as the conditional mean $E(U|\varepsilon)$ by the method of Jondrow *et al.* (1982).

The estimated coefficients are presented in Table 14.2. Except for five coefficients, all others are statistically significant at a 5 percent level. The 'RURAL' dummy carries a negative coefficient $\varphi_1 = -0.0776$, indicating a 7.76 percent lower operating cost for the rural FCUs. The 'BRANCH' variable has a positive coefficient that implies a higher operating cost for multiple branch offices. Other things being equal, an extra branch office incurs approximately an additional 8 percent cost, which likely results from duplicating administrative cost. On the other hand, the cost of branching might be outweighed by the belief in increasing returns to scale in operations, as is shown empirically. The coefficient φ_3 of the variable 'OTHER' is expected to be positive since it costs FCUs to render the remittance service and to process government agricultural loan programs. Since the stochastic shadow cost frontier approach focus on the quality-adjusted output and the allocative distortion factors on input prices, a further discussion on the implication of the coefficients δ is in order.

The value of δ_{11} determines how the quality of the nonfarm loans changes with increasing the defaults/arrears rate. The ratio of quality-indicates the degrees of distortion in output cost. The ratio is denoted as X_C. Since the estimate δ_{11} is positive, it implies an inverse relationship between the cost inefficiency and the defaults/arrears rate. As shown in

Table 14.2 Translog shadow cost frontier estimates

Variable	Coefficient	Estimate	Variable	Coefficient	Estimate
Constant	α_0	2.8149 (0.6613)	Rural	φ_1	−0.0776 (0.0259)
$\ln Q_F$	α_1	0.3653 (0.0444)	Branch	φ_2	0.0796 (0.0075)
$\ln Q_C^*$	α_2	0.2249 (0.0598)	Other	φ_3	0.0939 (0.0583)
$\ln P_K^*$	β_1	0.0986 (0.0337)	$(\ln Q_C)Z_Q$	δ_{11}	0.0010 (0.0005)
$\ln P_L^*$	β_2	0.4567 (0.0275)	$(\ln P_K)\,Z_U$	δ_{21}	0.0009 (0.0009)
$(\ln Q_F)^2$	α_{11}	0.0181 (0.0014)	$(\ln P_K)\,Z_R$	δ_{22}	−0.0094 (0.0013)
$(\ln Q_F)(\ln Q_C^*)$	α_{12}	−0.0316 (0.0029)	$(\ln P_L)\,Z_U$	δ_{31}	0.0030 (0.0006)
$(\ln Q_C^*)^2$	α_{22}	0.0481 (0.0030)	$(\ln P_L)\,Z_R$	δ_{32}	0.0035 (0.0010)
$(\ln P_K^*)^2$	β_{11}	0.0579 (0.0046)		σ_U^2	0.0469 (0.0201)
$(\ln P_K^*)(\ln P_L^*)$	β_{12}	−0.0258 (0.0024)		σ_V^2	0.1006 (0.0223)
$(\ln P_L^*)^2$	β_{22}	0.0518 (0.0059)		σ_{W_K}	0.0766
$(\ln Q_F)(\ln P_K^*)$	γ_{11}	0.0007 (0.0009)		σ_{W_L}	0.0575
$(\ln Q_F)(\ln P_L^*)$	γ_{12}	−0.0015 (0.0007)			
$(\ln Q_C^*)(\ln P_K^*)$	γ_{21}	−0.0010 (0.0021)			
$(\ln Q_C^*)(\ln P_L^*)$	γ_{22}	−0.0199 (0.0016)			

Notes: Asymptotic standard errors are in parentheses. Asymptotic standard errors for σ_U^2 and σ_V^2 are the moment estimates (Olson *et al.*, 1980: 82).

$\bar{R}^2$ on cost equation = 0.8301.

$\bar{R}^2$ on capital share equation = 0.2614.

$\bar{R}^2$ on labor share equation = 0.3898.

adjusted loans to the observed quantity,

$$\frac{Q_C^*}{Q_C} = Q_C^{\delta_{11} Z_Q} \equiv X_C$$

Table 14.3, the overall cost inefficiency due to defaults/arrears for the pooled sample is 3.27 percent of the total outstanding loans (Q_C^* / Q_C = 1.0327). Since the derivatives, $\partial X_C / \partial Q_C > 0$, and $\partial^2 X_C / \partial Q_C^2 < 0$, for $(\delta_{11}\, Z_Q) < 1$, the cost of loan quality is increasing at a decreasing rate with respect to the quantity of nonfarm loans Q_C. Using total asset value as the measure of size, the large FCUs with total assets greater than the sample mean are shown to be slightly less cost efficient due to larger defaults/arrears rates. This cost inefficiency is 3.68 percent for the large FCUs and 3.07 percent for the small FCUs. Rural and urban FCUs experience almost an identical distortion due to defaults/arrears loan problems.

Table 14.3 Distortion factors, cost of allocative distortion, and neutral inefficiency

Asset Size	$X_C = Q_C^*/Q_C$	$X_K = P_K^*/P_K$	$X_L = P_L^*/P_L$	AD	$E(U\|\varepsilon)$
Pooled	1.0327	0.5670	1.3812	0.0775	1.1620
	(0.0537)	(0.2319)	(0.2947)	(0.1764)	(0.0528)
Small	1.0307	0.5753	1.3933	0.0780	1.1647
	(0.0460)	(0.2386)	(0.3057)	(0.1856)	(0.0537)
Large	1.0368	0.5966	1.2920	0.0711	1.1408
	(0.0740)	(0.1682)	(0.1784)	(0.1503)	(0.0319)
Rural	1.0327	0.5602	1.4387	0.0795	1.1694
	(0.0536)	(0.2109)	(0.3336)	(0.1938)	(0.0619)
Urban	1.0327	0.5920	1.3294	0.0757	1.1554
	(0.0538)	(0.2487)	(0.2440)	(0.1596)	(0.0419)

Note: The sample standard deviations are in parentheses.

The price distortions due to the unsecured loans and the redeposit of loanable funds are measured as the ratios of shadow prices to the observed prices,

$$\frac{P_K^*}{P_K} = P_K^{\delta_{21} Z_U + \delta_{22} Z_R} \equiv X_K$$

$$\frac{P_L^*}{P_L} = P_L^{\delta_{31} Z_U + \delta_{32} Z_R} \equiv X_L$$

Table 14.3 also presents the price distortions. An efficient allocation of an input relative to loanable funds has the ratio of shadow price to observed price (relative to the price of loanable funds) equal to unity. For the sample as a whole, the shadow price of capital (relative to the price of loanable funds) is on average only 56.70 percent (X_K = 0.5670) of the observed price, while the shadow price of labor (relative to the price of loanable funds) is 38.12 percent (X_L = 1.3812) higher than the observed price. These deviations indicate a sever overutilization of capital, $X_K < 1$, and underutilization of labor, $X_L > 1$, relative to the utilization of loanable funds. Small and rural FCUs experience greater severity (measured as the deviation of X_K and X_L from unity) in overutilization of capital and in underutilization of labor. In fact the decomposition of the distortion indices in logarithmic terms,

$$\ln X_K = (\delta_{21} Z_U) \ln P_K + (\delta_{22} Z_R) \ln P_K$$

$$\ln X_L = (\delta_{31} Z_U) \ln P_L + (\delta_{32} Z_R) \ln P_L$$

shows that the overutilization of capital and the underutilization of labor are mainly due to the redeposit of loanable funds (Z_R) at the three agricultural banks. Evaluated at the sample means, the decomposition shows that the ratio $(\delta_{32} Z_R) \ln P_L / \ln X_L = 0.7785$. Over 77 percent of the underutilization in labor inputs is due to excessive redeposit of loanable funds. The ratio $(\delta_{22} Z_R) \ln P_K / \ln X_K = 1.0327 > 1$ since the ratio due to Z_U is negative, $(\delta_{21} Z_U) \ln P_K / \ln X_K = -0.0327$. This implies that the overutilization of capital is entirely due to the redeposit. Since the redeposit is a risk-free disposition of loanable funds, an inefficient FCU manager is more likely to opt for redeposit than to engage in a labor-intensive pre-loan credit screening and post-loan monitoring. This evidence suggests an agency problem in FCUs, which are a mutual form organization. An inefficient management is more inclined to make capital improvements in offices rather than make human capital improvements in loan officers.[6]

The overall cost of allocative distortion due to unsecured loans and the redeposit of loanable funds can be estimated from the comparison of the cost of the conditional input demands with and without the distortions. The conditional input demand functions can be derived by applying Shephard Lemma. In the absence of loan quality distortion, ($Q_C^* = Q_C$), the conditional demand functions for capital and labor are, respectively,

$$K(Q_F, Q_C, P_K^*, P_L^*) = \frac{C^*}{P_K^*}(\beta_1 + \beta_{11} \ln P_K^* + \beta_{12} \ln P_L^* + \gamma_{11} \ln Q_F + \gamma_{21} \ln Q_C)$$

$$L(Q_F, Q_C, P_K^*, P_L^*) = \frac{C^*}{P_L^*}(\beta_2 + \beta_{12} \ln P_K^* + \beta_{22} \ln P_L^* + \gamma_{12} \ln Q_F + \gamma_{22} \ln Q_C)$$

The cost of allocative distortion is then estimated as the ratio, denoted as *AD*,

$$AD = \frac{P_K[K(Q_F,Q_C,P_K^*,P_L^*)-K(Q_F,Q_C,P_K,P_L)]+P_L[L(Q_F,Q_C,P_K^*,P_L^*)-L(Q_F,Q_C,P_K,P_L)]}{P_K K(Q_F,Q_C,P_K,P_L)+P_L L(Q_F,Q_C,P_K,P_L)}$$

As shown in Table 14.3, the cost of allocative distortion is 7.75 percent for the sample as a whole, while the small and rural FCUs have higher distortion factors than do their large and urban counterparts. The loan quality, unsecured loans and redeposit of loanable funds all contribute to the output- and input-specific distortions on the shadow cost function of FCUs. Other neutral inefficiency may not be identified and accounted for, but nevertheless is still cost augmenting. The sample mean of the neutral cost inefficiency $E(U|\varepsilon)$ is about 16.20 percent over the frontier cost. The small and rural FCUs are about 2 percent more inefficient than the large and urban FCUs.[7] These results are not surprising because the small and rural FCUs are typically poorly staffed and trained, and because the management and operations are prone to political influence within its own FA organization.

As indicated in Table 14.4, there are increasing returns to scale in the sample and across the asset size. The estimates, SCALE, are all significantly greater than one. The estimates of the economies of scope is significantly greater than zero with an asymptotic t-value of 5.5755 (= $0.0591/0.2521/\sqrt{n}$). However, the decomposition of the within-sample SCOPE measure by the asset size reveals evidence of economies of scope at large FCUs and not small FCUs. Out of 142 measures, there are 130 of them, or 91.55 percent, with positive SCOPE in the largest 25 percent of FCUs, while there are 33, or 23.4 percent, with positive SCOPE in the lowest quarter. This implies there is little cost savings for small FCUs to engage in both farm and nonfarm loans within a credit union.

These findings, however, do not necessary translate into a policy recommendation of mergers and acquisitions among FCUs without a fundamental reorganization of the Farmers' Associations. A successful merger in improving cost performance rely on two preconditions: a high degree of local market overlapping between merging FCUs, and a more cost efficient acquiring FCU than the FCU being acquired (Berger and Humphrey, 1997). Neither of these preconditions are evident under the current FCUs' cooperative structure. Under the current FA cooperative charter and arrangement, FCUs' services are confined to their own members and townships. Intertownship banking activity by FCUs and investments other than loans are prohibited. Local market overlapping occurs, not among township FCUs, but between the FCUs and the local

Table 14.4 Economies of scale and scope

Asset Size	1st Quartile	2nd Quartile	3rd Quartile	4th Quartile	All FCUs
SCALE	1.6725	1.6400	1.6364	1.5794	1.6330
	(0.1546)	(0.1901)	(0.1925)	(0.1471)	(0.1748)
SCOPE	−0.1394	0.0022	0.1034	0.2666	0.0591
	(0.1620)	(0.1931)	(0.1858)	(0.2653)	(0.2521)
Percentage of	108/141	75/142	35/141	12/142	230/566
SCOPE < 0	76.60%	52.82%	24.82%	8.45%	40.64%
Percentage of	33/141	67/142	106/141	130/142	336/566
SCOPE > 0	23.40%	47.18%	75.18%	91.55%	59.36%

Note: The sample standard deviations are in parentheses.

commercial banks and financial institutions. Furthermore, an FCU is an integrated unit within a township Farmers' Association which provides, besides farm credit, marketing, farm extension and other social services to its members within the township. Any merger or acquisition of FCUs necessarily involves a consolidation of township FAs. The merger between a small rural and well-run FA, and a large urban FA may prove to be neither economically efficient nor politically viable. The policy issues regarding the FCUs in Taiwan are not if the merger shall take place, but whether Farmers' Associations shall be in the business of banking and credit services. To improve cost efficiency in banking service to farmers, there must be a separation of FCUs from FAs to allow FCUs to compete with other financial institutions in the market place.

4 CONCLUSIONS

The farmers' credit unions have played a vital role in the agricultural development in providing farm credit and banking service in Taiwan for the last three decades. The FCUs, followed by the poster saving banks, are the most popular financial institutions in rural townships. In the name of providing adequate and low-cost credit for farmers and for agricultural development, the FCUs in the past have enjoyed certain special legislation and regulation from the government to ensure their monopolistic status over financial services in rural areas. Although a great deal of effort has been made by the government to improve the operating efficiency of FCUs, the dominant position of FCUs has continuously been challenged and eroded recently due to deregulation and liberalization of the banking industry. Since the removal of interest rate control, and the liberalization of market entry, FCUs have to compete with other financial institutions for deposits and loans beyond the township farmers. Given that a primary goal of deregulation and liberalization is to improve the efficiency of the financial sector, the role and future of FCUs reserve a critical reevaluation.

This chapter uses the concept of a stochastic shadow cost frontier to investigate the cost efficiency, and the magnitudes of economies of scale and scope, among FCUs. The shadow cost frontier incorporates a measure for the quality of FCU loans to form a quality-adjusted shadow output and the factors that distort input allocation to form shadow prices in cost minimization. Empirical evidence based on a two-year panel of 283 FCUs has shown that there exists a great deal of output cost inefficiency due to quality of loans measured in the defaults/arrears rate, and the allocative distortions due to the unsecured loans and redeposit rate. Due to the large defaults/arrears rate, large FCUs are slightly less output cost efficient than the small FCUs. On average, FCUs tends to overutilize capital inputs and underutilize labor inputs, relative to the loanable funds input. The evidence suggests an agency problem in FCUs. Small and rural FCUs experience greater severity in the allocative distortion than large and urban FCUs. While all FCUs enjoy increasing returns to scale, there is evidence of economies of scope only for large FCUs. Although the stated objective of FCUs as rural financial institutions is to provide low-cost agricultural credit and banking service to their member farmers, in reality the business activities of FCUs are no different from those of regular commercial banks. Being geographically confined to within a township, FCUs are generally much smaller than commercial banks in assets, total deposits and loans, they appear to face constraint on benefitting from scale and scope economies. The evaluation of the future role of the farmers' credit unions as a banking institution in rural Taiwan must include an assessment of the effects on their cost structure of economies of scale and scope and of various types of cost inefficiency.

NOTES

1. See a study by Chang (1997) on the risk-adjusted production efficiency comparison of the FCUs.
2. The cost shares and the economies of scale measures are with respect to shadow prices P^* and shadow outputs Q^*. Both measures can be decomposed in terms of actual prices P and outputs Q as follow,

$$S_j = \frac{\partial \ln C^*}{\partial \ln P_j}(1+\frac{\partial \ln \theta_j}{\partial \ln P_j})^{-1} \text{ and SCALE } = (\sum_j \frac{\partial \ln C^*}{\partial \ln Q_j}\frac{\partial \ln Q_j}{\partial \ln Q_j^*})^{-1}$$

The decomposition thus permits the separate identification and estimation of the direction of the allocative distortion $1+(\partial \ln \theta_j)/(\partial \ln P_j)$, and the output-quality effect, $\partial \ln Q_j^* / \partial \ln Q_j$.

3. Since the shadow cost C^* and shadow prices P^* are not observed, the relation between C^* and the observed cost C technically is not additive. Kumbhakar (1996) observes that, $\ln C = \ln C_I^* + \ln(\Sigma_j S_j \theta_j^{-1})$, thus the neutral cost augmenting inefficiency U may contain an element of misspecification.
4. The lower quality loans may imply a short-run cost savings for the FCUs and hence δ_{11} is negative. However, as argued in Hughes and Mester (1993), the lower quality loans will at some point in time entail extra cost in order to resolve the bad loans. Furthermore, lower quality of loans are likely to incur a risk premium paid for the uninsured deposits.
5. Since the translog cost function is multiplicative in Q_F and Q_C, the predicted total costs are zero for the specialized FCUs engaged entirely on farm loans or on nonfarm loans. We therefore assume a one-NT dollar for those zero loans in the specialized FCUs.
6. Mester (1993) also found evidence of an agency problem at the mutual savings and loans industry in the USA.
7. Using a linear programming approach, Chang (1997) estimates the overall production efficiency for the FCUs to be 77.20 percent, or 22.80 percent inefficient. Jang *et al.* (1997) give an estimate of cost efficiency for the Taiwan small to medium-size banks to be 76.67 percent, or 23.33 percent inefficient. Neither studies take into consideration output quality and input allocative distortion factors.

REFERENCES

Atkinson, S.E. and R. Halvorsen (1986), 'The relative efficiency of public and private firms in a regulated environment: The case of U.S. electric utilities', *Journal of Public Economics*, **25**, 281-94.

Bauer, P.W., A.N. Berger and D.B. Humphrey (1993), 'Efficiency and productivity growth in U.S. banking', in H.O. Fried, C.A.K. Lovell and S.S. Schmidt (eds), *The Measurement of Productive Efficiency: Techniques and Applications*, Oxford University Press, 386-413.

Berger, A.N., and D.B. Humphrey (1997), 'Efficiency of financial institutions: international survey and directions for future research', *European Journal of Operational Research*, **98**, 175-212.

Berger, A.N., W.C. Hunter and S.G. Timme (1993), 'The efficiency of financial institutions: a review and preview of research past, present, and future', *Journal of Banking and Finance*, **17**, 221-49.

Bhattacharyya, A., A. Bhattacharyya and S.C. Kumbhakar (1996), 'Government interventions, market imperfections, and technical inefficiency in a mixed economy: a case study of Indian agriculture', *Journal of Comparative Economics*, **22**, 219-41.

Chang, C.-C. (1997), 'The nonparametric risk-adjusted efficiency measurement: an application to Taiwan major rural financial intermediaries', working paper, Institute of Economics, Academia Sinica.

Chang, C.-C. and T.-C. Hsieh (1997), 'The economic efficiency of the credit department of farmers' associations in Taiwan', *Applied Financial Economics*, forthcoming.

Hughes, J.P. and L.J. Mester (1993), 'A quality and risk-ajusted cost function for banks: evidence on the 'too-big-to-fail' doctrine', *The Journal of Productivity Analysis*, **4**, 293-315.

Jondrow, J., C.A.K. Lovell, I.S. Materov and P. Schmidt (1982), 'On the estimation of technical inefficiency in the stochastic frontier production function model', *Journal of Econometrics*, **19**, 233-38.

Kumbhakar, S.C. (1996), 'Efficiency measurement with multiple output and multiple inputs', *The Journal of Productivity Analysis*, **7**, 225-55.

Jang, S.-L., J.-T. Liu and C.-C. Chen (1997), 'Efficiency in the Taiwan SME banks: 1986-1994', *Academia Economic Papers*, **25**, 69-95.

Mester, L. (1993), 'Efficiency in the savings and loan industry', *Journal of Banking and Finance*, **17**, 267-86.

Olson, J.A., P. Schmidt and D.M. Waldman (1980), 'A Monte Carlo study of estimators of stochastic frontier production funcions', *Journal of Econometrics*, **13**, 67-82.

15. The Social Productivity of China's Town and Village Enterprises*

Clifford D. Clark and Jung-Chao Liu

1 INTRODUCTION

The township and village enterprises of China immediately interested western observers when they emerged two decades ago, and because of their performance, they remain a source of fascination today. In this chapter, we argue that these rural industries not only contribute to national output but also moderate the rate of urban growth, encourage entrepreneurship both in community government and industry, provide employment opportunities, demonstrate the effectiveness of incentives and help the country discover its comparative advantages. The town and village enterprises operate, often quite effectively, under rather confusing conditions. They utilize and derive incentives from market forces but they include representatives of local government in all major decisions. They negotiate through the ambiguities of controlling community assets and resources particular to each enterprise.

Whether they will continue to lead national economic development over the long term depends on their ability to become more mobile, to retain their entrepreneurship and to affiliate with other economic organizations. We acknowledge that the institutions may distort public priorities, particularly at the lowest levels of government, contribute to environmental deterioration and slow the forces of internal economic integration by limiting the area of primary influence to their original communities.

We believe on balance that the sum of their contributions is greater than the direct increment they make to national output. We refer to this extra contribution, which defies exact measurement, as social productivity.

*Thanks are due D. Gale Johnson, Eliakim Hasting Moore Distinguished Service Professor of Economics Emeritus, University of Chicago, for stimulating interest in China's rural industries and Dr. Linda Beale, Cleary, Gottlieb, Steen and Hamilton, New York, for manuscript suggestions.

With one possible exception, elements of the story told here about the town and village enterprises are familiar. We believe, however, that our interpretation of the context in which these elements operate and the relation of these enterprises to long-term development provides an important and new perspective on economic development in China.

2 BACKGROUND OF ENTERPRISES AND LOCAL GOVERNMENTS

China's business organizations may be classified into four categories. First are the state-owned enterprises, which are closely identified with the social values of the People's Republic and occupy favored positions in the hierarchy of industries. The large state enterprises produced about the same proportion of total industrial output throughout the past decade and a half. The medium- and small- state enterprises, however, have lost output share during the same period.

Second are the urban collectives, many of which were once worker-owned cooperative enterprises. Now, most are subordinate to other enterprises or to local governments. They also have lost output share in recent years.

Third are the town and village enterprises, also classified as rural collectives, which are under local government supervision and operated by managers from the community or region. The town and village enterprises were established during the commune movement of 1958 as commune and brigade enterprises, which took over the resources of handicraft operations and other sideline activities of farmers. In March 1984, a circular of the Central Committee and the State Council gave the enterprises the current designation. Acting together, the local officials and the managers serve as the planners and strategists, that is, the entrepreneurs of the town and village enterprises. The town and village enterprises have grown rapidly since the early 1980s and have gained in share of output, replacing in part the losses of the small- and medium-state enterprises.

Fourth are the private and other firms, including domestic joint ventures and foreign-invested firms. The foreign investment comes through foreign joint ventures or subsidiaries of foreign companies and companies registered in Hong Kong and Taiwan. During the early 1980s, private firms were limited in size, being allowed only five or seven employees, but in 1988 they were permitted to expand to more than eight employees. Nevertheless, private firms have remained small in size and continue to account for a small proportion of total industrial output. They have grown, however, relative to the small and medium state enterprises and have partially replaced them in share of total industrial output. In fact, the most rapid growth of any category in recent years has been registered by the foreign-invested private firms.

Since the late 1950s, the rural economy has been tied to the higher levels of government through the Communist Party but this has changed considerably with the economic reforms begun in 1978. The reforms established the production responsibility system in agriculture, which gave households partial rights to land and changed the distribution of income from determination by the collectives to direct earnings of households. The reforms also altered local governance, replacing communes with the new townships. The townships became a separate level of administration and public finance between 1984 and 1986. The villages, although not part of the official government hierarchy, are directly involved with the village enterprises and operate under authority delegated by the township governments. The village enterprises are similar to the town enterprises in most respects, although they are often smaller in size and have different product mixes.

The town and village enterprises are under the formal control of the township governments. The townships and villages have direct interests in the return to investment in the enterprises since profits and fees are important sources of revenue. In a sense, the arrangements between the governmental units and the enterprises are similar to that between a holding company and its operating units. The township governments establish the hiring systems for selecting managers, and they participate in planning new locations or new products, in obtaining financing and in acquiring materials used in production. The management team organizes production and often acts entrepreneurially to extend operations and to take advantage of changes in external circumstances (Byrd and Qinsong, 1990; IMF, 1996; Naughton, 1996a; Xiou Zhou, 1996).[1]

We focus our attention on the town and village enterprises because of their large contribution to national output and employment and because of their tentative acceptance by governing authorities all the way up the hierarchy. That support, however, on many occasions seems uncertain (Naughton, 1996a).[2] We are primarily interested in the enterprises because they give to those involved a degree of control over the circumstances of their personal lives that would not otherwise be available. We believe that, despite their unusual character as public and private entities, the town and village firms should continue to be an important part of China's economic landscape until more permanent forms of organizations emerge, whether they be private or some new and clearly defined form of productive institution. We will sometimes use 'rural industries' to refer to the town and village enterprises when such a label does not mislead, even though rural industries is a more inclusive term as noted above.

3 HISTORICAL DEVELOPMENT OF THE TOWN AND VILLAGE ENTERPRISE

In 1994, the town and village enterprises employed about 120 million people (about one fifth of China's labor force) and produced 30 percent of Chinese industry's gross output value (IMF, 1996: 11, 13; World Bank, 1966: 97). Employment increased more than tenfold from the beginning of reforms in 1978, when about 17 million persons worked in the commune and brigade enterprises, the forerunners of the town and village firms. (Ho, 1994: 19)

This rapid growth is generally attributed to national policies intended to balance agricultural expansion with development of rural industries. Whether these policies were in fact initiated by central authorities or simply the central government's acknowledgment that farmers had already found ways to establish nonagricultural industries (Xiao Zhou, 1996),[3] the stated purposes were to produce goods needed in agriculture and to permit production for nonagricultural uses in order to create new employment opportunities. This was seen 'as the only way rural China could absorb the huge number of surplus labor being released from collective agriculture by the widespread implementation of the household responsibility system' (Ho, 1994: 24).[4]

The town and village firms responded quickly to the new opportunities and to the incentives provided, as the production and employment figures show. Greater autonomy for the managers and new incentives associated with retention of earnings combined to create new directions and entrepreneurial energies. These unique organizations, owned by the villagers but controlled by the managers and local governmental officials (Chang and Wang, 1994), delegate authority in much the same way as the family responsibility system in agriculture. Performance contracts are drawn up between the town or village governments and the managers who are selected to achieve specific results (Chen, 1995: 57).[5] In effect, the local governmental personnel and the managers serve jointly as entrepreneurs. Despite ambiguities of ownership the organizational framework has provided powerful incentives and flexibility for the rapid expansion of the town and village enterprises.

Though the town and village enterprises are significant sources of employment they cannot accommodate more than a small share of those in search of full-time jobs. The number of people who have remained unemployed or less than fully employed in the countryside is still very large. Nearly a third of the 450 million people in the rural labor force are either underemployed or looking for jobs as part of the group of would-be migrants from country to city, or the 'floating population'. Although job creation was one of the reasons for their existence, the rural industries cannot be expected to create jobs singlehandedly, without the participation of other sectors of the economy (Perkins, 1996: 28). Either other employment opportunities must be created in rural areas or the cities must accept more migrants from the countryside than present policies permit. Perkins estimates that a national growth rate of 8-9 percent for the next 20 years will be required to absorb the unemployed and all new entrants into the labor force. He does not, of course, predict that such rates will continue (Perkins, 1996: 28). Given the age distribution of China's populations, the continuing prospects, and need, for job creation are high. It is likely that rates of growth in jobs will be considerably less than 8 or 9 percent and that high employment will not be obtained until growth of the labor force slows sometime well into the next century (Naughton, 1996b). How much the rural enterprises can contribute to the expansion of employment opportunities will depend on their ability to take on new organizational forms and expand into new locations.

Like other businesses, the town and village enterprises are attracted to those areas of economic concentrations on the periphery of relatively high-income cities. Only infrequently do they form in geographically remote regions of the country. The result is agglomeration of enterprises in urban areas. According to Ilo (1994: 292),

> The rural regions with the brightest prospects for rural non-agricultural development are those near urban industrial areas, where urban-rural linkages are strongest and where footloose industries producing standardized products are more likely to develop because such locations offer them the advantages of cheap land and labour and closeness to major markets and sources of technology.

Agglomeration is both advantageous and disadvantageous. On the one hand, the rural enterprises contribute to overall efficiency by participating in the concentrations of growth-enabling activities. On the other hand, they cannot help to bring vitality to inland areas unless they are better represented there.

4 THE TOWN AND VILLAGE ENTERPRISES, ENTREPRENEURSHIP AND ECONOMIC DEVELOPMENT

The town and village enterprises may be viewed in two ways. They may be seen as experimental institutions designed by government to test and to develop new production methods or they may be seen as economic organizations which emerged when entrepreneurs perceived that centrally administered controls had weakened. We subscribe to the latter view, much as argued by Xiao Zhou (1996) cited above, that the town and village enterprises were formed by the combined energies of public and private entrepreneurs from the bottom up and accepted later by central authorities who appreciated the resulting increases in productivity.

The initiative taken by the enterprises gave China assurances of its sources of trade advantage, led to rather impressive productivity gains within the enterprises, and contributed to economic growth in the metropolitan areas. As reviewed in two sections below, enterprises in Nantong City, in the northeast province of Jiangsu, provide insights into the linkages among entrepreneurship, management contracts, hiring processes and productivity advances.

4.1 Labor Intensive Products

China's manufacturing exports expanded by 19 percent per year from 1981 to 1994 as measured in constant valued dollars. As a share of national income, exports increased from about 6 percent in 1978 to over 30 percent in 1994 (Hu and Khan, 1996). Goods produced by labor-intensive methods, made to a large extent in the town and village enterprises, accounted for about 31 percent of total exports in 1978 and almost 57 percent in 1990. Although the exports of foreign-invested firms grew even more rapidly after 1985, they remained a relatively small proportion of total exports (Naughton, 1996b).[6] Regardless of relative rates of recent growth, the town and village enterprises became important exporters early in the post-reform era and established the country's comparative advantages in labor-intensive products in the international marketplace.

As a consequence, the rural enterprises may have protected the country from engaging in costly experiments with untested products in international competition. The composition of China's exports have developed in accord with comparative advantages which, despite slight increases in capital-intensive goods since 1990, continue to favor labor-intensive products (Yoshitomi, 1996).

4.2 Scholarly Appraisal of Productivity Advances

As labor-intensive goods encounter greater competition and as new products are demanded in the future, the town and village enterprises will need solid productivity improvements in comparison with potential competitors, including the state-owned enterprises, to remain viable. In comparison with the state firms, the town and village firms have shown favorable rates of advance in recent years. Whether they have reached comparable absolute levels of productivity remains in question. There is evidence, however, that they have surpassed the productivity levels of the state firms.

The rates of total factor productivity increase in the two sectors may have converged for a time during the 1980s, but by the early 1990s the town and village firms outpaced the state enterprises by a factor of two or more, according to Jefferson and Rawski (1994: table 4). Yanrui Wu agrees that the rates diverged from the mid-1980s to the early 1990s. In addition Wu notes that, while annual average increases in total factor productivity in the state-owned enterprises dropped from 4.9 percent to 1.8 percent from 1985 to 1991, productivity improvements in the town and village enterprises jumped from 3.6 percent to 5.2 percent during that same period (Wu, 1995: tables B1 and B2).

In 1989, a time of recession, critics and supporters of the town and village enterprises accepted the view that productivity in the town and village enterprises was relatively low. The critics cited the inferior level of productivity in their attack on the rural industries, while the supporters argued that the town and village enterprises' gap in productivity resulted from lack of easy access to raw materials, few of the subsidies accorded the state enterprises and limited amounts of fixed capital.

> [The supporters] were also quick to point out that while the state sector used five times more fixed capital per worker in 1987-1988 than did the TVE [town and village enterprises] sector, its labour productivity was only 1.7 times greater. Furthermore, in the 1980s labour productivity rose more than three times faster in the TVE sector than in the state sector. (Ho, 1994: 278)

Masaru Yoshitomi has reviewed work on the machine tool industry and considered findings on the differences in levels of labor productivity and in the ratios of capital to labor. He reports that the state-owned producers of machine tools in 1991 used over twice as much fixed capital per worker as the town and village enterprises. Yet the state-owned firms produced only about 10 percent more value added per worker. One of the reasons given by Yoshitomi for the difference is that the state-owned enterprises were more self-sufficient than the rural firms because state firms did not contract out as many activities as the rural enterprises. The ratios of outsourced components to intermediate imports were 11 percent and 22 percent, respectively, for large and medium scale state firms compared to 39 percent for the town and village enterprises (Yoshitomi, 1996: 59-60).

In short, a decade ago the general view was that labor productivity in the state enterprises exceeded labor productivity in the town and village units but that the degree of superiority was diminishing. According to a report of the World Bank, however, the performance of the state-owned enterprises has now fallen behind that of the nonstate sector. Value added per worker in the nonstate sector, which is greatly influenced by the town and village enterprises, is about twice the value added per worker in the state sector (World Bank, 1996: 15).

Our comparison between the labor productivity of the town enterprises (not including the village firms for which data are unavailable) with the state firms in Nantong City in Jiangsu Province substantiates that a cross-over in favor of the rural enterprises in that area occurred in 1994.

Comparisons of value added per employee in Nantong city show that the state enterprises had higher levels of productivity in 1993 than the town-run enterprises - 13 478 yuan per employee compared to 10 084 yuan. In 1994, value added per employee in the state enterprises, at 15 548 yuan per employee, fell slightly below the 15 878 yuan of the town enterprises. Although both figures decreased in 1995, the discrepancy grew. In that year, productivity in the state enterprises was 14 865 yuan compared to 15 547 yuan in the town enterprises. Fixed capital per employee, measured by the value of fixed assets transferred to net worth at the end of the year, was at least twice as great in the state enterprises as in the town enterprises in each of the three years Social and Economic Year of Nantong (1990, 1993, 1994, 1995). These data suggest that, despite more capital per worker in the state enterprises, productivity is greater at least in Nantong city in Jiangsu Province and, perhaps, generally in many of the town enterprises.

In addition to the differences between state and rural enterprises, some interesting contrasts exist between township enterprises and those run by the villages in Nantong city. Unlike the town enterprises the village enterprises are not reported in published governmental documents. Some comparisons can be made, however, from data gathered from both types of enterprises for tax purposes. The information used here was made available during a number of interviews with an economic development specialist from Nantong city. The data from submissions of all enterprises in Nantong show that the average value added per employee in the town enterprises for 1994 and 1995 was 16 500 yuan compared to 17 700 yuan in the village enterprises. But this average figure hides another difference. The town enterprises show larger amounts for value added per person in construction materials than village enterprises. The town construction materials firms were also larger than the village firms. The village enterprises, however, were more efficient than the town enterprises in those activities that are closely related to agriculture, such as aqua-culture and fisheries. The town enterprises seem to have scale advantages in producing construction materials while the village enterprises have location advantages in processing agricultural products.

4.3 Early Entrepreneurship in China

Economic historians report that entrepreneurs in China had created organizations to produce iron agricultural implements, established networks of communications among cities and developed private banking systems as early as the Ch'in era in 126 to 207 BC. Much later, during the Sung dynasty from the tenth to the thirteenth centuries, the iron and textile industries were productive and water-powered spinning machines were widely used. On the farms, 'many peasants worked full-time making paper, iron implements, and various other commodities. Others withdrew only part of their labour-time from food production, or only some members of a family withdrew' (Jones, 1993: 80). Thus, citizens of the Sung era would not be unduly surprised by today's rural industries and their entrepreneurial organizers.[7]

During the first half of this century, many of the larger and more profitable enterprises operated under foreign management. Firms owned by Chinese proprietors, although generally quite small, were nevertheless active. The firms milled flour and produced handicrafts and consumer goods such as cotton textiles, cigarettes and pressed oil. To get access to specialized components, they often formed linkages with, or subcontracted work to, other producing units (Riskin, 1995: 20-21). By the early 1930s, these types of nonagricultural entrepreneurial activities involved at least a fifth of the rural working population.

> A survey of 38,256 rural families in 101 representative localities selected from twenty-two provinces in China between 1929 and 1933 indicated that of the male population 7 years of age or older in the sample, 45 per cent worked only in agriculture, 27 per cent worked part-time in agriculture and part-time in other industries, and 20 per cent were engaged in non-agricultural pursuits only. (Ho, 1994: 13)

Today's town and village enterprises, following such precedents of at least a half century ago, have also developed linkages with other economic units, particularly in the coastal areas. Many of the rural firms accept orders from foreign trading companies and produce for a fee (Naughton, 1996b: 300). According to Masuri Yoshitomi, 'foreign companies have often entered Shenzhen through subcontracting the processing of products to local enterprises. An astonishing number of rural township and village enterprises have engaged in subcontracting manufacturing' (Yoshitomi: 1996: 60).

4.4 Concentration in the Suburbs

The concentration of economic activity in the urban areas near cities that is typical of China's town and village enterprises is common in other economic development. Among the advantages of such locations are access to markets for products, greater choice among suppliers, better chances to obtain specialized machinery (including used equipment), more sources of financing assistance, opportunities to learn from others in the same industry, access to pools of skilled employees and better technology. For example, in Jiangsu province the town and village enterprises have been assisted by utilizing engineers working on approved leave from state-operated firms, employing retirees from urban areas, developing cooperative institutions for research and vocational colleges, and joining in joint ventures. Similar linkages have been reported in other provinces. Yanrui Wu, for example, found positive effects of such externalities in the textile industry (Wu, 1996: 105, 106, 141; Ho, 1994: 129-131; Naughton, 1996a).

Advantages from locating near cities, as judged by the entrepreneurs, exceed the high costs of land and housing and the impact of congestion and crowding. Further, many linkages between China's rural enterprises and urban collectives, state enterprises or educational institutions, culminate in joint ventures and strengthen the participating units (Ho, 1994: 121-2). This concentration of the town and village enterprises near the cities does not imply that the enterprises pick up and move to such areas. Rather, their charter means that they have been established there. They may, of course, participate in jointly owned companies in the area even though their home base is somewhat distant.

4.5 Supply of Entrepreneurs

In economic literature the entrepreneur, among other things, is an organizer of productive work for economic return. Theorists inform us that entrepreneurial talents are widely distributed, are activated by opportunities and are strengthened by experience, education and health care. Joseph Schumpeter, Frank Knight, William Baumol, Theodore Schultz and others emphasize certain characteristics but draw up similar lists. The entrepreneur is viewed variously as owner, the primary decision maker, the one who puts new ideas into effect, the one who bears the risk and accepts the uncertainties, the innovator (of products, markets or organizational forms), the one who trades off assurances to others for rewards or the one who restores equilibrium following a change in his domain. Although they may differ in their points of emphasis, the theorists agree on the significance of entrepreneurship to developing and dynamic economies. Theodore Schultz (1990: 37) puts it this way:

> In thinking about what entrepreneurs do, it is imperative to hold fast to the basic reality that disequilibria are inevitable in a modern, ever changing economy. Such an economy is decidedly dependent on entrepreneurs who reallocate their resources.

Schultz gives attention, more than the others, to the supply of entrepreneurs and particularly to factors that enhance entrepreneurial abilities. His empirical studies lead him to the conclusion that:

> The supply is large in terms of numbers and the supply is widely distributed throughout the adult population at any given date. The quality of the supply is enhanced over time by investments in various forms of human capital. (Schultz, 1990: 91)

The emphasis given by Schultz to the entrepreneur as restorer of equilibrium includes all who want stable growth and development in their domains whether they are in government, members of a family or participants in business, farming or enterprise. In this enlarged way the concept is particularly applicable to the rural industries because they require the cooperative and joint efforts of government and market oriented individuals.

Entrepreneurs are activated by opportunity to gain monetary rewards or to improve their economic circumstances and status. The employment record of immigrants to the USA is instructive. Government reports on immigration show that immigrants are more likely to be self-employed than their native counterparts (US Government Printing Office, 1989: 24). The reason is that efforts to develop self-employment opportunities must be weighed against meeting the requirement of credentialing or customary practices of alternative employments. For immigrants, the balance frequently tips to self-employment. Similar choices may take place in the Chinese countryside but there self-employment is weighed against few alternatives. Agricultural employment has dropped and barriers to long-term employment in the cities have remained. Another consideration is that persons from outside may have limited leadership opportunities in family-controlled businesses. This characteristic of Chinese business is stressed by Fukuyama (1995: 75), who believes that many potential entrepreneurs would rather start their own businesses than join existing units. Whatever the supply of entrepreneurs in the past, indications today do not suggest shortages at least for the country as a whole. Young people of China appear to view business ownership more favorably. In a recent marketing survey of people aged 18 to 34 years 31 per cent agreed that owning a business signals personal success. This compares to 21 per cent for the older generation (*Asian Wall Street Journal*, 1997).

Reform and the prospects of establishing a risky business may have been attractive to rural dwellers in the late 1970s because they did not have the security or the same benefits that the urban residents had obtained. In this vein, Naughton (1996a: 38) has speculated that entrepreneurs were more readily available in the country at the time of reform than in the cities. He says:

> As a result of their somewhat more precarious economic position under the old system, Chinese rural dwellers may be less averse to the economic uncertainties implied by economic reform. In any case, the rural population came to be a more fertile soil for entrepreneurship and economic innovation than did the urban population.

The processes used by the town and village enterprises to select new managers also may contribute to the supply of entrepreneurial talent. Although the survey noted above suggests that there are many aspirants to entrepreneurship, it would help to know whether the processes for selecting enterprise leaders are weighted in favor of imaginative risk takers or tradition-bound administrators. A look at the criteria and processes suggest that the processes are balanced somewhat in favor of entrepreneurial talent In addition to these entrepreneurial characteristics frequently recounted, however, community involvement is an important aspect in China's town and village firms. Byrd (1990) in his case studies of entrepreneurs in rural industries, finds that commitment to the community is an important aspect of successful leadership.

4.6 Selection of New Managers or Directors

The manager selection processes and incentives contracts of the town and village enterprises in Jiangsu Province and Nantong City developed at the same time in the post-reform environment. In the early 1980s, Jiangsu began to experiment with a contract responsibility system similar to the household responsibility system in agriculture. By the end of 1983, most of the town and village enterprises in Nantong had adopted some form of a contract system which permitted managers to make decisions required by their obligations to accept risks and to receive residual income. Contracts assigned responsibilities and gave special attention to retaining workers, to wage reserves, and to the distribution of earnings or losses. The contracts between the local government and managers were usually for three years. Small firms with ten or fewer employees usually selected an individual who agreed to pay a fee for the chance to take over the firm. For larger enterprises, the contract was usually held by a management team drawn from aspiring executives in the area. The criteria used by the local government selection committees for choosing new managers emphasized experience, knowledge of the industry and commitment to the community. Education did not seem to be considered as a separate matter but only in connection with the development of proposed plans, including profits and costs targets. By the late 1980s nearly all the medium and large town and village enterprises in Nantong had adopted some form of the manager responsibility system (Yuanren, 1987: 182-3). [8]

In contrast, the manager responsibility system for the state-owned enterprises did not get underway in Nantong until 1984. That system was more complex, particularly in the processes for the selection of new managers. For example, promising managers gained positions through a competitive bidding or auction arrangement. The process was designed to stimulate managers to take advantage of new authority to improve performance and profitability of state firms. By the end of the decade, the auction system accounted for about one in seven appointments. Yet most managers continued to be appointed through bureaucratic channels in the usual way (Groves *et al.*, 1995). The town and village firms thus moved earlier and far more effectively than the state-owned companies to increase the influence of entrepreneurs in setting enterprise agendas. It is our view that the dissimilar productivity performances of the two sectors directly reflect these differences in entrepreneurship.

5 PROBLEMS OF THE TOWN AND VILLAGE ENTERPRISES

There are problems as well as gains associated with the town and village enterprises. In this section we give attention to two prominent issues: the biases that the enterprises introduce into local government public finance and the low rates of investment in interior regions of China.

5.1 The Bias in Public Expenditures

A potential drawback of the town and village enterprises is their impact on government expenditures, in particular, the effect of decentralization on sources of revenue for local governments. Local subprovincial governments now obtain much of their revenue from local businesses. Decentralization of public finances has redistributed both expenditure decisions and revenue authority from the center to lower levels of government (Blecher and Shue, 1996: 71-5; Park *et al.*, 1996). A report of the World Bank (1996: 39) describes the impact this way:

> The decline in government revenues and the desire to keep the budget deficit in check have led to a steady reduction in budgetary expenditures from 33.8 percent of GDP in 1978 to 14.1 percent in 1994. Extra budgetary government expenditures are estimated to be an additional 3.8 percent.

According to the report, expenditures have decreased in the aggregate and have been redistributed downward among levels of government. In 1994, central government expenditures amounted to only 40.2 percent of total government expenditures. This compares to two-thirds to three-quarters of total government expenditures in many industrial and developing countries. Park *et al.* (1996) argue that these changes have instilled new discipline in fiscal affairs at the local governmental level since new expenditures can be made only when new revenues are generated. Consequently the changes have released new entrepreneurial energies by local bureaucrats on behalf of rural industry. The authors observe, however, that local governments may overinvest in the expansion of industrial enterprises at the expense of activities with social and long-term economic benefits, particularly in the poorer areas (Park *et al.*, 1996: 751-78).

The World Bank (1996: 39) report likewise found that

> [s]ome high priority government activities have been underfunded, including health and education services, poverty alleviation, infrastructure development,

and environmental protection. Morever, some contingent liabilities associated with market reforms, such as pension payments, unemployment benefits, redundancy payments, and the monetization of housing benefits may eventually need to be borne by the budget.

Although the report does not distinguish among areas by level of income, it is highly probable that underfunding of social programs occurs more frequently in the poor rather than the affluent areas. Several alternatives could alleviate the biases against community-oriented services. First, as the World Bank suggests, that may require substantial increases in revenues. Although new taxes would surely be strongly resisted, such revenues would help to keep intact the incentives for local governments to support rural enterprises without neglecting community and long-term growth needs. Second, it may be necessary to separate the rural industries from their local governments and to allow each organization to pursue its own specific interests. Such a separation today would likely hamper the development of the town and village enterprises by withdrawing the support of local officials, but it may become more feasible in the near future. A compromise might be developed which would link increases in distributions from higher levels of government to local governments' commitments to fund certain neglected but important social programs affecting education, health, the environment and infrastructure.

5.2 Regional Integration

The lack of regional integration presents a different sort of problem. Regional integration brings advantages to the separate areas through specialization, economies of scale and the diffusion of knowledge. An increase in the flow of goods across China's internal boundaries should lower prices and, in the long run, equalize returns to human and physical capital. According to the World Bank, however, integration does not seem to be taking place. Between 1986 and 1991, regional price variations did not noticeably diminish and cross-provincial investment flows, relative to gross domestic product, decreased. From 1985 to 1992, the provinces increased trade with foreign countries more than with each other (World Bank, 1994: 37; Wu, 1995).[9]

Can the rural enterprises be changed so as to lessen the impact on the geographical distribution of investment funds generated by the industry? Luo Xiaopeng believes that the rural industries can be reformed only as part of a program to advance urbanization (Byrd, 1990: 170). A modest beginning, however, might be based on two changes: (1) make it possible for the enterprises to participate more fully than is common today in jointly-owned companies, including more contracts from the state-owned firms, and (2) permit the less-developed provinces to offer attractive investment packages similar to those offered to foreign-invested firms to attract entrepreneurs and to assist the development of the rural firms (Gao, 1996: 72; Cleary *et al.*, 1997: 5, 6).[10] Although participating in joint ownership of corporate-like companies might be of lasting value, the favorable location lures would not be appropriate in the long term, since ideal policies would be neutral with respect to sources of investment and locations.

6 CONCLUSION

We have argued that the town and village enterprises have brought returns to the Chinese economy above and beyond the direct additions of output. The enterprises have created a large number of jobs in the rural area. More employment in the countryside has slowed what otherwise would have been a surge of people to the cities well before the cities could accommodate them. The town and village enterprises have permitted China to discover its comparative trade advantages by showing their labor-intensive products to be internationally competitive. Hard budget constraints led the enterprises to develop responsibility contracts so as to tap entrepreneurial energies and to serve as models for the state-owned enterprises. The firms have enlarged their sphere of decision-making and strengthened management incentives. Hiring processes have been developed that seem to select managers with entrepreneurial skills. The greater autonomy accorded the town and village enterprises and the relative autonomy of the firms and their leaders have contributed to successful growth and relatively large productivity increases in recent years. The firms have contributed to the effectiveness of regional concentrations of economic activity and have participated in jointly run and owned enterprises and learned, thereby, new technological and managerial processes. The firms have interacted with other organizations, educational and business, to gain skills and knowledge required to upgrade operations. As a result the firms have demonstrated that substantial increases in productivity are possible in circumstances of incomplete markets and, in some areas, the firms have achieved higher absolute levels of output per person than have the state-owned enterprises. The most likely single factor accounting for these achievements is entrepreneurship.

The town and village enterprises have also provided new revenue sources to local governments, but in the process they have biased public expenditure decisions away from important social, environmental and long-term economic services and infrastructure, particularly in the poorer regions. They have clustered about the cities and have given and received from such growth-inducing environments. Their immobility, however, has prevented them from investing in the less-developed regions.

Two broad scale programs would help to resolve these problems while retaining the positive contributions and keeping the rural industries viable. First, the public expenditure biases could essentially be removed by providing more expenditures supported by a combination of revenues from higher levels of government and local revenues aimed at education, health, environment, poverty, and other social programs and infrastructure. Second, the reluctance of the local governments to see investment resources flow out the area could be removed by a program similar to many existing ones to attract foreign investment. The rural enterprises would be unlikely or unable to build branch facilities in the less developed areas, but they should be encouraged to form joint ventures with other kinds of business organizations.

The town and village enterprises, while serving as catalysts to economic growth and development in China, have given many participants and members of the communities a degree of personal autonomy that was not possible under the previous system of extensive controls. We believe that the town and village enterprises can continue to provide social returns for the foreseeable future. They may also give many individuals and members of the local communities a modicum of freedom and strengthen society's appreciation for greater personal choice in political as well as economic affairs.

NOTES

1. Sources for this section are the following: Byrd and Qinsong (1990, chapter 1) Naughton (1996a, chapter 4 and statistical appendix); Xiao Zhou (1996, chapter 5) and International Monetary Fund (1996). Statements in the text are our interpretations of the works cited above. Any errors are our own.
2. Naughton (1996a: 163) notes that Premier Li Peng showed doubts about the role of the town and village enterprises when after the Tiananmen incident he declared that the enterprises successes had been exaggerated by Zhao Ziyang and were due to preferential treatment and cheap labor.
3. Zhou emphasizes the influence of the farmers in bringing economic changes during the past few decades, particularly changes that gave greater opportunities to the farms and rural industries. She argues quite effectively that the farmers, beginning in the 1970s, negotiated deals with party cadre for opportunities to market output, to retain associated earnings and to manage without interference

from governmental authorities. Ultimately, the arrangement received official approval in early 1983 as the 'household responsibility system'.

4. Formally, the household responsibility system is a form of agricultural ownership and property rights in which households are tenants and landlords are the collectives, that is, the teams or villages. The responsibility of the household is to deliver quota to the State at a given price plus taxes, welfare and other expenses. The risk is born by the household because it is a fixed rent contract, not a sharing arrangement. The State and collective take their cut off the top and the residual belongs to the household.
5. Some historians of China find these agreements to be reminiscent of the contracting systems to collect taxes in the tenth century. See, for example, Chen (1995: 57).
6. Naughton (1996b: 299). See also comment by Nicholas R. Lardy on p. 339.
7. The town and village enterprises, however, may differ from historical precedent in that entrepreneurship is exercised by a team rather than by an individual. For analytical purposes, we assume that one person gives primary attention to the enterprise and its stakeholders while the other person addresses interests of the community. Undoubtedly the two viewpoints blend as the entrepreneurial team learns to work together. Nevertheless, those decisions critical to the survival of the enterprise would be expected to take priority over community needs. The more successful the enterprise, the more community goods can be provided, but first the enterprise must exist.
8. A memorandum by Ms LaiYi You of Nantong's economic development offices. Leaders of six enterprises and of the town of Guangyinshan, Nantong City, spoke to the authors about the importance of education to their employees and, apparently, to themselves.
9. Yanrui Wu in Chapter 8 of this book, however, finds that the regions are learning best practices from each other and are converging as measured by relative changes in technical efficiency.
10. Shangquan Gao, vice Minister of China's State Commission for Restructuring the Economic System, suggests that there is now flexibility in organizational arrangements for considerable experimentation. The need to encourage foreign investment to interior regions has been stressed recently. See, for example, the Hong Kong Office of Cleary *et al.* (1997).

REFERENCES

Asian Wall Street Journal (1997), March.

Blecher, M. and V. Shue (1996), *Tethered Deer*, Stanford, CA: Stanford University Press.

Byrd, W.A. (1990), 'Entrepreneurship, capital, and ownership', in W.A. Bird and L. Qingsong (eds), *China's Rural Industry*, New York: Oxford University Press, chapter 9.

Byrd, W.A. and L. Qinsong (eds) (1990), *China's Rural Industry*, New

York: Oxford University Press for the World Bank.

Chang, C. and Y. Wang (1994), 'The nature of the township-village enterprise', *Journal of Comparative Economics*, **19** (3), 432-52.

Chen, D. (1995), *Chinese Firms Between Hierarchy and Market: The Contract Management Responsibility System in China*, New York: St. Martin's Press.

Cleary, Gottlieb, Steen & Hamilton (1997), 'Foreign investment in China', memo, 20 June.

Fukuyama, F. (1995), *Trust: The Social Virtues and the Creation of Prosperity*, New York: Free Press.

Gao, S. (1996), *China's Economic Reform*, New York: St. Martin's Press.

Groves, T., Y. Hong, J. McMillan and B. Naughton (1995), 'China's evolving managerial labor market', *Journal of Political Economy*, **103** (4), 877.

Ho, S.P.S. (1994), *Rural China in Transition*, New York: Clarendon Press.

Hu, Z. and M.S. Khan (1996), 'Why is China growing so fast?', International Monetary Fund, IMF working paper WP/96/75, 14.

International Monetary Fund (1996), 'People's Republic of China - Recent Economic Developments' IMF staff country report no. 96/40, Washington, DC.

Jefferson, G. and T. Rawski (1994), 'Enterprise reform in Chinese industry', *Journal of Economic Perspectives*, **8** (2), 56.

Jones, E.L. (1993), *Growth Recurring*, New York: Oxford University Press.

Naughton, B. (1996a), *Growing Out of the Plan*, Cambridge, UK: Cambridge University Press.

Naughton, B. (1996b), 'China's emergence and prospects as a trading nation', in *Brookings Papers on Economic Activity*, 2, Washington, DC, 283.

Park, A., S. Rozelle, C. Wong and C. Ren (1996), 'Distributional consequences of reforming local public finance in China', *The China Quarterly*, **147**, 751.

Perkins, D. (1996), 'China's future: economic and social development scenarios for the twenty-first century', in OECD, *China in the 21st Century*, Paris: OECD, 28.

Riskin, C. (1995), *China's Political Economy: The Quest for Development Since 1949*, New York: Oxford University Press.

Schultz, T. (1990), *Restoring Economic Equilibrium*, Cambridge, MA: Basil Blackwell, Inc.

Social and Economic Yearbook of Nantong (1990, 1993, 1994, 1995).

US Government Printing Office (1989), *The President's Comprehensive Triennial Report on Immigration*, Washington, DC.

World Bank (1994), *China: Internal Market Development and Regulation*, Washington, DC.

World Bank (1996), *The Chinese Economy: Fighting Inflation, Deepening Reforms*, Washington, DC.

Wu, Y. (1966), *Productive Performance in Chinese Enterprise*, New York: St. Martin's Press.

Wu, Y. (1995), 'Productivity growth, technological progress and technical efficiency change in China: a three-sector analysis', *Journal of Comparative Economics*, **21** (2), 225-6.

Xiao Zhou, K. (1996), *How Farmers Changed China*, Boulder, CO: Westview Press.

Yoshitomi, M. (1996), 'The comparative advantage of China's manufacturing in the twenty-first century', in OECD, *China in the 21st Century*, Paris: OECD, **55**, 59.

Yuanren, M. (ed.) (1987), *History of the Development of Rural Industry in Jiangsu*, Nanjing: Nanjing Engineering College Press.

Index

F

G

H

I

L

M

O

P

R

S

T

U